The Encyclopedia of

THE CLASSICAL
WORLD

The Encyclopedia of
THE CLASSICAL WORLD

PRENTICE-HALL, INC. A SPECTRUM BOOK   Englewood Cliffs, N.J.

This book was originally entitled ELSEVIERS ENCYCLOPEDIE VAN DE ANTIEKE WERELD (Copyright by Elsevier—Amsterdam). It was translated from the Dutch by J. Muller-Van Santen, with emendations by Claire Jones. The author, *Dr. J. H. Croon,* received his doctorate from the University of Amsterdam and Cambridge, with concentration on the religious history of the Greeks. Many of his essays have appeared in periodicals in the Netherlands and elsewhere. He teaches classics in Leiden.

Current printing (last digit):

11   10   9   8   7   6   5   4   3   2

Preface

Dates. Where it is obvious from the context, the indication A.D. (*anno domini*) or B.C. (before Christ) has been omitted. The following rule also applies: mounting dates (for example, Augustine, 354-430) are always A.D.; declining dates (Aristotle, 384-322) are always B.C. The indication has, of course, been given when misunderstandings might arise.

Spelling of Greek proper names. The spelling made most popular by tradition or current use has generally been adhered to; that is, the Latinized form (for example, Corinth) when it is usually used, but the transcription (Samos) when it is not, or when the Latin form is entirely different from it (for example, Heracles: the Latin form is Hercules).

In general, a name not found under *C* should be sought under *K,* and vice versa. The same holds true for Roman names beginning with *I* and *J.* These rules also apply to the internal spelling of words; moreover, *ou* is sometimes interchangeable with *o* or *u; us* or *eus* with *os* or *ios; ae* with *e,* and so on. We have preferred what appears to us to be the most common form in most cases.

Roman names. Although as a rule the Roman citizen used the accepted abbreviation for his first name (*praenomen*), we have ordinarily written it out in this work. A few common abbreviations are:

Aulus (A.)
Gaius (C.)
Gnaeus (Cn.)
Lucius (L.)
Marcus (M.)
Publius (P.)
Quintus (Q.)
Tiberius (Ti.)
Titus (T.)

The second of his names (*nomen*) indicated the *gens* to which a Roman belonged (see GENS). His third name (*cognomen*) or his surname indicated the particular subdivision of the *gens.* An additional honorary name (*agnomen*) was sometimes given as a surname for a special achievement.

Cross-references. Most classical proper names and terms referred to in the entries have their own listings. Other references are indicated like GENS, above. Also note that after the first use within an entry, the subject of that entry is referred to by its first letter only; thus, Academy is thereafter denoted A.

Illustrations. Beginning on page 239 there is an Appendix of additional illustrations referred to in the text. Other maps and diagrams are to be found throughout the text, associated with the appropriate entries.

v

Abbreviations of the Names and Works of Classical Authors Referred to in the Text (With Common English Equivalents)

Caes. = Gaius Julius Caesar
  B.G. = *Bellum Gallicum* (The Gallic Wars)
Cic. = Marcus Tullius Cicero
  Ad Fam. = *Epistulae ad Familiares* (Letters to His Friends)
  De Deor. Nat. = *De Deorum Natura* (On the Nature of the Gods)
  De Fin. = *De Finibus* (On Ends *or* The Highest Good)
  De Leg. = *De Legibus* (On the Laws)
  De Off. = *De Officiis* (On Moral Duties)
  De Or. = *De Oratore* (On the Orator)
  In Cat. = *Orationes in Catilinam* (Against Catiline)
  Par. Stoic. = *Paradoxa Stoicorum* (Paradoxes of the Stoics)
  Phil. = *Orationes Philippicae* (Philippics)
  Tusc. = *Tusculanae Disputationes* (Tusculan Disputations)
Diod. Sic. = Diodorus Siculus
Eur. = Euripides
Hdt. = Herodotus
Hom. = Homer
  Il. = *Iliad*
  Od. = *Odyssey*
Hor. = Quintus Horatius Flaccus (Horace)
  Ars. Poet. = *De Arte Poetica* (The Art of Poetry, Epistle II,3)
  Carm. = *Carmina* (Odes)
  Ep. = *Epistulae* (Epistles)
  Epod. = *Epodi* (Epodes)
  Sat. = *Satirae* (Satires)
Juv. = Decimus Junius Juvenalis (Juvenal)
  Sat. = *Satirae* (Satires)
Liv. = Titus Livius (Livy)
Mart. = Marcus Valerius Martialis (Martial)
Ov. = Publius Ovidius Naso (Ovid)
  Ars Am. = *Ars Amatoria* (The Art of Love)
  Ep. ex Pont. = *Epistulae ex Ponto* (Letters from the Black Sea)
  Her. = *Heroides*
  Met. = *Metamorphoses*
  Rem. Am. = *Remedia Amoris* (The Remedies of Love)
Pers. = Aulus Persius Flaccus
  Sat. = *Satirae* (Satires)
Plaut. = Titus Maccius Plautus
  Poen. = *Poenulus* (The Carthaginian)
  Pseud. = *Pseudolus*
Plin. Maj. = Gaius Plinius Secundus (Pliny the Elder)
  Nat. Hist. = *Naturalis Historia* (The Natural History)

Plin. Min. = Gaius Plinius Caecilius Secundus (Pliny the Younger)
  Ep. = *Epistulae* (Letters)
Plut. = Plutarch
Quint. = Marcus Fabius Quintilianus (Quintilian)
Sall. = Gaius Sallustius Crispus (Sallust)
  Cat. = *Bellum Catilinae* (The Catilinarian War)
  B. Jug. = *Bellum Jugurthinum* (The War Against Jugurtha)
Sen. = Lucius Annaeus Seneca
  Apocol. = *Apocolocyntosis* (The "Pumpkinification")
  De Brev. Vitae = *De Brevitate Vitae* (On the Brevity of Life)
  Ep. = *Epistulae* (Letters)
Sil. Ital. = Silius Italicus
  Pun. = *Punica* (The Punic War)
Suet. = Gaius Suetonius Tranquillus
  Caes. = *Julius Caesar* (*from* The Lives of the Twelve Caesars)
Tac. = Cornelius Tacitus
  Ann. = *Annales* (The Annals)
  Hist. = *Historiae* (The Histories)
Ter. = Publius Terentius Afer (Terence)
  And. = *Andria*
  Heautont. = *Heautontimorumenos* (The Self-Tormentor)
  Phorm. = *Phormio*
Virg. = Publius Vergilius Maro (Virgil)
  Aen. = *Aeneid*
  Ecl. = *Eclogae* (Eclogues)
Xen. = Xenophon
  An. = *Anabasis*
  Hell. = *Hellenica*
  Memor. = *Memorabilia*

A

AB ACTIS. "Of the actions." Rom. editor of the senate reports (see ACTA DIURNA).

ABACUS.
—(1) The uppermost member of a capital of a column (see COLUMN).
—(2) A board for counting.

ABDERA. Gr. city on the Thracian coast, native city of Democritus and Protagoras. The Abderites generally had a reputation for stupidity.

AB ORIGINE. "From the origin." Compare with the Aborigines, the legendary original inhabitants of Italy.

AB OVE USQUE AD MALA. "From the egg to the apples" (as in Roman banquets); from the beginning to the end of a feast (Hor. Sat. I, 3, 6).

AB URBE CONDITA. See LIVY.

ABYDOS. Colony of Miletus on the Hellespont opposite Sestos, where Xerxes built a bridge during his expedition in 480 B.C.

ACADEMY. Originally a grove dedicated to the demigod Akademos (see HEROES) in Athens, where Plato founded his school in 387 B.C. Originally it was mainly an instruction center for political leaders. According to Plato's views, this implied a thorough training in mathematics and philosophy. Later more and more emphasis was put on theoretical philosophy. Leaders of the A. after Plato were Xenocrates and Speusippus. In a later period Carneades was a well-known leader. In the 5th cent. B.C. the A. was a center of Neoplatonism. In 529 Justinian closed it, along with the other pagan schools.

ACARNANIA. The westernmost Gr. province, on the Ionian Sea. It is very mountainous and has only one fertile strip, along the Achelous River; the inhabitants remained backward for a long time. They supported Athens during the Peloponnesian War. Like other western Gr. provinces (see ACHAEA; AETOLIA), A. did not acquire political significance until the Hellenistic period.

ACCIUS, LUCIUS (or ATTIUS) (c. 170-c. 85). The most important Lat. tragic poet, friend of Pacuvius; he wrote plays following Gr. examples, and also nationalistic Rom. dramas (Fabula praetexta); only fragments have survived.

ACHAEA. Province in the northern Peloponnesus, a refuge for the Achaeans after the immigration of the Dorians to Arcadia. In classical times A. was insignificant, but after 200 B.C. it became an important political center because of the formation of the Achaean League (see also ARATUS; SICYON), the most important political confederation, aside from the Aetolian League, in Hellenic Greece. Two strategists (later, one) presided over the league, assisted by an administering council of ten, and two representative bodies. Its politics were alternately anti-Macedonian and anti-Spartan. With the support of Rome, the league embraced almost the entire Peloponnesus (see PHILOPOEMEN) in the 2nd cent. B.C.; in 146 B.C. dissension with Rome led to its disbandment. For the history of civilization, the most important aspect of this was probably the fact that Polybius was taken to Rome. After the disbandment, A. was made a Rom. province.

ACHAEAN LEAGUE. See ACHAEA.

ACHAEANS. Homer's name for the Greeks. This name is also indicated in Egyptian and Hittite texts (probably for a part of Asia Minor inhabited by A.). The Gr. pre-Doric population, the bearers of the Mycenaean culture, are also generally called A. (see also ACHAEA).

ACHAEMENIDAE. The Persian royal house from Cyrus onward. After the death of Cyrus' son Cambyses, the succession fell to Darius I, who represented another branch of the family, to which Xerxes, Artaxerxes, and Darius III also belonged. The founder, Achaemenes, is semilegendary.

ACHELOUS. The longest river in Greece;

it formed the boundary between Aetolia and Acarnania.

ACHILLES. See TROJAN WAR.

ACROPOLIS. Gr. citadel, originally also center of defense, but particularly the place for the most important temples. The Athenian A., where the Propylaea, the Erechtheum, the Parthenon, and the temple of Nike were built after the destruction by the Persians in the 5th cent. B.C., is particularly well known.

ACROTERION. Ornament at the corners or on top of a fronton or on top of a stele (see ARCHITECTURAL ORDERS).

ACTA DIURNA. A daily newspaper in ancient Rome. During the imperial period the *Acta senatus,* founded in 59 B.C. by Caesar, contained transactions and decrees of the senate.

ACTIUM. Promontory in Acarnania with the temple of Apollo on it. It was here that the decisive battle between Octavian and Mark Antony (see ANTONIUS, MARCUS) was fought in 31 B.C.

AD CALENDAS GRAECAS. "Until the Gr. Calends" [to postpone]. As the Greeks had no calends (a designation in the Rom. calendar), this means "never."

ADHUC SUB JUDICE LIS EST. "The matter has not yet been decided" (Hor. *Ars Poet.* 78).

ADOPTIVE EMPERORS. The Rom. Emperors Nerva, Trajan, Hadrian, Antonius Pius, and Marcus Aurelius. So called because they, being wise through sad experiences with the earlier imperial dynasties, always adopted the man they considered best as a son and successor, most of them having no sons of their own. Due partly to this, the 2nd cent. was a period of rest and good government in the Rom. Empire, with flourishing culture (see TACITUS; PLINY; PLUTARCH; etc.) Marcus Aurelius broke with the tradition by appointing his own son Commodus as his successor, with disastrous results.

AEDILES. Rom. officials in charge of public works. Originally watchmen of the temple of Ceres (*aedes,* temple), the goddess of the plebs; later assistants to the *tribuni plebis.* Two A. curules were added to the two A. *plebis* (according to tradition this was in 367 B.C.), and these were, initially, always patricians. In this manner a council of four came into being.

Its task was primarily the maintenance of public works, maintaining order in the city, providing corn, and supervising the markets and the games. As this office was usually a link between the offices of quaestor and praetor in the *cursus honorum,* the A. frequently spent enormous sums on these games in order to gain public favor. During the imperial period they were no longer in charge of the corn provision and the games, which caused the office to lose its importance.

AEDUI. Gallic tribe in what is now Burgundy. They became faithful friends of Rome from 121 B.C., when they asked for help against the Arverni and the Allobroges; in 52 B.C., after long hesitation, they supported Vercingetorix. They were granted Rom. citizenship by the Emperor Claudius—the first Gallic tribe thus honored. They were also the first to send senators to Rome.

AEGADIAN ISLANDS. A group of islands to the west of Sicily, where the Carthaginian fleet was decisively beaten by Lutatius Catulus in 241 B.C., which terminated the First Punic War.

AEGAE. The first capital of Macedonia, originally called Edessa. After Archelaus, king of Macedonia, had moved the capital to Pella, A. was still esteemed as a religious center.

AEGINA. Island in the Saronic Gulf, opposite the coasts of Attica and Argolis; its importance during the Mycenaean period is reflected in the legends of Aias and his family. In about 1000 B.C. it became Doric, and in the 6th cent. it was an important naval and mercantile power. Pheidon of Argos had the first Gr. coins minted there. In the 5th cent., A. came into conflict with Athens, which would not tolerate the competition and forced A. into membership in the Delian League. During the Peloponnesian War Athens banished the inhabitants; later they were brought back by Lysander, but A. never flourished again. Pindar devoted lovely verses to A. The most important building was the temple of Aphaia, the statues from which, preserved in Munich, are showpieces of perfect archaic art, despite Thorvaldsen's drastic reconstruction. See Appendix.

AEGOSPOTAMI (or AEGOSPOTAMOS).

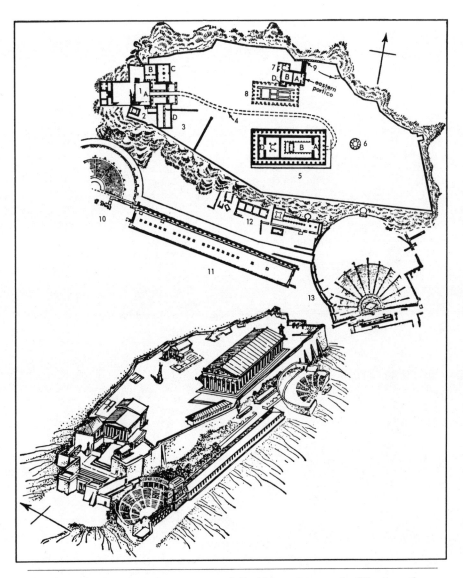

The Acropolis. 1. *Propylaea or entrance hall;* (A) *entrance arch;* (B) *pinacotheca;* (C)-(D) *unfinished halls.* 2. *Temple of Athena Nike.* 3. *Domain of Artemis.* 4. *Sacred way.* 5. *Parthenon, temple of Athena Parthenos:* (A) *vestibule;* (B) *cella with statue of goddess;* (C) *treasure chamber;* (D) *rear hall.* 6. *Roman temple of Roma and Augustus.* 7. *Erechtheum, temple of Erechtheus and Athena:* (A) *cella of Athena,* (B) *cella of Erechtheus,* (C) *north porch,* (D) *porch of the caryatids.* 8. *Hecatompedon, old temple.* 9. *Part of the wall in which columns of buildings destroyed by the Persians were incorporated.* 10. *Odeum of Herodus Atticus.* 11. *Hall of Eumenes.* 12. *Sanctuary of Asklepios.* 13. *Theater of Dionysus.*

Small river and town in ancient Thrace. Scene of Spartan victory over the Athenian fleet in 405 B.C., the last decisive battle of the Peloponnesian War.

AELIANUS. Name of:—(1) Author of a Gr. book on military tactics about A.D. 100. (2)—Claudius A. of Praeneste (c. 170-235), Gr. author; wrote a number of philosophical works, tinged with Stoicism, also an anecdotic *Variae Historiae*.

AEMILIANUS. See MILITARY EMPERORS.

AEMILIUS PAULLUS, LUCIUS. Name of several influential Rom. patricians:— (1) Consul in 218 and 216 B.C., killed in action near Cannae, after protesting in vain against his fellow consul's offensive strategy (according to the biased annalist version:—(2) Son of the preceding, consul in 182 and 168 B.C.; conqueror of Pydna. He was a typical representative of the group of Rom. notables who welcomed the Hellenistic influence in Rome, as long as the Rom. tradition was retained. His son was adopted by the son of Scipio Major, and was later known as Scipio Minor.—(3) Brother of Lepidus, consul in 50 B.C.; rebuilt the Basilica Aemilia in the Rom. Forum.—(4) His son, consul in A.D. 1; married Julia, granddaughter of Augustus; executed for conspiring against the Emperor.

AENEAS. See VIRGIL.

AEOLIANS. The northernmost group of Gr. tribes; settled in Thessaly and Boeotia, among other places, colonized the northern islands of the Aegean Sea (Lesbos, etc.) and the northwestern coast of Asia Minor (the Troas, etc.). Their dialect was used by Sappho and Alcaeus; traces of it can be found in Homer's epic poetry.

AERARIUM. Rom. treasury (Lat. *aes,* bronze, money); the A. Saturni was the most important, and was administered by the quaestors in the temple of Saturn at the base of the Capitol. During the imperial period the *fiscus* increasingly supplanted the A. During that time an A. *militare* for military pensions also existed.

AERE PERENNIUS. "More lasting than bronze." A quotation from Horace (*Carm.* III, 30,1); said of his own works.

AES. See COINAGE.

AESCHINES (c. 389-314). One of the ten Attic orators. He was first an administrative official, and then appeared as an actor; when Greece was confronted with the problems of rising Macedonian nationalism, A. was initially in favor of Demosthenes' politics, but was converted to the ideas of Philip II in 348. Because of this, Demosthenes hated him bitterly and accused him of high treason. A. narrowly escaped being condemned. When the city of Ctesiphon suggested bestowing a golden crown on Demosthenes in 337, A. tried vainly to impeach the proposer, and then fled to Asia Minor. Three of A.'s speeches have been preserved, which excel in simple clarity. His many allusions to "good" education can probably be attributed to an inferiority complex; to us, however, the fact that he is a "self-made man" is one of his most interesting characteristics.

AESCHYLUS (525-456). The first of the three great Athenian tragic poets; born of a Eupatrid family in Eleusis where he was probably initiated into the mysteries, he fought at Marathon and Salamis, twice visited the court of Hiero I in Sicily, and died during his second trip to Gela, where he was buried. His epitaph mentions the fact that he had fought for his country at Marathon, but not his achievements as a poet. A. wrote at least seventy-nine plays, most of which have been lost, with the exception of a few fragments. Large fragments of *Niobe* and the Satyric drama *Proteus* (dealing with the tragedy of the House of Atrius) have been found, written on papyrus. Seven of his plays have survived complete: *The Suppliants*—the flight of the Danaides to Argos (this used to be generally considered the first play because of its lyrical nature; recently found papyri, however, suggest that it was written in about 463); *The Persians* (472)—the impression the report of the battle of Salamis makes on the Persian court; *Seven against Thebes* (467)—the downfall of the children of Oedipus; the trilogy (see TRAGEDY) *Oresteia* (458), consisting of *Agamemnon* (his murder by his wife Clytemnestra), *Choephoroe* (Furies, Orestes' revenge), *Eumenides* (reconciliation because of the acquittal of Orestes by the Areopagus in

Athens). Just where *Prometheus* (the first part of a trilogy, in which Prometheus rebels against his vanquisher Zeus) fits into the chronology is uncertain.

A. is justly called the "creator of the tragedy." By introducing a second actor he makes a real drama possible. His own works show an evolution in dramatic technique. The chorus dominates less and less. It has been found that the very lyrical play *The Suppliants* is probably not the oldest, but in the *Oresteia* the dramatic element is completely dominant and, in imitation of Sophocles, a third actor has been added. Stage setting also probably originated with A. He went even farther than his successors in producing artificial stage effects. The story, on the other hand, is uncomplicated. The action follows a "straight line."

The most important characteristic of A.'s work is his gradually more perfect command of dramatic technique in conjunction with his gifts as a religious thinker, almost a prophet. In his dramas strong human personalities are confronted with the inexorable will of the gods, in particular that of the almost monotheistically described Zeus. Hybris of man leads to guilt, and guilt brings suffering for many generations. But even in suffering there is a lesson, which can bring man to reconciliation with the will of the gods. A.'s language is no less exalted than his personages. Even today, a part in one of his plays can be a rare experience for a talented actor.

AESCULAPIUS. See ASKLEPIOS.

AESOP [Gr. Aisopos] (6th cent. B.C.), Gr. freedman from Samos to whom fables were attributed, even in the 5th cent. B.C. He is said to have been a hunchback who came originally from Phrygia. The "Aesopic" fables may be traced back to him in some measure (see BABRIUS; AVIANUS; DEMETRIUS OF PHALERON; PHAEDRUS).

ÆTHIOPIA. An area on the upper reaches of the Nile, to the south of Egypt, already known in the time of Homer. At first the Greeks had only a vague idea of this country. After several of them had visited it after c. 625 B.C., they localized it in what is now Ethiopia. Under the Ptolemies it became better known, and was even slightly Hellenized.

AETIUS. Rom. general under the Emperors Honorius and Valentinian, who became the "strong man" in the West Rom. Empire. By cleverly playing the Germanic tribes off against each other, he managed to repel Attila's great attack on Gaul (Catalaunian Plains) with their support. When he later tried to marry his son to Valentinian's daughter, the Emperor himself murdered him.

AETNA.

—(1) The Rom. name of the volcano Etna in Sicily, and of the city of the same name at its base, where Hiero I founded a colony in 461 B.C., after forcibly driving out the natives.

—(2) Lat. poem in 646 hexameters about volcanic phenomena. It has been ascribed to Virgil but the ascription was disputed even in classical times).

AETOLIA. Area in western Greece, to the east of Acarnania (boundary line, the Achelous River); it remained completely undeveloped until the 5th cent. B.C., when the inhabitants united to repel an attack by the Athenian general Demosthenes (426). The Aetolians had, however, from ancient times had a common bond in the sanctuary of Apollo in Thermon (middle-A.). Calydon was also important, being a religious center. In the 4th cent. A. began to flourish, at the same time as the other formerly undeveloped areas (see ACHAEA) and the Aetolian League were founded. This league was politically anti-Macedonian and therefore initially pro-Rom., in the Hellenic period; after the league was subjected to Rome, however, it became disloyal and brought Antiochus III to Greece as a liberator (189 B.C.). The league had a dominating influence on the Delphic Amphictyons, particularly in the 3rd cent. B.C. A strategist, chosen yearly, led these, with the assistance of a representative body which chose an executive committee from among its members. It was an interesting example of the federal formation of states.

AFRICA. This name was given to the continent (called Libya by the Greeks) by the Romans. It referred to the northern part in particular, and sometimes, still more narrowly, to the Rom. province A., the former Carthage area (about what is now Tunisia). The Rom. capital was Utica; Caesar added Numidia after the battle of Thapsus, and the emperors enlarged the area even more. A. was an important source of wheat to Rome. Young Christianity found considerable support there, and many ancient Christian writers and philosophers came from A. Later, the Vandal empire was founded there.

AGAMEMNON. See TROJAN WAR.

AGATHOCLES (361-289). Statesman of Syracuse first a democratic leader, but a tyrant after 317. King from 304 on. He attacked the Carthaginians in Sicily, but was driven back to Syracuse and besieged. He broke out, and shifted the scene of the battle to Africa, without ultimate success. Later he marched on Sicily and Italy. At his death, he freed Syracuse, but only chaos followed. A. was a typical representative of the Hellenic idea of kingship (see Pyrrhus).

AGATHON (c. 425 B.C.). Gr. tragic poet of whose works only titles and fragments have survived. He appears in Plato's *Symposium*. According to tradition, he tried to modernize tragedy by using original (not mythological) plots and by reducing the choruses to interludes.

AGER PUBLICUS. Rom. public lands confiscated at the subjection of Italy. At first, the A.P. was partly allotted to patricians and partly (in very small shares) to plebeians, and some parts were leased by the censors in the name of the state. Another part was reserved for colonization. Although the famous *Lex Licinia Sextia* (Licinian Rogations) of 367 B.C. limited personal ownership of the A.P., large parts gradually fell into the hands of a few people. The Gracchi attempted to set this right and make small land ownership possible again, but they never fully succeeded in this endeavor. The agrarian problem was the most important social question of the later Rom. Republic. A new aspect was illuminated when the demobilization of the enormous civil war armies made it necessary to confiscate lands for the veterans. In the provinces, land in subjected areas and pillaged cities (Corinth, Carthage) was also declared A.P.

AGESILAUS (444-360). King of Sparta, son of Archidamus. In 396 he was sent to Asia Minor to protect the Ionians against the Persians, and there he fought successfully against Tissaphernes. When Sparta itself got into difficulties, he was recalled, and he defeated the Boeotians and their allies at Coronea (394)—without lasting results, however. After the battle of Leuctra he organized the Spartan defense. Then he again served abroad, to build up the state treasury, in Asia Minor and Egypt. He died on his way home. A. was a typical example of a Spartan general, a true fighter, but not a particularly good strategist. Xenophon, who served under him and admired him greatly, wrote his biography.

AGIS. Name of several Spartan kings:
—(1) A. II (reigned 427-401), son of Archidamus, retrieved Spartan prestige in Peloponnesus by a victory over the Argives at Mantinea (418). He occupied Decelea in 413, on the advice of Alcibiades. This was one of the most serious losses Athens suffered during the Peloponnesian War. In 405-4 he besieged Athens with Lysander.
—(2) A. III (reigned 338-331), organized the Gr. resistance to Macedonia during Alexander the Great's Persian campaign. However, Athens remained neutral and A. was conquered and killed by Antipater.
—(3) A. IV (262-241), king after 244, during a period in which Sparta's fame was receiving a setback and the state was bowed under social evils, and had far too few citizens. A. tried to carry through land reforms and debt redemption, but after the return of his fellow king and opposer Leonidas, whom he had exiled earlier, he was executed. Later generations regarded his death as that of a martyr.

AGON. The Gr. word for "contest." Contests, sports, and games were an important and essential part of Gr. culture (see PYTHIAN; ISTHMIAN; NEMEAN GAMES; PANATHENAEA; and OLYMPIC GAMES). Homer already paid great attention to the games, in the funeral drama for Patroclus (Il. XXIII), and in Phaeacia participation in the A. was the mark of the nobleman (*Od.* VIII, 159-164 in part). When the Ten Thousand Greeks had returned with Xenophon to familiar surroundings on the Black Sea, one of the first things they did was to hold an A. (Xen. *An.* IV, 8). In the Hellenistic world sports were an essential feature of the Gr. style of living in the eastern countries (see GYMNASIUM). Among the Romans, with their very different culture, the games took on another character entirely (see CIRCUS; GLADIATORS).

It is remarkable how seriously the *agones,* which were usually also services for a dead hero or a god (see HEROES), were taken. The *time* (worth) of the participant was involved when he won or lost. We may certainly speak of an "agonistic" element in Gr. culture. Glaucus and Achilles were sent to Troy by their fathers with the message "always to be the best and to go one better than the others" (Hom. *Il* VI, 208; XI, 784); here, they are the prototype of ancient man, striving for *time.* This can still be found among the peoples around the Mediterranean Sea, and the point may be argued whether this is an example of the unchanged nature of a people, or a specific heritage from ancient civilization. But in any case, this element was not limited to the contest itself in ancient times. It can be found in various other fields (see CRESILAS, for example), but particularly in the literature. Homer and Hesiod are represented as participating in an A. Above all, the A. dominates the Athenian performances of tragedy. During the festival of Dionysus three tragedians appeared on three consecutive days, each performing four plays. First, second, and third prizes were awarded. Euripides is said to have been extremely unhappy because his plays hardly ever won a first prize; Sophocles, on the other hand, was usually first, sometimes second, but never third. Another result of this element of competition was the imitativeness that is found throughout classical literature, though it seems very strange to us moderns. *Aemulatio* (rivalry) was a constantly recurring characteristic. The authors imitated each other freely, the emphasis being on doing the work "better" and "more beautifully." Thus writers worked in the way our scientists do, tak-

ing the work of one's predecessors as a starting point, to build on and improve upon. This is the answer to those who still cannot appreciate Virgil's *Bucolica,* for example, because "it is all Theocritus' work anyway," and the *Aeneid* because it is obviously in imitation of Homer and Ennius. It is useful to compare the main characteristics of classic and modern literature, but one cannot apply the same standards. The farther we advance in our study of ancient culture, the more we realize that ancient man is not *strange* to us, being our intellectual forebear, but he is certainly *different.* Fathoming this "difference" is one of the most interesting aspects of this study.

AGORA. Originally a meeting place and meeting of the people in Greece, later a marketplace. The A. in Athens has been entirely excavated by American archaeologists, who crowned their work in 1956 by reconstructing the Stoa of Attalus.

AGRICOLA, GNAEUS JULIUS (A.D. 40-93). Rom. general and proconsul of Britain (78-84), where he extended Rom. rule into Scotland. Domitian recalled him because the armies were needed elsewhere (but probably also because he was suspicious). His son-in-law Tacitus wrote a famous biography of him.

AGRIGENTUM [Gr Akragas]. City in southwestern Sicily, founded by Gela in 582 B.C. It flourished under the tyrant Theron, who supported Gelon in his struggle against Carthage (480). After Theron's son had been banished (471) A. became a democracy (Empedocles played a part, among others, in the drawing up of its constitution). It was still the most powerful city in Sicily after Syracuse. In 405 it was destroyed by the Carthaginians and, although it was again a rich city afterward, even under Rom. rule, it never regained its former power. A. was and is famous for its beautiful Doric temples.

AGRIPPA. Name of:
—(1) Marcus Vipsanius A. (c. 63-12 B.C.), friend, general, admiral, and son-in-law to Augustus. Supported Octavian in the war about Perusia (41-40); reorganized the fleet and with it defeated Sextus Pompey (36); planned the victory

of Actium (31); spent several years in the East and in Spain in order to settle affairs there. In 21 he married Augustus' daughter Julia, and for years he was Augustus' right-hand man and probable successor. He supervised the building of many large structures, among others the Pantheon. Both he and his sons Gaius and Lucius Caesar died before Augustus. —(2) A. Postumus (12 B.C.-A.D. 14), son of the preceding and Julia. He was judged unfit for the succession because of alleged faults of character; was banished to the island of Planasia and immediately after the death of Augustus was killed at the instigation of Livia and Tiberius.

AGRIPPINA. Name of:

—(1) A. the Elder (c. 14 B.C.-A.D. 33) sister of Agrippa Postumus and wife of Germanicus, to whom she bore nine children (among them Caligula and Agrippina the younger), and whom she accompanied on his marches to Germany and the East. There was constant tension between her and Tiberius, who had her banished to the island of Pandataria and starved to death. A.'s character was a strange combination of old-Rom. virtue and uncontrolled, hot-tempered passion. —(2) A. the Younger (A.D. 15-59), Daughter of Agrippina the Elder and mother (by her first marriage) of Nero. Banished by Caligula, she was recalled by Claudius, whose second wife she became in 49. She succeeded in persuading him to adopt Nero as his son and heir (see *Britannicus*), and when Claudius showed signs of revoking his decision, she poisoned him. During the first few years of Nero's reign she dominated him completely, but when Nero tired of her, he had her murdered.

AKRAGAS [Gr.]. See AGRIGENTUM.

ALABASTRON. See VASE FORMS.

ALALIA (Aleria). City in Corsica, founded by the city of Phocaea in 564 B.C.; the inhabitants were driven off by the Etruscans and the Carthaginians. This marked the end of Gr. colonization in the western Mediterranean region.

ALARIC (c. 370-410). King of the Visigoths. He raided Greece, Epirus, and Illyria in the service of Theodosius, who allowed his people to settled there. In 401 he attacked Italy and was repelled by Stilicho, who left Gaul and Britain undefended in order to do so. After his death (408), A. controlled Italy, took Rome in 410, and had it pillaged. He died while preparations were being made for taking the Visigoths to Africa.

ALBA LONGA. What is now Castel Gandolfo, the ancient capital of the Lat. League of cities (see LATIUM), destroyed about 600 B.C. by Rome (under Tullus Hostilius). It existed as early as the 12th cent. B.C., and, according to legend, was founded by Aeneas' son Ascanius (see VIRGIL).

ALBINUS. See MILITARY EMPERORS.

ALCAEUS [Gr. Alkaios] (c. 600 B.C.). Gr. lyric poet from Mytilene on Lesbos. As a youthful aristocrat he came into conflict with the tyrant Myrsilus; as a result he spent several years in banishment. Pittacus, who came into power after Myrsilus, was a friend of A. at first, but later A. opposed him violently, which made it necessary for him to flee again. Before his death he returned to Lesbos, where he and Pittacus seem to have become reconciled.

Fragments of his poems, real expressions of feeling, have survived, as have fragments of Sappho's, who was a contemporary and compatriot of his. His poems are songs of love and hate, drinking songs, and warrior's songs, written in the Aeolian dialect and often in a meter he himself created (the Alcaic meter; see METER). They were often sung in classical times, and were an inspiration for many (among the Romans, notably Horace).

ALCAMENES (c. 460-400). Gr. sculptor, contemporary, and possibly a pupil, of Phidias. A Rom. copy of a statue of Hermes by him is well known. A statue of Procne and Itys in the Athenian Acropolis Museum has been attributed to him, and also a section of the Parthenon frieze and the famous relief of Orpheus, Eurydice, and Hermes.

ALCIBIADES (c. 450-404). Athenian statesman and general, nephew of Pericles, alternately lauded to the skies, the darling of the Athenian public, and deeply reviled, abused as godless and a traitor. After the death of his father,

Pericles became his guardian; A. became a disciple of Socrates (as such he appears in Plato's *Symposium*), who was, however, unable to curb his impetuous nature. In about 420, after the peace of Nicias, A. became the leader of the radical-democratic faction. He acted as the strategist against Melos in 416-15. Afterward he succeeded in persuading the Athenians to undertake their greatest imperial adventure, the expedition to Sicily. When the fleet had arrived there, A. was called back, suspected of mutilating the hermae and of profaning the Eleusinian mysteries (the latter was probably true). He fled to Sparta, where he advised the government (a) to support Syracuse (see GYLIPPUS); this contributed not a little to the failure of the Athenian expedition; (b) to occupy Decelea permanently; this was one of the worst blows to Athens during the second half of the Peloponnesian War. When A. disagreed with the Spartans, he went to Persia, from which he returned during the oligarchic revolution of 411 (see PISANDER), to take command of the Athenian fleet near Samos. After several victories at sea (among them Cyzicus, 410) he made a triumphant entry into Athens. All was forgiven and forgotten, until his second in command suffered a defeat in 406. Again he was banished; in 404 he was murdered in Phrygia by the Persian satrap, at the instigation of the Thirty Tyrants (see CRITIAS) and Lysander. A. is the "perfect example" in Athenian history of the brilliant man of genius, passionately desiring fame and power, who has no conscience to offset this. It is tempting to speculate on the probable results of the Sicilian expedition if it had been led by A. instead of by Nicias, who was his opposite in almost all respects. It is, however, more honest to note that the whole plan was purely aggressive, and that the way in which A. put his genius at the service of Sparta was horrifying. In him the ideas of the younger Sophists are embodied. On the other hand, Thucydides rightly reproached the Athenians with dropping A. twice, at the moment when he was most needed, after having accepted him before.

ALCMAEON [Gr. Alkmaion] of Croton (c. 500 B.C.). Pupil of Pythagoras; au-thor of a book on nature. He is said to have performed the first eye operations, and discovered the connection between the eye and the brain.

ALCMAEONIDAE. Notable Athenian family, who claimed descent from Nestor. Clisthenes was of this family, and so were Pericles and Alcibiades on the female side (see also CYLON).

ALCMAN of Sardes (c. 625 B.C.). Gr. lyrical poet. He lived in Sparta and wrote choral songs for maidens (*Parthenia*), of which a fragment has survived.

ALEA JACTA EST. "The die has been cast" (Suet. *Caes.* 32). Caesar's words spoken on crossing the Rubicon.

ALESIA. City in Gaul, now called Alise-Sainte-Reine, where Vercingetorix was surrounded by Caesar's army in 52 B.C. The taking of A. put an end to the uprising in Gaul (Caes. *B.G.* VII, 69-89). The Rom. fortifications were rediscovered in the 19th cent.

ALEXANDER THE GREAT (356-323). King of Macedonia, conqueror of the Persian empire, builder of cultural bridges between the East and the West; son of Philip II and Olympias, educated by Aristotle. He defeated the handpicked Theban troops opposing him at Chaeronea in 338. In 336 he succeeded his father; and after some difficulties, was recognized as the leader of the Gr. League. When he subsequently left for the north to quell revolts, Greece rebelled against him. A. returned promptly, destroyed Thebes (except for the temples and the house where Pindar had once lived), and after this deterrent measure, treated Athens and other Gr. cities clemently. Afterward Philip's plan for invading Persia (see also ISOCRATES) was also revived. The prospects appeared to be quite good, certainly if the invasion were to be undertaken on a limited scale: the expedition of the Ten Thousand (see XENOPHON) had already brought to light the inner weakness of the Persian empire seventy years earlier. In 334, A. advanced with a Gr.-Macedonian army (only Sparta had remained neutral) of 30,000 infantrymen and 5,000 cavalry. (For the first part of the campaign, see GRANICUS; IOXNIA; GORDIUM; ISSUES; DARIUS III; PHOENICIANS; EGYPT; AMMON; ALEX-

ANDRIA; GAUGAMELA; BABYLON; SUSA; PEPSEPOLIS; ECBATANA.) The goal he had aimed for in the first instance had now been reached. The expedition of revenge was completed. After the battle of Issus (333), Darius had already offered to cede the territory west of the Euphrates River (see also PARMENION). But A. was not satisfied. The southward swing toward Egypt cost him a delay of almost two years, but (a) he could not afford to let the Phoenician fleet operate behind him, on his lines of communication, and (b) to proceed eastward [toward Persia] immediately would have been contrary to his intention of freeing the entire Near East from Persian domination. In the meantime another important development was seen. After he had been acclaimed "son of Zeus" (see AMMON), A. became more and more alienated from his Macedonian *hetaeri*. He wanted to be recognized in the East as an Eastern prince and to this end he did not merely play the part of a conqueror, but also tried to approach useful personages of the East; he appointed some of them satrap and had the Asians greet him with the Eastern *proskynesis* (kissing the dust in front of the king's feet). The mutual suspicion between A. and his Macedonian nobles led, later on, to trials for high treason, as a result of which some of the most faithful generals were killed (see PARMENION). After the capture of the principal Persian cities it became apparent that A. intended to conquer the rest of the East. Darius had fled to the East and been murdered by the satrap Besus. A. marched on to Bactria (where he married Roxana) and the Valley of the Indus, where King Poros marched to meet him with war elephants. An important mixture of Gr. and Indian culture originated in this area because of the Gr. settlements. When A. wanted to march on to the Ganges River, his troops refused, so he sailed down the Indus River to the Indian Ocean. From there (see also NEARCHUS), after suffering many hardships, he returned to the Persian capital. A. died at the age of thirty-three on the 13th of June, 323, of malaria in Babylon. It was rumored that he had also been planning a campaign to the West (Carthage), but this is doubtful. There are no differences of opinion on the importance of A. in the history of the world. He was the forerunner of Hellenism, and he was conscious of it. Founding Gr. cities in the East, having his Macedonians marry Asian women (setting the example himself), opening trade routes—these things were all done for one reason: the mutual penetration of the Gr. and Eastern civilizations. The Greeks and the Macedonians accepted this reluctantly. In 324 a serious rebellion broke out against the mixing of Macedonian and Asian troops. The Diadochi consciously took a different course, but many of A.'s ideas became reality in spite of them.

There are many differences of opinion on what A. saw as his personal task in life. Some say that he wanted to realize the fundamental unity between the peoples, and sweep away all boundaries between national characters, races, and cultures. Others suppose that he only wanted to create an *oikoumenē* (ecumenē, communal living area), in which all the peoples could live freely and learn from one another. In any case, much of the latter was realized in the Rom. Empire later on (see also PAX ROMANA; CALLISTHENES; PTOLEMY; ARRIANUS; CURTIUS RUFUS).

ALEXANDER SARCOPHAGUS. Monumental sarcophagus found near the Phoenician town of Sidon, now in Istanbul. On the frieze, Alexander the Great is depicted as fighting the Persians or hunting lions. These reliefs can be distinguished from earlier ones by the formation of the groups in various designs and the plastic rounding of the figures. The colors, which have disappeared from most of the Gr. sculptures, have partly survived here. The S. was made in 315 B.C. (see also LYSIPPUS).

ALEXANDER SEVERUS. See SEVERUS.

ALEXANDRIA. Name of several cities founded by Alexander the Great as points of contact for Gr. and Eastern cultures. The most famous of these is A. on the Egyptian coast, founded in 331 B.C., later the residence of the Ptolemies and of the Rom. governors. It was connected with Pharos by a dam, creating two beautiful harbors. The city was built according to a plan, in the style of Hippodamus. The various groups of the population, Gr., Egyptian, and a large Jewish community, lived in separate sections. The most important buildings were the palace of the kings (later the Rom. governors), the Museum with the adjacent library (see BOOKS) and the temple of Serapis. A. was one of the most important Hellenistic centers of the plastic arts, literature, philology, and natural science. Its most flourishing period ended with its conquest by Caesar in 47 B.C., when the Museum went up in flames. In the early imperial period there was a great deal of tension between the Greeks and the Jews (see PHILO), and later mainly between the various sects of Christians. This led to bloody conflicts. In the meantime, A. remained a center of scientific culture. In A.D. 642 it was conquered by the Arabs.

ALLIA. Tributary of the Tiber River, near Rome, where (according to tradition in 387 B.C.) the Rom. army was crushed by the Gauls (see BRENNUS). The day (July 18) was marked down in the Rom. calendar as a *dies ater* (black day).

ALLOBROGES. Gallic tribe in the Rom. province of Narbonensis. Their chief town was present-day Vienne on the Rhône, conquered in 121 B.C. In 63 B.C. they refused to agree to Catilina's proposal for a rebellion, which led, among other things, to the unmasking of his followers (Sall. *Cat.* 40-45).

ALMA MATER. "Feeding, life-giving, blessing mother." Name for such Rom. goddesses as Ceres, Cybele, and Venus; now one's university, college or school.

ALPHABET. See SCRIPT.

ALPHEIOS. The largest river in the Peloponnesus, flows past Olympia.

ALTERA PARS. "The other side"; compare *audi alteram partem* (hear the other side).

ALTIS. See OLYMPIA.

ALYATTES (c. 610-560). King of Lydia, who extended the empire to Halys; a war with Cyaxares was ended when a battle was interrupted by an eclipse of the sun (May 28, 585), forecast by Thales. A. also extended the Lydian authority to the Ionic cities by conquering Smyrna, among other places.

AMASIS. Name of:

—(1) King of Egypt c. 569-526. During his reign there were strong ties with Greece; he used the services of Gr. mercenaries, encouraged the growth of Naucratis, and maintained relations with various Gr. states. Making acquaintance with Egypt during this period (the so-called Saitic empire) was particularly fruitful for the archaic Gr. art of sculpture.

—(2) Athenian potter (6th cent. B.C.) who employed one of the most talented artists—now called the Amasis Painter—to decorate his vases with graceful black figures.

AMBARVALIA. Rom. rite during which a sacrificial animal was carried as a purifying sacrifice: (a) around the fields by the farmers' families, (b) around parts of the ground symbolizing Rom. territory. Sometimes thought to be identical with the ritual of the *fratres arvales* because of their similarity.

AMBIORIX. King of the Eburones, who attacked Caesar's winter quarters in 54 B.C. and annihilated the occupation troops. The next attack, on the camp of Quintus Cicero (brother of the orator), failed (Caes. *B.G.* V, 38-52).

AMBRACIA. A colony of Corinth to the north of Actium, later the capital of Pyrrhus.

AMBROSE (c. 337-397). Early Christian author, bishop of Milan. He was chosen by the people to be a bishop against his will, in 374. One of the most important fathers of the church after Augustine and Jerome. Of his many works on dogma, philosophy, etc., at least one, *De Officiis Ministrorum,* was written under the strong influence of Cicero. The influence of the Stoics can also be seen in other works of A.

AMMIANUS MARCELLINUS (c. 330-c. 395). The last important pagan Rom. historian. He wrote a history in thirty-one books on the period 96-378 (sequel to Tacitus' *Historiae*). Books 15-31 have survived. They contain the history of his own period and are mainly important for the history of the Emperor Julian. He wrote in rhythmic prose with a great virtuosity of style, the more remarkable for the fact that Latin was not his mother tongue.

AMMON. Egyptian god, who had an oracle in the Libyan desert near the oasis of Siwa, among other places, where the Greeks of Cyrene heard of him and identified him with Zeus; they portrayed him with the traditional head of Zeus, but provided him with ram's horns. The oracle was visited by many Greeks, even by Alexander the Great in 332. The priests hailed him as the son of the god.

AMOR. See EROS.

AMPHICTYONS [Gr. amphiktyones, neighbors]. Leagues of Gr. states around a holy place. The most famous are the twelve A. of Delphi, which administered the sanctuary of Apollo in cooperation with the Delphic priests and organized the Pythian Games. The league developed a form of international law, and initiated an early form of Panhellenism. Transgressors were punished by a so-called Holy War. This was one of the ways in which Philip II established and enlarged his sphere of influence in central Greece.

AMPHIPOLIS. City on the river Strymon, the most important Gr. city on the Thracian coast. It was colonized by Athens in 437 B.C. and became important for the exportation of gold from Mount Pangaeus (see also BRASIDAS; CLEON; THUCYDIDES). In 357 B.C., Philip II annexed it to Macedonia.

AMPHITHEATER. Place where the Rom. gladiators' games, etc., were held; elliptic arena surrounded by graduated rows of seats for spectators. The oldest A. (c. 80 B.C.) has been found in Pompeii; the most famous one in Rome was the Colosseum; amphitheaters were found in every part of the Rom. Empire; some (for example, Verona, Nîmes) have survived so nearly intact that performances are still given there. The A. does not exist in Gr. architecture. See Appendix.

AMPHORA. See VASE FORMS.

AMYCLAE. Town to the south of Sparta on the Eurotas River. According to tradition, the Achaeans here withstood attacks by the Dorians for a long time. The famous sanctuary and the throne of Apollo Amyclaeus were found here.

ANACREON of Teos (Asia Minor) (6th cent. B.C.). Gr. lyrical poet. He fled from his native city when it was invaded by the Persians, and helped found Abdera; afterward he lived at the court of Polycrates on Samos and, after the death of the latter, with Hipparchus in Athens, where a statue to him was raised on the Acropolis. His works were later collected and published by Aristarchus. They consisted of hymns to the gods and love poems; but he is most famous for his drinking songs, which gave him the reputation of a bibulous graybeard, forever in love. Only three poems and some fragments of A.'s work have survived. The many other poems he is said to have written, the so-called *Anacreontica*, are of a much later period. "Anacreontic" poetry was also written by many Romans (Catullus, Tibullus), and by poets of later centuries.

ANAPEST. See METER.

ANAXAGORAS of Clazomenae (c. 500-428). Gr. philosopher, the first to settle in Athens, where he became friendly with Pericles. He was accused by the latter's enemies of godlessness, and fled to Lampsacus in the Troas, where he conducted a school until his death. A., with Empedocles and the atomists, was one of the philosophers who wrestled with the problem of the one indivisible, and in contrast, the varying multitude of phenomena. He and Empedocles had some knowledge of the elements which make up the universe; he called them *spermata* (seeds). The unchangeable element in everything is, according to A., the *nous* (spirit). According to Plato, Socrates reproached him with seeing this "spirit" as a material substance moving the universe. His so-called godlessness consisted, in part, of not considering the sun a god, but a "glowing stone, even bigger than the Peloponnesus." A. is a typical representative of natural philosophy in the stage before the crisis that led to the appearance of the Sophists and Socrates (see ETHICS).

ANAXIMANDER of Miletus (611-547). Ionian natural philosopher of the school of Thales. He named the "infinite" (*to apeiron*) as being the protomaterial from which opposing powers split off, which are "unjust" to one another and must "do penance" for it: a partly rational, partly mythical natural law, to which

An amphitheater. Above: segment and floor plan of the Amphitheatrum Flavium (Colosseum) in Rome, which had three floors. Below: the cages for the wild animals under the Colosseum. The animals were brought in through an entrance (a). After the cage had been hoisted to an intermediate floor, the animal was driven to the arena by way of a plank and trap door. Center: gladiator, the person who performed as a public entertainer in the amphitheater.

13

the entire universe is subject.

ANAXIMENES of Miletus (c. 550 B.C.). Pupil of Anaximander. He went back to indicating an observable substance as the protomaterial—namely, the air, which can rarefy itself into fire, and condense itself into wind, clouds, earth, and stone. On the other hand, he went further than his teacher in completely ignoring the mythical elements in the natural laws.

ANCUS MARCIUS (640-616). According to tradition, the fourth king of Rome. His most important deed is supposed to have been building the *pons sublicius* (a wooden bridge on piles) over the Tiber River. He is probably a historical character.

ANCYRA. City in Phrygia, founded by Midas, according to legend. Capital of Galatia. Now known as Ankara.

ANDES. Village near Mantua; birthplace of Virgil.

ANDOCIDES. Name of:

—(1) One of the ten Attic orators (c. 440-c. 390), also played an active political role. He was banished in 415 for participating in a religious scandal, in which Alcibiades was also implicated. In 403 he returned, declaring himself to be an ardent advocate of democratic ideals. Four of his speeches have survived.

—(2) Athenian potter (c. 525 B.C.), for whom painters worked in the black-figure as well as in the red-figure style.

ANIO. Tributary of the Tiber River which separated Latium from the Sabine country; with large waterfalls near the Tibur.

ANNALES [Lat. yearbooks]. Originally lists of magistrates and state events, kept by the pontifices. In about 123 B.C. the *pontifex maximus* Publius Mucius Scaevola compiled a collection of A. in eighty books. A. is also the title of several Rom. historical works. see ENNIUS; TACITUS; ANNALISTS).

ANNALISTS. The writers of *annales,* first written in Greek (Fabius, Pictor, etc.). Cato (although he was not himself an annalist in the strict sense) wrote the first historical narrative in Latin. The A. often distorted Rom. history in favor of the tradition prevalent in senate circles. Livy, whose works are mainly based on that of the A., was greatly influenced by this.

ANTALCIDAS [Gr. Antal Kidas]. Spartan diplomat who, by craftily plotting at the court of the Persian king Artaxerxes II, was able to persuade the King to impose the so-called King's Peace on the Greeks (387 B.C.) This meant, in fact, total capitulation of Greece: (a) the Ionian cities were returned to Persia; (b) the Gr. cities were to be free and autonomous—that is, any concentration of power in the form of leagues, which could make things difficult for Persia, was forbidden; (c) Sparta was to supervise —that is, tyrannize, as Thebes was soon to find out. With this, everything for which the Greeks had fought against the Persians since 480 was undone.

ANTHESTERIA [Gr. feast of flowers]. Three-day festival in honor of Dionysus, celebrated in the spring in Athens and other Ionian cities, during which the new wine was festively consecrated. Small children were also permitted to join the festival, and were given small jars of wine. On the last day the spirits of the dead were invoked.

ANTHOLOGIA. Anthology, collection of Gr. epigrams and other poems. In the 1st cent. B.C. the first anthology entitled *Stephanos* (wreath) was compiled by Meleager. The collection now existing and known by the name of A. originated in the 10th cent. A.D., in Byzantium; this collection, the manuscript of which was found at Heidelberg, in the Palatinate, is called the A. *Palatina*. In the 14th cent. it was revised by the monk Planudes, after whom the revised edition was named A. *Planudea*. There is also the so-called A. *Latina* containing poems of late Lat. authorship.

ANTIGONE. See OEDIPUS; SEVEN AGAINST THEBES.

ANTIGONIDAE. The Hellenic royal house of Macedonia.

ANTIGONUS. Name of various persons:

—(1) A. I. Cyclops or Monophthalmus (c. 382-301). General of Alexander the Great, who made him governor of Asia Minor. After Alexander's death (323) he tried to unite the entire empire under his rule, which seemed possible, especially after the death of Antipater. A coalition formed against him by Cassander, Ptolemy, Seleucus, and Lysimachus was finally successful: A. was defeated and killed at Ipsus.

—(2) A. II Gonatas (c. 320-239). King of Macedonia from 276, son of Demetrius Poliorcetes and grandson of A. I. He reigned over Greece for a short time and waged war against Pyrrhus. He was also a philosopher and brought together many philosophers, poets, and historians at his court.

—(3) A. III Doson (c. 263-221). King of Macedonia from 227, was called to Greece by the Achaean League and defeated the Spartans at Sellasia (222); died just as he was to be recalled to drive the Illyrians out of Macedonia. He laid the foundation for the ambitious plans of his adopted son and heir Philip V.

—(4) A. Of Carystus on Euboea (3rd cent. B.C.). Gr. author and sculptor. He worked for Attalus I in Pergamum.

ANTINOUS. Gr. favorite of the Emperor Hadrian, who drowned in the Nile during a trip with the Emperor. In his memory, Hadrian founded Antinoopolis on the site and had many statues of A., who was famous for his beauty, placed throughout the Rom. Empire.

ANTIOCH. Capital of Syria under the Seleucid empire, on the Orontes River. It was founded in 300 B.C. by Seleucus I and extended by Antiochus III and IV. As in Alexandria, the different population groups (Greeks, Macedonians, Syrians, and Jews) lived in separate parts of the city. Pompey added it to the Rom. Empire (64 B.C.). The city still flourished afterward, and was one of the two largest in the East, the other being Alexandria. Its prosperity was due to its position as the administrative center and its excellent trade routes to the hinterland and overseas.

ANTIOCHUS. Name of various kings:

—(1) A. I Soter (324-362). King of Syria from 280; son of Seleucus I, the greatest founder of Gr. cities in the East after Alexander the Great. His nickname Soter (savior) was given him after his so-called victory of the elephants (276) over the Gauls (see GALATIA).

—(2) A. II Theos (287-247). Son of Antiochus I; king from 262.

—(3) A. III, called the Great (242-187). Son of Seleucus II; king from 224; tried to recover his shrunken empire and to extend it, which he was able to do in the east. In the south he was temporarily stopped by Ptolemy IV. However, when he again marched on Egypt after a secret treaty with Philip V, he came into conflict with Rome, which led to the Syrian War, during which A. was advised by Hannibal. A. crossed over to Greece, but was worsted by Rome. This ended the Seleucid empire's period of greatness.

—(4) A. IV Epiphanes (c. 215-163). Son of A. III; king after 175. Known primarily because of the revolt of the Maccabees against him in Palestine, which he was trying to Hellenize.

—(5) A. XIII Asiaticus. After several other kings of that name had reigned for longer or shorter periods, he was the last to reign over the Seleucid empire. He was deposed, and Pompey added the area to the Rom. Empire as the province Syria in 64 B.C.

ANTIPATER (397-319). Governor of Macedonia during Alexander the Great's Persian campaign. After the death of Alexander in 323, the Greeks revolted; he defeated them, after which Demosthenes committed suicide. A. was appointed regent in 321; his death two years later led to a bitter struggle between the Diadochi.

ANTIPHON. (c. 480-411). One of the ten Attic orators. He played a leading part in the oligarchic revolution in 411 (see also THERAMENES; ALCIBIADES). After the failure of the revolution he was condemned to death, in spite of his masterly speech of defense. He created the Attic style of oratory, and was also the first to use the well-known strict organization of a plea, later used by Cicero: (a) Introduction; (b) reconstruction of the facts of the case; (c) argument; (d) peroration.

ANTISTHENES of Athens (c. 444-366). Founder of the school of Cynics, pupil of Socrates, whose intellectualistic ethics (virtue is knowledge and thus can be learned) he adopted and elaborated. According to A., he who aims only at virtue in life cannot be touched by any external things as illness, pain, poverty, or slavery.

ANTIUM. City on the coast of Latium. For a long time it was the main city of the Volsci; it was a pirates' nest until the Romans captured the fleet in 338 B.C.—from the landward side (see ROS-TRA). Caligula and Nero were born there. At that time A. was a famous port with temples and villas. One of the famous sculptures found there is the "Apollo Belvedere," and also the "girl of A." (probably a Gr. original from the 3rd cent. B.C.), a young priestess with an offertory plate.

ANTONIUS LIBERALIS (2nd cent. B.C.) Gr. author. He wrote a book on mythology (*Metamorphoses*).

ANTONINUS PIUS (86-161). Rom. emperor from 138, one of the adoptive emperors, adopted by Hadrian. He himself adopted Marcus Aurelius and Verus. He was a sensible and mild ruler, with respect for the senate; he reigned economically; the government was centralized as much as possible. His policy was peaceful, on principle, but he still had to cope with revolts and riots, among the Jews and others. A temple dedicated to him and his wife Faustina stands in the Rom. Forum.

ANTONIUS, MARCUS (Mark Antony) (82-30). One of the triumvirate of 43 B.C.; accompanied Caesar in Gaul and commanded the left wing at Pharsalus. He was *magister equitum* under Caesar's dictatorship of 48 and in 44 he was his fellow consul. After the assassination of Caesar he delivered an impressive funeral oration and communicated to the populace Caesar's testament by which Octavian was named as Caesar's adopted son and heir. Octavian soon asserted his rights, and this led to tension between them. Lepidus and others brought about a reconciliation, after which the second triumvirate, officially recognized by law, was formed. First, though, those in opposition were eliminated by proscription. A. was emphatic in wanting Cicero, who had turned violently against him in his *Philippicae,* on the list of those doomed. The expedition against Brutus and Cassius (Philippi) followed. A. now left for Asia Minor— where he first met Cleopatra—and Egypt. In 40 the renewed tension between A. and Octavian was smoothed over at Brundisium, where A. married Octavia, sister of

Augustus. A. then governed the Eastern half of the Rom. Empire, Octavian the Western half. In 37 the triumvirate was renewed for five years in Tarentum. But the unity was not destined to be of long duration. Lepidus was pushed aside; in the meantime A.'s actions in the East were becoming more and more repulsive to Rome. An expedition against the Parthians was a serious failure. A. became more and more involved with Cleopatra, whom he finally formally married, and to whose insatiable lust for power he gave in time after time. Finally Octavian was able to persuade the senate to declare war on Cleopatra. A. was not mentioned in order to keep up the appearance that war was being waged against a foreign power. Cleopatra fled from the battle of Actium and was followed to Egypt by A.; both committed suicide there. The historical meaning of the struggle between A. and Octavian is basically that of the conflict between East and West on which it was founded. Cleopatra undoubtedly wanted to use A. as a figurehead for making Alexandria the capital of the area around the Mediterranean Sea. The Rom. Empire, as it had come into being in the 2nd and 1st centuries B.C., might be ruled as a single country, but was clearly divided into two cultural areas, a Lat. Western half, and a Gr. Eastern one. This Gr.-Hellenistic East was now to dominate Hellenized Rome and Italy, which were still fundamentally different by nature. It was important for the history of Europe that this process was temporarily held back. The ultimate split into an East and a West Rom. Empire, which would one day become unavoidable, would have come about even then if A. and Octavian had reached an impasse. So we can safely say that the battle of Actium gave three centuries of respite to the unity of the Rom. Empire.

APAMEA. City in Syria, on the Orontes River; of the Seleucid empire the second in importance after Antioch.

APELLA. See SPARTA.

APELLES. Renowned Gr. painter in the time of Alexander the Great. He painted portraits of several Macedonian princes. One of his most famous canvases was that of Aphrodite, rising from the sea foam. None of his paintings have survived; we know of them only through the descriptions given by ancient authors. Some of the paintings from Pompeii are sometimes regarded as copies of his work.

APHAIA, TEMPLE OF. See AEGINA.

APHRODITE. Gr. goddess of love, beauty, and fertility (Rom. name: Venus). Her name cannot be accounted for by the Gr. language; the Greeks themselves say it is derived from "born out of foam" (*aphros*). The cult comes from the East and is related to that of the Babylonian astarte or Ashtaroth, the Phoenician Ishtar. Thus Cyprus was one of the most important places for the cult; also Cythera, Corinth (where she was served by *hierodoules,* female temple slaves, who gave their love to strangers), Cnidus, and Mount Eryx in western Sicily. In Sicily, as in Cyprus, her Phoenician origin can be clearly seen). Her Eastern origin can also be seen in her role of protector of the Trojans (in the Iliad, etc.); she had been the beloved of the Trojan Anchises, and mother of Aeneas, and was thus his faithful protector in Virgil's *Aeneid.* Renowned sculptures and paintings of A. are: the "A. of Melos" (the so-called Venus of Milo), the "A. of Cnidus" of Praxiteles, and the "Ludovisi Throne."

APOLLINARIS SIDONIUS, GAIUS SOLLIUS (c. 430-c. 487). Lat. author, born at Lugdunum, son-in-law of the Rom. Emperor Avitus. Author of nine books of letters and poems valued as source material for Gallo-Rom. society of the 5th cent.

APOLLO. Gr. god of justice and order, of beauty and art (particularly of music). The origin of A. has been hotly debated. Now it is generally assumed that he comes from Asia Minor, although elements of a shepherds' god from the north can also be found in his person. (See also LYCEUM.)

In Greece his cult was practiced mainly in Delos, where, according to legend, he and his twin sister Artemis were born (see also LETO), and Delphi, where he was mainly a god of oracles (see also PYTHIAN GAMES). In addition to the functions named, he was also the cleanser of those laden with guilt, and the healer

(here we can see the ambivalence of the gods: A.'s arrows could also spread disease). Asklepios was his son. Later he was also seen as a sun-god (see HELIOS); this aspect is probably connected with his epithet Phoebus (radiant). In Gr. culture, the harmonious tranquillity personified by A. is in contrast to the ecstatic element Dionysus. A. was introduced to the Romans early, by way of Etruria and also by way of Magna Graecia itself. Augustus and his family, particularly, considered themselves to be under the protection of A. A famous original Gr. sculpture of A. is in the west façade of the temple of Zeus on Olympia. He was also often portrayed as an archer, as in the Rom. copy of the "A. Belvedere" in Rome. In his character of the god of beauty, A. was also the ideal figure of a young man (archaic art).

APOLLODORUS. Name of:

—(1) A. of Athens (2nd cent. B.C.). A versatile Gr. scholar, pupil of Aristarchus. He wrote on such subjects as history, geography, and theology. One of his books was the *Bibliotheca,* on Gr. mythology, which was mainly about the heroes. A book attributed to him, and with the same title, has survived. This book, however, was written in the 1st cent. B.C. Of A.'s actual work, only fragments have survived.

—(2) A. of Damascus, architect under Trajan, whose Forum he built, and under Hadrian, who banished him in 129 B.C. and later had him executed.

—(3) A. of Gela and A. of Carystus, poets of the New Comedy.

APOLLONIUS RHODIUS (3rd cent. B.C.). Gr. epic poet, pupil of Callimachus and the librarian of the renowned library of Alexandria. After disagreements with Callimachus, A. fled to Rhodes; Callimachus was an advocate of the short epic (epyllion), A. of the heroic epic, but there were probably other, more personal reasons for friction. Aside from his shorter works, A. wrote the *Argonautica* in four books, on the expedition of the Argonauts. The poem copies Homer's style and his hexameter, but otherwise it is a typical scholarly poem, a product of the Alexandrian school. It also lacks the unity of composition which characterized

Homer's poetry.

APOLLONIUS DYSCOLUS [the grouchy one] (2nd cent. A.D.). Gr. Grammarian, who had a great influence on later grammarians.

APPIANUS of Alexandria (2nd cent. A.D.). Gr. writer of Rom. history; he lived in Rome under Hadrian and Antoninus Pius. His books are mainly about the Rom. wars of conquest, which he describes in geographical order. The quality of the writing is not high, but it is nevertheless invaluable for some parts of history, for which he is the only source. His most valuable work is on the history of the Gracchi.

Gr. version has survived, called *Lucius or a Donkey;* both versions go back to a Gr. original.

APULIA. Province in southeastern Italy, renowned for its wool. It contained many Gr. colonies. In 317 B.C. it was subjected to Rome; later it became allied with Hannibal against Rome, and also fought against Rome during the Social War (War with the Allies) of 90-88.

AQUAE SEXTIAE. A seaside resort with hot springs (now called Aix-en Provence), where Marius defeated the Teutons (see CIMBRI) in 102 B.C.

AQUEDUCT. Rom. waterworks over arched bridges, bringing the water from

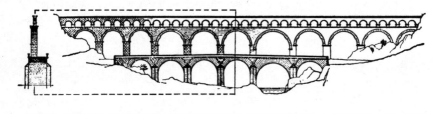

Aqueduct

APPIAN WAY (or VIA APPIA). See VIA.

A PRIORI. "From what is before"; from cause to effect (Vulgar Latin).

APULEIUS of Madaurus (c. 125-c. 185). Lat. novelist. He studied in Carthage, Athens, and Rome, afterward returning to Africa, where he was involved in a lawsuit; he was accused of having won a rich widow by using magic and of having poisoned her son by a former marriage. He won the case by means of a brilliant speech of defense, the *Apologia,* subsequently revised and called *De Magia,* which has survived. Later he was a traveling orator. His main book is *Metamorphoses* (better known as *The Golden Ass*) the only group of Lat. novels to survive. In the main character, Lucius, we often recognize the author. He is turned into a donkey and has all sorts of strange adventures. Finally he ends up in a procession in honor of Isis, which he describes enthrallingly, and she turns him back into his former self. A shorter

the mountains into the cities. The oldest aqueducts, however, such as the Aqua Appia were tunnels (see CLAUDIUS CAECUS). Famous examples of the A. are: the Aqua Claudia near Rome and the Pont du Gard near Nîmes.

AQUILEIA. City near Venice in northern Italy, an important sally port from Illyria to Italy. In the Rom. imperial period it was a very important city, sometimes called "the second Rome." In 452 it was destroyed by Attila.

AQUITANIA. Name for the part of Gaul between the Garonne River and the Pyrenees. A. was subjected by Caesar in 57 B.C.

ARA. Rom. altar; the A. Pacis (Augustae) is well known. It is a monument dedicated by the senate in honor of the restoration of peace by Augustus; it was put up on the Campus Martius (Field of Mars). The reliefs show the rite of the *suovetaurilia* at the dedication (9 B.C.), with pictures of the imperial family (including Augustus as the *pontifex max-imus*). See Appendix.

ARABIA. The Greeks hardly knew A. before the time of Alexander the Great, who organized a number of exploratory expeditions. During the Hellenistic period there was more contact, particularly with the Nabataei of Petra; the Romans continued with this, and under Trajan, Nabataeia became a Rom. province. The Greeks and the Romans imported mainly gold and incense, along the trade routes from the Near East.

ARATUS. Name of:
—(1) A. of Soli (Cilicia) (c. 315-240/ 39), author of an astronomical poem called *Phaenomena,* with a hint of Stoicism in it. A. adopted the story from Eudoxus. The book was greatly admired and was translated into Latin by Germanicus, Cicero, and Avienus.
—(2) A. of Sicyon (271-213) Gr. statesman. He became the strategist of the Achaean League, after he had enrolled his native city in it. By constantly changing his alliance, through tact and personal power, he was able to make the league's position a powerful one. The crisis came when Cleomenes III of Sparta defeated him in 227, which almost led to disbandment of the league. A. averted this by signing an alliance with Antigonus Doson. Cleomenes was defeated at Sellasia in 222. A., however, came into conflict with Antigonus' successor Philip V, because he did not share the latter's anti-Rom. views. He wrote memoirs, which were used by Plutarch and others. Plutarch's *Life of A.* is based on them.

ARAUSIO. City (now Orange) in the Rhône Valley, where a Rom. army was crushed in 105 B.C. by the Cimbri and the Teutons. Remains of Roman times include a theater in an excellent state of preservation and an arch of triumph.

ARBELA. See GAUGAMELA.

ARCADIA. Mountainous region in the central Peloponnesus, where the original population sought refuge after a Dorian attack, as in Achaea; the Arcadian dialect is therefore also related to Mycenaean Greek. There were only a few cities (see TEGEA; MANTINEA). During the classical period A. did not play any political role; Epaminondas tried to make it an active bulwark against Sparta (the founding of Megalopolis), and later it was a member of the Achaean League. Culturally too, A. remained backward, and many ancient ritual customs, festivals, and so forth, still existed there in much later times. These were extensively described by Pausanius.

ARCADIUS. The first East-Rom. emperor (reigned 395-408). He left most of the affairs of state to his wife, Eudoxia.

ARCHAEOLOGY. The science that illuminates the life, history, culture, and society of ancient times. Classical A. comprises two branches: (a) the history of ancient art (see ARCHITECTURE; SCULPTURE; MOSAIC; GEMS; and PAINTING); (b) the technique of excavation. The results of these excavations are still our main source of knowledge about a large part of ancient history before 900 B.C. This has been only partially changed by the fact that Mycenaean script has been deciphered (see CNOSSUS; PYLOS), because it only covers a limited field. A. also provides indispensable additions to and corrections of the data that have been handed down on paper (see, for example, HOUSES; PRIENE; TROY; OLYNTHUS; AGORA; POMPEII; HERCULANEUM). A. is also of great importance for the economic history of ancient times. The places where Gr. vases are found, for example, yield information about trade routes, export articles, and so forth. Our knowledge of the Etruscans is almost entirely derived from the results of A. Data on social life in the provinces under the Rom. Empire are acquired only by A. and epigraphy, which is usually also dependent on A. for new material.

ARCHAIC ART. The art of the 6th and 7th centuries B.C. (For painting, see VASE PAINTING; for temples, see ARCHITECTURE; TEMPLE.) Gr. monumental sculpture developed during this period. It is the period of the "Apollo" figures, the *kouroi* (young men) and the *korai* (young women). Characteristics are: decorative stylization, a stereotyped smile, and the frontal attitude. Many characteristics can be traced back to the influence of Egypt (see AMASIS; NAUCRATIS). At this time Egypt, under the Saite kings, had just been opened to Gr. colonists and traders and the art forms of the old empire were being revived. In about 500 B.C. a transitional form between archaic and classical art began to appear. We usually distinguish between the early archaic period (660-580), the middle archaic period (580-535), and the late archaic period (535-480).

ARCHELAUS. Name of:
—(1) Gr. philosopher (5th cent. B.C.), pupil of Anaxagoras and teacher of the Lampsacus school after the latter's death.
—(2) King of Macedonia from c. 413-399; he moved the residence from Aegae to Pella, and encouraged the Hellenization of his country by inviting Gr. men of art and letters (Euripides, etc.) to his court.
—(3) Gr. general of Mithridates (1st cent. B.C.) He was defeated at Orchomenus by Sulla (85). During negotiations he was suspected of treason by Mithridates, and deserted to the Romans.

ARCHIDAMUS. Name of several Spartan kings:
—(1) A. II (reigned 476-427). He put down the great Helot revolt after the earthquake of 464, and repeatedly attacked Attica during the first part of the Peloponnesian War in an effort to destroy it, although he personally had not wanted the war at all. He also led operations against Plataea.
—(2) A. III (reigned 360-338). He led the retreat of the army after the battle of Leuctra (see also AGESILAUS), and fought successfully against Epaminondas and the Arcadians. Called in by Tarentum to help fight the Lucanians, he organized an attack on Italy (compare PYRRHUS), during which he was killed.

ARCHILOCHUS of Paros (c. 700 B.C.). The first Gr. lyric poet, an extremely interesting character. As a mercenary he led a roving life and was killed on Naxos. In his poetry—mainly iambs and elegies (see METER)—he describes his life, writes poisonous things about his enemies, and disdainfully mocks conventions. Quite a large number of fragments of his work have survived. His poetry was greatly admired in his own time; he was even considered to be on a par with Homer. A. can be seen to have been one of the most striking representatives of rising individ-

ualism.

ARCHIMEDES of Syracuse (287-212). The greatest Gr. mathematician and physicist, killed when the Romans took his native city (see NOLI TURBARE). The story of how he devised the most fantastic war machines against the Romans is well known (Liv. XXIV, 34); his words, "Give me a place to stand and I will move the earth" are also famous. A. is credited with pioneering work in the fields of mechanics (lever, center of gravity) and hydrostatics. He is said to have uttered the famous exclamation "Eureka!" when he discovered, while bathing, the principle of buoyancy—that a solid submerged in water will be buoyed up by a force equal to the weight of the water it displaces. Of his many books, several have survived. Some of his theories were also handed down by way of Middle-Eastern Arabian science.

ARCHITECTURAL ORDERS. In classical Gr. temples, we can distinguish two orders: Doric (A) and the Ionic (B). In the Doric order, the column (2), without a pedestal, stands on the stylobate (1) formed by three steps, and is crowned by a simple capital (3). On the columns lies an architrave (4), a single horizontal beam, which gives an impression of massiveness. Above this there is a band of triglyphs (5) and metopes (6). The triglyphs are a relic from the time when temples were built of wood and the protruding ends of the crossbeams were ornamented. The metopes—the spaces between the triglyphs—were perfect for depicting a story in episodes (for example, the legend of Theseus, the labors of Heracles, etc.). The whole was crowned by a pediment (7) whose cornices enclosed the tympanum (8), a triangular space which was suitable for monumental representations (for example, Parthenon: the birth of Athena; Olympia: the battle between the Lapithae and the Centaurs); the space could be filled in a natural manner, for example by placing a god in the center and fighting figures and animals at either side, and filling in the corners with river gods or fallen warriors. In the Ionic order (B) the main difference, apart from those in the column, are that the architrave is divided into layers (usually three), which gives an impression of greater lightness, and that above it there is a frieze (9), an uninterrupted band of sculpture. The Corinthian order (C) can hardly be considered a separate order at all before the Rom. period. In Gr. A. it is no more than a variant form of the capital (10) (see COLUMN). The total impression given by Doric A. is heavy, massive; that of the Ionic is much lighter. After the 5th cent. B.C., Doric temples were given an Ionic aspect by making the columns more slender, and sometimes by adding Ionic building elements (see also PARTHENON; BASSAE; TEMPLE; ACROTERION).

ARCHITECTURE. For Minoan-Mycenaean A. see CNOSSUS; PHAISTOS; MYCE-NAE. For Gr. A. see ARCHITECTURAL ORDERS; TEMPLE; COLUMN; THEATER; HOUSES. For city planning see HIPPODA-MUS; PRIENE. For Rom. A. see (in addition to some of the articles cited above) POMPEII; OSTIA; AQUEDUCT; THERMAE; BASILICA; AMPHITHEATER.

ARCHITRAVE. See ARCHITECTURAL ORDERS.

ARCHONS. Gr. magistrates. The Athenian A. are the most famous ones, the dignitaries who took over the government after the dissolution of the monarchy. First there were three: the *basileus* (religious function); the *polemarchos* (military function); and the *eponymos* (after whom the year was named, as was the case with the Rom. consuls); soon

The three Greek architectural orders

six *thesmothetai* (with judiciary powers) were added. When the A. was no longer elected after 487, but chosen by lots, the office lost its political significance (see STRATEGIST). Ex-A. were life members of the Areopagus. The list of *eponymoi* was kept from 683 B.C. on.

ARCHYTAS of Tarentum (c. 400 B.C.). Gr. philosopher, mathematician, and physicist of the school of Pythagoras, friend of Plato. He studied mathematical progressions, among other things. In common with all the other Pythagoreans, he was greatly interested in music theory.

AREOPAGUS. A hill in Athens, dedicated to Ares; also the council of nobles which met on that hill. Originally, an advisory council of the kings, after the decline of the monarchy, the board of administration of ex-archons; it also acted as a court, especially for murder trials (compare Aeschylus, *Oresteia*). The A. retained this authority even after having lost its political importance, first through the practice of drawing lots for the office of archon (487 B.C.) and especially because Ephialtes divested it of its authority as a supervisory body (462 B.C.). In 480 B.C., however, the A. still had a great deal of prestige as a result of its courageous actions during the crisis of Salamis. In A.D. 50 St. Paul made his famous speech on A. hill (Acts 17: 19-34).

ARES. Gr. god of war, probably from Thrace, which was famous for its sturdy warriors. His cult was not nearly so extensive in Greece as it later became in Rome, where he was identified with Mars. In the *Iliad* he protects the Trojans, and is feared on the battlefields. His fellow gods hated his crude violence. He was also a rather odd partner for his wife (or mistress) Aphrodite.

ARGINUSAE. A group of three islands near Lesbos, where the Athenian fleet defeated the Spartan fleet in 406 B.C. This was the last Athenian victory of the Peloponnesian War. However, the Athenians, immeasurably blind, afterward condemned the strategists to death because a storm had prevented them from recovering the bodies of those who had been drowned or killed in action. Of the *prytanei* (see PRYTANEUM), who had to prepare the motion in the popular assem-

bly, only Socrates protested against this procedure.

ARGONAUTS. Members of an expedition of Gr. heroes under the leadership of Jason, who set sail in the ship *Argo* for Colchis, to find the so-called Golden Fleece—that is, the golden fleece of the ram on which Phrixus and Helle had fled from the attacks of their stepmother in Orchomenus. The heroes, among whom were the Dioscuri, Heracles, and Orpheus, met at Ioleus in southeastern Thessaly, and went from there to Lemnos, the Hellespont, and the Pontus, and thus to Colchis. Here, after undergoing many hardships, Jason acquired the fleece with the help of the Princess Medea. Medea fled with the A. from the wrath of her father Aeetes. The return journey is endlessly prolonged, especially in later versions. The *Argo* is said to have sailed up the Danube and returned by way of the Po (or even the Rhine!).

The story is narrated in the 4th-cent. Pythian ode of Pindar, and greatly expanded in the epic of Apollonius Rhodius. As many of the dwelling places of the Minyae are named in it, it is often assumed that the story originated with that tribe.

ARGOS. Gr. city on the plain of Argolis (northeastern Peloponnesus). It appears as the city of Diomedes in Homer's epic; it is also generally known as the kingdom of Agamemnon. In tragedy A. is identified with Mycenae. In about 1000 B.C. the Dorians settled in A.; in the 7th cent. B.C., Pheidon ruled it. After that period A. was always anti-Spartan and never became a member of the Peloponnesian League. During the Peloponnesian War, it remained neutral. The goddess of the city was Hera, of whom Polyclitus made the famous temple statue (the sanctuary was not in the city, but to the north of it).

ARION of Lesbos (c. 625 B.C.). Gr. poet at the court of Periander in Corinth; he invented the dithyramb, but no examples of his work have survived. According to legend, A. on a homeward voyage from Italy, was overpowered by members of the crew, but he jumped overboard and was saved by a dolphin (see also TRAGEDY).

ARIOVISTUS. King of the German

Suevi, who entered Gaul in 71 B.C. in order to support the Sequani against the Aedui. The Rom. senate temporarily recognized him as a "friend of the Rom. people," but in 58 Caesar picked a quarrel with him and defeated him badly. He fled across the Rhine and died soon afterward (Caes. *B.G.* I, 30-54; V, 29).

ARISTAGORAS (c. 500 B.C.). Tyrant of Miletus; regent for his father-in-law Histiaeus: instigator of the Ionian revolt against Persia (499). After the rebellion had failed (see LADE) he fled to Thrace, where he died.

ARISTARCHUS:
—(1) A. of Samothrace (c. 217-c. 145). Founder of scientific philology, pupil of Aristophanes of Byzantium; head of the library of Alexandria from c. 153-c. 145; from there he went to Cyprus, where he died. He edited the textual criticism of Homer's works, and of various other Gr. authors. He also wrote many commentaries and was a pioneer in the field of grammar. The arrangement of the *Odyssey* and the *Iliad* which we now use was devised by A.
—(2) A. of Samos (c. 250 B.C.). Gr. mathematician and astronomer. According to Archimedes, he declared that the earth rotates on its axis and revolves about the sun; however, this is not in harmony with what A. wrote in the only one of his manuscripts that has survived.

ARISTIDES (c. 525-c. 467). Athenian statesman, strategist at Marathon. He was banished by ostracism in 848 after a disagreement with Themistocles about the latter's naval plans. A.'s policy emphasized the role of the army. When he was recalled in 480, he was able to make use of his special talents during the assault on the island Psyttaleia in the battle of Salamis, and in 479 at Plataea. After the Persian Wars, he organized the Delian League and determined the contributions of the members. This justified his epithet "the Just." According to tradition, he died in poverty. This tradition (Nepos, Plutarch) gives a very one-sided, black-and-white picture of the relationship between him and Themistocles. Actually, apart from their quarrel in 484, only cooperation between them has been proved.

ARISTIDES, PUBLIUS AELIUS 2nd cent. A.D. Gr. rhetorician (see RHETORIC). Fifty-eight of his speeches have survived, written in pure Attic. He was greatly honored by later generations.

ARISTIPPUS of Cyrene (c. 435-356). Gr. philosopher, pupil of Socrates; either he or his grandson of the same name founded the Cyrenaic school.

ARISTOGEITON. See HARMODIUS.

ARISTOPHANES (c. 445-c. 385). The most important representative of the Attic Old Comedy; practically nothing is known about his life apart from his dramatic activities. Probably one or more of his plays were performed for Dionysius I in Syracuse; Plato makes him a good friend of Socrates in his *Symposium*. His plays show that he was a conservative; he particularly opposed radicals like Cleon, and was in favor of an honorable peace with Sparta. Making use of the unequaled freedom of speech possible in 5th-cent. Athens, he mocked all modernism, not only in the state and society, but also in art, religion, and philosophy. This criticism was not his goal, but only a means of educating his people. In his later plays he was forced to exercise restraint, and chose more neutral subjects; these were the transition to the Middle Comedy. Of his forty plays, eleven have survived; *The Acharnians* (425)—the "good citizen" Dicaiopolis negotiates a private peace with Sparta; *The Knights* (424)—a satire on Cleon; *The Clouds* (423)—a satire on the sophists, strangely enough represented by Socrates; *The Wasps* (422)— on the Athenian rage for trials; *The Peace* (421)—the goddess of peace is freed from imprisonment; this refers to the coming peace of Nicias; *The Birds* (414)—flight from the unpleasantness of Athenian society to a Utopian bird kingdom; *Lysistrata* (411)—"marriage strike" to force the men into peace. *The Thesmophoriazusae* (411)—the women at the Thesmophoria festival against Euripides; *The Frogs* (405)—Dionysus himself goes to the underworld to bring back a tragic poet, as all the great ones have died; Aeschylus wins in the contest with Euripides; *Ecclesiazusae* (389)—persiflage on the emancipation of women; *Plutus* (388)— the god of wealth is cured of blindness and thenceforth meets good people. A.'s language is poetic and powerful; his jokes, although often vulgar and obscene, show great ingeniousness. His people are often types rather than characters, but this is mainly a characteristic of the genre.

ARISTOPHANES of Byzantium (c. 357-180). Gr. scholar, successor of Eratosthenes as librarian at Alexandria, teacher of Aristarchus. He edited the texts of Homer and other poets, among which was the first collection of Pindar's works. He also made a selection of the best Gr. poets, on which the list of authors whose work was preserved in Byzantium by the scholars was based.

ARISTOTLE (384-322). Gr. philosopher and famous scholar, born in Stagirus, the son of a court physician to one of the Macedonian kings. He came to Athens in 367 to study at Plato's Academy. After the latter's death in 348, he and Xenocrates left Athens, since they did not get along with Plato's successor Speusippus, and pro-Macedonians were not favorably looked upon in Athens. They went to Assos, near Troy, and after three years A. left for Lesbos. Here Theophrastus was his host. A. devoted himself to the study of zoology, which was to remain his favorite subject. From 342-335 he tutored Alexander the Great, at the request of Philip II. After that, A. returned to Athens, where he founded the Lyceum. He taught there for thirteen years. When Alexander died in 323 and the anti-Macedonians returned to power in Athens, A. retreated to Chalcis, saying (with the death of Socrates in mind) that he did not want to give the Athenians a second chance to sin against philosophy. He died the next year.

A.'s work embraces very nearly the entire scale of Gr. thought and Gr. science, and has left ineradicable traces on the philosophy and science of later ages. He deals with logic, ontology, ethics, metaphysics (for A. this word only means that which follows physics in the outline of his work), biology, physics, psychology, astronomy, rhetoric, poetry, and politics. Almost none of those of his articles that have survived were written for publication. They are concepts for lectures at the Lyceum, and therefore

they lack Plato's brilliant style. None of his published dialogues have survived. Of writings in a third category, large collections of material for scientific works, there has been handed down a copy on papyrus of *The Government of the Athenians*. Together with descriptions of 157 other forms of government, of which only fragments are left, this is the preparatory study for *Politics*.

The enormous extent of his works makes it impossible to mention more than a few main characteristics here. A. was a pupil of Plato, and never entirely succeeded in dissociating himself from Plato's way of thinking. Still, he was too much of a realist to take over Plato's transcendent world of ideas. The ideas do exist, according to A., but *in* the world of the visible. In each thing, he distinguishes the matter which is capable (*dynamis*) of being controlled by an imminent "form," and thus becoming actuality (*energeia*). In spite of all the criticism of Plato implied by this, A. ranges himself on Plato's side, insofar as he demands to know, in the first place, to what *goal* every particle of the finite leads, what its *purpose* is (teleological thought). This striving for a goal (*telos*) can also be seen in A.'s picture of the cosmos, which has one god, an "unmoved mover," as its nucleus. This god is total "form" and total *energeia*. The most striking characteristic of his ethics is the doctrine of the "golden mean"; for example, courage is the middle road between recklessness and cowardice. This same thing can be seen in political science: the best form of state is again the middle way between monarchy and radical democracy. In metaphysics, too, A. tries to steer a course between idealism and materialism. Because of his great feeling for order, system, and clarity, ancient philosophy as a whole cannot be seen apart from A. The scholasticism of the Middle Ages was based entirely on his work, particularly as preserved by Arabian scholarship (see also PERIPATETICS; TRAGEDY; RHETORIC).

ARISTOXENUS. See MUSIC.

ARMENIA. Mountainous country in eastern Asia Minor, a satrapy of the Persian empire. Xenophon went through it with the Ten Thousand (*An.* IV, 4-6). During the Hellenistic period it was an independent kingdom, and later a vassal state of Rome, particularly after Lucullus' campaign against Tigranes. During the Rom. imperial period the Arsacidae and the Sassanidae reigned there successively.

ARMINIUS (c. 18 B.C.-A.D. 17). Prince of the German Cherusci. He had risen in the service of Rome, but led a revolt against Rome in A.D. 9 that resulted in the battle of the Teutoburger Wald. He was also able to arrest Rom. expansion on the right bank of the Rhine, against Germanicus.

ARNOBIUS (c. A.D. 300). Lat. Christian author from Numidia. He wrote a defense of Christianity against paganism, with many references to Lucretius.

ARNUS. Now the Arno River, in Etruria.

ARPINUM. City of the Volsci, subjected to Rome in about 300 B.C. Native city of Marius and Cicero.

ARRIANUS, FLAVIUS (c. 95-175). Gr. historian, our main source for the life of Alexander the Great. He was a pupil of Epictetus, whose *Discourses* and *Enchiridion* (a handbook of ethics) he published. He also wrote historical works, of which the most important is the *Anabasis of Alexander* (Alexander's Persian campaign). It is written in a very businesslike and matter-of-fact fashion; its importance, however, lies in the fact that its main sources were Aristobulus and Ptolemy I, both of whom had accompanied Alexander. He edited his material with a great deal of logic.

ARSACIDÆ. The Parthian royal house, c. 250 B.C.-A.D. 230. They declared themselves to be descendants of the Achaemenidae. Their capital was Ecbatana, their winter residence Ctesiphon on the Tigris.

ARSINOE. Name of several queens of Egypt, during the dynasty of the Ptolemies.

ARS LONGA, VITA BREVIS. See VITA BREVIS.

ARTAPHERNES. See DATIS.

ARTAXERXES. Name of several kings:
—(1) A. I Macrocheir, Longimanus (long hand). King of Persia from 464-

425; son of Xerxes. He was the king who negotiated the peace of Callias and offered Themistocles asylum.
—(2) A. II Mnemon (436-358, king after 404). The Persian king against whom Cyrus the Younger marched (see also CUNAXA); he made the peace of Antialcidas. One of his most influential satraps was Tissaphernes.
—(3) A. Ochus. Son of the last, king from 358-338; he restored central authority, which had been greatly weakened under the reign of A. II.

ARTEMIS. Gr. goddess of wildlife, and thus also of the hunt; protector of women in childbed (but also causer of the sudden death of women: ambivalence, see APOLLO). In mythology she is Apollo's twin sister (see LETO), but her origin is entirely different. She originated in the "ruler of the animals" in Minoan culture (see MYCENAE). She was represented as a proud virgin ("A. of Versailles," after Leochares); she was honored as a real goddess of nature, particularly in the more remote provinces of Greece (Arcadia, Aetolia; see also CALYDON). Later she was also looked upon as the moon-goddess, particularly after her identification with the Rom. Diana. A completely different A. figure was worshiped in Asia Minor (see EPHESUS).

ARTEMISIUM [Gr. Artemision]. Cape in northwestern Euboea, where the Gr. fleet fought against the Persians in 480 B.C., while Leonidas defended Thermopylae (see also THEMISTOCLES). A. is also the place where a lovely early classical statue of Zeus (or Poseidon) was found. It is a Gr. original, and is now in the National Museum in Athens.

ARVERNI. Gallic tribe in what is now Auvergne, which competed for a long time with the Aedui for hegemony in Gaul. Their capital, Gergovia, was besieged in vain by Caesar in 52 B.C. (see VERCINGETORIX).

ARYBALLOS. See VASE FORMS.

ASCRA. Town in Boeotia where Hesiod lived. He shudderingly described the unpleasant climate.

ASIA. In the writings of ancient authors this name usually meant Asia Minor, or the Rom. province Asia, the former kingdom of Pergamum, made over to Rome by testamentary disposition of Attalus III in 133 B.C. This once wealthy area (it was Croesus' empire) was fallen upon by Rom. governors and publicans. The terrible hatred of the inhabitants toward the plunderers led to rebellion in 88 B.C. (see MITHRIDATES). The imperial period restored prosperity to A., as it did to most of the other provinces.

ASINIUS POLLIO, GAIUS (76 B.C.-A.D. 4). Lat. statesman, writer, and patron of literature. He fought on Caesar's side at Pharsalus, and was a neutral mediator between Octavian and Antony. He devoted himself entirely to literature after the victory of Octavian. He was a friend of Horace and acted as the protector of Virgil; the latter dedicated his famous fourth *Eclogue* to him. He conducted a literary salon, and founded the first public library (see BOOKS) in Rome. Only a few fragments of his work have survived.

ASKLEPIOS [Lat. Aesculapius]. Gr. hero (see HEROES), later god of medicine; according to mythology he was the son of Apollo, educated by the Centaur Chiron, and killed by lightning sent by Zeus, for bringing the dead back to life. Homer still regards A. as a mortal, a Thessalian prince, whose sons are doctors in the Gr. army before Troy. It is certainly possible that the cult of A. as a hero originated in the Thessalian town of Tricca. When it extended to Epidaurus, A. was honored as a god in the classical period. From there the cult spread to many other places (to Athens in 420 B.C.; Sophocles played a part in its transmission); the sanctuary on Cos became very famous, and was the first of many temples of A. in the islands. About 280 B.C. the cult was introduced in Rome, as a result of an epidemic.

ASKOS. See VASE FORMS.

ASPASIA (c. 440 B.C.). Intelligent and learned woman from Miletus who came to Athens and was there first the mistress and later the second wife of Pericles, to whom she bore a son, Pericles the Younger. She was the target of many spiteful attacks, mainly by conservatives who did not dare attack the great statesman himself. Pericles even had to defend her on a charge of impiety (compare ANAXAGORAS).

ASSEMBLIES. See ECCLESIA; COMITIA. For the Spartan assembly (*apella*) see SPARTA.

ASSESSOR. Judicial assistant of a Rom. magistrate at trials.

ASTROLOGY. The belief that life on earth is controlled by the stars. This belief was adopted from the Babylonians by the Greeks and later by the Romans, as was astronomy. The philosophical foundation for A. is the picture of a world in which "sympathy," an all-embracing harmony, encloses the universe. This idea caught on, particularly in the Stoa. Ideas derived from A. can thus often be found in the works of great ancient authors (Tac. *Ann.* VI, 21-22). During the Hellenistic period the influence of A. was greatly widened. In Rom. times the so-called Chaldeans from time to time exercised great influence on various statesmen as well as the populace.

ASTRONOMY. A. was first practiced among the Greeks in Ionia, where the contact with the Near East, particularly with Babylonia, was close. Many pre-Socratic philosophers practiced A. Thales succeeded in predicting an eclipse of the sun in 585 B.C. After about 400 B.C., A. became the concern of specialists. The striking thing about this is that the most important results of the Gr. astronomers (the spherical form of the earth, its rotation on its axis, the heliocentric system, etc.) do not seem to have been known outside the closed circle of scholars. Everywhere else we find, in principle, the old mythological portrayal of the world. (For details see PYTHAGORAS; PARMENIDES; ANAXAGORAS; EUDOXUS; ARISTARCHUS; ARATUS.) The greatest Gr. astronomer was Hipparchus of Nicaea (2nd cent. A.D.), whose mathematical insight and technique of observation were highly developed, although he still propounded a geocentric system; his work is known to us through the handbook of Claudius Ptolemaeus.

ASTYAGES (585-550). The last king of the Medes, son of Cyaxares, dethroned by Cyrus (Hdt. I, 123-130).

ATELLANA. See FABULA.

ATHENA. Usually called Pallas A. or Athene. Gr. goddess, protector of cities and citadels, goddess of wise deliberation (also generalship), of social order (next to Apollo) of feminine handicrafts (and handicrafts in general). As the goddess of the citadel her origin goes back to Minoan-Mycenaean religion (see MYCE-NAE). In mythology she usually appears as the protector of heroes—of cunning Odysseus, as might be expected, but also of others, such as Perseus. She was also particularly the goddess of battle, who gave victory (this led to her being identified with Nike; see NIKE TEMPLE). Usually she is portrayed in battle array —as, for example, the "A. Parthenos" (see PARTHENON) of Phidias (see also PANATHENAEA; MINERVA).

ATHENAEUS of Naucratis (c. A.D. 200). Gr. author who wrote on widely diverging subjects. His work *Deipnosophistae* (The Banquet of the Learned) is a fictional account of a banquet at which all sorts of intellectual matters are debated.

ATHENS. The capital of Attica, the "Hellas of Hellas" during the flowering of Gr. civilization. There are remains there from the Mycenaean period. During the Dorian migration (c. 1100) Attica and A. remained more or less undisturbed, which made the Athenians call themselves *autochthones*. A. gained in importance when all Attica was united under its leadership (synoecism). This unification was attributed to Theseus, but actually it dates from the 9th cent. B.C. When the monarchy declined, A. became an aristocratic Republic (see EUPATRI-DAE; ARCHONS; AREOPAGUS); Solon took the first steps toward democracy, which was achieved by Clisthenes. In the 6th cent. A. was ruled by tyrants: Pisistratus, Hippias, and Hipparchus. This was also a period of prosperity for trade and (light) industry, due in part to Solon's work; for olive culture (see ATTICA). During the Persian Wars and the fifty years between them and the Peloponnesian War, A. was almost absent of Sparta in the struggle for power (see THEMISTOCLES; CIMON); it was during this period that the Delian League was formed. Soon Pericles became the powerful leader under whose leadership the

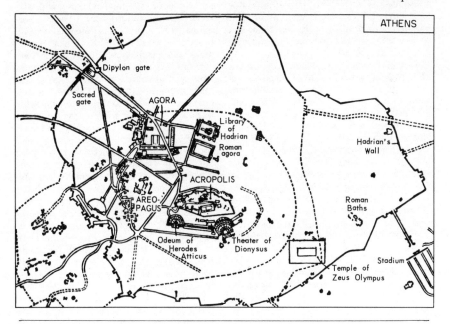

Plan of ancient Athens with the Acropolis

arts and sciences flourished as never before; from far and near, people of importance in the field of cultural achievement came to work in A. and live there with the native Athenians. The Piraeus (connected with A. by the Long Walls) was the most important center of trade in Greece. There was also, however, a dark side: a narrowminded policy of civic rights (see METICS) and increasing oppression of the allies, who were reduced to the condition of subjects, undermined A.'s position. The Peloponnesian War made an end to the empire. Nevertheless A. was still a center of cultural life in the 4th cent., and its trade prospered. It even founded a second League, but one with more independence for the members. A. was the heart of the opposition against rising Macedonian imperialism (see PHILIP II; DEMOSTHENES), but the days of independence were numbered. In the Hellenistic period A. remained relatively neutral in the face of the political turbulence; in 86 B.C., however, it was ravaged by Sulla. Under Rom. rule it was mainly a university town and an open-air museum, adorned with imposing buildings, the gift of Herodes Atticus and Hadrian. (See also ACROPOLIS; AGORA; AREOPAGUS; PNYX; and the map accompanying this article.)

ATHOS. Headland in Chalcidice, where the world-famous Monks' Republic is situated. (It was found in the 9th-14th cent. A.D.) After a Persian fleet commanded by Mardonius had foundered here in 492 B.C., Xerxes had a channel cut through the isthmus for his expedition of 480 (Hdt. VI, 44; VII, 22-23).

ATLANTIS. Legendary island in the Atlantic Ocean, swallowed up by the sea because of the immoral conduct of its inhabitants. The island was described by Plato in *Timaeus,* and more fully in *Critias;* here it is a myth, of importance insofar as it is one of the oldest Utopian stories (see also EUHEMERUS.)

ATLAS MOUNTAINS. Mountain range in northwest Africa. According to the myth, the giant who bore the vault of the heavens on his shoulders and guarded the gardens of the Hesperides had been turned into a mountain on that spot.

ATOMISM (or ATOMISTICS). A doctrine propagated primarily by Leucippus and Democritus, later adopted in a somewhat altered form by Epicurus, and known in this form from the Lat. poem of Lucretius. The doctrine encompasses these main elements: the universe is composed of invisible particles called atoms (literally: unsplittables) which glide through empty space like particles of dust in a beam of sunlight. By colliding, they become intertwined and form solid bodies in which many atoms are clumped together, and fluid or gaseous bodies in which they are thinly spread. The souls of humans and animals also consist of very fine and thinly spread atoms. This doctrine so surprisingly resembles the chemistry and physics of today (aside from very recent nuclear physics) that twentieth-century man finds it exceedingly modern, and the question arises whether modern physics is not derived directly from the Gr. theories.

This question can only be answered if A. is seen in the framework of pre-Socratic Gr. philosophy as a whole. It concerned itself almost exclusively with the study of nature, beginning with the Ionic nature philosophers (Thales, Anaximander, and Anaximenes). They posed the question, "What is the world made of?" and chose the answer, "One element." Their ideas may seem somewhat primitive to us, but at that time they were revolutionary. These philosophers saw nature as an *understandable* and *explicable unity,* in contrast to mythological thought, which still dominated the science of the Near East, the basis for many of their beliefs. A new phase began with Heraclitus. His "element" was not merely a basic material, but a dynamic principle, the foundation of the entire universe. Against his equally dynamic idea of endless change The Eleatics set their theory of the eternal immutability of being and thus created an impasse. The Eleatics could only validate their doctrine by totally rejecting sensory observation, which does perceive changes, in favor of pure thought (as they saw it). All the following systems—those of Empedocles, Anaxagoras, and the Atomists tried to combine the ever-changing and the never-changing elements that nature offers us.

There is still another dividing line. If you ask a number of people, "What is a hammer?" one will answer, "A wooden handle provided with an iron head." Another person will say, "A thing to hit nails with." These dissimilar answers are given almost intuitively, and originate in different manners of thinking, which may be called *materialistic* and *teleological*, respectively. For the Ionic school, however, the question of whether the universe was simply an explicable structure, or whether it was inspired with purpose (by a god, for example) had not yet arisen. This problem was not attacked until much later. The most consciously teleologic doctrine was that of Pythagorean school. This doctrine occupies a very special position, because of its religious content. The other schools were all more (Anaxagoras) or less (Empedocles) materialistic. The curious thing about A. is that it is the most consistent and carefully thought out in this direction. Its strict logic struck Aristotle particularly.

Going back to the original question, we can see that there is one fundamental difference between modern physics and the *entire* field of pre-Socratic natural science—not A. alone. Gr. thought was primarily speculative, contemplative; observation was sometimes resorted to, but an abstract schema was soon built up on it, from which the rest was logically deduced (deductive method). Modern physics, on the contrary, is empiric, drawing conclusions after experiment from observed fact to observed fact (inductive method). Gr. science used experimentation only incidentally until classical times (with the exception of medicine; see HIPPOCRATES). Still, there is a connection. It is certain that the founders of modern atomic doctrines in the 17th-18th cent. started by studying the ancient A. very carefully. A famous theoretical physicist concluded from this that modern theory originated in a combination of new, empirically found proofs and an a priori setting up of human ideas, which was also the method of Democritus and his disciples.

ATOSSA. Daughter of Cyrus I, wife of Darius I and mother of Xerxes. She is one of the principal characters in Aeschylus' drama *The Persians*.

ATRIUM. See HOUSES.

ATTALUS. Name of three kings:

—(1) A. I Soter (269-197). King of Pergamum after 241. He defeated the Galatians in 230, partly because of his friendship with Rome (he supported it against Philip V), he was able to make Pergamum one of the great Hellenic empires.

—(2) A. II Philadelphus (220-138). King of Pergamum after 160; continued pro-Rom. policies; however, it became more and more clear that this was just bringing in the Trojan Horse.

—(3) A. III Philometor (c. 170-133). Successor to Attalus II. He left his kingdom to Rome in his will (see ASIA).

ATTHIDOGRAPHI. The historians of Attica. They emphasized particularly the origins of religious usages (see also HELLANICUS).

ATTICA. The Gr. province of which Athens was the capital, united by synoecism under the leadership of Athens (see THESEUS; ATHENS) into one of the greatest *poleis* (see POLIS) of Greece. A. consisted of a number of small plains, separated by mountain ranges. The soil is poor in most places, as is the rule in Greece. The most important forms of agriculture in ancient times were the cultivation of wine and, particularly, olives. Solon saw to it that these became good quality export articles. The earth yielded marble (see PENTELIKON; HYMETTUS), silver (see LAURIUM), and potters' clay. Grain was grown mainly around Eleusis.

ATTIC COMEDY. See COMEDY.

ATTIC ORATORS. A list compiled during the Hellenistic period (probably in Alexandria) consisting of the most important representatives of Attic oratory (see ANTIPHON; ANDOCIDES; LYSIAS; ISOCRATES; AESCHINES; ISAEUS; DEMOSTHENES; HYPERIDES; LYCURGUS; and DINARCHUS).

ATTICUS, TITUS POMPONIUS (109-32). Friend of Cicero; the latter wrote him a large number of letters. He was strictly neutral in all political matters, and devoted his time to literature and publishing.

ATTILA. King of the Huns, reigned from 434-453. He ravaged the East Rom. Empire between the Euxine and the Adriatic (445-450) and invaded the West Rom. Empire in 450-452. He was defeated by the allied Romano-Gothic army, headed by Aetius and Theodoric, king of the Visigoths (see CATALAUNIAN PLAINS). Nevertheless, he invaded Italy from Pannonia in 452, but did not attack Rome.

ATTIUS. See Accius.

AUGUR. Rom. priest whose duty it was to observe the auspicia. Because no important military or political measure could be taken without consulting the *auspicia* first, the A.'s influence on politics and the army was sometimes very great indeed.

AUGUSTA TAURINORUM. The Rom. name for the city of Turin.

AUGUSTA TREVIRORUM. The Rom. name for the city of Trier (Trèves), founded by Augustus; during the latter part of the imperial period it was the capital of Gaul. There are many important Rom. remains there, among which are the *Porta Nigra,* an amphitheater, and baths (see THERMAE).

AUGUSTINUS, AURELIUS (354-430). Usually called Augustine. Lat.-Christian author, most important scholar of ancient Christendom. He was born in Thagaste in Numidia. His mother was a Christian, but he was originally a pagan. He studied Cicero and was influenced by Manichaeism and Neoplatonism. He went to Rome by way of Carthage in 383 and became professor of rhetoric in Milan in 384. He was baptized there by bishop Ambrose in 387. Afterward he returned to Africa, where he became a priest in 391 and the bishop of Hippo Regius in 395. He remained here until his death. His writings, which embrace a very large field, have had a great and permanent influence on Western civilization, as a result of their depth of thought and visionary power, combined with warm inner feeling. Apart from his dogmatic works, and his writings against heretics, the following are particularly noteworthy: (a) his letters and stenographically recorded sermons, in which he proves to be an inspired spiritual adviser. (b) the *Confessions,* in which he tells of the mental struggles and wanderings of his early years. (c) *De Civitate Dei* (the State of God), his most learned and elaborate book, written while he was deeply impressed by the conquest of Rome by Alaric in 410. In the last, A. sets forth a well-thought-out philosophy of history; here history is no longer regarded as a cycle, as in the writings of some pagan historians; it is presented as directed toward a final goal, and moving in a straight line. This decisively influenced all later histories, also those by non-Christians.

AUGUSTULUS, ROMULUS. Last emperor of the West Rom. Empire, conquered by German mercenaries in 475/6; he was deposed and was succeeded by Odoacer.

AUGUSTUS (63 B.C.-A.D. 14). First Rom. emperor. His original name was Gaius Octavius; after his great-uncle Caesar adopted him as a son by testamentary disposition in 44, and named him his heir, he called himself Gaius Julius Caesar Octavianus. At an early age he accompanied Caesar on his expeditions. When Caesar was killed, he decided to avenge his murder, won the sympathy of Cicero and senatorial circles, and soon Mark Antony became his opponent. They were reconciled in 43 and formed the second triumvirate with Lepidus. The first thing the *triumviri* had to do was get rid of opponents by proscription. A. proved to be just as merciless in that as Antony. Then Brutus and Cassius were defeated at Philippi. Again the two opposed one another, but were temporarily reconciled through the marriage of Antony to Octavia, which was decided on in Brundisium in 40. After that, A. had to fight hard from 38-36 against Sextus Pompey who dominated the sea. The fleet, built up for this war from almost nothing, served well in the ensuing conflict with Antony. A., supported by the whole West, was regarded as a favorite of Apollo. After Lepidus had been pushed aside, only the two rivals remained; the struggle ended in A.'s victory at Actium in 31 (see also AGRIPPA). A. spent the next three years consolidating his powerful position in Rome and in the Empire, under the pretense of restoring republican traditions. On January 13, 27, he resigned his special authorities as a triumvir; and the senate granted him the title "A." (the word "august" had a religious connotation). All republican institutions were restored in name, but actually the key government positions were kept for one person: (a) the *imperium proconsulare* (see PROCONSUL); (b) the *tribunicia potestas* (see TRIBUNI); (c) complete control of the "armed" provinces (see PROVINCIA). A. adopted the title "princeps." This was the beginning of the Rom. Empire. Primarily because the concentration of power was hidden behind a republican façade (with all possible cooperation from the senate), A. succeeded where Caesar had failed. The general longing for peace after the destruction of the Civil Wars also contributed to his success. "It was in the interest of peace that the government should be run by one person," said Tacitus (*Hist.* I, 1). It was to celebrate this peace that the Ara Pacis was erected in 13 B.C.

The feeling of relief, the feeling that a period of rest, happiness, and prosperity had dawned, is reflected particularly in the works of Horace and Virgil. Tacitus, by contrast, emphasizes the negative aspects of the concentration of power, particularly in the first few chapters of his *Annales,* even though he is convinced that it is unavoidable.

A.'s foreign policy was aimed at consolidation. There was only one (abortive) attempt at extending his territory (see VARUS); provinces were also reorganized, communications improved, colonies founded, and navigation made safe (see PIRACY). For the Rom. Empire outside continental Italy, the period that commenced with A. meant renewed prosperity. It was the end of being bled by governors and publicans (see PROVINCIA). In Rome itself, large structures were built (A's Forum, among others); laws were instituted for limiting the immorality that had increased alarmingly during the Civil Wars. The arts and sciences flourished (see MAECENAS; VIRGIL; HORACE; LIVY; OVID; PROPERTIUS; TIBULLUS). In his private life, A. was unhappy. His daughter Julia caused him great distress; her husband Agrippa and two of her sons died

before A.; the third grandson, Agrippa Postumus, was not considered fit to succeed. When his stepson Drusus died too, A. could do nothing but appoint Tiberius as his successor, particularly as Livia forcefully urged this course (see also MONUMENTUM ANCYRANUM).

AULIS. Port on the Euripos Strait, where the campaign against Troy started and where Iphigenia was sacrificed to Artemis (Eur. *Iphigenia in Aulis*).

AURELIANUS. See MILITARY EMPERORS.

AURELIUS VICTOR, SEXTUS (c. A.D. 370). Rom. historian. He wrote a history of Rome from Augustus to Constantius II.

AURI SACRA FAMES. "Accursed greed [literally: hunger] of gold" (compare Virg. *Aen.* III, 57).

AUSONIUS, DECIMUS MAGNUS (c. 310-393). Lat. poet of Gallic origin. He studied in Bordeaux and Toulouse and was called to Trier (Trèves) by Valentinian to tutor his son Gratianus. In the reign of Gratianus, A. became consul in 379. After Valentinian's death he returned to Bordeaux and devoted his time entirely to poetry. His style is very delicate; *Mosella,* a poetic description of the valley of the Moselle River, is well known. His poem about the teachers of Bordeaux is particularly interesting from the point of view of the history of education. A. was a Christian, open to the ideas of pagan civilization.

AUSPICIA. In Rom. culture, omens—particularly the omens taken from the birds; for these, the augurs outlined an imaginary space (*templum*) in the air, within which they observed the birds' flight. Other omens, such as the way the sacred fowls pecked, were also called A. There were A. *maxima* (greatest) and A. *minora* (lesser); the first could only be observed on the instructions of magistrates, the lesser were taken by aediles and quaestors (see also AUGUR).

AVARICUM. Gallic city now called Bourges, conquered by Caesar in 52 B.C., during the revolt of Vercingetorix (Caes. B.C. VIII, 14-28).

AVENTINE HILL. One of the seven hills of Rome, in the southern part of the city, on the Tiber, outside the pomerium in the republican period; it was assigned to the plebs in 476 B.C. The A. had close connections with the Lat. League (see LATIUM) from time immemorial.

AVERNUS, LACUS. Lake near Cumae, known as the entrance to the underworld, because of its depth and poisonous vapors (Virg. *Aen.* VI). Agrippa had the lake connected with the ocean by a tunnel, remains of which have been found.

AVIANUS (c. A.D. 400). Rom. writer of fables who also edited the fables of Babrius. He was often read during the Middle Ages.

AVIENUS, RUFUS FESTUS (4th cent. A.D.). Lat. poet. He wrote poems on astronomy (based on Aratus) and especially on geographical subjects. Among the latter are the *Ora Maritima,* a description of the South-Gallic and Spanish coasts; in it are incorporated data from the writings of ancient explorers (see PYTHEAS).

B

BAALBEK. See HELIOPOLIS.

BABRIUS (2nd cent. A.D.). Gr. composer of fables; editor of the so-called Aesopic fables (see AESOP).

BABYLONIA. The southern part of Mesopotamia. Its capital was Babylon, one of the most important politico-religious centers of western Asia. The Greeks first came into direct contact with B. during the New Babylonian empire (Nebuchadnezzar, 6th cent. B.C.) when the Chaldeans were the ruling people. Many Eastern ideas came into Greece by way of B. during that period. Thales, for example, must have obtained much of his knowledge of astronomy in that manner. In 538 B.C., B. was annexed by Persia (Cyrus I). It was an important part of the Persian empire. Babylon was the primary reason for the campaign of Cyrus (1) against his brother Artaxerxes II (see CUNAXA). Alexander the Great conquered it in 331. Seleucus I founded Seleucia to replace Babylon as the capital and center of trade.

BACCHANALIA. Festivals in honor of Bacchus/Dionysus, usually in the form of orgies (ecstatic rites, during which the participants, mostly women, wandered among the mountains and raw meat was torn apart and eaten) and Dionysiac mysteries. Euripides gave a striking description of this in his *Bacchae.* In 186 B.C. the Rom. senate intervened to suppress excesses during the B. in Italy. Their decree has been found in an inscription, and Livy (XXXIX, 8-18) gives a detailed report of the case.

BACCHIADAE. Aristocratic oligarchy in Corinth (8th-7th centuries B.C.), under whose rule Corcyra and Syracuse were colonized and ceramics flourished (see PROTO-CORINTHIAN POTTERY). Cypselus overthrew the oligarchy in 657.

BACCHUS. See DIONYSUS.

BACCHYLIDES (c. 505-450). The greatest Gr. lyric poet of choral songs after Pindar. He was born on the island of Ceos and worked at the court of Hiero I in Sicily, after traveling extensively in Macedonia, Aegina, and Athens. Twenty of his poems, odes, and dithyrambs have been found more or less intact. Fragments of other poems have been preserved. Unfortunately, B.'s work has always been compared with that of Pindar, to the detriment of his reputation. This is certainly unjust. Judged on its own merits, his work is very charming and has great clarity of style.

BAIAE. A town on the Bay of Naples, with medicinal sulphur springs, a fashionable resort town with beautiful villas; even in ancient times, however, it suffered earthquakes and its people were subject to malaria.

BALBINUS. See MILITARY EMPERORS.

BALEARIC ISLANDS. Group of islands off the coast of Spain, controlled first by the Phoenicians, then by the Carthaginians, and after 121 B.C. by the Romans. The inhabitants were capable slingers, and therefore greatly sought as mercenaries.

BARBARIANS [Gr. *barbaroi*]. "Those who speak a foreign language" (see PANHELLENIC IDEA; PERSIAN EMPIRE).

BASILICA. Rom. building with a rectangular roofed hall, usually with side aisles, used as a commercial and social meeting place, associated with a forum. A B. has been preserved in Pompeii. Other famous basilicas are the B. Julia and the B. Aemilia (see AEMILIUS) in the Rom. Forum (1st cent. (A.D.), and the B. Nova of Maxentius (c. A.D. 300) nearby. This manner of building had some influence on the architecture of Christian churches. See Appendix.

BASSAE. Site of one of the best preserved Gr. temples of Apollo, built by Ictinus c. 430-410. B. is in southwest Arcadia, near Phigalia. The Doric temple, which strangely enough has Ionic columns decorating the sidewalls of the cella (see ARCHITECTURAL ORDERS; TEMPLE) had its main entrance on the north side, a departure from the usual practice of having it face east.

BATAVI. German tribe, who settled on the Rhine delta. In about 15 B.C. they became (privileged) allies of Rome. They contributed auxiliary troops under their own commanders. In 69-70 they revolted under Julius Civilis, who cleverly made use of Rome's difficulties during the Year of the Three Emperors. He pretended to be supporting Vespasian, but when the latter came into power and sent his capable general Cerealis to the B., Civilis was forced to show his hand. After a battle that was in the main unfavorable to him (he was not, however, defeated), he started negotiations with Cerealis. Tacitus' detailed story breaks off at this point (*Hist.* IV, V). Later, the B. are again seen as allies of Rome. At this time, however, they probably have fewer privileges.

BATRACHOMYOMACHIA. One of the oldest parodies in classical literature, a mock-heroic poem describing in the Homeric style and hexameters, a battle between frogs and mice. It was probably written in the 5th cent. B.C.

BEATI POSSIDENTES. "Happy the possessors" (compare Hor. Carm. IV, 9, 45).

BEATUS ILLE, QUI PROCUL NEGOTIIS. . . . "Happy is he, who [lives in the country] far from cares . . ." (Hor. *Epod.* II, 1).

BEDRIACUM. See YEAR OF THE THREE EMPERORS.

BELGAE. The northernmost group of Gallic tribes, living in what is now northern France, Belgium, and southern Netherlands, of mixed Celtic and Germanic origin. Caesar calls them the most warlike of the Gauls (*B.G.* I, 1), because they were farthest removed from the civilizing influence of the Roman province and because of their German contacts. He conquered them in 57 B.C., but had to subdue them repeatedly afterward (see AMBIORIX; also VERCINGETORIX, who was supported by some of the B.) B. also lived in Britain.

BENEVENTUM. Town in southern Italy, first city of the Samnites, Rom. colony after 268 B.C., later a *municipium*. The Romans defeated Pyrrhus (see CURIUS) there in 275. It was an important stopping place and junction on the Via Appia.

BERENICE. Name of several queens of the House of Ptolemy.

BIBRACTE. A hill fort and original capital of the Aedui, where Caesar defeated the Helvetii in 58 B.C. and Vercingetorix was appointed commander in chief of the Gauls by a general assembly of the Gallic tribes in 52 B.C. (Caes. *B.G.* I, 25; VII, 63).

BITHYNIA. Province in northwestern Asia Minor, an independent kingdom during the Hellenistic period, whose kings (usually called Nicomedes or Prusias) founded many cities. In 74 B.C., Nicomedes IV died, having bequeathed his kingdom to the Rom. people. Under Augustus it was made a Rom. province.

BOEOTIA. Province in central Greece, bordered on the southeast by Attica. In the Mycenaean period, the most important cities were Thebes and Orchomenus, separated by Lake Copais. In 447 B.C., B. was united under the leadership of Thebes, in the Boeotian League, which played a leading role during the 4th cent.

B.C. The Boeotians are represented in Athenian literature as stupid and slow-thinking people. However, B. produced great poets (see CORINNA; PINDAR; also HESIOD, although he was not a native); music also flourished there (see also THEBES; ORCHOMENUS; CHAERONEA; TANAGRA; ASCRA; and PLATAEA).

BOETHIUS (c. 480-524). Rom. philosopher and a high official under Theodoric (consul in 510). He was accused of treason and was imprisoned and later executed. During his imprisonment he wrote his principal work, *De Consolatione Philosophiae*. This is a dialogue between B. and philosophy personified, written in the form of a Menippean satire (see MENIPPUS). He also wrote a book on music which is one of our main sources of information on Gr. music, and translated and wrote commentaries on the works of Aristotle and other authors. B. was a Christian, but his work contains many pagan elements.

BOII. Gallic tribe, who entered Italy in about 400 B.C. and settled there (capital, Bononia). After several defeats by Rome, they supported Hannibal in 218, but were definitely subjugated to Rome in 191. Another part of the tribe (probably from Bohemia, which is named after them) entered Gaul with the Helvetii in 58 B.C. and was then settled in the region of the Aedui by Caesar.

BONA FIDE. "In good faith"; the phrase *bona fides* was already in use as a legal term in ancient Rome.

BONNA. The Rom. name for Bonn on the Rhine, used by the Romans as a fortress against the Germans.

BONONIA. Italian city, now called Bologna. It was named by the Boii, who captured it from the Etruscans. In earliest times it had been a Villanovan settlement. In the 2nd cent. B.C. it became a Rom. *municipium;* in 43 B.C. the second triumvirate was created there. It was an important junction of Rom. roads.

BOOKS. The Greeks first published books in the form of rolls of papyrus, the material for which was imported from Egypt, although there are indications that prepared sheets of leather were also used at a very early time. Until the 3rd cent. B.C. the roll of papyrus remained the usual

form; then, it gradually became customary to bind the sheets of papyrus into books, following the example of the parchment code (bound book). Parchment is lasting, in contrast to papyrus, which has been preserved only in the very dry climate of Egypt. The word is derived from Pergamum, where, according to tradition, this material came into use when Ptolemy V forbade the export of papyrus. In Athens, booksellers were already known in the time of Socrates, but true bookstores originated in Alexandria and Rome. A book was copied by dictating the text to many slaves.

Until the 3rd cent. A.D., libraries were owned only by rich and influential persons. The first large public library was founded in Alexandria by Ptolemy I, and it was enlarged by Ptolemy II. The leading writers of Greece directed it or worked there. During Caesar's stay (48/47 B.C.) this library was almost entirely destroyed by fire. Other Hellenistic princes followed the example of the Ptolemies, principally those of Pergamum. In Rome too, the first collections were private ones; Asinius Pollio founded the first large public library there; this example was again followed by many emperors and rich benefactors. The story of Pliny the Younger, who gave a library to his native city of Comum, is well known. (*Ep.* 1, 8, 2).

BORYSTHENES. The Gr. name for the river Dnieper in the country of the Scythians, a channel of communications with the hinterland, for Gr. traders.

BOSPORUS. The entrance to the Black Sea, named, according to mythology, after Io, who crossed it in the form of a cow. The cities of Byzantium and Chalcedon were situated on the B. The ocean currents leading to Byzantium contributed greatly to its prosperity (see also CHALCEDON).

BRASIDAS. Spartan general during the Peloponnesian War. He was successful in Thrace, where he conquered Amphipolis in 423 B.C. In 422 he was killed near this city, at the same time as his Athenian opponent Cleon. This cleared the way for the peace-loving groups on both sides and led to the peace of Nicias. In the short time that he spent on the Thracian coast, B. won a remarkable amount of good will, and was even made a hero there (see HEROES).

BRENNUS. Name of:

—(1) The Gallic prince who defeated the Romans at the Allia about 390 B.C., occupied the entire lower city of Rome and plundered it, besieged the Capitol in vain, and departed upon receiving a monetary tribute (see VAE VICTIS).

—(2) Leader of the Galatians, who invaded Macedonia and Greece in 279 B.C.

BRITAIN. See BRITANNIA.

BRITANNIA. Rom. name for England and Wales, visited by ancient explorers (among others, Pytheas in the 4th cent. B.C.); in the last few centuries B.C. the Celts settled there (among them the Belgae); Caesar undertook two expeditions to B. without much success (see CASSIVELAUNUS). In the 1st cent. B.C. it became a Rom. province; the Emperor Claudius personally led the campaign of conquest (see also AGRICOLA). Under Hadrian a definite boundary between England in Scotland was demarcated by a wall (Hadrian's Wall). About A.D. 400 the Rom. troops were withdrawn.

BRITANNICUS (41-55). Originally named Claudius Tiberius Germanicus. Son of the Emperor Claudius and his wife Messalina. Agrippina the Younger succeeded in having her son Nero replace him as the successor to the throne. B. was poisoned by Nero. Racine wrote a tragedy on this theme.

BRUNDISIUM. City, now called Brindisi, in south Italy, the end of the extended Via Appia, and the best harbor on the east coast of Italy, the sally port to Greece.

BRUTTII. South-Italian tribe, after which the ancient Bruttium, the "toe of the boot" (modern Calabria) was named. Gr. cities: Rhegium, Croton, Sybaris near Thurii. The B. were subjected to Rome in 272 B.C.; they supported Hannibal and were punished by complete loss of their independence.

BRUTUS. Name of:

—(1) Lucius Junius B., the founder of the Rom. Republic (510 B.C.) and, according to tradition, the first consul. His fellow consul Collatinus is certainly legendary, and many of the other stories about B. are only legends (see LUCRETIA).

—(2) Marcus Junius B. (85-42), first a supporter of Pompey, deserted to Caesar's party after Pharsalus. When it seemed that Caesar was about to make an end to republican freedom, he conspired with Cassius to assassinate Caesar (March 15, 44). Their ideal, however, proved illusory. The republic was dead, and would not be revived. After the battle of Philippi, in which they were defeated by Octavian and Antony, both committed suicide.

—(3) Decimus Junius Albinus B. (c. 84-43), served under Caesar in Gaul; took part in the conspiracy against his life in 44. Afterward he turned against Antony and defended Mutina against him; then he attempted to join Marcus Brutus in Macedonia, but his soldiers deserted him and he was put to death at Antony's orders.

BRYAXIS (2nd half of the 4th cent. B.C.). Gr. sculptor. He worked on the Mausoleum in Halicarnassus and was said to have created the statue of Serapis for Alexandria. The base of a statue in the National Museum in Athens bears his signature.

BRYGOS (c. 500 B.C.). Athenian potter. He employed a master in the technique of red-figure vase painting whose style was very lively. Nine vases bear B.'s signature.

BURRUS, SEXTUS AFRANIUS (?-A.D. 62). *Praefectus praetorio* (see *Praetorians*) under Claudius and Nero; during the first year of Nero's reign, he and Seneca controlled practically the entire government of the Rom. Empire, to its advantage. They had a restraining influence on Nero; they made just enough concessions to keep him within bounds (Tac. *Ann.* XIII, 2). When Nero tired of this restraint, he pushed B. aside.

BYZANTIUM. City on the Bosporus, founded by colonists from Megara in about 660 B.C. It flourished quickly partly due to commercial fishing. It changed hands frequently during the struggles between the Greeks and the Persians, and between Athens and Sparta. When Xenophon arrived there with the Ten Thousand, it was ruled by Sparta. In the 4th cent., it was a member of the second Attic League. After 355 B.C. it was entirely independent; it voluntarily allied itself with Rome. During the Civil Wars it was completely destroyed and ravaged by Septimius Severus (A.D. 196), who later had it rebuilt. After it had been destroyed once more, Constantine the Great rebuilt it again, made it his capital city, and renamed it Constantinople. Nevertheless, the city was still called B., particularly when it was referred to as a cultural center. The East Rom. Empire was also sometimes called the Byzantine Empire. After the fall of the West Rom. Empire (A.D. 476), the Rom. traditions were preserved in B. The *Corpus juris,* for example, came into being here (see also THEODOSIUS; JUSTINIAN). The study of Gr. literature, too, was pursued in B. (see PHOTIUS; SUIDAS). Here countless Gr. texts were preserved for posterity, and excerpts of them were made, continuing the work of the Hellenistic schools (see ALEXANDRIA; BOOKS; ARISTARCHUS; ARISTOPHANES OF BYZANTIUM; ZENODOTUS).

C

CABIRI (or CABEIRI). Mystic deities of Samothrace, Lemnos, and Thebes. Their cult was of Eastern origin, probably from Phrygia. The C. are usually described as four in number. They were fertility deities and, like Demeter, were represented in mysteries. From the 5th cent. B.C. onward, they were worshiped particularly by mariners; thus they were often confused with the Dioscuri.

CAELIAN HILL. One of the hills of Rome, to the southeast of the city.

CAERE. One of the most important cities of Etruria, now called Cerveteri; originally a Villanovan settlement. Many Etruscan sepulchral chambers were found there, with murals and utensils in them, among which were many imported Gr. vases, the Caeritan hydriae (see VASE FORMS); all came, we now assume, from the same studio in Ionia.

CAESAR, GAIUS JULIUS (100 or 102-44). Rom. statesman, general, author. He prepared the ground for the empire. His family, of the *Julia gens,* was said to have sprung from Iulus, the son of Aeneas (see VIRGIL). C. was a nephew of Marius and narrowly escaped proscription by Sulla, who was said to have remarked, "Many Marii lurk in this young man." He served as an officer in Asia Minor, returned to Rome after Sulla's death in 78, and worked there as a lawyer. He studied at Rhodes from 75 to 73, then became quaestor (68) and aedile (65); in 63 he protested against the execution of Catalina's followers. He spent enormous sums on getting himself chosen *pontifex maximus.* He became *praetor urbanus* in 62; as propraetor, he was unable to leave for his *provincia* Spain until Crassus had promised to guarantee payment of his debts. In 60 he returned to Rome, where the senate opposed him when he tried for a consulship. He entered into the first triumvirate with Crassus and Pompey, who was also having trouble with the senate (see TRIUMVIRI). It was a purely private agreement.

C. became a consul in 59, together with the unimportant Bibulus (the populace talked about the consulship of Julius and C., instead of Bibulus and C.!). C. forced the senate to comply with Pompey's demands and to *assign* to himself the province of cisalpine Gaul and Illyria. The senate, which had become intimidated, added transalpine Gaul. This became the basis of C.'s conquest of Gaul (58-50). (For details see HELVETII; ARIOVISTUS; VENETI; BRITANNIA; AMBIORIX; LABIENUS; and VERCINGETORIX.) In the meantime, the triumvirate had been renewed at Luca in 56, but Crassus fell in 53 and a breach between C. and Pompey appeared, which became gradually deeper.

Pompey relied more and more on the optimates; they fearfully awaited the day on which C. would return with his ten legions, whose training during the Gallic War had made precision instruments of them. C. wanted to compete for the consulship for 48, but the senate and Pompey demanded demobilization of his armies beforehand. C. accepted the challenge, and crossed the Rubicon on January 10, 49. Pompey fled to Greece, but C. had no wish to pursue him, until he had protected his rear by defeating Pompey's army in Spain (Battle of Ilerda); when this was done, he crossed over to Greece and defeated Pompey at Pharsalus, in spite of initial setbacks and a numerical disadvantage (48). Next, C. followed the fleeing Pompey to Egypt, but did not find him alive. In Alexandria C. put Cleopatra on the throne and made her his mistress. A violent rebellion drove C. into a very tight corner. There followed operations against Pharnaces and the remains of the Pompeian party (see QUIRITES; THAPSUS; MUNDA). Now C. had become an absolute monarch. He had already been a dictator twice; he now became dictator for ten years, and later for life. He had himself chosen as consul several times; he had already been *pontifex maximus* for a long time; he was also given the immunity of the *tribuni plebis* and thus controlled the entire mechanism of the state. Now he started on his ambitious reforms: the foundations for many centuries of rule, which he planned not only in terms of Rome, but of all Italy, and the empire outside of Italy. The senate was increased to 900 members, among them being, for the first time, senators from the provinces. The cities in Italy were given a large degree of autonomy, and citizenship was granted on a wide scale. Colonies were founded everywhere; all sorts of buildings were started; the Julian calendar was introduced. Later emperors elaborated on many of these measures; C. can be considered to have laid the foundations for the Rom. Empire (the German word *Kaiser* is derived from the name C., French *empereur* and English *emperor* from Imperator, a title permanently conferred on C.). Yet C. was unable personally to create a stable government, something Augustus did succeed in doing. This can be partly attributed to the fact that during C.'s reign it was still possible to hope for the restoration of the Republic, but after his death this was seen to be an illusion, so that anti-monarchical circles were more inclined to resignation. But the most important cause of this failure lay in the person and the personal attitude of C.: he was probably more of a genius than Augustus, but he was certainly less of a diplomat. He did refuse the title of Rex, but the glorification that he willingly accepted ran counter to every republican tradition. Therefore, a conspiracy was formed against him, led by Cassius and Brutus, which cost him his life on the Ides of March, 44.

Two of his works have survived, *Commentaries* on the war in Gaul (seven books, the eighth being by Hirtius) and on the Civil War of 49-48 (three books); other writings have been lost. He also signed descriptions of other campaigns, written by his army officers. C.'s manuscripts are very tendentious, and invite critical reading; they are crystal clear and show the brilliant originality of his mind. Together with Cicero, C. is the most important representative of classic Lat. prose. The *Commentaries* are rightly used as primary reading matter for students of Latin.

CAESAREA. Name of various cities in the East and Mauretania, among others, C. Palaestinae, formerly Stratonis Turris, on the Palestinian coast, about 20 mi. south of what is now Haifa. The great revolt of the Jews against Rome took place here in A.D. 66.

CALABRIA. The old name for the "heel of the Italian boot" (what is now C. is the toe). Cities: Brundisium, Tarentum.

CALENDAR. In the oldest calendars, which originated in the Near East, the only system known was based on the motions of the moon. In Babylonia this moon calendar was made to fit into a sun calendar, the so-called lunisolar system. But since the year cannot be evenly divided into lunar months, a leap month was necessary. In Greece every polis had a system of its own: the best known was that of Athens, where they used alternate months of 29 and 30 days, making a year of 354 days, eleven days short of the solar year. The months were named after religious festivals, a reminder of the fact that the C. has a sacred origin. The month started with the new moon, and was divided into three periods. The Rom. year consisted of ten months, with four full months of 31 days (March, May, July, and October), and six months of 30 days (April, June, August, September, November, and December). However, as 304 days make up neither a solar year nor a lunar year, January and February were later added at the end (the Rom. year began originally with March, so that September [from *septem,* seven] was the seventh month for the Romans). These months were based on the moon's revolutions about the earth, so that the year had 355 days. Again a leap month was needed and an attempt was made to add the ten days needed for a solar year. Adjustments and records with regard to the C. were in such disorder, that Julius Caesar, in 46 B.C., had a new C. drawn up. The year 46 B.C. was lengthened and the new C. was introduced on the 1st of January, 45 B.C. This C., based on the Egyptian solar system, in which a year had 365¼ days, was called the Julian C., and remained in use until 1582. In designating the days of the month, the Romans reckoned backward from three points, the calends, the nones, and the ides. The Rom. month *Quintilis* was changed to *Julius* (July) in honor of Caesar, and later the month *Sextilis* was named *Augustus* after the Emperor Augustus (see also CHRONOLOGY; FASTI).

CALENDS. First day of the Rom. month.

CALIGULA (real name Gaius Caesar) (A.D. 12-41). Rom. emperor, son of Germanicus and Agrippina the Elder. His nickname ("Little Boot") was given to him because his mother, who accompanied her husband on his campaigns, put small soldiers' boots on him to gain popularity with the troops (Tac. *Ann.* I, 41). He was proclaimed emperor in 37 at the death of Tiberius, mainly as a result of the protection of the *praefectus praetorio* (see PRAETORIANS), Macro. At the beginning his government was reasonable, but within a year he began to become despotic (according to Philo this was the re-

sult of a disease which affected his mental powers); this got worse and worse. He was inclined to replace the principate by a Hellenistic form of monarchy (including demands of personal deification) but was only aware of its poorer aspects. Thus, his reign foreshadowed the dominate. By making a plan (which he later abandoned) for having a statue of himself erected in the temple at Jerusalem, he precipitated a violent rebellion, which led to pogroms in Judaea and Alexandria. After a number of conspiracies that failed, he was murdered in his own palace on Jan. 24, 41.

CALLIAS (5th cent. B.C.). Athenian nobleman who fought at the battle of Marathon (490). He was ambassador from Athens to Artaxerxes and negotiated a peace, humiliating to the Persians. On his return to Athens, the success of his mission was questioned; he was accused of high treason and fined fifty talents.

CALLIMACHUS of Cyrene (c. 305-c. 240). Gr. poet and scholar. He was appointed chief librarian of the library at Alexandria by Ptolemy II, and compiled a critical and historical catalogue of that library. He wrote short epic poems; he was against the long epic on principle (his pupil Apollonius Rhodius rebelled against this). His most important work was the *Aitia,* a typically learned poem on the origins of religious usages; important fragments of it have been preserved on papyrus. Hymns and epigrams have also survived.

CALLIOPE. See MUSES.

CALLISTHENES (4th cent. B.C.). Nephew and pupil of Aristotele. He accompanied Alexander the Great on his expedition to Persia. For criticizing Alexander's adoption of oriental customs, C. was accused of being an accessory to the plot to assassinate Alexander. It has not been ascertained whether he died in prison or was executed. He wrote a history of Alexander which was used by Diodorus Siculus and Curtius Rufus.

CALPURNIUS SICULUS, TITUS (c. A.D. 55). Lat. pastoral poet; wrote seven eclogues following Virgil's and Theocritus' example, partly court poems for Nero.

CALYDON. City in Aetolia, where the

legend of Meleager and the Calydonian wild boar takes place (compare Hom. *Il.* IX, 525 ff.; see also Epic); there was an important temple dedicated to Artemis Laphria, who was honored here as a nature goddess.

CAMARES. Village on Crete with an adjacent cave where the so-called C. vases from the Middle Minoan period were found (c. 1800 B.C.). These vases are ornamented with abstract designs, painted in white and red on a dull black background.

CAMBYSES. Name of:

—(1) the father of Cyrus I.

—(2) Son of Cyrus (c. 555-522). He succeeded his father in 529 and conquered Egypt in 525. He was not entirely sane; he acted scandalously, and also counter to the traditions of the Achaemenidae. Recalled from Egypt because of the revolt of a Magus (Persian priest) who posed as C.'s murdered half brother Smerdis, he died on his way home (Hdt. III, 61-66).

CAMEO. See Gems.

CAMILLUS, MARCUS FURIUS (c. 400 B.C.). Rom. hero who took Veii after a siege of ten years (396). He was banished to Ardea on a charge of having embezzled part of the spoils (the charge was never substantiated), but was recalled to become a dictator in the defense of Rome against the Gauls (see Brennus; Allia). He is said to have defeated the Gauls and to have embezzled once again the stipulated tribute in gold. Much of this is legend, but it has been proved that he had a large share in rebuilding Rome after the Gallic catastrophe. He also granted privileges to the plebs and suppressed the revolt of Manlius Capitolinus.

CAMPANIA. The most fertile region in Italy, south of Latium, capital Capua, other important cities: Cumae, Neapolis, Puteoli, Nola, Baiae. Various Gr. colonies were founded there in the 8th cent. B.C.; later the city was dominated by the Etruscans, Samnites, and Romans (after 343 B.C.). From the reign of Augustus onward, C. also embraced southern Latium.

CAMPUS MARTIUS. Field in Rome, which served as a parade ground for the army, as it lay outside the pomerium; for that reason it was also the meeting place of the *comitia centuriata*. Eventually, more and more public buildings were erected on it, so that by the imperial period it was completely built up. Some of the buildings were: Pompey's theater, Augustus' Mausoleum, the Ara Pacis and the Pantheon.

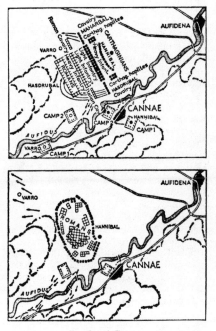

Battle of Cannae

CANNAE. Village in Apulia, where Hannibal destroyed the Rom. army in 216 B.C. (Rom. losses were as high as 50,000 men, according to some reports). The Carthaginians were in the minority, but had the marvelous Numidian cavalry on their side. The battle of C. has been studied endlessly, as being a perfect example of the so-called pincer strategy.

CANNINEFATES. German tribe in north and south Holland, who supported the Batavi during the revolt of Julius Civilis.

CANON [Gr. *Ranon.*, rule, rod]. Work by Polyclitus in which he described the ideal proportions of the human body. In harmony with these rules he sculpted a figure, the famous "Doryphorus" (spear holder). This figure was called the C. because its proportions served as an example for later artists. The word C. is also used in the field of literature; it is applied to collections (in the Alexandrine and Byzantine schools) of the work of classical authors, such as the ten Attic orators, the three great tragic poets, and others, which were to serve as classic examples.

CAPITAL. See COLUMN.

CAPITOL [Lat. Capitolium]. An important building of ancient Rome, situated on the south summit of *Mons Capitolinus*. The hill terminates at its southern side in a precipice, the Tarpeian Rock, over which traitors were thrown. On its north summit stood the *Arx* (citadel) of Rome.

The C. was founded by Tarquinius Priscus and completed by Tarquinius Superbus. It withstood the attack of the Gauls in 386 B.C. (see BRENNUS) when Juno's geese woke the watchmen. The C. was burned down in 83 B.C. and again in A.D. 69, the Year of the Three Emperors. Both times it was rebuilt, but burned a third time in the reign of Titus. It was magnificently restored by Domitian.

The Roman consuls made their sacrifices and took their oaths of office in the C. Victorious generals were borne there to offer thanks to Jupiter.

On the Capitoline Hill there stood the temple of Jupiter, flanked on either side by a temple of Juno and Minerva, respectively, and the Tabularium where the archives were stored.

CAPITOLINE HILL. See CAPITOL.

CAPPADOCIA. Province in eastern Asia Minor, a satrapy under the Persians (see SATRAP), later a Rom. vassal kingdom and, after A.D. 17, a Rom. province.

CAPREAE. Now Capri. Here Tiberius spent the last ten years of his life, urged to do so by Sejanus who was planning to take the government of Rome into his own hands.

CAPUA. The principal city of Campania, founded by the Etruscans in 600 B.C. and inhabited by the Samnites after 440 B.C. In 343 it became a Rom. ally, but after the Battle of Cannae it deserted to Hannibal and allowed his armies to spend the winter there, which had a demoralizing influence on the troops. In 331 it was reconquered by Rome. The Rom. senate, wanting to set an example here at all costs, did not even break off the siege when Hannibal appeared at the gates of Rome, and after C.'s capitulation, it was horribly punished; among other things, the entire rural area was confiscated. During imperial times it flourished again, mainly as a result of Augustus' favor. The Vandals plundered it in 456. What is now called C. was Casilinum in ancient times.

CARACALLA, MARCUS AURELIUS ANTONINUS (186-217). Rom. emperor, son of Septimius Severus. He had his brother Geta murdered in 212 and afterward ruled as absolute monarch. One of those killed during the persecution of Geta's followers was Papinianus. C. undertook expeditions to Germany and the East, where he wanted to found a Rom.-Iranian empire, following the example of Alexander the Great. During this expedition he was murdered by Macrinus (see MILITARY EMPERORS), who succeeded him. His most important act as emperor was the edict of 212, in which all free inhabitants of the Empire were given citizenship. This was a logical measure, which furthered the development of the Empire. On the other hand, citizenship lost its meaning as a privilege, and thus its political significance. C. built enormous thermae in Rome. He was known as a cowardly, cruel man.

CARIA. Province in southwestern Asia Minor. The native population was related to one of the pre-Gr. segments of the population on the Aegean Sea (see CYCLADES). The principal city of C. was Halicarnassus.

CARINUS. See MILITARY EMPERORS.

CARNEADES of Cyrene (214-129). Gr. philosopher, founder of the Third or New Academy. Under his leadership it became a center of skepticism—that is, the doctrine that certain knowledge concerning existence is impossible. He applied this when coming to Rome with a legation of philosophers in 156/155 to give lectures; he first built up a complete proof (namely, of justice as the fundament of the state) and then broke it down again, just as completely. So, according to C., our knowledge is no more than a scale of probabilities. In practice, however, the "probability verging on certainty" is a usable guide. C. opposed the Stoa—and particularly violently, its religious ideas. He had great influence on Cicero. (See also SKEPTICS.)

CARPE DIEM, QUAM MINIMUM CREDULA POSTERO." Enjoy the present moment, trusting the least possible to the future" (Hor. *Caron.* I, 11, 8). *Carpe diem* has come to mean "Embrace the opportunity."

CARRHAE. City in northern Mesopotamia, where Crassus was defeated by the Parthians in 53 B.C. (Rom. losses, 34,000 men) and was killed during negotiations for surrender.

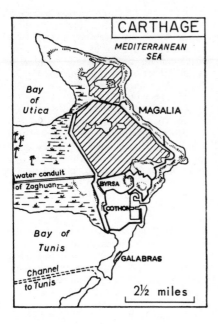

CARTHAGE (Phoenician Karthadshat, that is "New City," Gr. Karchedon). Colony of the Phoenician city Tyre, on what is now the Gulf of Tunis, founded in 800 B.C., the only Phoenician colony that developed into a large city. It was a trade republic, governed by an oligarchy. The highest magistrates were *suffetes*, judges, chosen for two years, with an advisory council, which the Romans compared to their senate. C.'s influence was extended to the western Mediterranean region in the 8th-6th centuries, including the large islands, particularly Sicily, which profited from the old Phoenician trading stations. The relationship with the second large power in this area, the Etruscans, was good. By concerted action of the two peoples, Gr. expansion was halted (see ALALIA). In Sicily, C. had been trying continuously to dominate the entire island since the 5th cent. (see GELON; THERON; DIONYSIUS; AGATHOCLES; PYRRHUS). When Rome succeeded Etruria as the most powerful Italian state, it also maintained friendly relations with C. Several treaties were concluded, in which it was determined that each would respect the other's sphere of influence. The first of these treaties was made as early as 508 B.C. The 250 years of friendship, however, were followed by more than 100 years of bitter war (see PUNIC WARS), which ended in 146 B.C. in the devastation of C. The area then became the Rom. province Africa. In 122 a first effort at rebuilding it was made (see GRACCHI) but it was Caesar and Augustus who made C. live again. Once more it became an important city with a flourishing culture; it fostered the Western type of Christianity as well (see TERTULLIANUS; CYPRIAN; and AUGUSTINE). Later it became the capital of the Vandal empire.

It is difficult to form an objective opinion on C., as almost all our data have been acquired from her bitterest enemies. It has been determined, however, that her policies were inclined to be easygoing rather than aggressive. At any rate, at least two of the three Punic Wars were caused by Rom. aggression. The Barcine family (see HAMILCAR; HASDRUBAL; HANNIBAL) favored militant action, but the imperialistic policies pursued by this group led to expansion of trade connections rather than to the Rom. type of conquest. Another group, typified by Hannibal's adversary Hanno, was more in favor of expansion in Africa, and exploitation of the agrarian riches of the land. When efforts in this direction proved very successful, in the 2nd cent. B.C., it was a thorn in the flesh of Rome (see CATO), and led to the catastrophe in 146.

CARTHAGO NOVA. Now Cartagena in Spain. It was founded in 228 B.C. by Hasdrubal (1) as a base from which to conquer Spain and taken in 209 by Scipio Major. It was known for the adjacent silver mines.

CARUS. See MILITARY EMPERORS.

CARYATIDS [From the Greek *Karyatides,* literally priestesses at the temple of Artemis in Caryae]. The term is applied to figures of women which take the place of columns. The most famous ones are the C. of the Athenian Erechtheum; also those of the treasure house of the Siphnians in Delphi.

CASILINUM. Now Capua, where the Via Appia crossed the Volturno River by means of a bridge.

CASINUM. City in Latium near what is now the monastery of Monte Cassino; it was already a place of strategic importance during the second Punic War.

CASSANDER (c. 358-297). Son of Antipater. He tried to keep control of Macedonia and Greece, which brought him into conflict with Antigonus I and Demetrius Poliorcetes. He killed Olympias in 316, and Roxana and her small son in 311. He founded Thessalonica and rebuilt Thebes.

CASSIUS, GAIUS LONGINUS. Rom. general who saved the remains of the Rom. army after Carrhae. He fought on Pompey's side, but was shown mercy by Caesar after Pharsalus. He and Marcus Brutus were the main conspirators against Caesar (44 B.C.); afterward he left for Syria, of which Caesar had made him proconsul. From there he joined Brutus in Macedonia and committed suicide after the first battle of Philippi, although at that time all was not yet lost.

CASSIVELAUNUS. King in Britain who opposed Caesar's second expedition to that country in 54 B.C. (Caes. *B.G.* V, 11-23). After his capital had been taken he reached an understanding with Caesar and agreed to pay tribute to Rome.

CASTRA. Rom. army camp. This was usually a rectangle, divided by two main roads (*via principalis* and *via quintana*);

the center contained headquarters or *praetorium,* with a platform (*tribunal*) and a parade ground. There were four gates in the earthen wall (*vallum*). A Rom. army was trained to build a C. in a few hours, after the day's march: the more permanent winter camps (*hiberna*) were, of course, more solidly constructed. Instead of tents, they had barracks. In the permanent camps built during the Rom. imperial period, there were stone buildings. Thus, the C. often developed into a real settlement. See Appendix.

CATALAUNIAN PLAINS. Plains near Châlons-sur-Marne, where Attila is said to have been defeated by Aetius; the actual scene of the battle was closer to Troyes.

CATILINA, LUCIUS SERGIUS (c. 108-62). Commonly called Catiline. The notorious conspirator, born of a patrician family. He acquired a bad reputation during Sulla's proscriptions, and made it worse as the governor of Africa. Accused of blackmail, he could not become a candidate for the consulship in 65; he therefore planned to murder the consuls elected. This plan failed; in 63 and 62 he also failed in his efforts to be elected consul. In 63 Cicero became a consul and C. then prepared for a real coup d'état, together with a number of fellow conspirators. Cicero reacted with his famous four Catilinarian orations. C. fled to his friend Manlius in Etruria; his fellow plotters in Rome were to carry on, but they were unmasked, particularly when they started negotiating with the envoys of the Allobroges, who promptly denounced them. The coplotters were executed under the *senatus consultum ultimum* (see CAVEANT CONSULES), which was not really legal. C. himself fell at Pistoria (Sall. *Catilina*).

CATO. Name of:

—(1) Marcus Porcius C. (Cato Major) (244-149). Rom. statesman and author. He followed the *cursus honorum,* becoming consul in 195; in 184, he became censor. C. was extremely severe in the execution of his duties, and took strong action against luxury and corruption (this earned him the surname "Censor"). In 157 (or 153) he went to Carthage as an envoy, saw its renewed prosperity, and expressed his views of this in the senate (see CETERUM CENSEO). He lived just long enough to see the beginning of the third Punic War.

C. was a typical representative of the resistance to the increasing Hellenization of Rome (see SCIPIO MINOR; LAELIUS); he wanted to retain the old Rom. traditions and to have Rome concentrate on the western Mediterranean region. The East was to be dominated, not integrated. He propagated his ideas in writing as well as in speech. His historical work *Origines* was lost, as were his orations. A work on agriculture has survived. Pronouncements such as "An orator is a good man, who has command of the art of speaking," and "Know your subject, and the words will come of their own accord" are typical of C.

—(2) Marcus Porcius C. (Cato Minor or Cato Uticensis) (95-46), great-grandson of the last. He remained loyal to the party of Pompey, even after the latter's death. Being an uncompromising republican and having Stoic ideals, he detested monarchy. After the battle of Thapsus he committed suicide in Utica. His memory was honored long afterward by republicans and Stoics.

CATULLUS, GAIUS VALERIUS (c. 84-c. 53). Lat. lyric poet. Born in Verona, he came to Rome in 62, where he fell in love with Clodia, the sister of Clodius. He honored her in his poems, as "Lesbia"; this woman, ten years his senior, proved to be unfaithful, which drove C. to despair. In his songs, which equal Sappho's in their depth of feeling, he expresses his love and his bitterness. In his descriptions of nature, too, he reached rare heights seldom equaled in classical poetry. He was capable of great sharpness in his satires (against Caesar, among others). Of his poems 116 have been preserved (three of which are wrongly attributed to him). His works show the influence of the Alexandrian school, and to a still greater extent his admiration for the older Gr. lyricism (especially Sappho); his own, fascinating personality, however, remains dominant. His influence on later Rom. poets (Horace, Martial) is great. Much of European lyric poetry in later ages, mainly after the Renaissance, was inspired by his work.

CATULUS. Name of:

—(1) Gaius Lutatius. Rom. consul (242 B.C.); commander of the fleet that defeated a daring attack by the Carthaginian fleet near the Aegadian Islands. He was the only real seaman to command a Rom. fleet during the first Punic War.

—(2) Quintus Lutatius C. Consul (102 B.C.); he defeated the Cimbri at Vercellae together with Marius. He is also known as one of the Rom. notables who continued to work for the ideals of the "Scipionic Circle" (see LAELIUS).

CAUDINE FORKS. Mountain passes on the road between Capua and Beneventum, where the Samnites trapped the Rom. army in 321 B.C., and made them pass under the Caudine yoke, a humiliation which the Romans never forgot.

CAVEANT CONSULES, NI QUID RESPUBLICA DETRIMENTI CAPIAT. "Let the consuls beware, that the state shall suffer no injury"; formula with which the Rom. senate decreed the *senatus consultum ultimum*, a sort of a state of siege; used mainly after dictatorship had become obsolete.

CAVE CANEM. "Beware of the dog." Warning on mosaics showing the figure of a dog, found at Rom. houses (in Pompeii, among other places).

CECROPS. Mythical king of Athens, under whose rule Athena and Poseidon were said to have competed for the position of patron of the city. His grave was said to be at the southwestern corner of the Erechtheum.

CELLA. See TEMPLE.

CELSUS (2nd cent. B.C.). The first critic of Christianity. The text of his book *The True Word* was extensively quoted by his opponent Origen. C. was a Platonist; he was also well acquainted with the Jewish religion.

CELSUS, AULUS CORNELIUS. Compiler of an encyclopedic work in the reign of the Emperor Tiberius, of which only the medical section (eight books) has survived. It is clearly written; since the Renaissance this work has been the most important source of knowledge on ancient medicine. C. himself was a layman, and wrote mainly for laymen.

CELTIBERI. Collective name for a

number of peoples in central and northern Spain (see HISPANIA). The Iberians probably came from North Africa in the 3rd millennium B.C., drove most of the Ligurians out of Spain and assimilated in the 3rd cent. B.C. with the Celts, who came from the North. Their most important city was Numantia. Their type of sword was adopted by the Romans as a weapon for the soldiers of the legions.

CELTS. See GALLIA, CELTIBERI; BRITANNIA.

CENABUM. Now Orléans; scene of the outbreak of the revolt (52 B.C.) that was soon to be led by Vercingetorix (Caes. *B.G.* VII, 3).

CENSOR. Name for two Rom. magistrates, who were elected every five years for a period of office of one and a half years. Their duties were various: they kept the census, that is, the estimate of each citizen's fortune and the designation of the class to which each belonged; they appointed the members of the senate, usually ex-magistrates, and were authorized to expel unworthy members of it; they awarded the contracts for public works. The census always ended in a lustrum. The office, which was established in 443 B.C., was at first limited to patricians, after 350, plebeians (see PLEBS) were also eligible. It was a high honor; in general, only ex-consuls were chosen. Sulla deprived it of most of its importance, by having the senate automatically supplemented by ex-quaestors. Under the Emperor Domitian it ended as a distinct office.

CENTAURS. Mythical figures, half horses, and half men, who lived, according to legend, in Thessaly and led wild, lawless lives. The Greeks believed that they were the personification of the animal and barbarian in man. The battle between the C. and the Lapithae, as portrayed on the west façade of the Temple of Zeus at Olympia, symbolizes the Persian Wars. There was also one wise Centaur, Chiron, who was the teacher of certain heroes (Jason and Achilles). He had a cult in Thessaly.

CENTURY. Section of nominally 100 infantrymen in a Rom. legion (see also COMITIA). The commander was called a centurion. This function corresponds to that of a modern junior-grade officer, as to the number of soldiers, but as far as the social position is concerned, they were more like noncommissioned officers. The centurions were the professional officers of the Rom. army; they came up from the ranks by personal merit, strength, and courage. They could reach the highest rank, that of *primipilaris* (supreme centurion) by seniority or by special achievement.

CEPHISODOTUS (4th cent. B.C.). Name of two Gr. sculptors. C. the Elder, a relative, and C. the Younger, the son of Praxiteles. A noted work of C. the Elder was the statue "Irene with the infant Plutus," of which a copy exists in Munich.

CEREALIS, QUINTUS PETIL(L)IUS. Rom. general, related to Vespasian, whom he supported during the Year of the Three Emperors; he was then sent to quell the revolt among the Batavi and, later on, to Britain.

CERES. See DEMETER.

CETERUM CENSEO, CARTHAGINEM ESSE DELENDAM. "I also believe that Carthage should be destroyed." The words with which Cato Major was wont to conclude all his speeches in the senate (compare Plut. *Cato* 27).

CHAERONEA. City in Boeotia, where Philip II of Macedonia defeated the Athenians and the Thebans in 338 B.C.; this battle marked the end of Gr. freedom. On the mass grave of the fallen Thebans, the marble "Lion of C." can still be seen. In 86 B.C. Sulla defeated Mithridates at C. It was the native city and dwelling place of Plutarch.

CHALCEDON (or CHALCHEDON). City on the Bosporus opposite Byzantium, founded in 685 B.C. by colonists from Megara on a site inferior to that of the opposite shore with regard to the current. For this lack of foresight, according to the Persian general Megazabus, the inhabitants were called "blind" (Hdt. IV, 144). The original colonists were more interested in good farm land than in trade. (See BOSPORUS.)

CHALCIDICE. Peninsula to the south of Thrace and Macedonia where the Greeks founded many colonies (among others, Potidaea and Olynthus); these cities were members of both Attic Leagues. For a time they called themselves the Chalcidian League, under the leadership of Olynthus. Philip II annexed C. to Macedonia. Most of the inhabitants were Ionians; only Potidaea, a Corinthian colony, was Doric.

CHALCIS. The main city of Euboea. Its period of greatest prosperity was in the 8th-6th centuries B.C., when C. founded many colonies (Chalcidice, Sicily, Magna Graecia) and successfully fought against Eretria in the Lelantic War.

In about 560-520 C. produced beautiful Chalcidian vases, some of which have been found in many Italian and Sicilian graves. In the 5th-4th centuries it was dominated by Athens. During the Hellenistic period, it was again an important trade center.

CHALDEANS. The dominant people in Babylonia during the New Babylonian empire (625-538) of Nebuchadnezzar. Astrology was extensively practiced in Babylonia, and knowledge of it spread to Greece in the course of trade relations. To the Greeks this science was the outstanding achievement of the people of Babylonia, and gradually the word "C." became synonymous with "astrologers," particularly among the Romans, even when entirely different peoples were concerned.

CHARONDAS (6th cent. B.C.). Lawgiver of the Gr. cities Catana in Sicily and Rhegium in Italy, among other places. His laws, about which we know a little through the works of Aristotle, were democratic in character, although C. himself was a patrician. He made special laws for the protection of family life, and forbade citizens to come to an assembly armed. It is said that he once accidently broke this law himself and then committed suicide.

CHERSONESUS. The Lat. word for peninsula, forming part of several Latin place names. The best known are:
—(1) C. Thracia, the Thracian peninsula on the Hellespont, colonized by the Greeks in the 8th-7th centuries B.C., later the domain of the Miltiades family, then Athenian and finally Macedonian and Rom. property.

—(2) C. Taurica, the Crimea, colonized by Miletus, important for its wheat supply.

CHIOS. One of the largest islands in the Aegean Sea; according to tradition, Homer was born there. It was colonized by Ionians and was an ally of Miletus, later a member of the Delian League, and usually friendly to Athens. During the 4th cent., C. was famous for its wine.

CHITON. Gr. tunic, hanging down from the shoulders, provided with armholes, held together around the waist by a girdle. The Doric C. was made of wool, the Ionian of linen. Indoors, a C. was usually the only garment worn. See Appendix.

CHLAMYS. Gr. short cape, worn by soldiers and when riding.

CHRONOLOGY. The science of measuring time by regular divisions. There were several Gr. systems of measuring time; these varied from city to city. The years were counted according to certain eponymous offices; that is, each year was designated by the name of the holder of that office for the year. In Athens, for example, the years were named after the *archon eponymos,* in Argos after the priest of Hera; a unified system was not established. The division into Olympiads was more practical. They were counted from 776 B.C., but this C. was used only by historians (Diodorus Siculus, for example). In Rome, years were counted after the consuls from the founding of Rome (*ab urbe condita*). This was fixed at 753 B.C. by Varro. In the East, there was a fixed measurement of time during the era of the Seleucids, running from 312 B.C. onward (see also CALENDAR).

CHRYSIPPUS (c. 280-207). Gr. philosopher, who succeeded Cleanthes as the leader of the Stoa; he gave the Stoic doctrine its orthodox form, and defended it against the attacks of the Academy. It was said of him that "if C. were not, there would be no Stoa."

CHRYSOSTOMUS. See DION.

CICERO, MARCUS TULLIUS (106-43). Rom. orator, statesman, and writer on rhetoric, statesmanship, and other philosophical subjects. He was born in Arpinum into a family of the *equites* class. Ambitious and talented, he went to Rome in his youth. Although he was a *homo novus,* he passed through the *cursus honorum* in a minimum of time. At first he only worked as a lawyer, and distinguished himself as early as 80, by getting a young man, Roscius, acquitted of patricide against one of the most powerful favorites of Sulla; for this, he needed not a little courage. He then studied in Athens (where he made a lifelong friend of Atticus) and at Rhodes, where he followed the lectures of Posidonius. In 76 he was quaestor in Sicily; in 70 he successfully prosecuted Verres; in 69 he was aedile, in 66 praetor (see MANILIUS). The peak of his career was his consulship (63), during which he foiled Catilina's conspiracy. When the first triumvirate was formed in 60 (see TRIUMVIRI) C. was approached, but he refused. This put an end to his leadership. In 58 he was driven into exile by Clodius, but he returned in 57 and devoted his time to study. During these years he wrote his most important works on oratory and statesmanship. In 51 he was proconsul of Cilicia; in the following Civil War, after long hesitation, he chose Pompey's side against Caesar. After the latter had granted him mercy, he again devoted his time to studying and writing philosophical treatises. After the murder of Caesar he returned, once more, to the political arena, to attack Antony in his *Philippicae.* At the next proscriptions, C. was one of the first victims; during an attempt to escape, he was caught and killed by the minions of Antony.

C.'s work can be divided into three categories: (a) The speeches (fifty-seven preserved). Besides those mentioned above, the following deserve special mention: the one for the poet Archias (62), which is also a warm plea for poetry in general, and the one for Milo, the murderer of Clodius (52). The latter, often considered the most perfect plea ever made during a suit, was never delivered. During the actual pleading, C. was confused by Clodius' henchmen, and Milo was banished. (b) The rhetorical-political writings (most of which are original) and philosophical treatises. The latter are not original, and C. did not pretend they were. They are edited writings of Gr. philosophers. C.'s great merit was that

he made Latin a medium for perpetuating philosophical ideas. (c) The letters, almost 800 in number, and ninety by his correspondents. Almost none of these were written for publication, and they were published after his death (most of them by Tiro). They give us an insight into his private life and intimate thoughts; we know him in a way in which we know no other personage from antiquity. We can read his immediate reactions to political events, and also cries from the heart, as, for example, his sorrow on the death of his beloved daughter Tullia.

The evaluation of C. has varied greatly in the course of the centuries; with Mommsen, in the 19th cent., it reached its lowest point. Today there are still scholars who conveniently use his letters to blacken his memory. He was certainly opportunistic and vain (witness his bad verses, in which he glorifies his consulship); but there are many positive points to offset this. As a young man, he dared to defy Sulla's followers, and in the last year of his life he attacked Antony with the courage of a lion. His ideal of a *concordia ordinum* (concord and cooperation between the classes) could, under Pompey's leadership, have been realized. C.'s greatest importance, however, lay in his literary work. In his orations and other works, he set the standard for classic Lat. prose. In his philosophical works he transmitted the ideas of Gr. philosophy after Aristotle in a manner all his own, so that Western civilization was also deeply influenced by it through the Lat. culture of the later classical period, early Christianity, and the Middle Ages. Thus, C. became one of the great educators of mankind.

CILICIA. Province in southeastern Asia Minor, south of the Taurus Mountains; capital, Tarsus. The coastal strip was notorious for its many pirates' nests, against which Pompey and others acted vigorously (see PIRACY).

CIMBRI. German tribe, originating in Jutland, which started migrating in the 2nd cent. B.C. (probably as a result of floods), and invaded southern Gaul with the Teutons about 110. In 105 they destroyed a Rom. army at Arausio. Later they invaded Spain, after which they re-entered Gaul on their way to Italy. Here the two tribes were separated. Marius defeated the Teutons at Aquae Sextiae; the C., who had penetrated to the Po Valley from the northeast, going around the Alps, were also defeated by Marius, at Vercellae in 101.

CIMMERIANS. The mythical Cimmerii, mentioned by Homer as living at the misty edges of the world, where the entrance to the underworld was thought to be. In about 700 B.C. the historical C. invaded Asia Minor from southern Russia, by way of the Caucasus; they terminated the kingdom of Phrygia and razed Lydia (Sardes was taken in 652 B.C.), after which they also attacked the Ionian cities. King Alyattes drove them off.

CIMON (c. 510-449). Athenian statesman and general, son of Miltiades. He helped Aristides to organize the Delian League, and commanded the fleet against the Persians regularly, from 478-465. His greatest victory was in the battle at the mouth of the Eurymedon River. In internal politics, he was the leader of the group that wanted to continue the fight against Persia at all costs, but strove after friendship with Sparta (in opposition to the policy of Themistocles. Therefore, when Sparta had to cope with a revolt of the Helots in Messenia, after a serious earthquake in 462, C. led an army to their aid. But Sparta, always suspicious as to C.'s motives, and afraid of foreign influence, sent him back ignominiously. This led to loss of influence in Athens, and in 461 he was ostracized. The democratic party under Ephialtes (and soon afterward under Pericles) now got the upper hand. C. was later recalled, and led just one more campaign against the Persians, in 449, which was to lead to the battle of Salamis in Cyprus; on that expedition, however, he died.

CINCINNATUS, LUCIUS QUINTIUS. Rom. hero, dictator 458 B.C., who was called from the plow to become dictator in a war against the Aequi (see VOLSCI). He defeated them in fifteen days and went back to his farm. He is the standard example of old-Rom. virtue, simplicity, and patriotism.

CINNA, LUCIUS CORNELIUS. Patrician leader of the *populares* in Rome against Sulla, consul 87-84. After Sulla's departure for the East, C. had him outlawed, and recalled Marius and his supporters. Banished by the senate, he forcibly returned to Rome and slaughtered many of the *optimates*. After Marius' death, he was, in fact, a dictator in Rome. When Sulla returned from the East, C. went out to meet him, but was killed in a mutiny at Brundisium.

CIRCUS. Rom. racetrack, U-shaped, surrounded on three sides by graduated grandstands. The stables for the teams of horses were at the straight end, and were distinguishable by the different colors. A fence, the *spina*, ran lengthwise along the track, dividing it into two strips, shut off at the end by a pole (*meta*). The oldest and most important C. in Rome was the C. Maximus, between the Palatine Hill and the Aventine. The C. of Maxentius, on the Via Appia, is the best-preserved one. There were also circuses in many other cities—for example, Constantinople, where the parties that organized the teams (the Greens, White, Blues, and Reds) had great political influence.

CITHAERON. Mountain on the frontier of Boeotia, the Isthmus of Corinth, and Attica. According to the legend, Oedipus was abandoned there as a foundling; it was also the place where the Bacchannalia took place (Eur. *Bacchae*).

CIVILIS, JULIUS. See BATAVI.

CLAUDIAN HOUSE. The patrician Rom. family (the *Claudia gens*), of which many members played leading parts in Rom. history during the period of the monarchy. They had come to Rome from the land of the Sabines. They possessed genius combined with perseverance and a will of iron; therefore, they often did not conform to the republican senatorial regime. They were either praised or reviled, depending on whether or not the results of their unorthodox conduct were successful. An example of the former was the courageous decision of Gaius Claudius Nero, consul in 207 B.C., to leave his *provincia* with his colleague Livius, without waiting for the senate's permission, in order to defeat Hasdrubal at the Metaurus River. An example of the latter is the conduct of Publius Clodius Pulcher,

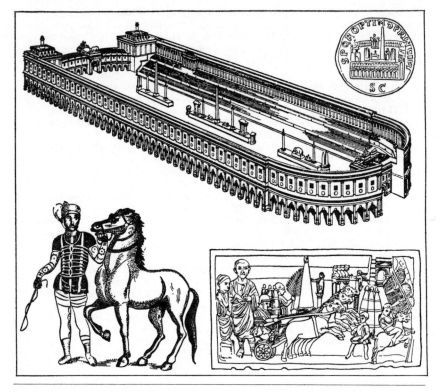

Reconstruction of the Circus Maximus in Rome. Above, right: the circus on a bronze coin, minted by Trajan. Below, left: mosaic depicting a charioteer. Below, right: 3rd cent. relief on a tomb, depicting a chariot race.

who lost a naval battle at Drepanum during the First Punic War, after he had thrown the sacred chickens, which refused to peck (see AUSPICIA), into the sea with the cry: "If they will not eat, let them drink" (*bibant, si edere nolunt*). (For other members of the same family, see CLAUDIUS CAECUS; CLODIUS PULCHER, PUBLIUS; TIBERIUS; CALIGULA; NERO.)

CLAUDIANUS, CLAUDIUS (2nd half of the 4th cent. A.D.). The last of the Lat. classic poets. He was born at Alexandria. At first he wrote in Greek; later he came to Rome and wrote Lat. poems and was court poet to Stilicho and Honorius. He had perfect command of Latin, and his poetry had great charm and power. He also wrote good political satire (often aimed at the leaders of the East Rom.

Empire). He died c. A.D. 408.

CLAUDIUS. Name of:

—(1) C. I (10 B.C.-A.D. 54). Full name Tiberius Claudius Drusus Nero Germanicus. Rom. emperor, brother of the Emperor Tiberius; to his consternation, hailed as emperor by the praetorians after the death of Caligula (A.D. 41). Before that, he had led a retiring life as a scholar (he wrote on the history of Etruria, among other things). The bad name history has given him (for example, Tacitus and Seutonius) can be ascribed to the antipathy toward him in senatorial circles. This was mainly due to the fact that C. appointed freedmen as government officials. The truth is that his government was excellent, a relief after Caligula's tyranny. We know this through the many decrees and inscriptions on papyri, found in the provinces. A negative side to his reign was the dominating influence of his wives; Messalina, the mother of Britannicus, and later Agrippina the Younger, who managed to have her son Nero adopted by C., and who murdered her husband in 54 with a dish of poisonous mushrooms (see also BRITANNIA).

—(2) C. II. Full name Marcus Aurelius C., surnamed Gothicus (see MILITARY EMPERORS).

—(3) Appius C. The most important of the Rom. decemviri, who framed the laws of the Twelve Tablets; he tried to mediate between the people of various ranks, like a Gr. *aisymnetes* (see SOLON; PITTACUS). His work was finally successful, although he personally was disappointed. According to tradition, he assaulted a certain Virginia, after which the plebs revolted and overthrew the decemvirate government.

—(4) Appius C. Caecus. Censor in 312 B.C., consul in 307 and 296. He approved of the same policy of emancipation of the plebs as Appius Claudius. He built the first aqueduct (the Aqua Appia), and the Via Appia. In his old age he was an influential senator, who persuaded the senate to reject the peace proposals of Pyrrhus in 280. He is also said to have been the first Rom. writer of prose.

CLAZOMENAE. One of the Ionian cities on the coast of Asia Minor, native city of Anaxagoras. It is famous for its sarcophagi, made of painted terra cotta in the archaic period.

CLEANTHES (3rd cent. B.C.) Gr. philosopher. He succeeded Zeno as the leader of the Stoa (c. 263) and gave Stoic philosophy its typically religious tone. He was also the author of the well-known hymn to Zeus, which was cited by St. Paul in his speech on the Areopagus. In his ethics, he contended that an evil thought is worse than an evil deed. His religious idea was that the divine forms the living soul of the universe.

CLEARCHUS (c. 450-401). Spartan general. He acted as ruler in Byzantium at the end of the Peloponnesian War. Cast out by Spartan troops as a result of his reign of terror, he went into the service of Cyrus the Younger. He was the most important commander of the former's Ten Thousand (Gr. mercenaries, see XENOPHON) and led the (Gr.) right wing at Cunaxa. After that, he was captured by the treachery of Tissaphernes and put to death.

CLEMENT OF ALEXANDRIA (Titus Flavius Clements) (c. 150-c. 215). Christian Gr. author. He was the head of the catechetical school of Alexandria, where converts were instructed in the Christian doctrine (C. was himself a convert). In his works, he defended the superiority of Christianity over pagan philosophy. Nevertheless, he was very well versed in pagan Gr. culture, and had great admiration for it. His work is an important source of knowledge on data that have been lost entirely, for example, the mysteries.

CLEOMENES. Name of:

—(1) C. I. King of Sparta, reigned 520-487. He helped drive Hippias out of Athens in 510 and afterward opposed Clisthenes, but was unsuccessful. C. was mainly responsible for the fact that Sparta did not want to support the Ionian revolt in 500. Formally, the reason was simply that a war with Argos was impending, but the real cause was certainly the general Spartan reserve toward venturing overseas. His principal opponent in Sparta was his fellow king Demaratus.

—(2) C. II. King of Sparta, son of Cleombrotus I, reigned 370-309.

—(3) C. III. King of Sparta, reigned 235-219. He opposed the Achaean League under Aratus; this led, after initial success, to the defeat at Sellasia (see also Antigonus III); C. afterward fled to Egypt, where he was imprisoned by Ptolemy IV; after an abortive attempt to escape, he committed suicide. C.'s internal policy is known mainly because he continued with the social reforms Agis IV had started, but less from real social idealism than as a foundation for Sparta's political expansion.

CLEON (?-422 B.C.), Athenian politician. Born of a middle-class family (he inherited a tannery from his father), he became the political leader in Athens on the death of Pericles. He constantly incited the populace to battle with Sparta in the Peloponnesian War. When a Spartan army was surrounded at Sphacteria in 425, he refused an offer of peace, was given command himself, and managed to force a surrender. In 422 he went to Thrace in order to recover Amphipolis from Brasidas, but fell in battle. The bad reputation which tradition has given him stems from the fact that Thucydides, and, to an even greater degree Aristophanes, disliked him. We must therefore make allowances for a certain amount of exaggeration; but, on the other hand, it has been determined that C. was capable of acting like a vulgar demagogue, and with reckless cruelty.

CLEOPATRA (68-30 B.C.). Macedonian princess, queen of Egypt; last queen of the house of Ptolemy. When Caesar went to Egypt after the battle of Pharsalus (48), she became his mistress in order to regain the throne, from which she had been driven. She bore him a son, Caesarion; later she spent some time in Rome, returned to Alexandria after Caesar's death, and had her brother and fellow king Ptolemy XII murdered. In 41 Antony summoned her to Tarsus, became her lover, and married her in 37. She and Antony made plans for dominating the Rom. Empire, which inspired hate and fear in Rome. Octavian declared war on her (and therefore on Antony) that ended in the battle of Actium. After C. had tried in vain to captivate Octavian as well, she committed suicide by letting an asp bite her. C. was an extremely intelligent and very domineering woman. Her love affairs with Rom. leaders were all in the cause of her immeasurable political ambitions. Horace (*Carm.* I, 37) portrays the almost indescribable relief in Rome at the tidings of her death.

CLERUCHIA [Gr. klerouchia]. A special Athenian colony, to which poor citizens were sent. They retained their Athenian citizenship and were given a piece of land to cultivate; they also had to act as *hoplites*. It was mainly a way of keeping troublesome or rebellious members of the Delian League under control.

CLIENT. In Rome, a citizen who was under the protection of a prominent person, his patron. This patron had to defend the C. before the court, and give him help and advice in all phases of life. The C., on the other hand, supported his patron in elections, and offered him homage, for example by a morning call to offer his respects. The relationship was fixed by law, and made sacrosanct by tradition. In the earliest republican times there was a regulated relationship between patrician patron and plebeian C. Eventually the relationship lost its religious and moral aspects, and became a purely material one. A freedman was automatically the C. of his former master.

CLIO. See MUSES.

CLISTHENES [Gr. Kleisthenes]. The founder of Athenian democracy (6th cent. B.C.); member of the Alcmaeonidae, who drove away Hippias with the aid of Sparta (see CLEOMENES) in 510; C. then formed a democratic party in opposition to the aristocratic Isagoras. In 507 he carried out his program. He abolished the four ancient Ionian *phylae* (tribal subdivisions) and established ten new ones, on a geographical basis, as a result the old family ties lost their conservative-political power. The Council of Four Hundred, established by Solon, was increased by C. in order to have fifty representatives from each tribe. The task of this council was to do the preliminary work on the decisions of the ecclesia. The phylae were subdivided into demes, or residential districts, the smallest units in which citizens' rights were exercised. C. gave a firm foundation to the democracy for which Solon had, in principle, created the necessary conditions.

CLITIAS. See FRANÇOIS VASE.

CLOACA MAXIMA. A canalized stream, which served as the main sewer in Rome. According to tradition, it was constructed by Tarquinius Priscus but most of it originated in the 3rd cent. B.C., and was improved by Agrippa in 33 B.C.

CLODIUS ALBINUS. See MILITARY EMPERORS.

CLODIUS PULCHER, PUBLIUS (1st cent. B.C.). Rom. political agitator. Though born of a patrician family (*Claudia gens*), he became a member of the plebs (thus the different, "popular" spelling of his name). He sent Cicero into exile, because the latter had had supporters of Catilina put to death without a *provocatio*. During Caesar's stay in Gaul he conducted a reign of terror against Pompey in Rome, with armed gangs. In 52 he was murdered by his opponent Milo, which led to still more riots in Rome.

CLUSIUM. Etruscan city near Lake Trasimenus, residence of Porsenna. Roman city after 300 B.C. Several beautiful tombs were found there (see FRANÇOIS VASE); it is also the place where many Etruscan canopics vases were found. The present-day Chiusi.

CNIDUS. Dorian city on the southwest coast of Asia Minor; flourished in the 6th cent. B.C. as a result of trade relations with Naucratis and Tarentum. In the 5th cent. it was a member of the Delian League. The city was famous chiefly for its school of medicine, for Praxiteles' statue "Aphrodite," of which several Rom. copies have survived and which was the first statue of the naked female figure, and for Eudoxus' observatory.

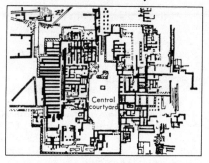

The palace of Cnossus

CNOSSUS. The most important center of Minoan culture on Crete, already inhabited in the *Neolithic* period. We can speak of a culture after about 3000 B.C.; even then C. was flourishing through contact with Egypt and Asia Minor. In about 2000 B.C. the first "Palace of Minos" came into being; it was destroyed (by an earthquake in about 1700 B.C., and again in 1600 B.C.; in 1400 B.C. it was destroyed by fire, probably in the course of a conquest by a new group of Achaeans); each time it was rebuilt, enlarged, and beautified. When this palace was excavated in about 1900 by British archaeologist Sir Arthur Evans, three types of written texts were found, which could not be deci-

phered. It was not until 1950-53 that the Englishman Ventris succeeded in deciphering the third type, the so-called Linear B, which had also been found on the Gr. mainland (particularly in Pylos). The language turned out to be Greek. So we must assume that already in the 15th cent. the Greeks were established in C. and maintained the Minoan culture there. The palaces are unevenly built around a courtyard (explaining the legend of the Labyrinth); they were not fortified by strong walls, which indicates that the inhabitants felt secure, probably because they had control over the seas (see also MINOAN CULTURE; CRETE; SCRIPT).

CODRUS. Mythical king of Athens (if he is historical, he probably lived in the 11th cent. B.C.). During a Dorian attack on Attica, the Delphic oracle prophesied that Athens could only be victorious if C. were to die at the enemy's hands. It is said that C. then disguised himself, went among the enemy, and in an act of patriotism, provoked a fight and was killed.

COHORT. In the Rom. army, originally a section of *socii;* after the 3rd cent. B.C. a section of Rom. infantry (one tenth of a legion, consisting of 600 men). (For the *cohors praetoria* see PRAETORIANS.)

COINAGE. Originally, coins did not exist in the antique world. The value of goods was expressed in cattle, for example (Hom. *Il.* VI, 236); the Lat. term *pecunia* (money) is derived from *pecus* (cattle) or in a weight of precious metal (talent, Gr. *talanton,* actually means "scales," and thus "weight"). Later, iron staves were used (*obolos,* literally "roasting spit"). The first coins were minted in Lydia in about 800 B.C.; their usage was adopted by the cities of Ionia who minted coins made of electron. In about 700 the Greeks also began to mint coins, first on Aegina (see also PHEIDON); here, silver was used (Gr. *augurion* "small silver," meaning "money"); Corinth and Chalcis soon followed; Athens started in about 600 and came into prominence when Solon changed over from the heavier Aeginetan to the lighter Chalcidian standard. The Athenian "owls" cornered the money market in the 5th and 4th centuries B.C. Then golden coins were minted, which had formerly been monopolized by the

Persians (see DAREICUS). Bronze was first used in Sicily and was introduced in Greece in about 400. Only Sparta continued to use iron staves. In Rome the first coins of bronze (*Aes*) were introduced (289 B.C.); shortly afterward pieces of silver came into use. After about 200 B.C. gold was minted sporadically, not coming into general use until Caesar's time. The devaluation of money posed a serious problem in ancient times, in Greece in the Hellenistic period, after Alexander the Great had put the treasures of Persia into circulation, and in Rome in the 2nd-1st centuries B.C., when enormous capitals from the East, flowed into Italy, and foreign minted money also went into circulation.

The most important Gr. coins are: the *drachma* (4.36 gr. of silver), consisting of 6 *oboles*; 100 drachmae were equal to one *mina;* 60 *minae* equaled one *talent.* In Rome the monetary unit was the *aes* (originally 327 gr. of gold, but devaluated to about 30 gr. in c. 125 B.C.); 2.5 aes were a *sestertius,* 10 a *denarius.*

Coins are an important source for the history of politics, art, and especially religion. Numismatics is devoted to the study of these aspects of coins. Through coins we can trace the degree of colonization and the expansion of trade relations, we can follow the Rom. soldier on his campaigns, study daily life, verify conquests and victories. Sometimes we also find important lost works of art depicted in miniature on coins (for example, the statue of Zeus by Phidias in Olympia).

COLCHIS. Province on the east coast of the Black Sea, south of the Caucasus (see ARGONAUTS).

COLONIA. Rom. settlement of citizens, founded for strategic reasons near large roads or on the coast. There were also *coloniae Latinae,* only partially inhabited by Romans; these had their own civic rights. Often, veterans were settled in a colony, as a reward for faithful service.

COLONIA AGRIPPINA. Rom. settlement on the Rhine, now Cologne, capital of Germania Inferior, founded by the Emperor Claudius in A.D. 50, on the site upon which Agrippa had already allowed the Ubii, who were friendly to Rome, to settle in 38 B.C.

COLONIZATION. A significant new wave of C. started in the 8th-7th centuries B.C., following the earlier Dorian migration (see IONIANS). When Greece, overpopulated, began to suffer from social disturbances everywhere within her territory (see TYRANT; LEGISLATORS), groups of Greeks swarmed to all the coastal areas of the Mediterranean Sea (see particularly MILETUS; CHALCIS; PHOCAEA; SICILY; MAGNA GRAECIA; ORACLE). Their leader was usually an aristocrat who was celebrated as "the settler" (*oikistes*), and who, after his death, often was venerated as a hero. The colony became an independent city-state, but usually maintained friendly relations with its founding city. The poor relationship that existed between Corinth and Corcyra was an exception. A significant civilizing influence emanated from many of these cities, for example, Cumae in Italy and Massilia in Gaul (for Athenian C. in connection with the Delian League see CLERUCHIA; for Phoenician C. see PHOENICIANS; for Rom. C. see COLONIA).

COLOPHON. Ionian city on the coast of Asia Minor, one of the cities that claimed to be the native city of Homer.

COLOSSEUM. The largest amphitheater in Rome; the name (dating from the Middle Ages) originated from the colossal statue of Nero which stood there. The Rom. name was *Amphitheatrum Flavium,* built by Vespasian and Titus, dedicated in A.D. 80. The approximate measurements are: length, 615 ft.; breadth, 510 ft.; height, 160 ft. It could accommodate 45-50,000 spectators. See Appendix.

COLUMN. One of the most distinctive elements of architectural orders. There are three types: the Doric, Ionic, and Corinthian C., the only difference between the second and the third lies in their capital. The C. is constructed of cylindrical discs (drums), with a hole in the center, and are decorated with vertical fluted grooves; the edges between these grooves are sharp in Doric columns and flat in Ionic ones. The Doric C. has no base and is comparatively thick and heavy; the Ionian C. has a base and is more slender. Both types have a bulge (*entasis*) in the middle, reminiscent of the construction of the ancient wooden temples (a wooden C. expands in the middle as the result of pressure by the dome), which also produces a harmonious line. The capital of the Doric C. is a "cushion" with a square slab above it, the Ionic one is decorated with two large spirals (volutes), the Corinthian one with acanthus leaves. This capital is the easiest means of distinguishing architectural style at first glance. The C. was used for monuments (see also STELE) as well as for temples. The columns of Trajan and Marcus Aurelius in Rome, which are decorated with reliefs, are well known.

COMEDY. Gr. C. had its origin in the festival of Dionysus. During a gay procession (*komos*), the participants sang and jested—always keeping the reactions of the audience in mind. The Doric inhabitants of Megara are said, according to tradition, to have been the founders of Gr. C., because they claim to have been the first to form the jokes and antics of the *komos* into a type of farce.

The Old C., had its beginning with Epicharmus of Cos (c. 540-450 B.C.) who developed this local Doric C. in Sicily to its literary form. His subjects for caricature were not only gods and heroes but everyday people as well. These early comedies did not have a chorus.

Old C. reached Attica (probably by way of Megara) where a chorus, which had sprung up from the *komos,* was an important element. Masters of the Old C. are Aristophanes, Cratinus, and Eupolis. From the comedies of Aristophanes it is apparent that plays of this period of the Old C. were primarily patriotic and political in nature. In his later work there is evidence of the curtailment placed on political free expression. It was necessary to give up the elaborate and expensive chorus due to the disastrous financial results of the Peloponnesian War, and with it the *parabasis* in which the chorus addresses questions of the day to the audience. Consequently, the decline of the Old C. was inevitable.

The so-called Middle C. (from c. 400-338 B.C.) took its place with a less prominent chorus as its characteristic form. There is also less political significance and no criticism of political figures. It deals with characters rather than individuals.

The drama of the New C. (from c. 330-B.C.-the 3rd cent. A.D.) offered humor, rarely concerned with public life. There is a definite plot revolving around definite social types—there is a tendency to moralize and philosophize. The chorus is no longer concerned in the action, it sings small parts written in lyric meters. The greatest figures of this period were Menander, Diphilus, and Philemon. Euripides exercised a strong influence on the New C. which in turn greatly influenced Rom. C. (see FABULA; MIME; PLAUTUS; and TERENCE).

COMITIA. Rom. popular assembly, in which the suggestions of the magistrates were accepted or rejected, without debate or the right of amendment. The following kinds were known: (a) C. *curiata,* meetings of the nobles of the *curiae;* who met, during the period of the monarchy, to choose the king. A survival of this function is found during republican times in the meetings of the assembly to give the newly chosen magistrates the *imperium.* (b) C. *centuriata*—literally, assembly of the army (which is why it met on the Campus Martius). The delegates voted by century and according to financial status. At first, the richest classes dominated absolutely; after a reformation in the 3rd cent. B.C. this domination was slightly lessened. The main functions of this C. were to elect the *magistratus cum imperio* (see MAGISTRATE), to decide on war or peace, and to sit as a court of appeals (*provocatio*). (c) C. *tributa* or *concilium plebis,* classified by tribes; this was the most democratic popular assembly, in which the lower magistrates were chosen and, eventually, most of the proposed laws were dealt with. The Emperor Tiberius transferred the elections to the senate, after which the importance of the C. quickly waned.

COMMODUS, LUCIUS AELIUS AURELIUS (161-192). Rom. emperor. He succeeded his father Marcus Aurelius in 180 (see ADOPTIVE EMPERORS) and soon proved to be a selfish, cruel man, luxuriating in his power. He considered himself to be a reincarnation of Heracles and enjoyed being portrayed as such; during this period a revival of the Heraclean cult was noticeable in every corner of the Rom. Empire. One of his concubines poisoned him; but as the poison worked slowly, ordered him strangled by an athlete.

COMUM. Now Como in northern Italy, a native city of Pliny the Elder and the Younger.

CONON (c. 444-392). Athenian admiral, the only one of the commanders (strategists) to escape from Aegospotami. After the defeat of the Athenians, he put himself at the service of the Persians and persuaded them to send their fleet, under his command, to operate for Athens against Sparta. In 394 he destroyed the Spartan fleet at Cnidus. He then entered Athens in triumph and had the Long Walls connecting Athens to the Piraeus rebuilt. His policy, however, came to naught as a result of the cunning diplomacy of the Spartan Antalcidas; soon after the latter's first contact with the Persians, C. died.

CONSTANS, FLAVIUS JULIUS (323-350). Youngest son of Constantine the Great; West-Rom. emperor from 337 on; reigned despotically and was murdered by his rival, Magnentius.

CONSTANTINE THE GREAT (Flavius Valerius Constantinus) (c. 280-336). Rom. emperor; son of Constantius Chlorus. On his father's death (306) C. was proclaimed "Augustus" in Britain, after which he was forced to wage a number of bitter civil wars against several pretenders, the last against Maxentius, whom he defeated in the battle of the Pons Milvius near Rome (312). During the battle C. was said to have seen a cross in the sky, and to have heard the words *In hoc signo vinces,* "In this sign, you will conquer."

C. had now become the ruler of the West. At first his relations with Licinius, the ruler of the East, were friendly, but in 323 a war broke out during which Licinius was defeated and killed (324); C. thus became the absolute ruler of the entire Rom. Empire. In the government, he adopted Diocletian's policies and developed them further. The dominate was given its definitive form by C., with more centralization of the governing body and greater development of bureaucracy. On

the Danube, the Goths were driven back and the frontiers were consolidated. C.'s importance in the history of the world is founded on two facts: (a) He laid the foundations for the Christian empire. He had inherited a tolerant disposition from his father. He himself had come to a vague monotheism by way of an interest in the philosophical trends of his time. Just when he became a Christian at heart is open to dispute, but he must have supported the idea of a Christian state church early in his reign, partly from conviction and partly as a matter of opportunism. In 313 he and Licinius proclaimed the Edict of Milan, which permitted the Christian faith equal rights with the other religions. This was followed by more and more privileges. It was also in the interests of the state that the now officially recognized church should preserve its unity. Heretical trends were therefore vigorously combated, and the Council of Nicaea (325) effected a unity of creed. This meeting of the interests of church and state also contributed to the fact that the Christian Church was organized in the 4th cent. on the model of the Rom. Empire. C. himself was not baptized until he lay on his deathbed. (b) C. moved the seat of government to Constantinople, which he built (see also BYZANTIUM). Rome was definitely dethroned. Thereafter, even in the West Rom. Empire, Milan, Ravenna, Trier, and other cities were often government centers.

CONSTANTINOPLE. The city founded by Constantine the Great on the site of Byzantium (324-330), capital of the East Rom. Empire. The Rom. tradition, particularly in the field of Rom. jurisprudence (see CORPUS JURIS), and the heritage of Gr. and Hellenistic culture were preserved here for centuries (see BYZANTIUM).

CONSTANTIUS. Name of:

—(1) C. I Chlorus (Flavius Valerius Constantius) (c. 250-306). Father of Constantine the Great. He was proclaimed "Caesar" in the West by Diocletian in 293. When Diocletian abdicated in 305, he became "Augustus." C. was victorious in Gaul and in Britain, where he died.

—(2) C. II (Flavius Julius Constantius) (317-361). Third son of Constantine the

Great. East Rom. emperor from 337 on, also ruler of the West after the death of Constans and the defeat of Magnentius (see CONSTANS). At his death he recognized Julian as his successor.

CONSUL. Title of the two highest Rom. magistrates. According to tradition the office was created in 510 B.C. (see BRUTUS); however, it is certain that these officers were at first called praetor, and that the title C. appeared later. It is also probable that, at least in internal government, there was initially a single incumbent, although he held office for only a year. Until 367, only patricians were eligible for this office; in that year the *Lex Licinia Sextia* (Licinian Rogations) determined that at least one of the consuls had to be a plebeian. In 172 B.C. two plebeian consuls were elected for the first time. The consuls had *imperium;* they were chosen in the *comitia centuriata;* the year was named after them; they were accompanied by twelve lictors; they presided over the senate and the *comitia,* had executive powers, and commanded armies. During the imperial period consulship gradually became an honorary office. In order to honor as many deserving men or favorites as possible, the term of office was limited to three months. The year was named after the first pair of consuls (see also CURSUS HONORUM; PROCONSUL).

COPAIS. Lake in Boeotia. Drainage works were executed in prehistoric times; an important Mycenaean settlement has been found on an island. In classical times the lake was famous for its eels.

CORBULO, GNAIUS DOMITIUS. Rom. general under Claudius and Nero. Appointed governor in 47 B.C., he entered what is now Holland (Frisia, etc.), where he constructed a canal, the *Fossa Corbulonis,* between the Meuse and the Rhine. Later, he was sent to Armenia to quell a revolt. In 67 he committed suicide at the order of Nero. He wrote memoirs, which were used by Tacitus and others.

CORCYRA. Island on the west coast of Greece (modern Corfu), usually considered to be the island Scheria of Homer's *Odyssey.* The first colonists came from Eretria; they were driven out by Corinthians in 733 B.C. Corinth found C. a troublesome colony; there were many quarrels between the colony and the founding city. This was most unfavorable for Corinth because C. was very necessary as a halting place in the trade relations with the West (Syracuse). In 433 one of these conflicts led to the Peloponnesian War, as Athens supported C. against Corinth. In 427-425 a bloody civil war between the oligarchies and the democracies broke out, which is described extensively by Thucydides (III, 70-85); he sees an occasion in this for a penetrating analysis of Gr. moral degeneration during the Peloponnesian War. Later C. was a bone of contention between the Hellenistic princes (Pyrrhus and others). It became a Rom. possession in 229 B.C. and later part of the Rom. province Macedonia.

CORDUBA. Now called Cordova, in Spain, native city of Lucan and both Senecas.

CORFINIUM. Capital of the Paeligni, a people of central Italy, near the present Pentima; it was made the seat of government by the *socii* during the Social War of 90-88, and renamed Itali(c)a.

CORINNA (c. 500 B.C.). Gr. lyric poetess from Tanagra. She wrote narrative songs in simple verse forms on Boeotian legends. Two of these have been preserved on papyrus.

CORINTH. Large port on the Isthmus of Corinth, which flourished as a result of its excellent position for land trade between the Peloponnesus and central Greece and for sea trade between the Near East and the West by way of Greece. C. had two harbors, Lechaeum on the western and Cenchreae on the eastern side of the Isthmus. C. existed as early as the Mycenaean period. About 1100 B.C. the Dorians settled there, and assimiliated some of the earlier Achaeans. In the time of the Bacchiadae, Cypselus, and Periander, C. prospered. It took an active part in the colonization of the 8th-6th centuries (Corcyra, Syracuse, Potidaea); art also flourished (see PROTO-CORINTHIAN; ARION). After the fall of the tyrants C. became allied to Sparta in the Peloponnesian League. When Athens began to outstrip C.'s trade in the 5th cent., mainly as a result of Athens' expansion to the

West, C. became the bitter enemy of Athens. It was one of the main inciters to the Peloponnesian War (431-404). Afterward, however, it fought with Athens against Sparta in the so-called Corinthian War (395-387), during which the battles of Coronea and Cnidus (see CONON) took place. In the Hellenistic period C. was once more a rich trading city, a city, too, of amusements, in which the temple slaves of Aphrodite played a large part. It became a member of the Achaean League; in 146 B.C. it was destroyed by Mummius. In 44 B.C. it was rebuilt, and regained its position as a center of trade and (immoral) amusements. St. Paul founded an important Christian community there. In A.D. 395 it was pillaged by Alaric, and in 521 it was destroyed by an earthquake.

CORINTHIAN COLUMN. See ARCHITECTURAL ORDERS; COLUMN.

CORIOLANUS, GNAEUS MARCIUS (c. 500 B.C.). Legendary Rom. hero. He was given his surname in honor of his having taken the city of Corioli of the Volsci. Later, having been banished from Rome because he had tried to prevent the distribution of grain to the plebs, he led the Volsci in an attack on Rome. He was finally persuaded by his mother Veturia and his wife Volumnia to withdraw his army; thereupon the Volsci put him to death. The legend inspired Shakespeare to write his play of the same name, and Beethoven to compose his "Coriolan Overture."

CORNELIUS. Name of a very distinguished patrician Rom. family, of the *Cornelia gens* (see SCIPIO; SULLA; CINNA). Cornelia, the daughter of Scipio Major, and mother of the Gracchi, was also a member of this family.

CORONEA. Town in Boeotia where in 447 B.C. the Boeotians defeated the Athenians and in 387 B.C. Agesilaus defeated the Athenians and their allies. On the latter occasion Xenophon fought against his native city, and as a result was banished.

CORPUS JURIS CIVILIS. The name of the large, summarizing codification of Rom. law, which originated in the 6th cent. A.D. on the orders of the Emperor Justinian, under the supervision of the jurist Tribonianus.

The work consists of four parts: (a) the *Institutiones*, an introduction to jurisprudence; (b) the main section, the *Digesta* or *Pandectae*, embracing more than 20,000 decisions and rulings on concrete legal questions by Rom. lawyers from "classical" times (for Rom. law that is mainly the 2nd cent. A.D.; see below); (c) the *Codex*, a collection of laws made by Justinian himself; (d) the *Novellae*, an "appendix" of laws added later.

The C. J. is the conclusion of a thousand-year development, which started with the notation of the laws of the Twelve Tablets by the *decemviri legibus scribundis* (see also CLAUDIUS, APPIUS) in 451/450 B.C.; actually, it was earlier than that, as this oldest Rom. Code of law was not much more than a codification of the old common law of the as yet small Rom. farming community, which had formerly been in charge of the *pontifices*. The Twelve Tablets were never formally abolished, but they were, of course, greatly developed in the course of time, as the Rom. state expanded and came into contact with foreign states and their juridical systems. One of the important factors in this development was the edicts of the praetors; but eventually the praetors did little more in this field than take over the edicts of their predecessors, possibly incorporating a few minor changes; about A.D. 130 a definitive text of an *edictum perpetuum* was prepared by Salvius Julianus under Hadrian. A second factor in the development of the law was the lawmaking of the *comitia*. A third was the rise of systematic, scientific jurisprudence, particularly after 150 B.C. (see SCAEVOLA); here Rom. ideas of law are distinguishable from those of the other ancient peoples. Jurisprudence was also widely studied during the imperial period, and the 2nd cent. A.D. was, in fact, considered the "classical" period; it was at this time that such men as Gaius, Papinianus, Paulus, and Ulpianus lived and worked. The development of the law was also promoted by imperial legislation, the so-called *Constitutiones;* these laws were eventually collected in codes, of which the Code of Theodosius II is the most important. The entire development is crowned by the C.J.

This Rom. juridical system was adopted, particularly after the 12th cent., by most of the peoples of the western European continent, for whom it superseded native law. Rom. law exerted its greatest influence by means of Napoleon's *Code Civil*. This significant development requires explanation. A European expert on Rom. law writes: "The reason lawyers still looked to Rom. law for solving legal problems in the 17th, 18th, and 19th centuries is the practically ineradicable idea that Rom. law embodies the principles of natural justice." Certainly this legal system embraces an almost ideal union of *ius* (positive law) and *aequitas* (equity). But there is more. To quote the same author: "Rom. law, and its view that the science of law is based principally on the interpretation of written edicts and laws . . . have made such a deep, almost ineradicable impression on our European judicial way of thinking, that we can hardly disengage ourselves from them even when studying ancient and modern Eastern juridical systems or the laws of primitive peoples." This is the heart of the matter. Other juridical systems—even, in principle, the common law found in England and America—work from case to case, and *precedent* rules; Rom. law, on the other hand, distilled a *hard and fast rule* from a number of individual cases, kept applying it, and *did so from the Twelve Tablets on.*

From the viewpoint of originality, the Romans made no great contribution to ancient culture (but see SATIRE, PORTRAITURE); their task was rather to conserve, to adapt, to transmit (see esp. CICERO) and to create the living conditions which would permit civilization to expand (see PAX ROMANA). But particularly in the field of law, they were able to make a significant contribution to Western civilization, as a result of their gift for systematizing and organizing, their craving for order and clarity, and their feeling for strict logic.

CORSICA. Island in the Tyrrhenian Sea, originally inhabited by Ligurians. After the expulsion of the Gr. colonists (see ALALIA) it was Carthaginian from 535 B.C. on. In the period between the First and Second Punic Wars it came under Rom. domination by threatening war with Carthage, which was in the throes of an internal crisis: a hypocritical example of political blackmail; Rome made it part of the province Sardinia. Later the Vandals and the Goths ruled it.

CORTONA. City in Etruria near Lake Trasimenus.

COS. One of the islands off the southwest coast of Asia Minor (Sporades), probably colonized from Epidaurus (with a Thessalian bent); a member of both Attic Leagues; a center for science and art (Theocritus worked there) under the Ptolemies. C. became famous mainly through the temple of Asklepios with which many physicians (the so-called Asclepiads) were connected. In the 5th cent. B.C., Hippocrates laid the foundations for medical science there.

COUNCIL. For the boule in Athens see SOLON; CLISTHENES; PRYTANEUM. For *gerousia* (C. of elders) see SPARTA. For the Rom. C. see SENATE.

CRASSUS, MARCUS LICINIUS (c. 112-53). One of the *triumviri* of 60 B.C.; had a big share in the conquest of Sulla at the Porta Collina (82) and then enriched himself immeasurably during the proscriptions by buying up cheaply the estates offered for sale everywhere by those outlawed. In 72 he defeated Spartacus as praetor; in 70 he was a consul with Pompey (of whom he was suspicious); in that year they abolished most of Sulla's laws. When Pompey then left for the East (see also MITHRIDATES), C. tried to extend his influence in Rome, in order to gain strength against the time of his rival's return. He observed Catilina's plotting with tongue in cheek: he is believed to have intended to use the agitator to further his own ends. In young Caesar he soon saw the man of the future, and he helped him by guaranteeing his debts. When Pompey returned, Caesar managed to reconcile them, and so the first triumvirate was formed. After Caesar's departure for Gaul, C. at first retired from the political scene, although he secretly supported Clodius. After having been a consul with Pompey again in 55, he left for the East in 54, to win some laurels himself as the head of an expedition against the Parthians. This led, however, to the catastrophe of Carrhae where he was slain. C. was a typical example of a climber without ideals; his power and influence were only due to his unequaled wealth.

CRATES OF MALLUS (Cilicia) (2nd cent. B.C.). Gr. philologist, head of the Pergamum library (see Books); in direct opposition to his contemporary Aristarchus, he did not apply purely materialistic criticism to Homer's text, but an allegorical interpretation with Stoic coloring. During a visit to Rome he broke a leg in the Cloaca Maxima and gave lectures during his recovery. As a result of these lectures the Romans became interested in the study of philology and literary criticism.

CRATINUS (c. 520-423). Poet of the Old Comedy. Some of C.'s plays, which have all been lost with the exception of Aristophanes, was a conservative.

CREMONA. See YEAR OF THE THREE EMPERORS.

CRESILAS (2nd half of the 5th cent. B.C.). Athenian sculptor. He is known chiefly for his head of Pericles, of which copies have survived in the Vatican and the British Museum. He also created a statue of a wounded Amazon; according to tradition, this work was said to have been his contribution to a contest with Phidias and Polyclitus. This statue, now in the Capitoline Museum in Rome, is considered the original one of several Rom. copies that have been found.

CRETE. The largest island in the Gr. archipelago; since very ancient times, an important point of contact for trade and cultural influences with Egypt and the rest of the Near East on one hand, and for the Cyclades and continental Greece on the other. A municipal civilization developed at the beginning of the Bronze Age (c. 2700 B.C.), which reached its

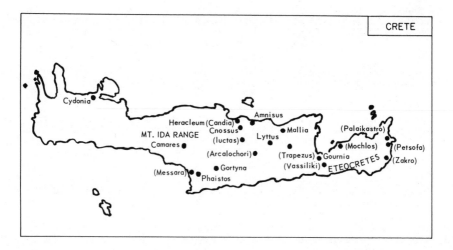

a few fragments, were satires aimed at individuals or the political order; some were mythological parodies. The content of one play, the *Dionysalexandros*, has been found on a papyrus. In this work Dionysus takes over the role of Paris with the golden apple, and causes the Trojan War (this episode alludes to Pericles, who brought Athens into the war): C., like highest peak about 1600-1400 B.C., and was mainly concentrated in the cities of Cnossus and Phaistos (see also HAGIA TRIADA). Invaded by the Achaeans in the 15th cent., C.'s power diminished, although the civilization of Cnossus continued to flourish (see MINOAN CULTURE). About 1100 B.C. the Dorians, who introduced the polis form of government to C., settled there; Homer mentions "one hundred cities." Next to Cnossus, Gortyna and Cydonia became important centers. The aristocratic form of government reminds one strongly of that of Sparta; the Spartans themselves believed that their government was adopted from C.'s; several contemporary scholars agree with this theory. In classic times, C. lay outside the main cultural stream, although it remained important for transient trade. It often supplied mercenaries for Gr. armies, particularly archers. In 69 B.C. the Romans conquered C., at which time Cnossus was destroyed.

CRITIAS (c. 460-403). Athenian politician; one of the Thirty Tyrants appointed in 404 by the Spartans. (See OLIGARCHY.) As a rich aristocrat he hated the radical democracy of the last years of the Peloponnesian War violently. He was banished and went to Thessaly, where he incited the slaves to rebellion. After the fall of Athens (404) he became the most important of the Thirty, had the more moderate Theramenes killed, and was killed himself by Thrasybulus. C. had been a follower of Socrates; this contributed not a little to the suspicions the latter held under restored Athenian democracy (see also ALCIBIADES). C. wrote poems and tragedies, and was a Sophist; he is also one of the characters in Plato's dialogues.

CRITO. Faithful friend to Socrates; Plato has him discuss an escape from prison with Socrates in the dialogue named after him. C.'s affection is the more touching, as he really doesn't understand Socrates' ideas at all.

CROESUS. King of Lydia from 561-546; he completed the subjugation of the Ionian cities, but afterward maintained friendly relations with them; his empire was conquered by Cyrus of Persia even before C. was able to call Greece and Egypt to his support (see HALYS). Of the many legends about him, the most famous is his talk with Solon, however, it is definitely not a historic fact due to a forty-year discrepancy in date. His proverbial wealth (Lydia had tremendous natural resources, see also ASIA) and his good relationship with Greece, particularly with the Delphic Oracle, to whom

he sent gifts, were facts, however.

CRONUS [Gr. Kronos]. In mythology, the most important of the Titans, father of Zeus. The legends about him are often contradictory: he is pictured as a cruel man, who swallowed his own children (Zeus was saved through a ruse by his mother, after which C. was forced to disgorge the other children; there is a curious parallel between this story and a Hittite epic); he is the ruler of the Golden Age (the mythical, paradisiacal prehistoric age), when everyone was happy. Most probably C. was a god of agriculture for the ancient Greeks. This is reflected in his festival, the Kronia, celebrated at harvest time, when slaves and masters fraternized (see also SATURN; SATURNALIA).

CROTON. Colony of Achaea in southern Italy, founded in 739 or 710 B.C., soon prospered greatly, was famous for its doctors, athletes, and the school of Pythagoras. In 510 it destroyed Sybaris. Later it weakened as the result of wars with the neighboring Lucanians and Bruttii and became a Rom. colony (194 B.C.). The famous temple of Hera (Juno) Lacinia stood near C.

CTESIAS (c. 400 B.C.). Gr. physician from Cnidus; private physician to Artaxerxes II, whom he accompanied during the battle of Cunaxa. He wrote a history of Persia and a work on India; Photius made excerpts of them in his works.

CUI BONO. "For whose advantage?"; to what end? of what use? (Cic. Pro Sex. Rosc. Amer. 30.84).

CUMAE. The oldest Gr. colony in Italy, founded before 721 B.C. by Chalcis on the coast, near Naples (the ancient Neapolis was founded by C.). Gr. culture in Italy expanded from there to Etruria and later to Rome. The Etruscans were driven out by the inhabitants in 505, under the tyrant Aristodemos. In about 400 B.C. it was dominated by the Osci, in about 340, by Rome. It remained loyal to Rome against Hannibal and during the Social War. The cave of the Sybil that Aeneas visited (compare Virg. Aen. VI) is still there. Eventually C. was overshadowed by Puteoli. The opinion—often heard—that the Romans got their alphabet (see SCRIPT) from C. is probably incorrect; it came to them by way of Etruria, which, in all probability, did not receive it directly from C. either.

CUM GRANO SALIS. "With a grain of salt"; with some allowance (Plin. Maj. *Nat. Hist.* XXIII, 149).

CUM LAUDE. "With honors"; honors given for excellence in examinations and upon graduation from a University.

CUNAXA. Town in ancient Babylonia, where Cyrus (2) fought his brother Artaxerxes II in 401 B.C. The Ten Thousand (see XENOPHON) vanquished the Persians' right flank; the center and left flanks of Cyrus' army were completely defeated by Tissaphernes and Cyrus himself fell. The Gr. commander Clearchus made the fatal mistake of giving chase, and leaving the rest of Artaxerxes' army unmolested (Xen. *An.* I, 8; 10).

CUPID. See EROS.

CURIA.

—(1) The first political division of the Rom. people, thirty in number (ten per *tribus*); they met first during the regal period, in the *comitia curiata*.

—(2) The Rom. senate building near the Forum, built, according to tradition, by Tullus Hostilius (C. Hostilia); burned down in 52 B.C. during the riots after Clodius' murder; in its place Faustus Sulla erected the C. Cornelia. Caesar interrupted this work and ordered the C. Julia to be built in its place.

CURSUS HONORUM. The predetermined order in which a notable Roman could succeed to the degrees of office (see MAGISTRATUS); regulated by law in 180 B.C. in the *Lex Villia Annalis*. A minimum age was determined for each office: quaestor twenty-eight (later thirty), praetor forty, and consul forty-three. The age limit for the office of aedile was not legally set, but usually fell between those of quaestor and praetor. Cicero prided himself on having held all the offices at the minimum age, even though he was a *homo novus*.

CURTIUS RUFUS, QUINTUS (1st cent. A.D.). Rom. historian. He wrote a history of Alexander the Great in ten books (the first two are lost); the remaining eight have little historical value because there are chronological and geographical inaccuracies. However, the work is written in a rhetorical style that may well be considered the precursor of numerous novels on the subject of Alexander.

CURULE MAGISTRATES. See MAGISTRATUS.

CYAXARES. King of Media, reigned c. 624-584, who brought an end to the Assyrian empire by destroying Nineveh, with the aid of Nabopolassar, the founder of the New Babylonian empire (see BABYLONIA). He waged war against Lydia in 585, during which the famous battle of the Halys River took place (see THALES).

CYBELE. Mother goddess of Phrygia; the Romans called her the "Great Mother" (*Magna Mater*) of all natural life, of mountains; C. was sometimes also called "Mother of the Gods." The C. cult goes back to a Minoan *Potnia* figure (see MYCENAE); she was worshiped with ecstatic dances, and believed to grant immortality. In Greece she was identified with Rhea, the wife of Cronus. Her cult was brought to Rome during a crisis in the second Punic War (205 B.C.). There she found many worshipers, particularly during the Rom. imperial period when Eastern rites in general were very popular (see MITHRAS); the sacramental sacrifice of a bull made in her service (*taurobolium*) can be found very often, portrayed in Gallo-Rom. art. (see GAUL). C. was usually depicted riding on a cart drawn by lions, and wearing a mural crown.

CYCLADES [from Lat. *cyclus;* Gr. *kyklos* circle]. Group of islands in the Aegean Sea, which formed a circle around Delos. Originally inhabited by Carians (see CARIA) who, according to tradition, were driven out by the king of Crete, Minos. In the 2nd millennium B.C. the C. were an important Aegean cultural center connecting Crete with Mycenae. The culture of the C. was under the strong influence of Crete, as appears from articles found in Phylakopi on Melos. In about 1000 B.C. Ionians settled there. In 490 B.C. they were forced to capitulate to the fleet of Datis; after the Persian Wars the C. were members of the Delian League, and later of the second Attic League (see ATHENS). During the Hellenistic period they were tossed back and forth between the Diadochi empires. Augustus restored peace

CYCLE, EPIC. A series of epic poems which were written about the Trojan, Theban, and other groups of sagas, after Homer had written his epos; the C. only appeared as a complete series in the first few centuries A.D. The *Cypria,* poems in which Aphrodite (worshiped mainly on Cyprus) plays a large role (introduction to the Trojan War), were an important part of the C. as were the *Small Iliad* (sequel to the *Iliad*) and *Iliu Persis* (the destruction of Troy). The oldest of these poems was written shortly after Homer, 8th-7th centuries B.C.; we know the contents from Proclus' anthology, included in the works of Photius.

CYLLENE.
—(1) Mountain in Arcadia, where Hermes was born, according to myth.
—(2) Port in Elis, with an important Asklepios cult.

CYLON. Athenian nobleman who conspired to become tyrant in about 630 B.C. His efforts failed and he fled; his friends took refuge at the altar of Athene. They were forced to surrender and were killed on the orders of the archon Megacles, one of the Alcmaeonidae. As a result, the latter was exiled. Since then, there was a curse on the house of the Alcmaeonidae, which was exploited in the Spartan propaganda against Pericles when the Peloponnesian War broke out.

CYNICS [Gr. from *kynikos,* doglike]. The followers of Diogenes (who, in turn, was influenced by Antisthenes). The C. were not a school of philosophers in the actual sense of the word, but they maintained the life of a "dog," which was expressed in their asceticism, indifference to social morality and conventions, also often in uncivilized crudeness (in antiquity the dog was not the symbol of loyalty, but that of shamelessness). The C. stated that they only strove after virtue (as Antisthenes had preached) and believed that one had to give up all worldly comfort in order to do so. The wandering mendicant philosophers of Rom. imperial times, who often irritated the emperors with their bold criticism, were also C.

CYNOSCEPHALAE. Two hills in a low range in Thessaly where Philip V was defeated by Flamininus in 197 B.C. This defeat limited his empire to Macedonia proper and ended Macedonian imperialism.

CYPRIANUS, THASCIUS CAECILIUS (c. 200-258). Christian writer and martyr; originally a teacher of pagan rhetoric, he was converted and became bishop of Carthage in A.D. 248. His schooling ininvolved extensive reading of the classical authors, to which he owed his clarity of style.

CYPRUS. Island of the eastern Mediterranean Sea, to the south of Cilicia. It had extensive contacts with Greece from the Mycenaean period on. At Salamis, the capital during this epoch, Mycenaean remains were found. Achaeans were already settling there at that time, and brought with them a form of Mycenaean script. This Cyprian syllabic writing remained in use in a modified form until classical times, and was used to express Greek. C. was part of various Near Eastern empires between the 15-16th centuries (Hittite, Egyptian, Assyrian, Persian); the Phoenicians established trading centers there. During all those centuries the rich copper mines on C. were exploited (our word copper is derived from C., the Gr. *kupros*). Cimon liberated C. from Persian domination; in 411 Evagoras, the national hero, was able to set himself up as king, with the support of Athens. As a result of the "King's Peace" (see ANTALCIDAS) of 387, the Persians returned, but Alexander the Great definitely ended their domination in 333. After that, C. was Ptolemaic, and then Roman. The main cult was of an Astarte figure, identified by the Greeks with Aphrodite (see PAPHOS).

CYPSELUS. Tyrant of Corinth from c. 655-625 (according to some sources, somewhat later). He overthrew the rule of the Bacchiadae. The kind of government he conducted was a matter of controversy, even in ancient times; it is certain that Corinth underwent a period of economic prosperity; colonies were founded on the west coast of Greece as way stations for trading with the West. (Leucas, Ambracia). The transition from proto-Corinthian to Corinthian pottery was made during his reign. Herodotus

(V, 92) tells a romantic tale about C.: after his birth, he escaped death at the hands of the Bacchiadae who had been warned by an oracle that he would prove their ruin; his mother was said to have hidden him in a chest (Gr. *kypsele*), hence his name. When he came to power, he dedicated the chest and a statue of Zeus at Olympia as a thanks offering.

CYRENAIC SCHOOL. School of philosophers founded by Aristippus, who taught that "enjoyment" (Gr. *hèdonè* thus, hedonists) should come before all else. The school did not exist for long, but it is, nevertheless, interesting for its connection with Epicurean philosophy.

CYRENE. The most important Gr. colony in Lybia, founded in 630 B.C. by colonists from Crete and Thera, later reinforced by a second group of colonists. C. expanded greatly, established subsidiary towns and flourished greatly in this fertile area. The kings, Battus and Arcesilas, maintained friendly relations with the Egyptian Saitic empire (see AMASIS); corn, wool, and particularly a native product, silphium (a kind of vegetable) were exported. Pindar sang of the victories of Arcesilas IV in the *Pythian Games*. C. was a republic since the 4th cent., a center of cultural life (see ERATOSTHENES; CALLIMACHUS; CARNEADES). Later it was dominated by the Ptolemies and Rome. Under Trajan's reign serious revolts took place among the many Jews who lived there. Significant remains of Gr. and Rom. buildings have been found there.

CYRUS. Name of:
—(1) C. the Great or the Elder (d. 529 B.C.). Founder of the Persian empire of the Achaemenidae. In 550 he banished Astyages from the throne of the Medes in Ecbatana, defeated Croesus and annexed Lydia (546), and later Mesopotamia, Syria, and Palestine (539); fell during an expedition to the northeastern section of his empire. He pursued a wise policy of tolerance regarding the customs and manners of subjected peoples, which was later adopted by Darius I. Thus, when in Babylon, he sacrificed to Marduk, the god of the city, and he allowed the Jews to return to Palestine from their banishment in Babylon.

The Greeks were always fascinated by C.'s character. Herodotus relates his background, birth, and youth in a romantic story (I, 107-122); Xenophon saw him as the ideal ruler (described in his *Cyropedia*).
—(2) C. the Younger (d. 401 B.C.). Youngest son of Darius II and brother to Artaxerxes II. As satrap in western Asia Minor, he supported Sparta in the Peloponnesian War (407-405), by giving Sparta money for a fleet (see LYSANDER), which was one of the main causes of Athens' defeat. When his brother became king, he revolted against him with the support of the "Ten Thousand" (see XENOPHON; CLEARCHUS); this led to his defeat and death at Cunaxa. His great opponent was Tissaphernes (Xen. *An.* I).

CYTHERA. Island to the south of the Peloponnesus, known in ancient times for its purple dye. Aphrodite was worshiped there; it is said that she rose out of the foam of the ocean there (see LUDOVISI THRONE).

CYZICUS. Gr. city on the Propontis, founded by Miletus in about 675 B.C., renowned for its coins made of an alloy of gold and silver (see ELECTRON).

D

DACIA. Ancient country situated in the loop of the lower Danube, about where Rumania is now. A Thracian people lived there, who threatened the Rom. Empire under Decebalus, in the 1st cent. A.D. He was defeated by Trajan in two campaigns (101/2 and 105/6), after which it became a Rom. province, adapting many Rom. customs. Rumanian is the only Romance language in the entire, large area. Trajan's campaigns were immortalized in reliefs on his column in Rome. Aurelianus gave the province up as the result of invasions by the Goths (see MILITARY EMPERORS).

DACTYL. See METER.

DALMATIA. Region on the Adriatic Sea, seceded from Illyria, of which it was originally a part, and was separately subjugated by Octavian (35-33 B.C.). The main town of the Rom. province was Salona, the native town of Diocletian, who had a huge palace built there.

DAMOCLES. Courtier of Dionysius the Elder, who was jealous of the ruler; Dionysius allowed him to sit on his throne; luxuries within reach. When D. looked upward he found a naked sword suspended above his head by a single horsehair. The expression "the Sword of Damocles" has become proverbial with danger. (Cic. *Tusc.* V, 61.)

DAMON AND PHINTIAS (not Pythias). Pythagoreans from Syracuse, devoted friends. Condemned to death by the tyrant Dionysius for assault, Phintias was granted a short respite in order to arrange his affairs. Damon pledged his life for the return of his friend. When Phintias returned in time, the tyrant gave them both their freedom. They were the symbol of firm friendship in ancient times (Diod. Sic. X, 4; Cic. *De Off.* III, 45).

DANAOI. The name Homer uses for the Greeks in general. Correctly the name for the inhabitants of Argos, the descendants of Danaos, their king.

DANUVIUS. The Rom. name for the upper course of the Danube. The lower course was called Ister. The fact that it was the same river was unknown until the 1st cent. A.D. Strabo was the first to describe its course more or less accurately.

DAREIKOS. Persian gold coin with the head of Darius I on it; it was *the* gold coin until the 4th cent. B.C.

DARIUS. Name of several Persian kings:
—(1) D.I (c. 550-485); reigned for thirty-six years. He is regarded as one of the greatest Eastern rulers. He ascended the throne after quelling the revolt of the pseudo-Smerdis (see CAMBYSES). D. divided the empire into twenty satrapies, had a beautiful network of roads constructed, improved communications, and had a canal dug from the Nile to the Red Sea. He continued Cyrus the Great's policy of tolerance toward subjugated peoples. In 512 he led a punitive expedition against the Scythians (See HISTIAEUS); in about 500 he had the Ionian revolt quelled and then organized campaigns to Greece. The first (492), under Mardonius, gave the Persians a good base in Thrace and Macedonia, but to no avail, as their fleet was shipwrecked near Athos. The second campaign by way of the Aegean Sea (see DATIS) ended in the battle of Marathon (490); D. died before a third expedition could be undertaken.

In Aeschylus' *The Persians,* D. appears as the wise and good king who rises from his tomb to lecture his degenerate son Xerxes on his presumptuousness. Naturally, in 472 the Athenians knew very well that D. had threatened them, as well as his son. But Aeschylus needed a dramatic contrast, moreover, D.'s excellent rule had been recognized in Greece too.
—(2) D.II Nothos or Ochos; king from 425-404; under his rule Cyrus (2) and Tissaphermes intervened successfully in the Peloponnesian War.
—(3) D.III Codomannus; king from 336-330; was defeated by Alexander the Great, fled to the eastern part of his empire and was murdered there by the satrap Bessus.

DATIS. Commander along with Artaphernes, of the expedition Darius I sent out in 490 B.C. to punish Athens and Eretria for supporting the Ionian revolt; their real aim was doubtless to subjugate the Greeks; they succeeded in taking the Cyclades and destroying Eretria, but the Athenians defeated the Persian army at Marathon.

DEATH CULT. See HEROES.

DECELEA. Small city in Attica which ruled the plains up to Athens. In the second part of the Peloponnesian War the Spartans occupied D. from 413-404, on the advice of Alcibiades, they did so permanently as a "pistol to the head" of Athens.

DECEMVIRI. A Rom. college of ten persons, with various functions, legal and religious. The following are well known: (a) the D. *sacris faciundis* that consulted the Sibylline Books (see SIBYL) when inauspicious omens were reported (*prodigia*); (b) the D. *legibus scribundis* that (according to tradition, in 451/50 B.C.) composed the laws of the Twelve Tablets. The D. had unlimited power. The first college, in 450 embraced patricians only; the next year a second college was formed, which also contained plebeians. The tyranny of the D. caused a riot, which led to its dismissal. (For legislation see CLAUDIUS, APPIUS and CORPUS JURIS.)

DECIUS. See MILITARY EMPERORS.

DECIUS MUS, PUBLIUS. Name of three Romans, father, son, and grandson, who sacrificed their lives (*devotio*), according to tradition, and threw themselves among the enemy, winning the battle for Rome. Only the death of the second D. can be considered a historical fact. He performed this act of heroism during the battle of Sentinum (295 B.C.).

DECURIO. Member of the city council in a Rom. *colonia* or *municipium*. In the later imperial period, the office of a D. became compulsory and hereditary. It included collecting taxes from the municipalities and was therefore not coveted.

DE FACTO. "In fact"; actually; in reality (as distinguished from *de jure*), and often used attributively.

DEINOS. See VASE FORMS.

DE JURE. "By right"; by a lawful title (as distinguished from *de facto*).

DELIAN LEAGUE. League of Gr. cities on the islands in the Aegean Sea and on its coasts, formed in 478/77 B.C. under the hegemony of Athens, to continue the

naval war against Persia. The league was organized by Aristides, who determined the contribution for each member in ships or, if desired, in money. There was a general assembly (in which each member, including Athens, had one vote) on Delos; the exchequer was also established there. From the beginning, many members preferred to contribute cash, probably for economic reasons or because of inertia—this made them more or less tributary, a situation that became more affirmed when the exchequer was moved to Athens in 454, supposedly because the Aegean Sea lay open to the Persian fleet after a serious defeat of the Athenian fleet in the delta of the Nile (see EGYPT); but after the danger had passed, the money stayed in Athens, which was slowly becoming a domineering, instead of a leading force. Deserting allies were punished more and more severely. They were given a *cleruchia* to keep them under her thumb. The league, therefore, started falling apart during the Peloponnesian War, and was officially disbanded when peace was made (404). Sparta—with its slogan "Liberty for the Greeks"—was successful in subjugating many allies (see LYSANDER).

DELOS. Small island in the Cylades where, according to the myth, Artemis and Apollo were born. Since the 8th cent. B.C. it was a place of pilgrimage to the temple of Apollo for whom festivals were given. The island was respected as neutral territory by Datis; as a sacred island it was "cleansed" twice by the Athenians, that is, all graves were removed. In the Hellenistic period it flourished greatly through trade, particularly after Rome had declared it a free port, under control of Athens, which drove off the populace and founded a *cleruchia* there. D. was known mainly as a slave market. After it had been destroyed by the general Archelaus in 88 it declined.

Excavations by the French brought to light impressive remains, among which the temple of Apollo with its outbuildings is particularly noteworthy. D. also yielded many inscriptions.

DELPHI. The main sanctuary of Apollo on the Gr. mainland, in Phocis, on the southern slope of Mount Parnassus. It was already a sanctuary of an earth goddess in the Mycenaean period; the Greeks themselves preserved the recollection of the fact that Apollo had "conquered" D. by killing the Python, an earth demon in the shape of a snake. Since 650 the sanctuary was administered by the Amphictyons. Philip II of Macedonia was able to penetrate to this college by participating in the so-called Holy War against Phocis; this gave him a foothold in central Greece. D. was plundered by the Gauls in 279 B.C., and later, by Sulla; in general, the Rom. emperors had great respect for the sanctuary. In A.D. 390 it was closed by Theodosius (see also ORACLE).

Like Delos, the other large sanctuary of Apollo, D. was excavated by the French. The third temple of Apollo stands in the center (the other two were destroyed in 548 and 373 B.C.); the "Sacred Way" with twenty so-called treasure houses leads to it: the Gr. states each having had storeroom for the gifts brought by their citizens (see THESAURUS). The stadium and the theater have also been well-preserved. The museum contains, among other things, the famous "Charioteer." D., as well as Delos, is rich in interesting inscriptions, which give insight into Gr. administration, among other things.

DEMARATUS. King of Sparta c. 510-491, opponent of Cleomenes I, who succeeded in deposing him by disputing his legitimacy. D. fled to Persia and accompanied Xerxes as an adviser in 480. The latter awarded him the governorship of Pergamum.

DEME. A term used to designate a township in Attica (see CLISTHENES); the *demes* kept a register of members; a certain number of members from each D. were chosen for the Council of Five Hundred. The purely territorial classification disappeared eventually, as one kept one's father's D. when one moved.

DEMETER. Gr. goddess of agriculture, particularly of grain (Rom. Ceres). Her name appears in the recently deciphered Mycenaean documents (see MYCENAE; CNOSSUS; PYLOS). As the goddess of fertility and agriculture she does not play a role in Homer's epic poetry, however, one of the oldest and most important "Homeric" hymns is devoted to her. It tells the story of the abduction of her daughter Kore (Persephone), the central myth of the Eleusinian mysteries. She was worshiped—sometimes as the earth-goddess in general—in many places, particularly in the country, in the isolated regions of the Peloponnesus. One of the most famous statues of her is the "D. of Cnidus," an original Gr. statue of the 4th cent. B.C. (see also THESMOPHORIA).

DEMETRIUS. Name of:

—(1) D. of Phaleron (c. 350-c. 283). Athenian scholar and statesman, pupil of Theophrastus; he was made tyrant of Athens by Cassander, and tried to carry through Aristotle's political ideas. When Demetrius Poliorcetes took Athens in 307, D. fled to Alexandria, where he advised Ptolemy II (foundation of the Museum); later he fell into disgrace. In addition to philosophical and philological works, he wrote a collection of proverbs and fables.

—(2) D. Poliorcetes [besieger] (336-283). One of the Diadoch, son of Antigonus I; supported his father in wars until the latter's death at Ipsus, after which D. became king of Macedonia and retained the mastery over Greece. However, when Lysimachus and Pyrrhus marched into Macedonia, his subjects deserted him. D. went to Asia Minor, where he died as a prisoner of Seleucus I.

He owes his surname Poliorcetes to the gigantic machines he devised to assail the walls of the city during his assault against Rhodes (305)—without, incidentally, being able to take the city. We can say, without much exaggeration, that the "scientific" method of besieging started with D.; almost all earlier conquests of fortified cities were brought about by treachery, strategy, or famine.

DEMOCRITUS of Abdera (c. 460-370). Gr. philosopher; only more or less legendary stories about his life are known. He remained in his native city to work; in his youth he is said to have made long journeys to the East, but his works were produced in his native city. In later antiquity he was known as "the laughing philosopher." For his doctrine (see ATOMISM, also LEUCIPPUS).

DE MORTUIS NIL NISI BONUM. "Of the dead [say] nothing but good." Origin of the proverb unknown.

DEMOSTHENES. Name of:

—(1) Attic orator and statesman (384-322); considered the greatest of the ten Attic orators. He was seven years old when his father died, leaving D.'s inheritance in trust of guardians who abused this trust. Inspired by the orator Callistratus, and eager to bring his dishonest guardians to justice, the young D. studied rhetoric with Isaeus. In 364 he delivered a speech against Aphobus, one of the guardians, and won his case. However, D. received only a small part of the money due him, and to support himself he wrote speeches for others. He also appeared in person as a lawyer in the courts. His first two speeches were complete failures; partly due to his weak voice, a speech defect, and lack of confidence. It is said that to overcome these handicaps and improve his delivery, D. spoke with pebbles in his mouth, declaimed poetry while running uphill, and spoke on the seashore during storms. About 355, D. gained renown as an orator with his celebrated speech against the Law of Leptines; two years later he began his political career, giving up his law practice. His most famous speeches, the *Philippics* and *Olynthiacs* (see OLYNTHUS) were directed against Philip II of Macedonia. (Philip is reported to have said that he was fighting D.—not the Athenians.) When the city of Ctesiphon (see AESCHINES) wanted to honor D. for his services to Athens during the times of conflict (before and after the battle of Chaeronea in 338, in which D. fought personally), his most violent adversary, Aeschines, opposed this gesture. In his oration *On the Crown,* D. defended Ctesiphon. This speech is a review of his entire political career—a masterpiece of oratory. In 324 D.'s enemies brought a charge of bribery by Alexander's receiver-general (see HARPALUS) against him; D. was unable to pay the fine and was incarcerated but managed to escape. On the death of Alexander, the Gr. states rose against Macedonia and D. returned to Athens. However, in the following year the Greeks were defeated, and—being in power once more—Macedonia demanded D.'s surrender. Pursued by the emissaries of Antipater, vice-regent of Alexander, D. sought asylum in the temple of Poseidon on the island of Calauria. It is said that he took poison before his enemies could capture him.

—(2) Athenian general in the Peloponnesian War, who made prisoners of the Spartans on Sphacteria (425 B.C.). In 414 he was sent to reinforce the Athenian forces at Syracuse with a fleet and an army; when his immediate night attack failed, he advised a retreat, but was overruled by Nicias. When the retreat finally was begun, the division under D. fell behind, was cornered and surrendered. D. was imprisoned and put to death by the Syracusans (see NICIAS).

DENARIUS. See COINAGE.

DENTATUS, MANIUS CURIUS d. e. 270 B.C. Hero of the Rom. plebs, consul four times; defeated the Samnites, Sabines, and Pyrrhus (Beneventum 275). He started the construction of the second Rom. aqueduct. Many legends were spread about him, by Cato Major.

DEUS EX MACHINA. [Lat.] "The god from the machine." This expression alludes to the ancient Gr. theater where a separate stage (*theologeion*) was used on which a god could appear who, by his intervention, gave a decisive turn to the plot. This procedure was employed by Sophocles (*Philoctetes*) and, on a larger scale, by Euripides (for example, *Iphigenia in Tauris*). Another stage was the *ekkuklèma,* a platform on rollers, on which things that happened indoors were shown. The expression is applied now to mean the introduction of a mechanical device into an author's plot.

DIADOCHI [Gr. successors]. Name given to the generals of Alexander the Great, who divided his empire after his death in 323 B.C. and laid the foundations for the Hellenistic empires. (For the fates of the various D. see ANTIGONUS I; ANTIPATER; CASSANDER; LYSIMACHUS; PTOLEMY I; SELEUCUS I; DEMETRIUS POLIORCETES.) An important turning point in the conflict over the boundaries between the D. was the battle of Ipsus (301); the boundaries were not definitely fixed until the battle of Corupedion (286).

DIANA. See ARTEMIS.

DICTATOR. Rom. special magistrate, appointed by the consuls in times of emergencies. He was always appointed for a specified purpose; and held office (with absolute *imperium*) for six months at the most. As a rule, the D. resigned as soon as his particular task was accomplished. The other magistrates served concurrently, but were forced to honor the higher *imperium* of the D. The D. (also called *magister populi*) had an assistant, a *magister equitum*. A D. could be appointed for various tasks; the most important was the D. *rei gerundae causa,* who had military power in times of war. A D. was also appointed for purposes other than dealing with external or internal crises, or judicial problems. For example, a D. was appointed to hold elections in the *comitia centuriata* when both consuls were absent, or to take charge of games and religious festivals. This class of D. was usually only in office for a few days. In the 3rd cent. B.C. the office declined; it was revived when Quintus Fabius Maximus became D. (unconstitutionally, as he was elected, not appointed). After that, it was replaced by the practice of *senatus consultum ultimum* (see CAVEANT CONSULES). The dictatorships of Sulla and Caesar, who was named perpetual D. before his death, were unconstitutional. Sulla resigned of his own free will. After Caesar's death the office of D. was completely abolished by Marcus Aurelius.

DICTYS of Crete. One of the heroes of the Trojan War. In the 4th cent. A.D. a certain Lucius Septimius claimed to have translated a so-called eye witness report by D. of this war, using a Gr. version. This story influenced the tales of Troy in the Middle Ages.

DIDIUS JULIANUS. See MILITARY EMPERORS.

DIDO. See VIRGIL.

DIES ATER [Lat. black day]. A day of catastrophe, officially marked down on the Rom. calendar—for example, the days of the battles of the Allia and Cannae. Such days were *dies nefasti,* on which no popular assemblies or administration of justice might take place, as opposed to the *dies fasti* (see FASTI).

DIGESTA. See CORPUS JURIS.

DIMINI. Small town in Thessaly, where very important prehistoric remains have been found, dating from the 2nd half of the third millenium B.C. (see also SESCLO).

DINARCHUS (c. 360–after 290). One of the ten Attic orators. He was born in Corinth and went to Athens in 342; was an opponent of Demosthenes. Three of his speeches have been preserved, the last specimens of Attic oratory.

DINOS. See VASE FORMS.

DIO CASSIUS COCCEIANUS (more correctly Cassius Dio) (c. 150-235). Gr. historian from Nicaea (Bithynia). He held office under Commodus and wrote a history of Rome from its beginnings to 229 B.C. in eighty books, of which books 36-60 (covering the period from 68 B.C.-A.D. 47) and books 79-80 (in part) have survived; fragments of other books have also been preserved. For his history of the Republic he used the tradition of the annalists Polybius and Livy. His history of the Empire is of great value; in its preparation he used not only Tacitus (or his sources) but also memoirs, and his own experiences as a government official were extremely useful. He wrote his works in twelve years, after ten years of study—a measure of the seriousness and sense of responsibility with which he performed his task.

DIOCLES. See MILITARY EMPERORS.

DIOCLETIANUS, GAIUS AURELIUS VALERIUS (c. 243-316). Commonly called Diocletian. Rom. emperor, founder of the dominate. He was the commander of the life guards at the time of Numerianus' (see MILITARY EMPERORS) death (284), and the soldiers hailed him as emperor. He appointed Maximian first as "Caesar" (vice-emperor) and later (286) as "Augustus" (coemperor) to rule the West; he had Constantius Chlorus for his "Caesar" in Gaul and Britain, while D. himself appointed Galerius as "Caesar" to govern Illyria. The Caesars were to succeed the Augusti, and then choose other Caesars themselves, so that the continuity of the government would be assured for the future. During their reign the four rulers had to suppress constant riots and wage border wars. In internal government, bureaucracy was carried to extremes, and military and civil government were separated. The city of Rome lost its privileged position, and Italy its freedom from taxes. The administration was so expensive, as was the augmented army, that taxes began to weigh very heavily indeed. An ambitious financial reform only led to catastrophic inflation. The municipal governments were made responsible for paying a previously determined amount in taxes; it was no longer an honor to be invested with local office, but a heavy obligation, passing from father to son. Farmers were no longer allowed to change their calling; this measure was taken in order to check the flight from the agricultural sector, in which the tax pressure was the heaviest. This whole system was later ameliorated by Constantine the Great; it is impossible to tell, with precision, what improvements can be attributed to Constantine or to D. The old Rom. religion was greatly stimulated by D.; the Christians were heavily persecuted after 303. In 305 D. abdicated and forced Maximian to do the same, so that the Caesars could take over the government. D. retired to Salona.

D.'s importance was based on two main points: (a) He carried through the complete deification of the emperorship; (b) By his classification of the Empire into two executive areas, each divided again into two zones, he created the fundamental separation into an East Rom. and a West Rom. Empire, although in name the Empire was still one political unity. Culturally, the division had existed for centuries (see ANTONIUS, MARCUS), and the formal political separation was not to be long in coming.

Of the enormous buildings that D. erected, his palace in Salona and the thermae in Rome are particularly noteworthy.

DIODORUS SICULUS (1st cent. B.C.). Gr. historian. He wrote a history of the world from mythical times to 60 B.C. in forty books, of which books 1-5 and 11-20, and some fragments have survived. His idea, not to write from the point of view of one particular people or state, but to give a real history of the world, is very interesting, but the results leave much to be desired. The work is chaotic; sometimes it is possible to discover what source he has used; then we often have a valuable excerpt from one of the lost authors (for example, Timaeus or Philinus, one of the few ancient authors who was pro-Carthaginian—see CARTHAGE). But this cannot be credited to D. He follows the method of the annalists, and uses the chronology of the Olympiads.

DIOGENES:

—(1) Gr. philosopher, surnamed "the Cynic" (400-c. 325); founder of the philosophical school of Cynics. He was born in Sinope and came to Athens, included in the exile of his father, the mintmaster of Sinope, who had been accused of counterfeiting. D. then began to teach unconventional concepts in the field of ethics. He adopted many of Antisthenes' ascetic ideas, particularly that of autarchy," or self-sufficiency; he applied that principle to his entire way of life, which explains the many anecdotes about him—his life in a barrel and his reply to Alexander, when the latter offered to grant him a wish, "Do not stand between me and the sun." The story of his searching for an "honest man" in the marketplace with a lantern in the full light of day is also well known. It is difficult to discover his real doctrine, as the Stoics liked to attribute their theories to him, in order to strengthen their claim to a spiritual descent from Socrates.

—(2) D. Laertius (3rd cent. A.D.). Gr. author of a book on the lives and doctrines of Gr. philosophers. His work is uncritical, yet it is valuable as a source of information about the lives of many Gr. philosophers.

DION. Name of:

—(1) D. of Syracuse (c. 408-354). Brother-in-law and minister to Dionysius the Elder. He tried, aided by Plato, to put the latter's political ideas into practice in Syracuse; under the reign of Dionysius the Younger, his endeavors to this end were unsuccessful, and he was banished in 366. He returned in 317 with an army, drove Dionysius off, and became a tyrant in spite of himself, after having vainly tried once more to institute the Platonic ideal state. Finally he was murdered by dissatisfied leaders of the people.

—(2) D. of Prusa in Bithynia (c. 40-c. 120). Surnamed Chrysostomus (golden mouth). Gr. orator and philosopher. He went to Rome and, after being banished by Domitian in 82, made long journeys and delivered public lectures on ethical and literary subjects in many places. Before his banishment he had been almost exclusively a rhetorician; now he became primarily a philosopher, a follower of the Stoa and the Cynics. He was recalled under Nerva and achieved a position of honor under Trajan. As a propagandist for Gr. ideas, during the Rom. Empire, he can be compared to Plutarch. Eighty of his orations are extant; essays on political and philosophical subjects.

DIONYSIUS. Name of:

—(1) D. the Elder (c. 430-367). Tyrant of Syracuse. He distinguished himself in a period when Carthage was again obtruding upon the Gr. cities of Sicily, was legally invested with power and soon proved to be a born monarch, a precursor of the Hellenistic type of king. His court was one of opulence and flattering courtiers (see DAMOCLES), men of letters and philosophers were entertained by him (Plato among others). D. himself wrote tragedies, which the poets of the Middle Comedy ridiculed. He fought against the Carthaginians with varying success; after a defeat, the aristocracy attempted a revolt, but he was able to suppress it and ruled with the help of an army of mercenaries. He recommended the practices of the old Syracusan tyrants (see HIERO I; GELO) by depopulating entire cities, and settling his hirelings there. He also expanded in southern Italy, where he destroyed Rhegium and combated Etruscan piracy. But eventually his extravagance and his expensive army of mercenaries inspired great dissatisfaction as the citizens were increasingly burdened with taxes. He died during the course of a new war with Carthage.

—(2) D. the Younger (c. 397–after 344). Eldest son of Dionysius the Elder. He succeeded his father as tyrant in 367, but was inexperienced, irresolute, and weak, although quite intelligent. He relied completely on his mercenaries and his advisers (among others, Dion, who brought Plato to Sicily). Dion drove him out in 356; he came back in 346, but had to surrender to Timoleon, who sent him to Corinth, where he lived for many years.

—(3) D. of Halicarnassus. Gr. orator and historian (1st cent. B.C.). He taught in Rome from 30-8; and wrote a history of Rome from the most ancient times to 266 B.C. (the point at which Polybius' work begins). Far more important than this are his rhethorical and critical works; in them, he proves himself to be a master of literary criticism.

DIONYSUS. Gr. god of young plants in spring, particularly of the vine, and thus of wine; also the personification of the ecstatic element in religion and culture (compare APOLLO). Under the alternative name Bakchos (Lat. Bacchus), he was identified with the Italian god Liber, god of fertility and vineyards. Until recently D. was assumed to be a late-comer among the gods. Now, however, his name (the proper name Dionysios) has been found in Mycenaean documents (see MYCENAE; CNOSSUS; PYLOS). According to the myth, he was originally a hero (see HEROES), but was soon given the status of a god. The fact that Homer hardly mentions him can be attributed to the sphere of interests of the Ionian nobility (as with Demeter); D. was, first and foremost, a god of the people. His cult probably came from Thrace (partly, perhaps by way of that country from Phrygia); in Greece his most important center was Thebes, which is also the scene of the story of Pentheus, who is punished for refusing to recognize D. (Eur. *Bacchae*). In Athens comedy and tragedy were performed in his service. He also had a place in the Eleusinian mysteries; other mysteries took place entirely in honor of him (see also ANTHESTERIA; LENAEA; BACCHANALIA; SATYRS; DITHYRAMB; ZAGREUS).

DIOSCURI [Gr. *dioskouroi*, sons of Zeus]. The twin brothers, Kastor and Polydeuces (Lat. Castor, Pollux), sons of Zeus and Leda, brothers of Helena; according to tradition, only the first was a son of Zeus and therefore immortal, Castor was mortal; out of brotherly love,

they agreed, when it came time for Castor to die to take turns in Hades. They were worshiped mainly as the protectors of mariners; the so-called St. Elmo's fire was considered a manifestation of the twins. Their cult was native to Sparta. Later they were also identified with the Cabiri. A temple dedicated to them stood in the Rom. Forum.

DIPYLON VASES. See GEOMETRIC ART.

DIS. See HADES.

DIS MANIBUS. See MANES.

DISTICHON. See METER.

DITHYRAMB. Hymn of praise to Dionysus. It originated as a popular song, sung alternately by a leader and a choir, and was thus divided into strophes and antistrophes. The D. was introduced into literature by Arion of Lesbos and later brought to Athens, where it was recited at the Dionysian festivals in the form of a competition (see AGON). Sometimes the D. was addressed to other gods than Dionysus. Pindar and Bacchylides were masters of this form. To reach a true judgment of the D., we would have to be able to reconstruct the music (mainly that of the flute) as well; unfortunately, none of the music has survived.

DIVIDE ET IMPERA. "Divide and govern," a principle often attributed to Rome in her treatment of the Italian cities. The Romans, it was argued, gave the cities various rights (see COLONIA; MUNICIPIUM; SOCII) in order to create mutual jealousy which would keep them disunited. This is probably incorrect; the differences originated in the constantly varying circumstances of subjugation. On the other hand, we can assume that the Romans, when they saw the results of this development, were aware of the advantages of their policy.

DODONA. Town in Epirus, where there was a very ancient oracle of Zeus (mentioned by Homer); the will of the god was revealed through the rustling of an oak.

DOMINATE. The absolute Rom. emperorship, as established by Diocletian. There were prototypes before him; after him it was the rule. The emperor was "lord and god," and ruled, with a bureaucratic machine, over subjects who had no say at all. In contrast to this, the earlier emperorship established by Augustus is called principate (see PRINCEPS).

DOMITIANUS. Full name Titus Flavius Domitianus Augustus, commonly called Domitian (51-96). Rom. emperor (81-96), youngest son of Vespasian. He was in Rome during the Year of the Three Emperors, and narrowly escaped death in the last days of Vitellius; when Vitellius was killed, D. was given a foretaste of power, as he was appointed commander of Rome until the return of his father's army. During the reign of Vespasian (69-79) and of his younger brother Titus (79-81) he was deprived of all power; after Titus' death, D. succeeded him on the throne. The earlier years of his reign were good ones, but as he grew older he ruled with atrocious cruelty—persecutions were the order of the day. Yet even under this hated tyrant, the provinces were governed as efficiently as under most of the other emperors. Wars were waged, mainly on the Danube front and in Britain (see AGRICOLA). D.'s murder by a group of conspirators among his own entourage was instigated by his wife.

DONATUS. Name of:
—(1) Aelius D. (4th cent. A.D.) He wrote a grammar for beginners and one for advanced students, as well as commentaries on Terence and Virgil. Almost all of the last has been lost, but it was later used by Servius.
—(2) Tiberius Claudius D. (c. A.D. 400). Author of a commentary on the *Aeneid*. His work, mostly a prose paraphrase, is not of great value.

DORIANS. The last of the Hellenic tribes to settle in Greece (11th cent. B.C.) Their invasion—called the Dorian migration—is an offshoot of the general migration which took place in the entire eastern Mediterranean Sea basin about 1200, and was evident in Egypt also, where the "seafaring peoples" tried to invade the Nile delta, but were driven back. However, the invasion of the D. should not be visualized as a mass attack, but rather as an infiltration; still, there is a difference from the earlier invasions of the Indo-European tribes (Ionians, Achaeans): the D. were much more warlike, and destroyed Mycenaean culture. They mainly occupied the Peloponnesus, except for Arcadia and Achaea, then the southern islands of the Aegean Sea (Thera and Rhodes in particular), Crete, and the southwest coast of Asia Minor. In most places they were more or less assimilated by the earlier inhabitants; in Crete and Laconia, however, they were subjugated and made Helots (see SPARTA). They were much less sensitive to art and science than the Ionians, although their stalwart character was manifest in architecture. They also achieved considerable skill in choral lyric poetry (see ALCMAN): even in Attic tragedy, the choruses are written in a dialect derived from the Doric. In the field of politics, they took the initiative in the development of the city-state (see POLIS).

DORIC COLUMN. See ARCHITECTURAL ORDERS.

DORIC TEMPLE. See ARCHITECTURAL ORDERS.

DRACHMA. See COINAGE.

DRACO (or DRACON). The first Athenian legislator, who codified the existing laws (621 B.C.)—unwritten and administered arbitrarily. His laws were proverbially severe (for example, the death sentence for the slightest theft); later it was said that they had been written not in ink, but in blood. Because of their harshness, Solon drew up new laws (594), reducing their severity in most instances, but retaining the laws relating to murder. Nevertheless, D.'s work represented a great improvement, because (a) the laws were now objectively determined and not exposed to the arbitrary interpretation of a class judicature, and (b) vendettas were brought to an end, since criminal law was now administered entirely by the state.

DRAMA. D. is the Gr. word for action, and is used particularly for the action of the figures on the stage, the *dramatis personae*. Various aspects of the Greek and Roman stage are discussed in this encyclopedia, under TRAGEDY; COMEDY; THEATER; FABULA; MIME; PANTOMIME; and under the names of the various dramatists. Two aspects will be discussed more fully here: the dramatic aspect of classical literature in general, and the religious character of the D.

The D. was not in any sense limited to the theater alone. This is also true of modern literature, but to a lesser degree,

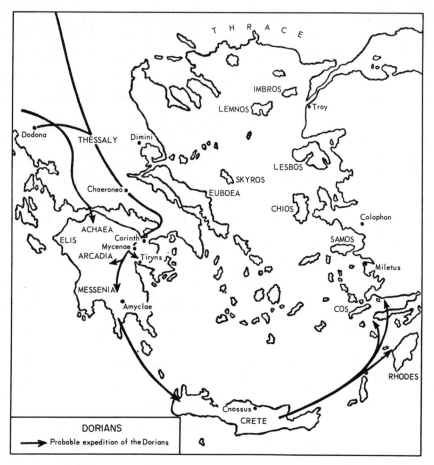

DORIANS
→ Probable expedition of the Dorians

for two reasons: (a) the dialogue in a novel has a fundamental nature of its own, and (b) historical writing has come to partake more of the characters of science than of literature. Every D. is based on a conflict, and the ideal dramatic conflict is essentially unresolved, as both parties are "right" from their own point of view. Nonetheless, the sympathy of the dramatist can be obviously with one of the parties; in *Antigone*, Sophocles is clearly on the side of the heroine, although the part of Creon preserves the dramatic balance. The conflict may lie between a hero and his environment, between a hero and higher powers (Fatum) and in the heart of the hero, himself.

There are many examples of each situation in classical literature; we shall cite one of each. The first may be found in Homer's *Iliad*: Achilles in conflict with his environment, represented by Agamemnon. At a matter of fact, one has only to ask a narrator or scenarist to present the first book of the *Iliad,* in modern theatrical style, and the result would be a veritable D. The second occurs in Herodotus' story of King Croesus (Book I) and his conflict with his fate (for dramatic concepts of Herodotus' entire work see HERODOTUS). The works of almost all other ancient historians contain this element of D. in some form (see particularly LIVY). The third type can be found, for example, in Book IV of Virgil's Aeneid—the conflict in the heart of the hero, between his vocation and his human desires. Finally, in all three of these heroes—Achilles, Croesus, and Aeneas—we also find indications of one or both of the other types of conflict.

It is curious, particularly in the light of the reserve with which the theater is treated in some religious circles even now, that European D. originated in religion at two different epoches: in ancient times in the festivals in honor of Dionysus later becoming secular, and again in the Middle Ages, in the mystery, or liturgical drama of the Christian Church. The religious origins of the Gr. D. are discussed under COMEDY and TRAGEDY. It is important to note that the D. remained a ceremony connected with a cult until well into the 5th cent. B.C.—primarily in worship of the god Dionysus, at whose festivals the performances were given, and, more generally, in honor of those gods who could guarantee the welfare of the city-state. It should be of great interest to us that the D., and especially tragedy, carried a religious message—still valuable today. That explains why classical tragedy still plays an important part in our theater (the technical mastery of the Gr. dramatists is a contributing factor) and why its themes are found again and again in modern forms, in the works of contemporary dramatists (Anouilh, O'Neill, etc.). This message is difficult to sum up in a few words, but one of its main points is that it shows man "at the border": man, represented by the tragic hero reaches, at critical points in his life, the frontiers of the world of the "Other" (God, Fate, supernatural power, cosmos), and is faced with inner disharmony, which leads him to suffering and death, or to the verge of it. But above and through the suffering, the tragedy also points the way to human dignity in reconciliation and harmony with the "Other."

DRAMATIS PERSONAE. "The persons [roles] of the play."

DREPANUM. Port on the Western tip of Sicily, Carthaginian naval base in the first Punic War. D. and Lilybaeum were kept out of Rom. hands throughout the war by Hamilcar Barca. In 249 B.C., D. was attacked by Publius Clodius Pulcher with a large fleet. However, the fleet was undermanned and the tactics were badly executed; as a result, the Romans suffered a severe defeat, with the loss of a great many ships.

DRUIDS. The caste of priests in Gaul (and Britain); it was a privileged class (paid no taxes, for one thing) and had a wider range of functions than ordinary priests. The D. were entrusted with the education of young noblemen, whom they instructed in the oral traditions. They also had great political influence, and acted as judges. The Romans persecuted them, mainly on account of this political power (Caes. *B.G.* VI, 13-14).

DRUSUS:

—(1) Marcus Livius D., who, as a *tribunus plebis,* vetoed the proposals of Gaius Sempronius Gracchus (see GRACCHI) during the latter's second tribunate. He tried to outbid him with twelve *coloniae,* which were never founded.

—(2) Marcus Livius D., son of the preceding, who made some extreme proposals as a *tribunus plebis* in 91 B.C.; his aim was to reconcile the senate and the *equites,* in the spirit which Cicero was later to advocate; he also proposed giving the *socii* Rom. citizenship, which testifies to his very wise statesmanship. However, he was murdered, which was the immediate cause of the Social War.

—(3) Nero Claudius D. (38-9 B.C.). Brother of Tiberius, with whom he campaigned in Raetia; later proconsul of Gaul. Augustus appointed him to invade Germany (12 B.C.); in preparation for this invasion he constructed the D. canal, which was named after him. He penetrated as far as the Elbe, but died on the way back, as the result of a fall from his horse.

—(4) Julius Caesar D. (13 B.C.-A.D. 23). Son of Tiberius. He suppressed a revolt of the legions in Pannonia after the death of Augustus (Tac. *Ann.* I, 16-30). He was considered the probable successor to Tiberius, but was poisoned by his wife, who had been seduced by Sejanus.

—(5) Julius Caesar D. (7-33 B.C.), Son of Germanicus. After the death of the latter in 19 and of Drusis (4) in 23, he was considered the probable successor to Tiberius; Sejanus therefore arranged for him to die as well.

DURA-EUROPOS. Military colony of the Seleucids on the Euphrates, founded c. 300 B.C. (the old Babylonian name was Dura, and Europos was the native city of Seleucus I in Macedonia). At first Greek, it was later orientalized and dominated by the Parthians. In A.D. 165 it was conquered by the Romans, who made it an important fortress on the Euphrates line; in 257 it was destroyed by the Sassanidae. Archaeological excavations have brought to light a wealth of data concerning this outpost of Hellenism in the East, alternately under the influence of Gr., Parthian, and Rom. culture. In addition to the excavated buildings, there are many inscriptions, papyri, and other documents which give an insight into the life of the people and of city administration. The murals (in a synagogue, among other places) are extremely valuable to historians of religion.

DURIS. Athenian painter of vases (about 490 B.C.), master of the red-figure style (See VASE PAINTING) One of his most famous works is a group of Eos and Memnon (an antique *Pietà*) on a kylix (see VASE FORMS) in the Louvre.

DYRRHACHIUM. See EPIDAMNUS.

E

EAST ROMAN EMPIRE. See BYZANTIUM.

EBURONES. Germanic tribe in what is now Belgium, capital Aduatuca (Tongeren); after the revolt of Ambiorix they were nearly exterminated (Caes. *B.G.* VI, 29-44).

ECBATANA. Capital of the empire of the Medes, summer residence under the Achaemenidae; conquered by Alexander the Great in 330 B.C., when enormous treasures were also captured. It was also the residence of the Arsacidae.

ECCLESIA [Gr. ekklēsia]. Popular assembly in which Gr. citizens met to discuss and vote on all political matters. In an oligarchy those with a certain fortune or birthright were admitted, in a democracy, all adult male citizens; this was the case in Athens, among other places, where democracy was planned, extended, and radicalized by Solon, Clisthenes, Ephialtes and Pericles, respectively. Consequently, in keeping with democratic ideas, during the trial about the Arginusae, the slogan was used that no one, not even those invoking the law, could "stop the people from exercising their own free will." The E. met on the average of once a week, on the Pnyx. Under Pericles, and since then, an attendance fee was paid; anyone could attend without great financial hardship. Preliminary work on decisions was done by the *boule*—(council, see CLISTHENES), that is, in practice, by the *prytaneis;* one of them presided over the E. There was complete freedom of speech and right of amendment. Decisions were made by a simple majority when the issue concerned an individual's rights (see OSTRACISM), a special E. was assembled.

EGYPT. The history of the predynastic period, the Old Empire (c. 2800-c. 2250), the Middle Empire (c. 2000-c. 1700), and the New Empire (c. 1560-c. 1100, as well as the following period of decline to 712) is outside the cadre of this book. No doubt there was contact with the world surrounding the Aegean Sea during the times of the pharaohs, namely by way of Crete, but it was not until the Saitic period (663-525) that direct and active relations with Greece were established (see AMASIS; NAUCRATIS; ARCHAIC ART). Other connections were made by way of Cyrene (see also AMMON). In 525 E. was conquered by the Persians (see CAM-

BYSES); it revolted against the new masters several times, sometimes with the support of Athens, which in 459-454, sent a strong fleet to the Nile Delta which suffered a serious defeat (see DELIAN LEAGUE). Many Greeks visited E., among others Plato and Herodotus, who gives us an exciting account of his voyage in his second book. In 332 B.C. Alexander the Great invaded E. and founded Alexandria, after which the period of the Ptolemies followed that ended with Cleopatra. Augustus did not annex E. to the Rom. Empire, but, as the prize of conquest, he treated it as part of his personal domain. The country, a rich source of corn, was subjected to systematic exploitation, in violent contrast to the welfare the Rom. Empire was bringing other provinces.

Culturally, the direct influence of E. on Greece before 300 B.C. was limited to a few areas (see ARCHAIC ART, for example); far more important, was the influence of Egyptian civilization on the Near East, so that cultural goods came into Greece indirectly, by way of Phoenicia, Syria, and Mesopotamia. In the period of the Ptolemies there was social apartheid between the Macedonian-Gr. and native inhabitants. A religious experiment (see SERAPIS) supported by those in power, failed completely. In the Rom. period, the worship of Isis, which was general in Egypt, spread, as did other cults (see also APULEIUS), to the Mediterranean world. (See CALENDAR; PAPYRUS.)

ELAGABALUS (203-222). Rom. emperor, reigned from 218 on. He was called E., or Heliogabalus, because in childhood he was made priest of the Syrian sun-god. His reign was inefficient and corrupt; he established a state cult in Rome for his god (*Sol Invictus*), which involved licentious rites. An ex-actor was made the head of the Praetorians, the food supply was controlled by a barber. The Praetorians finally murdered him, and Alexander Severus became emperor.

ELEA. See VELIA.

ELEATIC SCHOOL. A Gr. school of philosophy. It took its name from Elea (Lucania), home of its chief exponents, Parmenides and Zeno. The school is said to have been founded in 540 B.C. by Xenophanes; it reached its fullest development under Parmenides. It is probably more correct to regard him as the founder. The main tenet of their doctrine was monism, the doctrine that there is only one ultimate unchangeable reality or substance; the natural changes in the universe are only illusory.

ELECTRON.

—(1) An alloy of gold and silver mainly used for coins.

—(2) Amber, imported from the area surrounding the Baltic Sea, as early as Homer's time, through the agency of the Phoenicians; used for jewelry.

ELEGY. Gr. or Lat. lyric poem, recited with a flute accompaniment, consisting of alternating one hexameter with one pentameter (distichon, see METER); was used as a drinking song, a call to battle, or as a historic-narrative song; epitaphs and other poems could also be in elegiac form. The style originated in Ionia (c. 700 B.C. see ARCHILOCHUS). From being used for epitaphs, the E. developed particularly as a dirge—our interpretation of the word stems from this fact. Of the Romans, it was mainly Ovid who employed the E. for his dirges, but also for historic-folkloristic poems (for example, his *Fasti*) and others. The love E., of which traces can be found in the works of the Gr. poets, and particularly in Alexandrine lyric poetry, flourished among the Romans (Tibullus, Propertius).

ELEUSINIAN MYSTERIES. The myths of Demeter and the abduction of Kore, (see ELEUSIS) who passed three months of each year in the underworld, are associated with death and rebirth of nature. The festivals were celebrated twice a year: the lesser mysteries in the month of February to symbolize Kore's return to earth, which marked the beginning of spring. The ceremonies started with purification rites, during which the initiates bathed in the sea, followed by a procession along the "Sacred Way." The actual mysteries took place in the hall of initiation (*Telesterion*). The greater mysteries were celebrated in September, when the initiates took part in a drama—its subject probably the abduction of Kore. A sheaf of barley, symbolizing the new forces of nature, was presented in complete silence. The secret of the rites was well guarded —only a few allusions to them are made by Christian authors of antiquity. This cult of nature took on an eschatological character: as early as the 8th cent. B.C., the "Homeric" hymn to Demeter promises a better life in the "beyond"—this belief was accepted by Pindar. The excavations at Eleusis brought to light the *Telesterion,* which, after the earlier hall had been destroyed, was designed by Ictinus and replaced in the 6th cent. B.C.

ELEUSIS. City in Attica to the northwest of Athens, on a fertile plain. It already existed in the Mycenaean period, and became dependent on Athens in the 7th cent. B.C. It was famous mainly because of the mysteries, a festival with initiation rites in honor of Demeter (Ceres) and Kore (Persephone).

ELIS. Country in the northwestern Peloponnesus, the capital bore the same name; principal cities were Olympia and Pisa. After the First Peloponnesian War, E. was involved in most of the wars of Greece, usually but not always as ally of Sparta. In the Hellenistic period it was friendly to the Aetolian League.

ELOQUENCE. Old Peleus gave Phoenix the task of teaching his son Achilles to be "a speaker of words and a doer of deeds" (Hom. *Il.* IX, 443), before Troy. That a Homeric hero should have to be a man of action is obvious; but it is astonishing that he should also have to be a "speaker," and that this attribute is given precedence. Long before rhetoric had become a special art, E. was already an essential element in antique culture. The history of Greece and of Rome cannot be divorced from E., which was used for persuasion. Peitho, the personification of persuasion, was a Gr. deity. Clearchus, Xenophon and the other Gr. commanders after him did not command the Ten Thousand—they persuaded them. The Gr. verb "to obey" means literally "to be persuaded." E. plays a very important part in most antique literary genres—outside of rhetoric—especially in the epic and historical works. The fact that the historians were so fond of inserting speeches was not due to their need of documenting the words of the main characters of their narrative—even as objective a historian as Thucydides did this. They wrote, in their own style, the words their characters might have used and employed this method to illuminate the background of the historical events. All this is typical of a society which considered beautiful words not only as a means, but also as a goal, desirable in itself.

ELYSIUM. In classical Gr. literature, an abode to which specially favored mortals are carried by the gods, usually without having died, in order to live a life of perfect happiness. This abode was imagined as a beautiful meadow (Homer) at the western extremity of the earth near the river Oceanus, or identified as the Islands of the Blessed (Hesiod). This belief probably originated in the Minoan cult (see MYCAENE). Much later the E. was seen as part of the underworld, where the souls or shades of the blessed dead dwelled; as for example in Virgil, *Aeneid* VI.

EMPEDOCLES of Akrages (Agrigentum) (c. 490-c. 430). Gr. philosopher, an almost legendary figure, a curious combination of philosopher, miracle worker, and statesman. Probably a political revolution caused him to leave his country and he settled in the Peloponnesus, where according to some sources, he died; other stories exist, usually wondrous tales about his wanderings and death. In his epic poem in three books *On Nature* and *Purifications* (considerable fragments remain) he proclaims a pluralistic world, as opposed to the monism of the Eleatics. There are four elements (E. calls them "primordial elements"): fire, air, water, and earth; their manifold minglings and separations originated all species, man included. The mingling is a result of the elementary power, Love, the separation, of the other elementary power, Hate. These powers invest the doctrine with a mystic religious feature, which is entirely in accordance with E.'s complex, fascinating personality. The fact that E. accepted the principles of Orphism (see PYTHAGORAS), particularly as related to metempsychosis, can also be attributed to his religious attitude. He also practiced rhetoric (Gorgias was his pupil) and medicine.

ENNA. See HENNA.

ENNIUS, QUINTUS (239-169). The "father of Lat. poetry." Although he was Greek by birth (born at Rudiae, in Calabria), and had received a Gr. education, he was a subject of Rome and served in the Rom. army. In 204 he was taken to Rome by Cato Major, where he became Scipio Major's valued friend (see LAELIUS). He translated and edited Gr. tragedies, comedies, poems, and fables. His own, most important literary work was the *Annales,* a history of Rome beginning with the destruction of Troy up to the poet's own time. It was the first Lat. epic written in Gr. hexameters; unlike the work of his predecessor Naevius, who wrote in his native Italian Saturnian meter (see METER). Some of the fragments of E.'s *Annales* that have survived, can only be distinguished from prose by their metrical style; others are of more refined form. His achievement was nonetheless praised by all the scholars; Cicero admired him greatly; Lucretius and Virgil often copied him.

ENTASIS. See COLUMN.

EPAMINONDAS (?-362 B.C.). Theban statesman and general. Follower of the Pythagoreans (see PYTHAGORAS) in his youth. When the Theban democracy was established, E. was one of its strongest supporters. In 371 he participated in the congress of Gr. states held at Sparta and spoke in defense of the Theban policy of maintaining a united Boeotia. Agesilaus demanded that the Boeotian cities make peace separately, and not as a league under the hegemony of Thebes, by virtue of the regulations governing the King's Peace (see ANTALCIDAS). E. refused, Sparta then declared war and he was appointed commander in chief of the Theban army. The Spartans were defeated at Leuctra in 371, the victory being mainly due to E.'s military tactics. This battle brought the supremacy of Sparta to an end. In 370 E. and Pelopidas invaded the Peloponnesus and dissolved the Peloponnesian League. Arcadia was restored to its former independence, Megalopolis was founded, and Messenia was freed. For the first time, an enemy army appeared in the valley of the Eurotas. In 368 E. made a second expedition into the Peloponnesus and in 366 a third. In

364 he risked interfering with Athens' sea power, with a fleet on the Aegean Sea. Before he could be successful, he was recalled to Arcadia, where fighting had started anew. In 362 he undertook a fourth expedition, a coalition of Sparta and a number of states opposing him. A major battle was fought at Mantinea, which the Thebans won; E. himself died of the wounds he had received there.

E. was esteemed by his contemporaries, particularly for his integrity, his simplicity, and his unselfish patriotism. For history, his importance is twofold: (a) his military reforms (Leuctra); (b) his political changes in the Peloponnesus, which broke Sparta's supremacy forever, and laid the foundation for the political constellation of the Hellenistic period on that peninsula (see ACHAEA; ARATUS; PHILOPOEMEN). Afterward, Sparta was forced to concentrate on its own internal problems, and solve them under its own power (see CLEOMENES; AGIS). However, E. having raised Thebes to the supremacy of Greece, she nevertheless lost it soon after his death.

EPHEBUS. Gr. designation of a youth of Athens after he had attained the age of eighteen years. The *ephebi* then had two (later one) years of military training, at the end of this term, they were enrolled as full citizens. The E. could be recognized by their short hair, wide-brimmed hat (*petasos*) and *chlamys.* At the end of their training, the *ephebi* were given a sword and shield, and swore an oath not to bring shame on his weapons (ephebic oath).

EPHESUS. Ionian city in Asia Minor, which competed with Miletus for a long time, and finally eclipsed it. Founded in the 11th cent. B.C., according to tradition by a son of Codrus. Conquered by Croesus, who presented the columns for the first large temple of Artemis (see below), then subjected to Persia, and later a member of the Delian League; in 415 B.C. it associated itself with Sparta; during the Hellenistic period it was part of the kingdom of Pergamum, and later, of the Rom. province Asia. Under the Rom. Empire, it was a metropolis, the capital of Asia Minor.

E. became famous mainly through the

cult of the mother goddess of Asia Minor (fertility goddess, see CYBELE), that the Greeks identified with Rhea and later with Artemis, although she showed no trace of the young, virginal image normally associated with Artemis. The resemblance lay mainly in the fact that both goddesses gave fertility to fields, humans, and animals. The temple was destroyed in 356 B.C. (see HEROSTRATUS), rebuilt, and was considered one of the Seven Wonders of the World (see also SCOPAS). The excavations (by Austrians) brought to light significant parts of the Hellenistic E., in addition to the temple.

EPHIALTES. Name of:

—(1) The Malian who betrayed the Greeks at Thermopylae in 480 B.C., by leading Xerxes over the mountain path of Anopaea.

—(2) Athenian statesman, fierce democrat, who dissolved the Areopagus in 462 B.C. with the help of Pericles, who was then only a young man; this made him so hated in aristocratic circles, that E. was murdered, which automatically left the leadership of the democratic wing to Pericles.

EPHORS [Gr. *ephoroi,* overseers]. A group of five Spartan magistrates, elected annually from among all the citizens. The year was named after the senior ephor. The E. had absolute authority over the whole country, including the kings. Two of them accompanied the king on his campaigns and had the right to bring him to trial if they felt that his actions were not in Sparta's best interest. It was the duty of the E.'s to summon and preside over the assemblies and decide on questions of foreign policy (see also SPARTA).

EPHORUS of Cyme (Asia Minor) (c. 405-330). Gr. historian, pupil of Isocrates. He wrote the first universal history attempted in Greece, from the return of the Heraclidae (that is, the Dorian migration, see DORIANS) to 340 B.C., a period of 750 years. E. used all available sources, not entirely uncritically; the work was a great success. It was lost, but we have extensive excerpts made by Diodorus Siculus.

EPIC. Heroic poem, long narrative poem in hexameters (see METER). For us, the Gr. epic begins with Homer, although there are definite traces of pre-Homeric epics (*Il.* IX, 527-599, for example, certainly goes back to a separate Meleager-E.). The Homeric E. was created orally, and narrated by *rhapsodoi.* This tradition was maintained for centuries by a family called the *Homeridae,* who claimed descent from him and recited his poetry at festivals. Hesiod's *Theogonia* falls between the E. and the didactic poem; his *Shield of Heracles* is a true E. in smaller form. In the 8th-7th centuries the first poems of the Epic Cycle (see CYCLE) were written. In the 6th cent. the recitation of Homer became a tradition in Athens; the creative period of the E. was then at an end. It was revived in Alexandria, not as recitation but as literature (see APOLLONIUS RHODIUS); the small E. (epyllion) was also popular then (see CALLIMACHUS). The E. flourished once more in the 4th-5th centuries A.D. (see QUINTUS SMYRNAEUS; NONNUS).

In Rome, epic poetry was first written by Livius Andronicus, who also translated the *Odyssey* into Italian Saturnian meter (see also NAEVIUS). The hexameter was first used by Ennius. The grand master of the Lat. E. was Virgil. Work by Lucan, Valerius Flaccus, Silius Italicus, and Statius has survived from imperial times. Claudianus also still used the epic style.

EPICHARMUS (c. 540-c. 450). The main representative of Sicilian comedy. In contrast to Attic comedy, E.'s plays do not embrace political satire. They are more in the nature of burlesque farces, parodies on myths and sagas, and middle-class comedies. Prototypes of the later Attic New Comedy, they have no chorus. Only fragments have survived.

EPICTETUS. Name of:

—(1) Athenian vase painter (c. 510 B.C.), one of the first masters of the art of painting red-figured vases.

—(2) Stoic philosopher (c. 55-c. 135), freedman from Phrygia, pupil of Musonius Rufus in Rome, exiled with a group of other philosophers in 89 by Domitian. He founded a school in Nicopolis (Epirus), where he worked until his death. E. revived the ideas of early Stoicism (that is, of Chrysippus) with the difference that he addressed himself expressly to the masses, and preached the brotherhood of man; there are quite a few points where his doctrine touches on the Christian one. Of the early Stoic ideas, he emphasized independence of action. Only that which is dependent on our own will and strength should touch us; the stroke of fate cannot hurt us, because it does not belong to the things that "depend on us." E.'s doctrine was preserved for posterity by Arrianus; Marcus Aurelius was greatly influenced by it.

EPICUREANS. See EPICURUS.

EPICURUS [Gr. Epikouros] (341-270). Gr. philosopher, founder of the Epicurean school, one of the most important Hellenistic schools of philosophers. He was born on Samos, the son of a school teacher who came of a prominent Athenian family. After his first stay in Athens, E. studied in various places, settled at Mytilene, and there first won recognition as a philosopher; at Lamsacus a few years later he became the head of a school. In 306 he revisited Athens, bought a beautiful garden which he used as the seat of the school he had founded there (his followers were called "the philosophers of the garden"). Here he lived in retirement, in a very modest style, surrounded by his pupils.

E.'s doctrine consists of two connected parts: (a) his natural philosophy is borrowed from Democritus' Atomism. The main difference was that E. assumed that the atoms collided and that, as a result, these movements and minglings formed new beings. Sensual perception is made possible because tiny particles falling from these bodies, are absorbed by our senses. This perception is the only real source of true knowledge. The gods also consist of very small atoms, and lead blessed lives in the areas between the worlds. They are not interested in life on earth; thus, they need not be feared. Death need not be feared either, as the soul consists of atoms, which separate as life ceases. (b) in his ethics also E. wants to liberate man from all fear. Pleasure is the ultimate good; he adopted this idea from the Cyrenaic school, but he elaborated on it, to him the supreme pleasure consisted of imperturbable peace of mind (*ataraxia*) and freedom from pain. Happy

is the man who, far from political and social struggles (preferably without family ties), is able to rise above his desires.

One of the most striking characteristics of this philosophy, is its individualism. The Epicureans reject both the traditional world of the gods, and the service to the community in state and society. There are points here, which resemble the doctrine of Cynics, however great the differences between them may be. The doctrine found many disciples in the Hellenistic world, in which the polis had gone under, but was less popular with the Romans than the Stoic doctrine, which agreed more with the traditional concept of Rom. virtue. Still, E. found prophets in Rome, too. Lucretius is our most important source for natural philosophy, and Horace called himself a follower of E.'s ethics, although he certainly was not a consistent one. A number of aphorisms and three of E.'s letters have been preserved.

EPIDAMNUS. Colony of Corcyra and Corinth, founded in 625 B.C. on the coast of Illyria; the dispute over it between the two founding cities was the cause of the Peloponnesian War. In about 300 B.C. it was renamed Dyrrhachium; later it was a Rom. army base (now Durrës, Italian Durazzo).

EPIDAURUS. City in Argolis, owes its fame to the cult of Asklepios; rightly called the Gr. Lourdes. The sick came to E. from far and near, to ask the god to cure their afflictions. Numberless inscriptions, in which the grateful and happy cured people give thanks, have been found; among them are a number of songs of praise by the poet Isyllus (c. 280 B.C.). These are invaluable material for the study of Gr. piety and Gr. medicine (see also COS). After observing special rites: purifications, baths, sacrifices, and fasts, the pilgrims passed the night in the temple, and the god prescribed for them in their sleep. E. has the best preserved Gr. theater, where even now, ancient dramas are regularly enacted.

EPIGRAM. Originally, a short, concise poem, usually engraved on stone (see EPIGRAPHY). In ancient Greece, the E. generally assumed an elegiac form (see ELEGY). It was not until later, with the

Romans, that the E. became satirical in nature, a genre very popular in the Hellenistic-Rom. period. Martial distinguished himself as a writer of epigrams (see ANTHOLOGIA).

EPIGRAPHY. The science of studying Gr. and Lat. inscriptions on durable materials (excluding coins, see COINAGE). This was already done in ancient times; Herodotus, for example, was very interested in inscriptions and often copied them. In Europe, since the Renaissance this interest was renewed, many travelers who visited Greece while it was still governed by Turkey, collected inscriptions. E. did not become a systematic science until the 19th cent.; that is when the large *Corpora Inscriptionum* appeared, supplements were added later, covering special collections of diverse types. Inscriptions throw a completely new light on the history of antiquity and on life in various epochs. They are invaluable for our knowledge of the Gr. alphabet (see SCRIPT), Gr. and Italian dialects, Gr. music, and some aspects of religion (see, for example, ASKLEPIOS; BACCHANALIA). Some highly important examples of historical inscriptions are: the *Parian Chronicle* (see PAROS), the lists of contributions to the Delian League, and the *Monumentum Ancyranum*. Almost all we know about social life in the provinces under the Rom. Empire, is based on this type of inscription. For the study of literature inscriptions in verse are especially valuable.

EPIRUS. Province in northwestern Greece, to the north of Aetolia and Acarnania. Important places were Ambracia and Dodona. It was inhabited by Illyrian tribes, of whom the Molossi were the strongest. Olympias and Pyrrhus were descendants of the Molossian royal house. In 167 B.C. the area was destroyed by the Romans and 150,000 prisoners were deported.

EQUITES. Term used for:
—(1) The cavalry of the Rom. army; originally Rom. citizens with a fortune, sufficiently large, to guarantee the upkeep of the horse that the state provided. Eventually, however, Rome used almost entirely foreign cavalry (mainly Spaniards and Gauls).

—(2) The Roman knighthood; there was a census (the estimate of each citizen's fortune) for them, too, even though the E.'s function was no longer thought of as a military one. The E. were, since Gaius Gracchus (c. 121 B.C.), a separate class, the second after the senators. Gracchus made them the jurymen in the tribunal and tax collectors in Asia. They formed a veritable "financial nobility," and often amassed enormous fortunes as bankers, publicans, and traders. Sulla took away many of their privileges. Under the emperors, high officials were often chosen from that group. The tokens of office of the E. were a tunic with a narrow purple border and a golden ring.

ERATO. See MUSES.

ERATOSTHENES of Cyrene (c. 275-194). Versatile Gr. scholar, pupil of Callimachus. E. was in charge of the library in Alexandria. He wrote philological works (about comedy, among others), studies on mathematics, astronomy, philosophy, history, and other subjects. His most famous work is his *Geographica,* of which only fragments have survived. It was the first handbook on general geography, used extensively by Strabo.

ERECHTHEUM. Sanctuary in the Attic-Ionic style (see ARCHITECTURAL ORDERS) on the Athenian Acropolis. The original temple, said to have been built by the legendary king Erechtheus, was burnt by the Persians in 480 B.C. The restoration of the new temple, possibly begun as far back as the time of Pericles, was—according to an inscription now in the British Museum—still not quite finished in 409 B.C. The building deviates from the classical order of Gr. temples, but attained a rare perfection nevertheless. A small hall, supported not by pillars, but by caryatids, is justly famous for its beauty.

According to tradition, the E. was also the place where Athena and Poseidon had their dispute for the possession of Attica.

ERESUS. City on Lesbos, native city of Sappho and Theophrastus.

ERETRIA. City on Euboea. Like its neighbor Chalcis, E. founded colonies in the west and north of Greece. Vanquished by Chalcis during the Lelantic

War; it never regained its former prosperity. With Athens it supported the Ionian revolt of 498 B.C., and was destroyed by the Persians in 490 B.C. in reprisal (see DATIS). The city was rebuilt and was a member of both the Delian Leagues. Under Rom. domination it fell into insignificance. For a short period under Mark Antony it was a possession of Athens.

ERGOTIMUS. See FRANÇOIS VASE.

ERINYES. Gr. avenging goddesses, particularly avengers of deeds of violence committed against a relative. They punished the sinner both in this world and after death (see HADES). The E. ascended from the underworld, relentlessly pursued the offender, and finally drove him mad (as, for example, Orestes, in Aeschylus' *Oresteia,* and in Euripides" *Iphigenia in Tauris*). When the anger of the E. had been soothed, people did not dare call the goddesses by their real name, but worshiped them as Eumenides (well-disposed). The Romans called them Furiae or Dirae.

EROS. Gr. god of love. (Rom. Amor or Cupid). In mythology the son of Aphrodite and Ares. In classical Gr. literature, E. is more a primeval and benign power (thus regarded in Orphism) than the mischievous little god as he was later represented. The chorus dedicated to E. as an elementary power in Sophocles' *Antigone* (781-801) is famous. Plato, in his *Symposium,* likens E. to the aspiration of beauty. The most famous temple of E. is located in Thespiae in Boeotia. The popular representation of the little child, armed with bow and arrow, dates from the Rom.-Hellenistic period.

ERRARE HUMANUM EST. "To err is human" (Cic. *Phil.* XII, 2, 5).

ESQUILIN HILL. One of the seven hills of Rome, to the east of the city, where the park of Maecenas was situated.

ETHICS [Gr. *ethikos*]. Not until Aristotle did the term *ethica,* meaning the systematic knowledge concerning moral actions according to a certain standard of good and evil, come into use. Of course the Greeks were aware of the theory of ethics before that. Already in Homer we find *diké,* for example, "the normal pattern of human actions"; *nomos* and *themis* are also clear conceptions belonging to the category of E. Before Socrates, Gr. philosophers were interested in "natural" philosophy first and foremost, with some exceptions: Xenophanes, for example, protested violently against the immoral aspects of polytheism. In the 5th cent. B.C., Gr. philosophy entered the crucial period which led to the shift in emphasis from the study of nature to the study of man and his moral actions. The reasons for this crisis were multiple: there was no way to reconcile the contradictory theories of the Eleatics and the atomists; democracy, developing further, made the citizen an active participant in the life of the state, and he began to demand definite directives of behavior for his public life as a citizen and as an individual. The disaster of the Peloponnesian War made social and moral ideals a problem. This raised the subject of *aretè* (virtue) with which the Sophists, vehemently opposed by Socrates particularly, were occupied. After that, E. became a definite part of philosophic thought (see also PLATO; ARISTOTLE; ANTISTHENES; CYNICS; STOICS; EPICURUS; and DIOGENES).

ETHIOPIA. See AETHIOPIA.

ETRURIA. Now Tuscany in Italy, the central lands of the Etruscans (Lat. also Tusci, Etrusci; Gr. Tursènoi).

ETRUSCANS. The most important and powerful tribe in Italy, before the expansion of Rom. power. From their central lands (see ETRURIA) they dominated Italy from Bononia to the south of Campania during their most prosperous period, the 6th cent. B.C. Since ancient times there have been various theories concerning the origin of the E. The main ones are: (a) they emigrated from Asia Minor (mainly Lydia); this goes back to Herodotus (I, 94); (b) they are the autochtonous inhabitants; this goes back to Dionysius of Halicarnassus. Both theories have drawbacks: the one against (a) is that there are no essential differences between the Villanovan culture and that of the E.; against (b), what little we know about the E.'s language shows clearly that there is a relationship with very early Gr. forms (probably those of Asia Minor, especially the Carian forms,

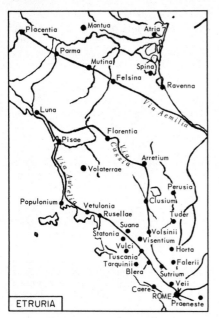

Etruria and its most important cities

see CARIA); also that several Etruscan customs are clearly Eastern in origin. The solution may well be, that the E. infiltrated overseas from the East in small groups in about 800 B.C., and settled as the dominating caste over a Villanovan population, with which they eventually assimilated. Etruria was not one state, but a confederation of twelve cities (the most important were Veii, Tarquinii, Vulci, Clusium, and Caere). At the height of their power (c. 500 B.C.) they also dominated Rome and Campania. After that they were pushed back (see CUMAE; TARQUINIUS; PRISCUS; TARQUINIUS SUPERBUS; and VEII); Hiero I of Syracuse broke their naval power. From the north, they were threatened by the Gauls (see BONONIA). In the 3rd cent. B.C. they were gradually dominated by the Romans. The cities of the E. were governed by aristocrats, with a king at their head.

The art of the E. was strongly under Gr. influence; still, it had a pronounced character of its own, in rapport with the national temperament; it is rigid, without excessive ornamentation—majestic, and at the same time, barbarian. The murals in the sepulchral chambers and statues like the "Apollo of Veii" and the "Chimaera of Arretium" are well known. The temples stood on elevations, had frontal orientation, with a deep peristyle (patterned after Rom. temples). The paintings in the sepulchral chambers have, understandably, mainly life after death as their subject. They are cruel in character, showing demons of death, and bloody funeral ceremonies. Yet alongside are scenes of games and a joyous, lighthearted and luxurious life, probably the privilege of the upper class. The E. were also masters in arts and crafts. See Appendix.

The many inscriptions that have been found are readable (resembling ancient Gr. characters) but are impossible to interpret, the language being still unknown; at any rate it was not an Indo-European language.

The influence of the E. on the Romans was very strong. Examples of adoptions are: the lictors, gladiators, haruspices, and in architecture, the erection of arches, domes, and temples.

EUBOEA. Large island off the coast of Boeotia; main cities: Chalcis and Eretria; also Carystus, known for its marble. E. came under Athenian rule very early (end of the 6th cent. B.C.), and after a revolt in 446 B.C. an Athenian *cleruchia* was established there. In the 4th cent. B.C. it had its own Euboean League, reestablished by Flamininus after Macedonian domination; after 146 B.C. it was part of the Rom. province Macedonia.

EUCLID. Name of:

—(1) A Gr. mathematician who taught at Alexandria c. 300 B.C. and founded its mathematical school. His chief extant work is *Stoicheia* (*Elements of Mathematics*) in thirteen books. We also have his *Data,* containing geometrical propositions as an introduction to geometrical analysis, and an astronomical work entitled *Phaenomena.* Until today his work is considered the basis for all geometrical textbooks.

—(2) Athenian archon in 403/2. During this time democracy was restored (see THRASYBULUS) and the Ionic alphabet (see SCRIPT) replaced the old Attic one for inscriptions. Consequently, the period of E.'s archontate is important for epigraphers.

EUDEMUS of Rhodes (4th cent. B.C.). Gr. mathematician. He wrote works on the history of astronomy and mathematics, which, with the works of Theophrastus, are the foundation for all the later works on these subjects. Only fragments have survived.

EUDOXUS of Cnidus (c. 408-355). Gr. philosopher and astronomer. He founded a school in Cyzicus which he later brought to Athens. His theory of concentric spheres in which the planets move around the earth, is well-known. Some of his mathematical theories have been transmitted to us in the works of Euclid.

EUHEMERUS of Messene (c. 300 B.C.). Author of *Sacred History,* a story of a fictitious journey to an island in the Indian Ocean; a Utopian paradise where Zeus was said to have reigned as king. On this, E. based his theory that all ancient myths were historical events and that the gods were deified mortals who originally were historical personages. The word "euhemerism" is derived from his name. E.'s book is a particularly interesting example of an ancient Utopian manuscript.

EUMENES. Name of two kings of Pergamum:
—(1) E. I, reigned from 263-241.
—(2) E. II, king from 197-159.

EUMENIDES. See ERINYES.

EUPATRIDAE. Descendants of the Athenian nobility, comparable to the Rom. patricians. Solon deprived them of most of their privileges (the supreme authority of the three highest ranking archons, and, consequently, exclusion as members of the Areopagus). However, they still kept certain prerogatives of the priesthood.

EUPHRONIUS (c. 500 B.C.). Athenian potter and vase painter, one of the greatest masters of the red-figured vase painting; twelve of his signatures as a potter are known, and five as a painter. He also employed the painters Panaetius, Pistoxenus, and Onesimus. Well-known works: krater depicting Heracles and Antaius (in Paris), and a drinking cup showing Heracles and Geryones (in Munich).

EUPOLIS (446-411). Gr. author of comedies, with Aristophanes the chief representative of the Attic Old Comedy. He treated Alcibiades badly in one of his plays; the story that Alcibiades threw him into the sea out of revenge has not been attested. Only fragments of E.'s plays have survived.

EUREKA! [*heurēka*]. "I have found [it]!" Exclamation attributed to Archimedes when he discovered his famous law of buoyancy while taking a bath.

EURIPIDES (c. 480-406). Last of the three great Athenian tragedians; born on Salamis, of a prosperous Attic family; we have little definite information about his life; he is said to have devoted his early years to athletics and paintings; then, influenced by Anaxagoras, Protagoras, and Socrates, he studied philosophy. In 455 he first staged a tetralogy, but did not win a prize until 441 (see AGON). In about 408/7 he left Athens, it was said, because he could not bear the spiteful attacks of writers of comedies and of the conservative critics. He lived at the court of King Archelaus in Macedonia, where he produced *Bacchae,* among other plays. He died there, and was buried near Pella. Of his ninety-two plays, nineteen (of which one, *Rhesus,* was probably not written by him) have survived. In probable chronological order: 1) *Alcestis* (438), performed as the fourth play, in place of a Satyric drama (E. often did this), the play is a little lighter—Heracles releases Alcestis from the death—she had volunteered to die for her husband; 2) *Medea* (431)— the mother who murders her children to revenge herself on Jason, her unfaithful husband; 3) *Hippolytus* (428)—the "Potiphar" motif; 4) *Hecuba* (c. 425)—her fate after the fall of Troy; 5) *Andromache* (c. 419, not performed in Athens)—her life as the wife of Achilles' son Neoptolemus and her hatred of his second wife Hermione; 6) *Heraclidae*— Athens protects the descendants of Heracles against the persecution of the Peloponnesian Eurystheus: definite political background; 7) *Supplices*—Theseus protects the mothers of the heroes that fell at Thebes; 8) *Troades* (415)—the fate of the women after the fall of Troy; 9) *Heracles*—in a fit of madness sent to him by Hera, he kills his children; 10) *Iphigenia in Tauris*—she and her brother Orestes flee from the Crimea, reconciliation after the curse on the family of Atreus; 11) *Ion*—a play that foreshadows the Attic New Comedy; 12) *Helena* (412)—on the way back from Troy, it is discovered that she was in Egypt all the time (probably an allusion to the expedition to Syracuse, the "great illusion") (see also STESICHORUS); 13) *Electra*—the same subject as Sophocles', but divested of its heroics; 14) *Phoenissae*—the battle of the Seven against Thebes; 15) *Orestes* (408)—the traditional theme, seen from a pathological angle; 16) *Iphigenia in Aulis*—the sacrifice of Iphigenia; staged after the death of E., as was: 17) *Bacchae* (407/6)—the saga of Pentheus in Thebes, see also BACCHANALIA; 18) *Cyclops*—Satyric drama about Polyphemus, date unknown; 19) *Rhesus* (see above).

With E., the social, philosophical, religious, and political problems of the years before, during, and after the Peloponnesian War, make their entrance on the dramatic stage. Aeschylus had been profoundly religious; Sophocles attached great importance to traditions, and although his philosophy is a matter for argument, his characters, at any rate, took on superhuman dimensions; E. draws man as he is, with all his greatness and his weakness, and he is passionately interested in him. This resulted in two facts: (a) it is more difficult with E. than with other dramatists, to distinguish between his own philosophy and the thoughts spoken by his characters—the characters frequently voiced current popular opinion, for example, or defended Sophist theories; (b) it exposed E. to much unjustified criticism. He, who spent his whole life fighting for a purer religious concept than that offered by tradition, who pleaded for the emancipation of women, was decried as an atheist and a woman hater. There are additional criticisms pertaining to his works; for example, the slight connection he creates between the chorus and the action, reducing the singers' importance; this only

appeared to be the case. Also, it is said that E. was often incapable of working out a plot, resorting to a *deus ex machina* to solve the problem. His critics forget that he did this deliberately. Finally, he is accused of not assimilating the exposé into the plot, but of explaining the story in a prologue connected loosely with the play; this only appears to be awkward, actually it helps the spectator to concentrate entirely on the human drama, of which the facts are only the point of departure.

EURIPOS. Strait near Chalcis between Euboea and Boeotia.

EUROTAS. River in Laconia on which Sparta was located. The E. flows between the Thornax and the Taygetus mountains; is said to have been named after king E., who is said to have dammed the lower reaches of the river.

EURYBIADES. Spartan admiral of the Gr. fleet at Artemisium and Salamis (fought against the Persians in 480 B.C.). In spite of the fact that Athens had much the stronger contingent, tradition dictated that a Spartan command the united fleet. However, he wisely followed Themistocles' advice, but opposed the latter's plan (if it is historical) of cutting off Xerxes' retreat by destroying all the bridges over the Hellespont (Hdt. VIII, 108).

EURYMEDON. River in Pamphylia, where Cimon achieved his greatest victory over the Persian army and fleet, in 446 B.C.

EUSEBIUS (c. 263-339). Bishop of Caesarea Palestinae, father of church history. He worked in a time of violent persecution of the Christians (303-310); later he was a favorite of Constantine the Great whom he baptized. A most important work for information on antiquity is his *Chronicle* (*Chronicon*), a work founded on the now lost writings of previous historians. His greatest work, *History of the Christian Church,* is an invaluable source of information on Christianity from its rise to A.D. 314. He also wrote a biography of Constantine (strongly influenced by his personal feeling).

EUTERPE. See MUSES.

EUTROPIUS (2nd half of the 4th cent. A.D.). Lat. historian. As the archivist of

Valens, to whom the work is dedicated, E. wrote a short history of Rome in ten books, from the foundation of the city to A.D. 364, the year of the latter's accession. The history was a compendium, concise and well written. It became very popular because, by comparison to a long, complete work of Livy, a summary proved to be timesaving for busy Romans.

EXECIAS (c. 540 B.C.). Athenian potter and vase painter, master of black-figured vase painting. Nine of his signatures are known (two as a ceramist and painter); famous works: amphora with Aias and Achilles, playing dice (Vatican) and kylix with Dionysus (Munich).

F

FABIUS. Name of:
—(1) Quintus F. Maximus, surnamed Cunctator (delayer), rose to the dictatorship after he had been defeated by Hannibal at Lake Trasimenus in 217 B.C. He owes his surname to his delaying tactics in the Second Punic War. He avoided all direct encounter with the enemy and never fought a decisive battle, giving Rome time to assemble her strength. His caution was misinterpreted in Rome and the people gave Minucius Rufus, his *magistrate equitum,* equal power. When, soon afterward, Rufus was entrapped by Hannibal, F. rescued him, and the two men reconciled their differences. F.'s tactics appear to less advantage in the closing years of the war—more aggressive generals were in command. F. opposed Scipio Major in his plan to invade Africa while Hannibal was still in Italy (Liv. XXVIII, 40-42). F. did not live to see Scipio finally triumph; he died in 203.
—(2) Quintus F. Pictor (c. 225 B.C.). The first Rom. annalist; was sent to Delphi to consult the oracle after the battle of Cannae. He wrote a history of Rome, written in Greek, beginning with the arrival of Aeneas in Italy down to his own time. The work was used by Polybius and Livy.

FABRICIUS LUSCINUS, GAIUS. Rom. commander against Pyrrhus, consul in 282 and again in 278 B.C. He is said to have been a model of incorruptibility.

FABULA. Lat. play. We can classify it mainly into the *F. Atellana,* the ancient Italian farce, with stereotype, comical characters; the *F. palliata,* Lat. adaptation of a Gr. comedy of the Attic New Comedy; the *F. praetexta,* Rom. historical drama; the *F. togata,* Lat. adaptation of a Gr. comedy, in which the actors wore the Rom. toga instead of the Gr. *pallium,* and the subject was completely adapted to Rom. life.

FASCES. The bundle of rods, having among them an ax (*securis*) with the blade projecting, carried on the left shoulder by Rom. lictors. The F. were for beating, the ax for decapitating. They were originally the symbol of royal power, later of the *magistratus cum imperio.* In Rome the ax had to be removed (except in the case of a dictator) because the magistrates did not have the power to inflict the death penalty. Like the lictors of the *imperatores* under the Republic, the lictors in the imperial period carried F. bound with laurel twigs. The F. probably originated in Etruria.

FASTI. The Rom. calendar, originally the lists of *dies fasti et dies nefasti* (see DIES ATER). The word F. was further applied to the annual lists of the names of important officials, priests, and persons who had been honored with a triumph. Some of these lists which have come down to us are fairly complete; others are fragments, such as the F. *Capitolini,* inscribed originally in 36 B.C. on the marble walls of the official residence of the *ponitifex maximus.* The celebrated F. of Ovid are a poetic description of the Rom. festival calendar.

FATUM [Lat. fate (literally: an utterance, oracle), the Greeks used *moira, aisa* (literally: one's share or lot in a thing)]. Homer already speaks of Fate; he generally writes of the Moira spinning the thread of life at man's birth. However, he also mentions several Moirae—their relation to the gods is not clearly defined; Fate is the power who rules over men and gods, yet elsewhere in his *Iliad,* Homer describes Zeus and other gods—and even men—as being able to change fate's course. In general, the ancients believed there were three goddesses of fate, Clotho who spun the thread of man's life, Lachesis who measured it, and Atropos who cut it off. The Romans called them Parcae or Fata.

A fatalistic belief manifests itself throughout ancient culture: in tragedy, the curse on certain families; in philosophy, in the doctrine of the Stoics especially (destiny results from the cosmic law); in astrology, these ideas form the basis for studies and interpretation (compare Virgil's *Aeneid;* see also LUCANUS).

FESTINA LENTE. "Make haste slowly." Motto of Augustus, according to Suetonius, *De vita Caesarum, Aug. 25.*

FESTUS. Name of:

—(1) Marcus Porcius. Rom. procurator of Judaea, who bore testimony to the innocence of the Apostle Paul, when the latter defended himself (see PROVOCATIO), and appealed to the emperor (Acts 25).

—(2) Sextus Pompeius F. (c. A.D. 300). Rom. author; wrote an abridgment of a lexical work of Verrius Flaccus, *De verborum significatu.* A considerable part of this work has been preserved.

FETIALES. College of twenty Rom. priests, instituted in the time of the kings; they advised on treaties and gave their opinion upon the question of war or peace. If war was decided on, their speaker, the *pater patratus,* in a special ceremonial, threw a spear into enemy territory, at the same time uttering a formal declaration of war.

FIAT. "Let it be done." A formulae of sanction; F. being the word to express that authority is given.

FIRMICUS MATERNUS of Syracuse (4th cent. A.D.). Lat. author. About A.D. 336 he wrote a work on astrology in eight books. Later he was converted to Christianity, and about A.D. 347 he wrote an apologia, *De Errore Profanarum Religionum,* in which he called on Constans and Constantius II to extirpate paganism.

FISCUS [Lat. little basket, chest]. The term used for the private treasury of the emperor, as distinguished from the public treasury (*aerarium*). The F. gained importance under the Emperor Claudius, and was entrusted to one of the most clever freedmen, Pallas. Since Hadrian, one of the *equites* managed it. The income from the imperial provinces (see PROVINCIA) and other monies, flowed into the F. Although the F. was theoretically the emperor's private treasury, it eventually became the state treasury, completely superseding the *aerarium.*

FLACCUS. See VALERIUS.

FLAMINES. Rom. college of sacrificial priests, with fifteen members, classified as three F. *majores* and twelve *minores;* the former were the F. of Jupiter, Mars, and Quirinus. The highest rank was held by the *flamen Dialis* (of Jupiter), who—to protect him from ritual contamination—was bound by all kinds of strict regulations. The rules governing the lives of the other F. were less severe. The F. all had to be patricians, and had many privileges.

FLAMINIUS, GAIUS (3rd cent. B.C.). The greatest Rom. democratic leader before the Gracchi; *tribunus plebis* in 232. In spite of the opposition of the senate, he carried the measure to divide the newly conquered land in Gallia Cisalpina among poor citizens. In 223 he was consul; defeated the Insubres on the other side of the Po and was awarded a triumph which the people had demanded. The senate had issued a decree against it, but popular clamor was too great. In 220 he was censor and built the Via Flaminia; in 217 he was again consul; he fell at Lake Trasimenus. Livy's derogatory description of his actions can be attributed to the traditional hostility reflected in the accounts of the annalists in senate circles. F. certainly tried to combat the social evils in Rome, which were already beginning to make themselves felt at that time; he was a courageous and energetic man; the fact that he did not take into account the interests of the Gauls in the valley of the Po, is typically Roman; it was no coincidence that it was an Insubrian horseman who stabbed him at Lake Trasimenus. (Liv. XXI, 6).

FLAMINIUS, TITUS A. QUINCTICUS (c. 225-174). The conqueror of Philip V. As a consul, he led the Rom. army against Macedonia in 198, defeated Philip at Cynoscephalae (197), limited him to Macedonia proper. At the Isthmian Games of 196 he declared all the Greeks, who had been under Macedonian rule, free and independent. He later fought against Antiochus III and defeated him at Thermopylae (191). In 183 he went to King Prussias of Bithynia as an ambassador, to demand that Hannibal be handed over. F. is a striking example of Rom. philhellenism, which was represented mainly in the circles of Scipio Minor. It is easy to view the "declaration of freedom" of 196 as typical Rom. hypocrisy, but that is seeing it too simply. The love F. and his circles bore the Greeks and their culture was certainly real. The fact that Greece still was not freed, and that it was subjected to Rome, was the result of political complications, which were then difficult to prevent.

FLAVIAN HOUSE. The imperial dynasty formed by Vespasian, and his sons and successors Titus and Domitian.

FLAVIUS JOSEPHUS. See JOSEPHUS.

FLORIANUS. See MILITARY EMPERORS.

FLORUS, LUCIUS ANNAEUS (2nd cent. A.D.). Lat. historian; came to Rome from Africa by way of Spain, where he became a favorite of Hadrian. He compiled, chiefly from Livy, a short history of Rome, emphasizing her wars. From similarities of style he has been identified with Publius Annius F., author of a rhetoric dialogue about Virgil, and a poet named F.; some sources attribute *Pervigilum Veneris* to him.

FLUTING. See COLUMN.

FORUM. Rom. marketplace. The term F. was applied by the Romans to the large, rectangular space in the central part of any city. Small villages and towns also had a F., for example, the F. Hadriani in

what is now Voorburg in the Netherlands and the F. Julii in present-day Fréjus in France. Ultimately the F. became the political rather than the commercial center (see AGORA). It served as a place where court was held, as well as public meetings and elections. The most famous F. is the F. Romanum, the center of Rome, surrounded by the Palatine, the Capitoline, and the Quirinal Hills; originally a marshy plain, first used as a cemetery, then drained in the 6th cent. B.C. In the course of time it was surrounded by large public buildings; the most important art: the *curia,* the *rostra,* the basilicas, the temples of Saturn and Castor, and the triumphal arch of Septimius Severus. The area in front of the *curia* was called *comitium,* the Tullianum (prison) was nearby. The emperors had the number of *fora* increased with new so-called imperial *fora,* of which those of Augustus and Trajan (with its famous column) are the best known.

FRANÇOIS VASE. The greatest masterpiece of black-figured vase painting (c. 570 B.C.), found in a sepulchral chamber in Clusium, and named after the finder. The vase is signed by the potter Ergotimus and the painter Clitias. The decorations consist of more than two hundred figures in six horizontal friezes. It shows mythological scenes (Trojan sagas, the Calydonian wild boar hunt, etc.). Now in Florence.

FRATRES ARVALES [Lat. field brethren). College of twelve Rom. priests; they held rites in May in honor of the goddess of the crops, Dea Dia, at which an ancient song, *Carmen Arvale,* was sung. This song is dedicated to the Lares and to Mars, and was supposed to promote fertility. It betrays a Gr. influence (though it originated in the 5th cent. B.C.). Significant fragments of the rites of the college have been preserved in inscriptions that include this song.

FREGELLAE. City in Latium, for many years a bone of contention between Rome and the Samnites. In 125 B.C. it revolted against Rome in the struggle for citizenship (see GRACCHI), and was destroyed.

FRIEZE. The band above the architrave (see ARCHITECTURAL ORDERS) in a temple. When F. of triglyphs and metopes in a Doric temple is described, the word F. is used in a limited sense; it designates a continuous band of figures, as in Ionic architecture and, for example, the F. around the cella of the Parthenon. Next to this F., which shows the parade of the Panathenaea, and was made under the direction of Phidias, the F. of the altar of Zeus in Pergamum is particularly well known. It depicts the struggle of the gods against the giants; it is one of the most impressive monuments of Hellenistic sculpture.

FRISII. German tribe in what is now Friesland, a province in the north of the Netherlands. They once inhabited the north sea coast from the Zwin to the Weser rivers. In 12 B.C. they became allies of Rome. They paid taxes in the form of cowhides; in A.D. 28 they revolted against the demands of the Rom. exploiters, which were becoming more and more excessive. In 47 they were subjugated again, by Corbulo; in 70 they supported Civilis (see BATAVI). The many Rom. coins found in Frisian mounds, bear witness to the lively trade.

FRONTINUS, Sextus Julius (c. 40-104). Lat. author; held various offices under Vespasian and Nerva. In addition to works on geology and strategy, which have been lost, he wrote: (a) *Strategematicon* (strategies), a handbook for Rom. officers, which is important for certain historical facts that have been inaccurately reported by other authors; (b) a work on Rom. waterworks that is instructive with regard to the technique of building aqueducts.

FRONTO, MARCUS CORNELIUS (c. 100-c. 166). Rom. orator; held office (consul in 143) under Antoninus Pius, Marcus Aurelius, and Verus. He acted as teacher of rhetoric to Marcus Aurelius. Their correspondence was found in the 19th cent. in two palimpsests. In those letters, F. tried in vain to persuade his pupil that rhetoric is more important than philosophy. This, however, had no effect on their warm friendship.

FRONTON. Another name for tympanum (see ARCHITECTURAL ORDERS).

G

GADES. Now Cadiz, in Spain. According to tradition, it was founded in 1110 B.C. by the Phoenician city of Tyre. In any case, in the 6th cent. B.C., it was a Phoenician trading post; it superseded the native Tartessus. Trade routes to the hinterland led from G. by way of Baetis (Guadalquivir) and overseas, at least as far as Britain (particularly for tin). Under the Carthaginians and the Romans the city continued to flourish.

GAIUS (2nd cent. A.D.) Rom. lawyer about whose personality almost nothing is known. In about 160 he wrote the *Institutes,* an excellent, concise abridgment of Rom. law. He was not greatly appreciated in his own time; he was valued all the more by Justinian. He also wrote juridical commentaries and other works.

GAIUS CAESAR. See CALIGULA.

GALANTIA. Country in central Asia Minor. It was named after a body of Gauls, a Celtic tribe, which had first roamed in Greece and Macedonia, plundering under the leadership of Brennus, had broken off from his army and invaded Asia Minor by way of the Hellespont in about 278 B.C. After they were defeated by Attalus I in 230, they settled permanently in this region, retaining their national Celtic character for many centuries. In 25 B.C. the country was made a Rom. province. The Apostle Paul addressed his *Epistle to the Gallatians* to the Christian communities in this area.

GALBA, SERVIUS SULPICIUS (5 B.C. -A.D. 69). Rom. emperor from June A.D. 68 to January, A.D. 69. He held high offices under Caligula and Claudius; was consul in 33, governor of northern Spain in 60. After the death of Nero he went to Rome with Otho and was proclaimed emperor. He wanted to be an emperor of the old school, but he incurred the hatred of the Praetorians by his miserliness—he refused to pay them a reward promised them in his name—and was hated by the people for his dislike of display. When G. adopted Piso as his son and heir—a man with the same qualities—Otho, who had counted on being the successor, had them murdered and was proclaimed emperor by the Praetorians. (Tac. *Hist.* I; Plut., *Galba;* see also YEAR OF THE THREE EMPERORS.)

GALEN (130-c. 201). The most celebrated physician in antiquity after Hippocrates. He came to Rome in 162, and became the court physician to Marcus Aurelius. Before he began to write medical textbooks, he devoted his time to philosophical studies. A monotheist, he believed his medical work served god. His theories on physiology and anatomy were the authority of medical science for many centuries. His doctrine of the four humors, blood, phlegm, choler (yellow bile), and melancholy (black bile)—on their mixture a person's temperament was said to be based—is well-known. The philosophical background of his theories can be seen clearly; compare, for example, the elements. See EMPEDOCLES.

GALERIUS VALERIUS MAXIMIANUS (c. 260-311). Rom. emperor from 305-311. In 293 Diocletian conferred on him, along with Constantius Chlorus, the title of "Caesar" and gave G. the governorship of Illyria. On the abdication of Diocletian (305), G. assumed the title of "Augustus." In 306, after the death of Constantius, G. hoped to become sovereign of the entire Rom. world, but Constantine (afterward Constantine the Great), the son of Constantius was acclaimed by the troups in Gaul and Britain in G.'s stead (see also MAXENTIUS). G. was known as a fanatical persecutor of the Christians.

GALLIA. Classified by the Romans into: (a) Gallia Cisalpina, northern Italy, especially the Po valley; (b) Gallia Transalpina, mainly what is now France and Belgium. (a) the Po valley was occupied at the end of the 5th cent. B.C. by the Celts (Gallatians), who marched to Rome (see ALLIA; BRENNUS; CAMILLUS), and were then pushed back further and further north. In the period between the First and Second Punic Wars, they were completely defeated by Rome, but became allies of Hannibal in 218. In the 2nd cent. B.C. they were conquered again, Rome founded several *coloniae* there; Sulla organized Gallia Cisalpina into a *provincia;* (b) Gallia Transalpina was divided into three parts by Caesar (*B.G.* I, 1): Aquitania, and territory of the Belgae, and G. in a narrower sense (central France and the Provence). The Provence (Lat. *provincia Narbonensis*) was the first to be occupied and colonized by Rome (end of the 2nd cent. B.C.) because in this region, Massilia (Marseille) had been friendly to Rome for a long time; a significant Hellenizing influence emanated from this city said to have been founded by Roman Greeks. After the Rom. conquest this area was thoroughly Romanized. Caesar later conquered the rest of G., between 58 and 51; Latin became the literary language, furthering the assimilation and helping to establish an entirely separate Gallo-Rom. culture there.

GALLIENUS. See MILITARY EMPERORS.

GAUGAMELA. Ancient village in northern Mesopotamia, where in 331 B.C. the army of Darius III was decisively defeated by Alexander the Great. The battle is sometimes erroneously called the battle of Arbela, a neighboring town.

GAUL. See GALLIA.

GELA. Gr. city on the south coast of Sicily, founded in 690 B.C. by colonists from Crete and Rhodes, mother city of Agrigentum. In about 500 B.C. it was the most powerful city in Sicily, under the tyrants Cleander and Hippocrates. Gelon relocated most of the population to Syracuse. After the people returned (466), G. flourished again until its destruction by the Carthaginians in 405, which was followed by a massacre organized by Agathocles (312); Aeschylus died in G. in 456 B.C.

GELLIUS, AULUS (2nd cent. A.D.) Rom.

author; held a judicial office in Rome. While on a visit to Athens to study philosophy, he collected material for his *Noctes Atticae* (*Attic Nights*) during the long winter evenings. It is a curious work, it contains excerpts from many Gr. and Lat. authors no longer extant. Although it has little literary merit, it is nevertheless valuable because it answers questions of historical and social interest.

GELON (c. 540-478). Tyrant of Gela and Syracuse; first a cavalry commander, later the successor to Hippocrates (see GELA). When the banished aristocracy of Syracuse asked for his help in 485, he became master of this city. In a very short time he made Syracuse the most prosperous and powerful city in the Gr. world; his power became even greater when he allied himself to Theron of Akragas (Agrigentum). When Xerxes attacked Greece, the allied Greeks asked for help from G. (Hdt. VII, 157-162). G., certainly aware of the fact that Carthage was preparing for war and caring little to leave his country, made conditions he knew would be unacceptable before he would render assistance: he was to be named chief general (Sparta refused), or commander of the fleet (this Athens refused). In 480 G. and Theron defeated the Carthaginians at Himera, while the Greeks in the motherland were defeating the Persians at Salamis. G. was hailed as the savior of the Gr. West.

GEMS. Engraved (intaglio) stones and stones cut in relief (cameo). Originally intaglios, the G. appeared already in Minoan-Mycenaean art. The designs had a naturalistic character (scenes of games, religious ceremonies) but became more and more abstract and stylized. Meanwhile this art form enjoyed a revival in the 7th-6th centuries B.C., when, influenced by the Egyptian scarab (sacred beetle), the G. took on oval form and borrowed their themes from oriental culture. Gr. mythological subjects were also represented. In the 5th-4th centuries B.C. scenes from daily life are found and, in the Hellenistic period, portraits as well. The G. from Roman imperial times are especially important to us for their portraits. Usually, the G. served as stones for signet rings (see POLYCRATES); later,

also as amulets and ornaments.

GENIUS. According to the Romans, a protecting spirit of every man (that of the woman was Juno); originally, the G. symbolized the power of reproduction, and continuity of the family and was worshiped particularly by the father (*pater familias*). On his birthday, sacrifices were made to his G. To revere the G. of another, or to swear by it, was a mark of profound respect. Eventually not only individuals, but also localities, communities, and even the entire Rom. people had a G. (*genius populi Romani*). The G. was often depicted as a snake (well-known symbol of life in antiquity).

GENS. [Lat. clan, tribe, family, race]. In Rom. society this term designated a group of families with a common ancestor. The middle of the three names borne by Romans was that of his G. The members of a G. were closely united; they made sacrifices to their ancestors, celebrated the same rituals, and helped one another in emergencies. Originally the properties of a G. were inalienably collective. Decisions were made by a council whose rulings all abided. About the 2nd cent. A.D. these traditions fell into disuse and the families became independent.

GEOMETRIC ART. Gr. art from the 10th-8th centuries B.C., in which linear motifs played a large part. A human or animal figure, for example, was built up from geometric forms (circle for the head, triangle for the torso, etc.). These characteristics are found in small bronzes, terra cottas, and other objects, but this art form in its highest development is mainly represented by Dipylon vases (named after the Dipylon gate of Athens where they were found). These vases combine all the elements of the style, particularly its cerebral-abstract aspect. For instance, a shroud does not cover the corpse, but is draped above him, so that both body and shroud may be seen; see also HORROR VACUI. The art reached its climax in the 8th cent. B.C. during Homer's time.

GERGOVIA. Capital of the Arverni near what is now Clermont-Ferrand, besieged in vain by Caesar in 52 B.C. (see VERCINGETORIX; Caes. *B.G.* VII, 32-53).

GERMANIA. For the Romans: (a) the

land on the right bank of the Rhine, outside the Rom. Empire; (b) the Rhine basin, mainly inhabited by Germans, and divided into two Rom. provinces in Augustus' time, G. Inferior, on the lower course, capital Colonia Agrippina, and G. Superior on the upper course, capital Mogontiacum (Mainz). An effort to conquer the area further to the east, up to the Elbe River, failed as a result of the battle of the Teutoburger Wald. The Germans were a constant threat to the Rom. Empire, even before the subjugation of Gaul (for example, the invasion of the Cimbri and the Teutons), but more so after Gaul had been conquered by Caesar; he was hindered by tribes that had invaded Gaul (see ARIOVISTUS) and he organized a few campaigns over the Rhine. The Rhine frontiers were later consolidated by the institution of the two provinces, and the construction of frontier fortifications (see LIMES). During the imperial period, whenever the vigilance of the legions was relaxed because of internal difficulties (the first time was during the Year of the Three Emperors), the threat from G. became acute (for the later invasions of the German tribes, see GOTHS; VANDALS; MARCOMANNI). About the independent G., the Romans knew comparatively little; Caesar and others made efforts to describe their institutions and mores (Caes. *B.G.* VI, 21-28 and Tach. *Germania*).

GERMANICUS, JULIUS CAESAR (15 B.C.-A.D. 19). Rom. general, son of Nero Claudius Drusus and husband of Agrippina the Elder, adopted son of his uncle Tiberius. By making great concessions, he quelled a mutiny among the legions along the Rhine after the latter's ascendance to the throne (A.D. 14). After that he led several expeditions across the Rhine; was then sent to the East by Tiberius to establish order there, who, at the same time, appointed Piso, who was always getting in G.'s way, proconsul of Syria. G. died at Antioch; it was generally believed that Piso had poisoned him. The relationship between Tiberius and G. was always strained; the Emperor was certainly jealous of the very popular young man who symbolized for the people the heroes of freedoms of the old Republic. Yet he had to concede his great capability, and it was logical that G. was the one to be appointed to do the difficult work of calming down the eastern provinces. It was typical of Tiberius' careful, suspicious attitude, that he sent Piso along as a watchdog. If it is correct that the latter poisoned G, Tiberius was indirectly responsible for G.'s death (Tac. *Ann.* I-II). G. is not only remembered as a great general but also as a cultured man; among other works, he translated *Phaenomena* of Aratus into Latin.

GERMANY. See GERMANIA.

GEROUSIA. See SPARTA.

GETA. See CARACALLA.

GLADIATORS. Swordsmen who fought to the death during Rom. games. The custom came from Etruria, where games of this type took place during funeral rites. In 264 B.C. they first appeared in Rome during the celebration of private funerals; later, c. 105 B.C., they took on the form of public amusement. These games were usually given by the magistrates (mainly aediles) to win favor with the populace, later by the emperor (see MORITURI TE SALUTAMUS). The G. were usually prisoners of war, slaves, or convicted criminals. They were instructed by a trainer (*lanista*) at a special school (*ludus*). The defeated man might be either spared or killed, depending on the mood of the people or the emperor. Seneca describes the demoralizing influence of this spectacle in a famous letter. (*Ep.* 7).

GNOSTICISM. The name given to a religious movement which arose outside the Christian Church in the 1st cent. A.D., soon entered the church, and reached its peak in the 2nd cent. It was a syncretistic philosophy, built on Jewish, Christian, and Eastern (pagan) ideas. The doctrine taught that emancipation came to the initiates through knowledge (gnosis) of the esoteric system.

GORDIANUS. See MILITARY EMPERORS.

GORDIUM. Capital of Phrygia, founded, according to legend, by Gordius, mythical king of Phrygia. The pole of his chariot was fastened with a skillfully devised knot. This, it was said, could only be untied by a future conqueror of the world. Alexander the Great cut it with his sword (334 B.C.); hence, figuratively speaking, a gordian knot is a complicated problem that can be overcome only by a bold action.

GORGIAS of Leontini (c. 480-380). Gr. orator and Sophist, founder of Gr. rhetoric art. He came to Athens in 427 B.C. and there excited the people by his eloquence. His style was oratorical, assonant, poetical, and lyrical; in his opinion, this made it possible for prose to compete with poetry. As a Sophist, he propagated skepticism, which can be seen by the title of his (lost) book, *On Nature, or on the Nonexistent* (an obvious polemic argument aimed at Parmenides); in this treatise he stated: (a) nothing exists; (b) if anything existed, it could not be known; (c) did anything exist, and could it be known, it could not be communicated.

GORGONS. See MASK; PERSEUS.

GORTYNA. Ancient city on the south coast of Crete, where an inscription of the city's legal code was discovered in 1884. The inscription has been dated c. 450 B.C., its contents, however, cover a period going back to the 7th cent. B.C. This inscription is our most important source for the knowledge of archaic Gr. law. The laws deal with penal and social matters, as well as with the tenure of land and slaves. It is interesting to note that slaves were permitted some rights of ownership and were even allowed to marry free women. There is also a prohibition against "playing the judge."

GOTHS. Germanic tribe, originally from southern Sweden (Götaland), which started to threaten the Rom. Empire in about A.D. 238. After they had been beaten by the Emperor Claudius II (see MILITARY EMPERORS), in about 269, they split into the Ostrogoths and Visigoths (East and West). These groups invaded the Rom. Empire successively. The Visigoths defeated Valens at Adrianopolis in 378, invaded Italy under Alaric, and finally settled in Spain and Gaul. The Ostrogoths, driven off their lands in southern Russia by the Huns, migrated to the West (see THEODORIC). The G. embraced Christianity.

GRACCHI. Members of the celebrated family of the *Sempronia gens.* Rom. social reformers in the second half of the 2nd cent. B.C., whose actions led to the quarrels between the *optimates* and the *populares* in the 1st cent. B.C.:

—(1) Gracchus, Tiberius Sempronius, son of Cornelia, the daughter of Scipio Major; educated according to the Gr. ideals of the "Scipionic Circle" (see LAELIUS), ideals which he wanted to uphold in the field of politics. On the way to Numantia, where he served under Scipio Minor, he is said to have seen the appalling conditions on the *latifundia;* when he returned he allowed himself to be elected *tribunus plebis* (133). Moved by the fate of the proletarians, he proposed a bill to renew and enforce an old agrarian law (the Licinian Rogations) which prohibited people from having more than a certain share of the *ager publicus;* the rest of the land was to be divided into small parcels, and rented to proletarians. G. proposed to divide the legacy of Attalus III among the poor—a violation of the senate's right to control finances and foreign relations. This infringement gave the senators who were big landowners a weapon against him. They persuaded one of G.'s fellow tribunes to pronounce his veto over the proposed law; G. then succeeded in getting the people to dismiss the other tribune (a revolutionary act), after this the law was passed by the *comitia tributa* but not enforced. When the time came for the election of the tribunes, G. wanted to be reelected (the senate declared this illegal), a riot followed, during which Scipio Nasica murdered G. Three hundred of his followers were also killed.

—(2) Gracchus Gaius Sempronius, brother of the preceding, was elected *tribunus plebis* in 123. He decided to avenge Tiberius and to promote the latter's plans even more energetically. His first act was to enforce his brother's agrarian law. More calculating and clever than his brother, he tried to weaken the power of the senators by driving a wedge between them and the wealthy nobility, which was soon to be known as the *equite* class. He allotted to the latter the right to farm the taxes in the newly established province of Asia and gave judicial offices of those courts which tried extortion cases, to members of the *equites.* He first won the people's acclaim by passing a law for the sale of grain at reduced prices and then decided to execute his extensive plan to found farming colonies in Italy as well as outside of Italy, especially on the lands of Carthage, destroyed in 146. The senate opposed this plan and was able to get another tribune, Marcus Livius Drusus, to veto the plans. Drusus offered the people more than G., and the latter's popularity began to wane during his second tribunate (since his brother's death, re-election had become possible). A proposal to give Rom. citizenship to the *socii* as a compensation for land they had to yield, was voted down by the short-sighted populace. G. ran for office a third time, but in vain. Serious rioting broke out; the senate proclaimed the *senatus consultum ultimum* (see CAVEANT CONSULES) for the first time; while fleeing, G. was killed by a slave who then took his own life (121). Many of G's followers were hounded to death.

The actions of the G., those of Tiberius with more idealistic, those of Gaius with more political motives, had unforeseeable consequences. Both recognized the profoundness of the existing social evils in Rome and Italy, but the time was not ripe for combating them effectively, certainly not against the egotistical opposition of the *optimates*. Many of their aims were not to be realized until imperial times: Rome was first to go through the trials of the Civil Wars, to which the G. also gave impetus. They proved, however, that it was possible to attack the oligarchy of the *nobiles* through political agitation. One big difference between their social politics and those of the later emperors existed. Gaius, for example, without a scruple, threw the population of the province (Asia) to the wolves, in order to help the Rom. proletarians. Moreover, there was no question of socializing private property; only land was involved, which was already state-owned. It is incorrect to consider the G. prototypes of socialists, as has occasionally been done.

GRAECIA MAGNA. See MAGNA GRAECIA.

GRANICUS. Small river in northwestern Asia Minor, emptying into the Hellespont; place where Alexander the Great won his first victory over the Persians after his crossing to Asia (334 B.C.).

GRATIANUS, FLAVIUS AUGUSTUS (359-383). Rom. emperor, son of Valentinian I. He ruled in the West after 375, alongside of Valens in the East; held a beautiful court in Trier (Trèves), where the poet Ausonius worked.

GRATTIUS FALISCUS. Author of a poem in 540 hexameters, on hunting (*Cynegetica*); contemporary with Ovid. The poem describes methods of hunting, the best breeds of horses and dogs, and various species of game.

GREECE. See HELLAS.

GUTTA CAVAT LAPIDEM, CONSUMITUR ANULUS USO. "The droplet hollows the stone, the ring is worn out by use." (Ov. *Ep. ex Pont.* IV, 10, 5).

GYGES. King of Lydia from about 685-657, the first ruler to be called *tyrannos* (see TYRANT). He came into power by murdering his predecessor Candaules, and then married his widow. A legend (related by Plato, Cicero, and others) says that he possessed a magic ring, with which he was able to make himself invisible; that is how he is said to have taken Candaules by surprise. It was in his reign that coinage began; soon afterward to be introduced in Greece (see COINAGE). He was the first Lydian king to attack the cities of Ionia.

GYLIPPUS. Spartan general. During the Athenian invasion in 415 B.C., he was sent to the aid of Syracuse. The defeat of Athens can be mainly attributed to his talent for organization.

GYMNASIUM. Gr. school of sports, often situated outside the city, near a sanctuary. It had training fields for various sports; usually there was also an adjoining palaestra (wrestling arena). A G. was used for exercises by the *ephebi* during their two years of military training. There also were rooms or halls for conversation and discussion where philosophers often taught. The three great gymnasia of Athens were the Academy, where Plato taught; the Lyceum, frequented by Aristotle; and the Cynosarges. The professional trainers were called: *paidotribes,* the head was the *gymnasiarchos.* Exercises were under the direction of *gymnastae.* The young men's conduct was supervised by *sophronistae* (in Athens ten in number, elected annually).

During the Hellenistic period, participation in the life in a G. was a mark of Gr. civilization, especially in the East. The Greeks in Egypt and in Syria proudly called themselves "those of the G." to distinguish themselves from the native population. The prudish Easterners did not approve of the Greeks' custom of exercising and playing games naked.

H

HABENT SUA FATA LIBELLI. "Books have their own [strange] adventures": Terentianus Maurus (2nd cent. A.D.) in his work *De Litteris, Syllabis, Metris*.

HADES. Among the Greeks, the underworld, the realm of the dead. It was ruled by a king (also called Hades, Minos, or Pluto) and by Persephone (Kore). The Greeks pictured H. as a gloomy and unpleasant place but later the influence of the mysteries becomes apparent (see ELYSIUM). In Orphism the thought of reward and punishment in the abode after death became a dogma. The principal description of H. can be found in the *Odyssey*. Later, in his *Aeneid* (VI), Virgil developed a completely new concept. The Romans called this underworld Orcus, Dis (also a name for Pluto), and poetically, Avernus.

HADRIANUS, PUBLIUS AELIUS (76-138), commonly called Hadrian. Rom. emperor, one of the adoptive emperors. Adopted by Trajan, he accompanied him on his campaigns; in 117 he succeeded him. H. strove to preserve peace with foreign nations and spent the greater part of his reign traveling through the provinces of the empire in order to consolidate the frontiers. Consequently he abandoned several of Trajan's conquests. Four influential ex-consuls—displeased with H.'s course of action in this respect—conspired against him while he was in Dacia. The four were killed by order of the senate.

H. also visited the Netherlands, crossing from there over to Britain; the wall he had erected there bears his name. On a visit to Egypt H.'s favorite, Antinous, was drowned (see ANTINOUS). In Judea, H. lacked judgment with regard to his peace policy by having a temple of Jupiter built and by establishing a Rom. colony by the name of Aelia Capitolina on the ruins of Jerusalem, previously destroyed by Titus. The result was a revolt of the Jews (132-135).

H. was a highly literate and artistic man, with a great love of Gr. culture. He enriched Athens with lovely buildings: library, completion of the temple of Olympian Zeus, the Olympieum (for his activities in the field of law, see SALVIUS JULIANUS). From 131-138 he lived in Rome, in peace and quiet, devoting himself to the centralization of the federal government. He adopted Antoninus Pius as his successor. His mausoleum in Rome forms the foundation of the present-day castle of St. Angelo. H.'s villa, the famous country seat near Tibur has been excavated; numerous works of ancient art have been found.

HAGIA TRIADA (Holy Trinity). The present name of a place near the south coast of Crete, where a Minoan palace has been excavated. One of the most important finds is a sarcophagus, on which a tree cult is depicted; this is one of the main sources of our knowledge concerning Minoan religion (see also MYCENAE).

HAIR STYLES. As a rule, Gr. women dressed their hair simply; a center part with a bun at the nape of the neck, sometimes tight tresses above the ears also. The very elaborate hair style of patrician ladies, with row upon row of curls, did not become fashionable until the Rom. imperial period. Gr. men originally wore their hair in long locks (Homer refers to the "long hair wearing Achaeans"); only slaves were required to cut their hair short. In about 550 B.C., a shorter cut came into style, the hair being combed forward from the crown, and then back over the ears. See App.

HALICARNASSUS. City in Caria, birthplace of Herodotus; colonized in about 1000 B.C. by Greeks from Argolis; the population retaining a strong Carian character. In the 6th cent., tyrants reigned, among them Princess Artemisia, who accompanied Xerxes in 480 B.C. and commanded a contingent of the fleet at Salamis. She advised Xerxes to beat his hasty retreat. In the 5th cent., H. was a member of the Delian League (for the later history see MAUSOLEUM).

HALYS (Kizil Irmak). Large river, flowing through central Asia Minor and emptying into the Black Sea. In Croesus' time, it was the boundary between Lydia and Persia (Hdt. I, 72), therefore, when Croesus crossed the H., it signified aggression toward Persia.

HAMILCAR BARCA (or BARCAS). Carthaginian general in the First Punic War. He directed the expedition against Sicily, which was then almost entirely in the hands of the Romans. Victorious at Drepanum, but defeated at Panormus and in the Aegadian Islands in 242 B.C., he negotiated a peace in 241. Although he was forced to abandon Sicily to the Romans, he refused to consider himself beaten. Recalled to Carthage to quell a revolt by his mercenaries, his anger mounted when Rome, exploiting Carthage's weakness, grabbed Sardinia and Corsica. After crushing the revolt, H., on his own responsibility, undertook with his son Hannibal, the conquest of Spain. H. doubtlessly felt the need to thus compensate for the losses sustained. By insinuating arbitrarily that the Carthaginians were also preparing for an act of aggression against Italy, Rome paved the way for the Second Punic War. H. remained in Spain for eight years, securing extensive territories. In 228 he drowned in the course of a campaign.

HANNIBAL (246-182). Carthaginian general, son of Hamilcar; followed his father to Spain, where he succeeded his brother-in-law Hasdrubal (1) as commander in chief of the army in 221. He attacked Saguntum, which, situated south of the Ebro, was not under the protection of the treaty which had been made between Hasdrubal and the Romans. It had, however, concluded an alliance with the Romans, who considered the attack a violation of this treaty. H.'s action thus precipitated the Second Punic War. Rome's plan to attack Africa was foiled by H.'s fast action; Rome could not finish its preparations. In 218, at the head of an army of 40,000 men, well-trained and organized, and employing elephants in warfare for the first time, H. crossed the Pyrenees, the Rhône, and finally the Alps. He made this crossing near the narrow St. Bernard Pass, a route which, even today, is considered difficult. Arriving in Gallia Cisalpina, his army shrunk to half its size, it soon regained strength through an alliance with the Gauls. In 218 H. defeated the Romans during the battle of Trebia and in 217 at Lake Trasimenus; the road to Rome seemed open. However, he followed a different strategy: he counted on getting the Roman *socii* to side with him, thus forcing Rome to capitulate. For the present, that failed. Quintus Fabius Maximus Cuntator avoided a direct battle for the rest of that year in order to gain time to consolidate the Rom. forces. After the battle of Cannae many cities in the south of Italy, led by Capua and Tarentum, allied themselves with H.; but central Italy remained loyal to Rome, which recovered and defended itself energetically on three fronts: Italy (Marcellus), Spain (Scipio) and Greece (against Philip V). Capua and Tarentum were reconquered and H. was forced far back into southern Italy. His brother Hasdrubal (2), who came to his aid with an army from Spain, was defeated at the Metaurus River. When Scipio Major invaded Africa on a daring expedition and attacked Carthage while H. was still in Italy, he was recalled by the Carthaginian government and defeated at Zama in 202. This defeat marked the end of the Second Punic War. Carthage was forced to accept a humiliating peace: the loss of Spain, Sicily, and the greater part of her fleet. After the war, H. tried to reorganize his country by enforcing constitutional reforms, which were a thorn in the side of the Carthaginian oligarchs. They slandered him in Rome and H. fled to the Court of Antioch III of Syria who was about to go to war against Rome. When the latter, too, had been defeated (190), and Rome demanded H.'s surrender, he fled to Prussia's king of Bithynia, and committed suicide when Prussia could not resist the demand that he be handed over to the Rom. ambassador (see FLAMININUS).

HARMODIUS AND ARISTOGITON. Athenian youths who conspired to kill Hippias and Hipparchus in 514 B.C. Only the latter was killed, and Hippias then really became a "tyrant" in the present sense of the word. When Hippias was expelled four years later, the Athenians regarded the pair as patriots—their names were toasted in drinking songs (*scolia*)—their descendants also were publicly honored.

HARPALUS (c. 355-323). A Macedonian; appointed receiver-general in charge of the treasury, and administrator of the satrapy of Babylon by Alexander the Great. Having embezzled considerable sums, H. absconded to Greece in 325. Allegedly, he bribed Demosthenes in Athens to support him aganist Alexander and his viceregent Antipater. H. fled to Crete and was murdered there.

HARUSPICES. Roman soothsayers, whose function it was to interpret the future from the internal organs (particularly livers) of sacrificial animals, *prodigia* (see also DECEMVIRI), and lightning flashes. Their craft originated in Etruria and the East (the Hittites and Babylonians also inspected entrails to ascertain the divine will).

HASDRUBAL. Name of:
—(1) Son-in-law of Hamilcar and his successor as commander in chief of the army in Spain (228 B.C.); he founded Carthago Nova and concluded the so-called Ebro treaty with Rome (see HIBERIUS).
—(2) Brother of Hannibal, who was left in command in Spain when Hannibal set out for Italy (218 B.C.); H. defeated Pub-

lius and Gnaeus Scipio in 212, and both fell in battle. A new Rom. military commander, Scipio Major, was victorious and H. was compelled to leave Spain. In 207 he went to Italy to help his brother. His messengers, sent ahead to Hannibal, fell into his hands of the Rom. consul Gaius Claudius Nero who, assisted by his fellow consul Livius Salinator, defeated him at the Metaurus River. His army was destroyed and H. was killed.
—(3) The son of Gisco, commander in Spain 214-206; also fought against Scipio Major in Africa.
—(4) The defender of Carthage in the Third Punic War, surrendered unconditionally to Scipio Minor in 146 B.C.

HEBE. Gr. goddess of youth. She married Heracles after he had taken his place among the gods. She was the handmaiden of the gods on Mount Olympus, filling their cups with nectar.

HECATAEUS of Miletus (c. 500 B.C.). Gr. genealogist and geographer. He was one of a group of logographers and took part in the Ionian revolution of 500-494. Well aware of the inexhaustible resources of the Persian empire, he pointed out the risks of the undertaking to the Ionians. He made long journeys to Europe and Asia, as well as to Egypt, and gave interesting descriptions of countries and people. Herodotus consulted his works, although he criticized them severely. The opening words of his works on genealogy reflect Ionian thought during this enlightened period: "I, Hecataeus, describe things the way I think they are; for the many tales of the Greeks, are only nonsense." Numerous fragments of his works have been preserved.

HECATE. Gr. goddess with power over sky, earth, and sea. In later times she was confused with Persephone who invoked ghosts from the underworld. Her statue with three bodies and three faces (one for each of the phases of the new moon) was placed at crossroads, especially where three roads met. Hence her Lat. name Trivia (having three ways).

HECATOMB [Gr. *hekatombē*]. Sacrifice of 100 oxen or cattle at one time; hence in modern usage, a great slaughter.

HECATOMPEDON. Ancient temple of Athena on the Acropolis in Athens, exactly 100 ft. long. Built by order of Pisistratus in the 6th cent. B.C., it was later replaced by the Parthenon. Fragments of sculptures (polychromed limestone) have been found.

HECTOR. See TROJAN WAR.

HELENA. See TROJAN WAR; STESICHORUS; EURIPIDES.

HELIAEA. Peoples' court in Athens, established by Solon; it became the authority in place of the Areopagus in 462 B.C. (see EPHIALTES). There were 6,000 *Heliastae,* or members of the court, or jurors; 600 being taken from each tribe (*phylae*). In some instances only a part of a division would try a case; in important trials more members served.

HELICON. Mountain in Boeotia; thought by ancient Greeks to be the abode of Apollo and the Muses. The famous springs Aganippe and Hippocrene flowed here. The city of Ascra lay on its slopes.

HELIOGABALUS. See ELAGABALUS.

HELIOPOLIS. Gr. name for the modern Baalbek, city of Syria; in ancient times seat of the worship of Baal, whose symbol was the sun. (In Gr. mythology: Helios, the god of the sun.) The population of H. was mostly Greek. The temples, particularly the one of Jupiter Heliopolitanus, built under Antoninus Pius and Caracalla (H. was a Rom. colony from the time of Augustus), are an impressive monument to Rom.-Hellenistic architecture. See Appendix.

HELIOS. The Gr. sun-god. In his cult, celebrated primarily in Rhodes, the sun itself was worshiped, not an anthropomorphic god. Much later H. was given human form on decorated vases where he is depicted in his chariot circling the heavens. People also swore by H. who "sees and hears everything." In the Hellenistic period and especially in Rom. times, under the influence of Eastern rites, the sun cult saw a marked revival, although by then Apollo was identified with the sun. During the Rom. imperial period, *Sol Invictus* (see ELAGABALUS) was worshiped.

HELLADIC CULTURE. The Bronze Age culture of the Gr. mainland (as opposed to the Minoan culture of Crete, and the Mycenaean culture in general) lasting from about 2500-1100 B.C.

HELLANICUS of Mytilene (5th cent. B.C.). Gr. logographer, precursor of the *Atthidographi.* Along with a work on Attic history, he wrote on mythology and attempted to write in chronological order the ancient history of other cities.

HELLAS. Originally this name only designated a district in Thessaly, later all of central Greece (to the north of the Isthmus of Corinth), still later, it was applied to Greece itself); today it is still the name the Greeks use for their country. The word Greeks comes from the Rom. *Graeci,* derived from *Graikoi,* a tribe of western Greece. The history of H. in ancient times, is described in this volume under the various entries; see particularly MYCENAE; ATHENS; SPARTA; CORINTH; THEBES; IONIA(NS); TYRANT; PERSIAN EMPIRE; PELOPONNESIAN WAR; DELIAN LEAGUE; PANHELLENISM; PHILIP II; ALEXANDER THE GREAT; POLIS; HELLENISM.

HELLENISM. In its narrow application, the civilization beginning with Alexander the Great and ending with Cleopatra, covering about the 3rd-1st centuries B.C. During that period, the Greeks spread into the areas that had formerly been part of the Persian empire, and brought their culture to places pervaded with the civilization of the ancient Near East. This was simplified by the opening of new trade routes (see, for example, NEARCHUS) and particularly by founding many cities in the East, which was first done by Alexander himself, later by the Seleucids (see ALEXANDRIA; ANTIOCH; APAMEA; SELEUCIA). In a broader sense, H. means the spread of influence of Greek civilization in general. In this sense, the innate characteristics of H. can already be noted in the 4th cent. B.C., in the secularization of the plastic arts (see PRAXITELES) and the loss of interest in idea of the polis (see also PANHELLENIC IDEA; EPAMINONDAS). H. continued to spread well past the 1st cent. B.C., mainly in the direction of the West, where Gr. cultural influences had already been felt since the colonization in the 8th-6th centuries. In this broader sense, a large part of the civilization in the Rom. Empire including the Latin speaking West, was reached by H. And it was precisely by way of Hellenized Rome that Gr. civilization and Gr.

ideas invaded western Europe, even before the fall of Constantinople (1453) caused the Byzantine scholars to flee to the West, where they were to introduce a new and direct interest in Gr. civilization.

However, if we confine ourselves to H. in its limited meaning, we see the first period (c. 325-170) marked by the advance of Gr. culture in the East, followed by a powerful counteroffensive of Eastern nationalism, which was expressed, among other ways, in riots among the natives in the empire of the Ptolemies, by the revolt of the Maccabees in Palestine (see ANTIOCHUS IV), and by the invasion of the Parthians. Still, the influence of Gr. civilization had taken deep roots, particularly in Syria and Asia Minor—it was no longer possible to uproot it. This H., in the Near East and in ancient Macedonia and Greece itself, had an aspect of its own. This can be seen particularly regarding man's place in society. The Greek had moved out of the closed circle of the polis into a larger environment and had lost many of his old traditions; even if he lived in the East, in what was called a polis, it was no longer the autonomous city-state of classic Hellas. The most typical characteristics of H. are said to be its cosmopolitanism and individualism. The latter particularly, the being forced back on one's self and one's own family circle, is manifested in art: interest in the individual—the playing child, the portrait. This is accompanied with a tendency toward pathos (the "Laocoön" group, the "Dying Gaul," the latter a sculpture in honor of Attalus' victory over the Gauls; see also FRIEZE; PERGAMUM); in literature we have the New Comedy with its emphasis on middle-class subjects. In philosophy we note that attention is paid to personal spiritual welfare (see EPICURUS; STOICS; CYNICS); the same holds true for religion, in the mysteries (see also ISIS; MITHRAS).

Of the many aspects of H. we will discuss one more fully: the form of government. It was a *monarchy,* but an entirely new type. The Macedonian-Gr. rulers of the Hellenistic empires had been called "king." The Greeks had always known kings of other peoples in addition to their own royal house before it was abolished. No one ever spoke of the king "of Macedonia," "of Thrace," etc., but always of "king *of the Macedonians,*" etc. (the way we use the term "king of the Belgians"). There was one exception: the Persian ruler was always called "The King" or "The Great King." What were the new-style kings in Alexandria, Antioch, etc. to be called? The ancient Macedonian dynastic names could not be applied, nor was, for example, "King of the Egyptians" suitable in places where their privileged subjects were Macedonians and Greeks. The solution was sought in a purely personal royalty, with whom each subject, Greek or Jew, Syrian or Lydian, could have his own relationship. This ideology of a personal king contains a mystical and religious element, reflected in the surnames with religious content like "savior" or "benefactor." At first glance, it is curious that it was the Greeks who accepted this personal deification of the ruler easily enough. It becomes less surprising if one remembers how, in ancient Greece, leaders were also heroized (see HEROES) during their lifetime (Brasidas, Lysander, the founders of colonies). Generally, it may be said that the idea that king*ship* is sacred originated mainly in the East, but the idea that the *king* is sacred came largely from Greece.

This leads to the following conclusion: H. used to be described mainly as a mutual penetration of Gr. and Eastern elements. At the present time, we are more inclined to consider the Gr. element predominant, although it is evident that Eastern elements can be detected in certain areas, especially in religion (mysteries) and philosophy (Stoicism), perhaps also in the development of a powerful bureaucracy.

HELLESPONT. The ancient name for the Dardanelles. The cities on the H. (particularly Troy in the Mycenaean period, later Sestos, Abydos, etc.) profited from the abundance of fish in the waters, and above all, from the heavy traffic between the Aegean and the Black Sea.

HELOTS. See SPARTA.

HELVETII. Celtic tribe, which migrated

from South Germany to what is now the north of Switzerland in about 200 B.C. Some segments of the tribe took part in the invasion of the Cimbri. In 58 B.C. they went to Gaul en masse, but were driven back by Caesar at Bibracte—those who survived went back to their own country. Because they had opposed Vitellius, Vespasian granted them special privileges. For this reason they enjoyed a period of prosperity beginning with A.D. 70.

HENNA. Ancient site of principal temple of Demeter (Ceres) and, in mythology, her birthplace; headquarters of slaves in First Servile War (132 B.C.).

HEPHAESTUS. Gr. god of fire, metallurgy, and pottery-making. Among the myths in which he plays a part is the birth of Athena and the birth of Erechtheus, who claimed H. for his father, and whom the Athenians considered as their ancestor. The Romans identified H. with Vulcanus.

HERA. Gr. goddess of marriage. Three towns were said to have been her favorites—Argos, Sparta, and Mycenae. Her cult flourished in Argos before the Gr. invasion; her name is probably pre-Hellenic also. She was worshiped in Samos, and in Olympia remains of her temple—the oldest Gr. temple yet found —have been preserved. The Romans identified her with Juno, ancient Italian protectress of women (see GENIUS).

HERACLES [Lat. Hercules]. The most celebrated of Gr. heroes. He had to perform twelve labors for Eurystheus, king of Mycenae, by command of the Delphic oracle. The tales of his heroic deeds lead to the supposition that H. was originally a historical figure who, like Perseus, for example, goes back to the Mycenaean period. In that case, he is certainly a composite of different figures, probably also of lesser gods. In his cult he was worshiped partly as a hero, partly as an Olympian deity (see COMMODUS). The most ancient representation of his labors are the metopes of the temple of Zeus in Olympia.

HERACLITUS of Ephesus (c. 535-475). Gr. philosopher; descendant of a royal family. Author of a work on nature, which, to judge from the fragments extant, consisted of aphorisms. Already in antiquity, his proverbs were famous for their obscurity, which earned him the surname of *skoteinos* (obscure). Unfortunately, we do not possess the complete work of which these fragments are a part, and so cannot determine whether his pronouncements were part of his positive doctrine, or intended to be haughty criticism aimed at others—philosophers, poets, and authors. He certainly criticized all sides: "being knowledgeable does not educate the mind," he writes, "otherwise, it would have educated Hesiod and Pythagoras, Xenophanes and Hecataeus." On the contrary, according to H., one must find *logos* (reason) through self-examination—the imminent truth, the fundamental principle on which the universe is based, is found in one's own mind. His most violent criticism was of the Eleatics, particularly Parmenides; he set the latter's monism against his own doctrine of constant change in nature. "Everything flows (*panta rhei*) and nothing remains constant, and one cannot step into the same river twice," is his most famous proverb. "War is the father of all." Peaceloving souls reproached H. for this concept, but by "war" he meant "struggle"—the clash of opposing principles; nature only comes to life through tension, as a bow derives its propellent force from the opposing stresses of string and horn.

Like the Milesians (Thales, Anaximander, Anaximenes), H. sought an ultimate principle on which all existence is founded. This element he believed to be fire. Fire is the always present dynamic principle—it periodically consumes the universe, which renews itself each time. Later, the Stoics adapted this doctrine to their teachings.

HERCULANEUM. City at the foot of Mount Vesuvius, inhabited by the Osci, Etruscans, and Samnites, but strongly under the influence of the Greeks (who probably came by way of Neapolis in the 6th cent. B.C.); in 307 B.C. it came under Rom. rule. H. was ravaged by an earthquake in A.D. 63, and was destroyed in 79, along with Pompeii, by an eruption of Vesuvius; both cities were completely buried under ash and mud. H. has been systematically excavated since the 18th and particularly the 19th centuries and it was seen that H. was built according to a much more regular plan than Pompeii, and that it was also more of a residential city; the commercial characteristics of Pompeii are lacking. Luxurious houses, a basilica, and a theater have been found there.

HERCULES. See HERACLES.

HERMAE. Name given to stone pillars surmounted by a bust of the god Hermes; many hermae were placed in streets and squares, especially in Athens. In 415 B.C. a number of H. were mutilated and this sacrilege was attributed to Alcibiades. Later, H. were also crowned with busts of other deities and eventually with those of celebrated persons, for instance, poets and philosophers. A famous herm, sculptured by Alcamenes, was set up in the Propylaea.

HERMES [Lat. Mercurius]. Gr. god of flocks, commerce, invention, and athletics; patron of roads and travelers, as well as thieves. In Arcadia, the original seat of his cult, he was a pastoral god, and is thus described in the *Iliad*. In the *Odyssey,* however, he is depicted as the messenger of the gods, and the conductor of the shades of the dead to Hades. As a messenger he became the god of roads and protector of travelers. In many places he was worshipped also as the god of mining. The pillars raised in his honor (see HERMAE) originally were ungainly heaps of stones at crossroads to which each passing traveler added a stone. A lucky find was considered his gift and call *hermaion.* His statues were common in the stadia and gymnasia. The most famous statue of H. is the one by Praxiteles.

HERMOCRATES (5th cent. B.C.). Statesman and strategist of Syracuse. In 424 B.C. he opposed the efforts of the Athenians to gain influence in Sicily. In 415-413 he and Gylippus fought the Athenian invasion, causing the defeat of the Athenian army. On Sparta's side, he participated in the Peloponnesian War, commanding a Syracusan fleet which was sunk near Cyzicus in 410 (see ALCIBIADES). H. was exiled from Syracuse and was killed in 407 during an effort to return. H.'s greatness lies mainly in his efforts (especially during a conference in Gela in 424, see above) to unify the Gr. cities on Sicily. It is true that the endless squabbles between these cities were the main cause of their weakness, toward the Carthaginians as well as other invaders, and later, toward the Romans.

HERMUS. Important river in Lydia. Magnesia and Sipylum, among other places, were situated on its bank. Next to the Maeander, it was the most important route connecting Ionia with its hinterland, Caria and Lycia.

HERODAS (or HERONDAS) (3rd cent. B.C.). Gr. poet of mimiambi (mimes, written in so-called iambic scazons). Eight of them have been found almost intact on a papyrus; popular types are sketched in a masterly way.

HERODES. Name of:
—(1) H. the Great. Commonly called Herod. King of Judaea (73-4 B.C.); appointed proconsul of Galilee in 47, king of the Jews under Rom. domination; in 37. With Rom. support, he held his own against the last of the Maccabees (see ANTIOCHUS IV) and the other native aristocrats. His government was effective, but tyrannical; the Jews considered him to be a stranger, and despised his efforts at Hellenization.
—(2) H. Antipas, son of the preceding (the H. of the Gospels), ruled from 4 B.C. to A.D. 39. He was appointed tetrarch (that is, vassal king) by Augustus, was a favorite of Tiberius; dethroned by Caligula, when he claimed the title of king.
—(3) H. Atticus of Marathon (101-177). Gr. orator and author of works on philosophy. He taught elocution in Athens and Rome, was highly esteemed and very rich. The remains of buildings he had constructed can be found in every center of culture in Greece; in Athens, the odeum, which bears his name, on the slopes of the Acropolis, is now being used for the presentation of Gr. dramas —the theater of Dionysus is too dilapidated to be useable.

HERODIANUS. Name of:
—(1) Gr. historian (3rd cent. A.D.). He wrote a history of the Rom. emperors

from the death of Marcus Aurelius to the accession of Gordianus III (180-238).
—(2) Aelius H., Gr. grammarian from Alexandria (2nd cent. A.D.), son of Apollonius Dyscolus. He worked in Rome under Marcus Aurelius and wrote more than thirty works on grammar, two of which have been preserved along with fragments of other books. He was mainly an authority on the patterns of Gr. accents.

HERODOTUS (c. 485-c. 425). Gr. historian; born in Halicarnassus, where the educated classes lived in an atmosphere of Ionian culture, although it was a Dorian city. As a result of civil strife, H. took refuge in Samos, point of departure for many of his extensive trips which took him to Egypt, Libya, Mesopotamia, the south of Russia, and other regions. In about 455 he went to Athens, where he was befriended by Pericles and Sophocles; here, he recited excerpts of his works in public, and had great success. In 444-3 he took part in the founding of Thurii. He settled in this colony, made several more journeys to the Gr. West, returned to Thurii and died there. It is most probable that there he formed the material he had collected into a single work, but whether it was finished or not is a matter of opinion. He may easily have intended the abrupt ending. But then again, the fact that in a certain place a reference to a digression occurs which cannot be found in this work could imply that a fragment may well have been lost.

The work was certainly written in sections, and divided into episodes (logoi, stories) by H. himself. The Alexandrine scholars later classified it into nine books, which were given the names of the Muses in the 2nd cent. A.D. The subject, interesting for its grand concept, covers the history of the Persian Wars (see PERSIAN EMPIRE) from 500 (the Ionian revolt) to 478 (the taking of Sestos). H. sees this conflict as a drama, a world-shaking clash between Hellenes and barbarians, of which he wants to give a historiès apodexis (publication of his historical investigation) for posterity. His many journeys made it possible for him to see this conflict not as an isolated event, but as the final drama of the age-old struggle between the East and the West. Almost half of his work is taken up by the history that preceded these wars, starting in mythical times. Whenever a people that played a part in the conflict (or in the history preceding it) is mentioned, an extensive historical and ethnological digression follows (for example, the entire second book on Egypt). It is evident that H. possesses the inquiring mind so characteristic of the Greeks, and the Ionians in particular, the curiosity that continually makes him ask "why." It is no accident that he chooses as the main theme in his introduction the question of the causes of the entire conflict with Persia. The many digressions only appear as unmethodical work to the casual reader; more profound study shows them to have their own place in an organic unity.

H. is a master storyteller. His dramatic concept of the entity, as well as the composition of the separate stories, make it understandable that his listeners were spellbound. His style, too (the so-called lexis eiromenè, strung-together narrative style) is a typical storyteller's style. H.'s language is literary Ionian, because of his origin and because Ionian had been the language of the ethnographic genre since Hecataeus. H. had a warm and sensitive personality; he deeply believed in the justice of the gods; his belief in the "anger of the gods," which knocks down proud mortals, is very striking, as is also his theory of the punishment of hybris. He sincerely tried to relate the truth, but did not always succeed, because of his great credulity. He also often tried to evaluate various accounts, and to choose the most trustworthy one. But his methods were not based on research; Thucydides was to become the first scientific historian; but H. can still be called, in Cicero's words (De leg. I, 1, 5), "the father of history."

HEROES. For the Greeks, beings who held a place between gods and mortals. The hero cult originated in the death cult, because certain illustrious dead were honored not only by their families, but by whole tribes or cities. Sacrifices were brought to their graves, and they were thought to have influence on prosperity and fertility. The sacrifices were about the same kind given the chthonian gods (underworld gods from *chthon,* earth), namely black sacrificial animals, burned entirely, not only certain parts. The hero cult started in the Mycenaean period and was practiced extensively during classical times. Homer, however, does not mention it at all; the word *heros* in the epos means "hero" or "nobleman" in the modern sense; the reason for this may be that the Ionian nobility scorned this earthy cult, which was practiced more in rural circles and by the general population. There were three main groups of H.: the real ancestors (princes, etc.), fictive ancestors, and gods reduced to a lower rank. Transitives between H. and gods were, for example, Heracles, Asklepios, and Dionysus. Mythology generally regards H. as children of gods; thus they can be called "demigods" in mythological terminology.

HERON of Alexandria. Gr. mathematician and technician. His date of birth has not been definitely established; it is usually placed between the 2nd cent. B.C. and the 3rd cent. A.D. Author of many works, mainly on mechanical contrivances operated by water, steam, or compressed air; among them a "coin automat" and a hydraulic organ.

HEROSTRATUS. Citizen of Ephesus who set fire to the temple of Artemis in 356 B.C., because he wanted to become famous. He succeeded, but only through the coincidence that Alexander the Great was born that same night.

HESIOD (8th cent. B.C.). Gr. poet who, with his father and his older brother, Perses, emigrated from Aeolis (N.W. Asia Minor) to Ascra in Boeotia. After his father's death, Perses, having bribed corrupt judges, was awarded his brother's share of the patrimony, an injustice which prompted H. to write *Works and Days.* This work consists of myths and fables, interspersed with exhortations to his brother that wealth should not be gained by trickery but by honest labor. H. also lays down precepts for agriculture and other fields, for instance, navigation, and specifies the days for special tasks. He was the first Gr. poet to ex-

pound his personal views. His other principal work is the *Theogony,* an account of the origin of the world and the gods. Other writings, including the *Shield of Heracles,* of which only fragments have survived, are erroneously attributed to him. H., who employs the hexameter, is classed as a didactic poet, even though his work often approaches the epic—like epic poetry, it also includes religious subjects. H. writes about the justice of the gods in which he firmly believes.

HESTIA. The Gr. goddess of the hearth. Although mythology regards her a sister of Zeus, she was insignificant, and hardly anthropomorphous; she had few, if any, temples. Her altars were placed in sanctuaries of other gods and she was worshiped within the family circle. The cult of her Rom. counterpart, Vesta, was much more important.

HESYCHIUS of Alexandria (5th cent. A.D.). Gr. lexicographer. His lexicon is an inexhaustible source for our knowledge of Gr. dialects and proverbs.

HETAERAE [Gr. *hetairai*]. Women courtesans or concubines mainly of Athens, who because of their culture and education, enjoyed great social standing and frequently attracted men of eminence. The Greeks did not often find in their own home the intellectual equivalent of the H. due to the secluded life enforced on the legitimate wives (see MARRIAGE). Famous H. were: Aspasia, Rhodopis, Thais, and Phryne, who was Apelles' model.

HETAERI [Gr. *hetairoi,* companions]. A privileged class, especially of noble landowners in Macedonia, who served as lifeguards of the king. In the army of Alexander the Great, H. formed a special guard.

HETAERIAE [Gr. *hetairiai*]. Political clubs with various objectives in the interest of the state. The oligarchic H. played a large part in the 5th cent. B.C., particularly in the revolution of 411 (see THERAMENES; ANTIPHON; OLIGARCHY). There were also H. on Crete, military men's leagues, comparable to the "tent associations" in Sparta.

HEXAMETER. See METER.

HIBERUS. The Rom. name for the Ebro River in Spain. Hasdrubal (1) made a treaty with Rome, in which it was agreed that the land to the north of the H. would be within the Rom. sphere of influence, and that the land to the south would be left to Carthage. The position of Saguntum, however, was decided separately.

HIC ET NUNC. "Here and now"; *hic et ubique:* "here and everywhere"; *hic iacet (jacet):* "here lies"; used on tombstones.

HIERO. Name of:

—(1) H. I (?-466 B.C.). Tyrant of Syracuse; succeeded his brother Gelon in 485 in Gela, and in 478, in Syracuse. He expanded his influence into southern Italy, where he saved Cumae from the Etruscan threat, by a great victory at sea (474), which put an end to Etruria's sea power. In Olympia, in commemoration of this conquest, he dedicated an inscribed helmet, which has been found. He "founded" Aetna by forcibly ejecting the population of Catana, and settling his mercenaries and followers there. The allegiance with Akragas (Agrigentum), which had been made in Gelon's time, was terminated. Philosophers and poets, including Pindar (who sang of H.'s victories at the Olympic Games), Xenophanes, Bacchylides, and Aeschylus gathered at his court.

—(2) H. II (c. 306-215). Tyrant (later with the title of king) of Syracuse. He came to power c. 275 and was proclaimed king after a victory over the Mamertini (c. 265); during the First Punic War he became an ally of Rome (after having chosen the Carthaginian side for a short while, under pressure from the Mamertini), and remained Rome's ally until his death, during the Second Punic War. It was a period of great prosperity for his city.

HIERONYMUS. Name of:

—(1) Grandson and successor of Hiero II, reigned over Syracuse 215-214 B.C.; took Carthage's side, but was soon assassinated in Leontini; still Syracuse remained disloyal to Rome, which led to the siege and the conquest by Marcellus in 212.

—(2) H. of Cardia (c. 300 B.C.), historian of the wars of the Diadochie, which he experienced himself.

HIEROSOLYMA. The Gr.-Rom. name for Jerusalem (see also JUDAEA).

HIMATION. Cloak, usually woolen; a rectangular piece of cloth, which Gr. men and women draped over the chiton.

HIMERA. City on the north coast of Sicily, on the river of the same name, founded by Zancle (see MESSANA) in 648 B.C.; native city of Stesichorus. There, in 480 B.C., the Carthaginians were defeated by Gelon and Theron. H. was destroyed in 408 B.C. by the Carthaginians, who founded a new city to the west of the ruins, near the neighboring warm springs (thermae himeraeae); however, this city became Greek too, but later it came under Rom. rule. It was the native city of Agathocles.

HIMERIUS (4th cent. A.D.). Gr. orator. Twenty-four of his speeches have survived in a complete form.

HIMILCO. Carthaginian navigator, who made a voyage of discovery from Gades in about 480 B.C. He may have reached the British Isles. He wrote a book about this voyage, which was used by Avienus.

HIPPARCHUS. Name of:

—(1) Son of Pisistratus and tyrant of Athens; governed the city with his elder brother Hippias. He greatly encouraged the plastic arts and literature, he invited Anacreaon and Simonides to come to Athens. Under his patronage, the first phase of red-figured vase painting flourished in Athens. He was murdered by Harmodius and Aristogiton in 514 B.C.

—(2) H. of Nicaea (c. 190-c. 120). The greatest Gr. astronomer (see also ASTRONOMY).

HIPPIAS Name of:

—(1) Eldest son of Pisistratus, tyrant of Athens from 527-510. He continued the government on the same principles as his father and tried to extend the influence of Athens to the gateway to the Black Sea; to achieve that, he sent Miltiades to the Chersonesus Thracica. After Hipparchus had been murdered, he became a "tyrant" in the present sense of the word; the Alcmaeonidae succeeded in expelling him from Athens in 510; H. fled to Persia, and returned from there with a fleet under the command of Datis, undoubtedly, with the idea to rule Athens as a Persian satrap. This plan was foiled

by the outcome of battle of Marathon.
—(2) H. of Elis, Gr. Sophist, famed
itinerant teacher, who asserted that he
was *autarkès* (self-sufficient). His achievements in geometry were particularly impressive (among other things, he trisected
an angle by a curve). Two dialogues of
Plato are named after him.

HIPPOCRATES (c. 460-c. 380). Founder
of scientific medicine. Little is known
about his life, except that he was born
on Cos and died at Larissa. A collection of numerous writings, the *Corpus
Hippocraticum*, bears his name, however,
the majority of these works is of a later
period and attributed to the school which
followed his teachings—the ancients
themselves were aware that only a small
part belonged to H. The text of these
writings does not agree with the facts
known about H., from pre-Hellenistic
times, which have come down to us
(mainly through Plato). And yet, the
content of some of the writings corresponds with the ideas of H. In one of
the most important parts of the *Corpus,*
for example, the work on the "Sacred
Disease" (epilepsy), it is stated that this
disease is not at all "sacred," is not
caused by demons but has a natural
cause, which can be determined empirically. This is exactly what we know
about H.—he practiced medicine as a
natural science. The "Hippocratic oath,"
taken to this day by recipients of the
M.D. degree, was already in use in ancient times.

HIPPODAMUS of Miletus (5th cent.
B.C.). Gr. architect. He was the first to
lay out towns on geometrical principles,
with streets crossing at right angles.
Pericles commissioned him to draw plans
for Thurii and Piraeus (about 440). His
system was subsequently used in the
foundation of other towns.

HIPPONAX (c. 540 B.C.). Gr. lyric
poet; born in Ephesus, exiled to Clazomenae, where he lived like a beggar. In
his *choliambic* verses (scazons), he
mocked everything and everybody in
colloquial language; he is even said to
have driven two of his victims to suicide;
he also parodied (was perhaps the first to
do so) the Homeric epic (compare BA-
TRACHOMYOMACHIA). Only fragments of
his works have survived.

HIRTIUS, AULUS (1st cent. B.C.).
Rom. general and author; served as *legatus* under Caesar in Gaul. In 43 he was
consul with Pansa. Cicero stirred them
up against Antony, but both died in the
battle of Mutina. H. added an eighth
book to Caesar's *Commentarii de Bello
Gallico,* and was probably the author of
the *Bellum Alexandrinum,* which was
attributed to Caesar.

HISPANIA [Gr. *Iberia*]. The Rom. name
for the Iberian peninsula. The original
inhabitants were mainly the Celtiberi.
The Phoenicians, who maintained trade
relations with the kingdom of Tartessus,
founded Gades near it. In the 7th cent.
B.C. colonists from Phocaea (partly by
way of Massilia) settled on the northwestern coast. The Phoenician sphere of
influence was eventually eclipsed by Carthage, mainly after the First Punic War
(see HAMILCAR). During the Second
Punic War, Rom. influence, which until
then had been limited to the north of the
Hiberus, began to spread over all of H.
Still, it was very difficult indeed to conquer the warlike population; the fall of
Numantia marked the end of the resistance (see also VIRIATHUS). The Romans
divided the country into two provinces,
H. Ulterior in the south (capital Corduba) and H. Citerior in the north (capital Tarraco); later Lusitania also became
a Rom. province. Eventually, particularly
in early imperial times, H. was thoroughly Romanized. Many Rom. authors
were born there; among others, Seneca,
Lucan, Martial, Quintilian, also the Emperors Trajan, Hadrian, and Theodosius
I, as well as many senators.

HISSARLIK. See TROY.

HISTIAEUS (d. 494 B.C.). Tyrant of
Miletus. When the Persian king Darius
I, on his campaign against the Scythians,
had a pontoon bridge built over the
Danube, he relied on H. to guard it.
Against the advice of Miltiades, H. did
not destroy the bridge by which the Persians must return. For this service he was
rewarded by Darius with a rich territory
in Thrace. Later, Darius, fearing H.'s
growing power, called him to Susa and
then prohibited him to leave. H. then
incited Aristagoras to launch the Ionian

revolt (500), and was sent by Darius to quell the uprising, because he had persuaded the king that he alone could do so. He left for Miletus in 498, failed, and was driven to establish himself as a pirate at Byzantium. He was captured by the Persians and killed by Artaphernes at Sardis.

HITTITES. Indo-European people, which invaded and dominated a part of Asia Minor, and established a powerful empire in the period from 1500 to 1200. They also came into contact with Mycenaean Greece and influenced her culture, namely her mythology (the labrys and the cult of Cybele can be traced back to the H., for example). The prototype of the stories about Cronus, for example, was probably found in a Hittite epic.

HOC VOLO, SIC JUBEO, SIT PRO RATIONE VOLUNTAS. "This I wish, thus I command, be my will sufficient reason" (Juv. *Sat*. VI, 223).

HOMER. Traditional name for the poet or poets of the *Iliad* and the *Odyssey*, two masterly and fully realized epic poems (see EPIC), with which Gr. literature, and at the same time European literature, begins. Seven cities claimed H. as a citizen (actually, there were more, because the lists we possess are not quite identical). Smyrna and especially Chios are the most plausible; the latter was in Ionia, and the epic poem was certainly a creation of the Ionian spirit; moreover, it was situated on the boundary of the Aeolian-speaking area, which could explain the many Aeolic forms in Homeric dialect. In later centuries, there was also a school of *rhapsodoi*, the *Homeridae*. Exactly when H. lived has been a point of argument, even in ancient times. Now, we usually assume a date somewhere in the 8th cent. B.C., although some scholars still believe in dating him at around 850 B.C., which coincides with the date mentioned by Herodotus. Nothing is known about H. with certainty, except that possibly he was blind; it is not improbable that the poet gave us a self-portrait in Demodocus, the blind singer of the Phaeacians (*Od*. VIII). We may also assume that he was not a member of the nobility, for whom the poems were recited; in the many comparisons with which H. interrupts and enlivens his narrative, he often faithfully portrays the lives of the common fishermen, the poor widow, etc., which do not belong in heroic narratives at all; apparently he knows all about the lives of everyday people.

The *Iliad* (almost 16,000 hexameters, see METER) describes several weeks of the ninth year of the Trojan War; the conflict itself, although it is extensively portrayed, is only the background for a dramatic tale of human passion. It is the story of the grudge of Achilles, whose pride was hurt by Agamemnon; he withdraws from the field of battle and only lets his friend Patroclus fight when the need makes it imperative. When Patroclus is killed, desire for revenge overrides his stubbornness; he goes into battle again and kills the great Trojan hero Hector, but nobly delivers his body to the aged king Priam.

The *Odyssey* (about 11,000 lines) also covers only a few weeks of the wanderings of Odysseus, the period just before his return, and the return itself. By using an ingenious literary format, H. has the hero relate his earlier adventures to the Phaiacians (probably on the island of Corcyra), while in the first books, when Telemachus goes in search of his father, almost all the important happenings after the end of the *Iliad* have been just as cleverly woven into the story; the taking of Troy with the aid of the Wooden Horse, the return of the principal heroes, etc.

In ancient times, it was believed that only one H. existed, the author of both epics. Several philologists in Alexandria propounded the theory that each epic was created by a different author; these scholars were known as the *chorizontes* (*separators*). Their theories were not accepted by the leading interpreters of H. (Aristarchus among them), and the situation remained unchanged until the German scholar F. A. Wolf (who had had a French predecessor who passed almost unnoticed) raised the "Homeric question" in his *Prolegomena ad Homerum* in 1795. Since then, critical judges of Homer have been divided into analytics, who assume various separate songs, were brought together by one or more editors (for example under Pisistratus' rule at Athens), and the unitarians, who believe in one Homer, or at least in one poet for both epics. While the former point of view, with many variations, dominated the 19th cent., the scholars of the 20th cent. are more inclined to unitarianism. Even if one is an extreme unitarian, believing that H. composed the *Iliad* while in the prime of life, and the *Odyssey* when he was older, one must admit that a long history preceded and followed this H. In many places it can be seen that older epic poems are incorporated by H., sometimes too, it is assumed that they are known to the hearer (not reader: the epic poem is *essentially* recitative). Consequently, H. is based on an epic tradition which is certainly very ancient. After him, many parts were definitely added (interpolations, see RHAPSODOI); the language too, an artful dialect based on the Ionian, became interspersed with newer forms (particularly Attic) in the course of time.

H. soon became the national poet of Greece. His work was interpreted in schools; his influence on the conception of deities was enormous, compared with that of Hesiod. His authority was almost unquestioned, in spite of incidental criticism (see XENOPHANES). He was even seen as a source of knowledge on subjects unrelated to poetry (Plato, *Ion*). He was copied by many, but never surpassed —not even by Virgil. And all later ages determined with amazement and admiration that Gr. literature, in contrast to plastic arts, philosophy, and other aspects of Gr. culture, commenced with a mature work of such magnitude: two poems, among the greatest of mankind's creations, by virtue of their poetic power as well as their unity of composition (see also CYCLE; HYMNS; BATRACHOMYOMACHIA).

HOMO NOVUS. Term used by the Romans for someone who was the first member of his family to hold a curule office (see MAGISTRATUS), thus entering the oligarchic caste of the *nobiles; a* H.N. was usually a member of the *equites.* The most famous examples are Cicero and Marius.

HOMO SUM, HUMANI NIHIL A ME ALIENUM PUTO. "I am a man; nothing of what is human do I count foreign to myself" (Ter. *Heautont.* 25).

HONORIUS, FLAVIUS (384-423). Rom. emperor; became emperor of the West Rom. Empire on the death of his father, Theodosius I (395). In 403 he brought his court to Ravenna. Stilicho, his guardian, was the *de facto* ruler until H. had him murdered in 408. Under his reign, in 410, Alaric plundered Rome (see ALARIC; GOTHS; VANDALS).

HOPLITES. Heavily armed forces of the Greeks; the nucleus of the infantry troops of the polis. Not all heavily armed soldiers could be called H.; the word indicates a specific formation. *Hoplon* originally meant an oval shield in bronze, furnished on the inside with a center strap through which the arm was passed and with a handle for the hand at the rim. For this reason, the diameter of the shield was twice the length of the forearm, so that with a shield of this size, the wearer could protect his left side, as well as his neighbor's right. The tactics of the H. consisted of attacking in an unbroken line, several ranks deep (the phalanx of the H.). These tactics were first developed in the 7th cent. B.C., during the Second Messenian War (see MESSENIA). The oldest representation of this formation is that on the so-called Chigi vase (proto-Corinthian c. 650 B.C.). Because a Gr. soldier paid for his own equipment, the H. were prosperous citizens (for example, farmers); the richer people could afford the upkeep of a horse, and so joined the cavalry. The rise of the H. as the nucleus of the army, was coupled with beginning political awareness of the middle class. Beside the shield, a hoplite's equipment consisted of armor, a helmet, shin protectors, lance about 6 ft. long, and a short sword.

HORACE. See HORATIUS.

HORA RUIT, TEMPUS FLUIT. "Time flies" (compare Pers. *Sat.* V, 153; Sil. Ital. *Pun.* XV, 64).

HORATIUS FLACCUS, QUINTUS (65-8 B.C.) Commonly called Horace. Greatest Rom. poet after Virgil; born at Venusia in Apulia, the son of a freedman. His father sent him to Rome, where he received lessons from Orbilius; later he studied in Athens. After Caesar's murder, he supported the republicans and fought for Brutus at Philippi. As a result of Octavian's agrarian division, he lost his patrimony and supported himself by becoming a clerk in the quaestor's office. During that period (c. 41-31) he wrote his *Epodes* in iambic verses (see METER) in the style of Archilochus. In the same period he started on his *Satires* or *Sermones,* taking Lucilius as his model. The *Satires* were generally written in a genial style (see RIDENTEM DICERE VERUM, QUID VETAT?); not as biting as his *Epodes.* In the meantime, H.'s circumstances had improved. Virgil had discovered him, and introduced him to Maecenas, who became his patron, and gave him a splendid country house near Tibur. From then on H. was able to lead a carefree life and devote himself entirely to his poetry. Then he began to write his *Odes* (*Carmina*), which brought him fame, and made him the greatest Lat. lyric poet. The first three books were written in about 31-23. Meanwhile, Augustus had become the ruler, and H., who had lost the republican illusions of his youth, set about supporting the social ideals of the principate; the first few odes in the third book have a particularly national character. Most of the poems, however, speak of nothing but love, wine, and the joy of living. H. adapts the strophes (see METER) of Alcaeus and Sappho to Lat. poetry in an elegant manner; he showed himself to be equal to Catullus and sometimes surpasses him. Now the *Letters* (*Epistulae*) followed, long poems in hexameters, a continuation of the *Satires,* but with a more settled philosophical note. From the ideas of Epicurus, H. turned more and more toward the doctrines of the Stoics. The most famous parts of the second book are the *Epistula ad Pisones,* commonly called *Ars Poetica;* a theoretical contemplation of poetry. In about 13, a fourth book of *Odes* followed. The *Carmen Saeculare,* composed in 17 on a commission from Augustus, as a festival song for the regular games, occupied a special place in his work; its prosaic tone clearly shows that it was composed for an official occasion.

H.'s poetry is very varied, not only in genre, but in technique, subject, and tone. Contentment, joy of living, friendship, and love resound on the strings of his lyre. In the *Satires* and *Letters,* we are aware of his wisdom and knowledge of people. Long after antiquity his influence remains apparent; no other poet of this epoch had so many significant maxims adopted from his works.

HORROR VACUI. "Horror of a vacuum"; term used in the history of art (see GEOMETRIC ART) to convey that all space, for example, between the legs of horses and the wheels of chariots, are filled up with rosettes, swastikas, and other ornamentation.

HORTENSIUS. Name of:
—(1) Quintus H., Rom. dictator c. 287 B.C. His *Lex Hortensia* put an end to the struggle between the patricians and the plebs; the decisions of the *concilium plebis* (see COMITIA) were made binding for all the people.
—(2) Quintus H. Hortalus, Rom. orator and Cicero's greatest rival. He defended Verres, with Cicero as prosecutor in the case; later, however, he and Cicero were on the same side in the defense of Murena and others. H. represented the "Asiatic" school of eloquence—a flowery style, bordering on the bombastic.

HORUS. See ISIS.

HOUSES. In Homeric Greece, the most important part of the house was the *megaron* (men's quarters), a rectangular room with a hall; this vestibule led to an aulè (courtyard), surrounded by sleeping chambers and servants' quarters. This type of house dates from Mycenaean times, and traces of even earlier ones have been found (see SESKLO). The upper rooms could be reached by way of the *megaron,* and served as women's quarters. This division of the H. into men's and women's quarters remained in existence for centuries. In the cities several H. were often built around one courtyard; verandas and colonnades were luxuries. The quality of the H. was usually poor (for example, clay walls); smoke escaped through holes in the walls, through windows and doors—the Gr. word for "burglar" literally means "he who crawls

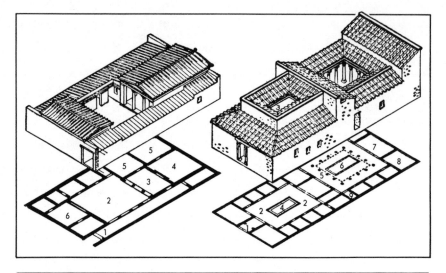

Reconstructions of a Greek (left) and a Roman house. In the Greek house we see:
1. entrance, 2. aulè (courtyard), 3. vestibule, 4. megaron (mens' quarters), 5. sleep-
ing quarters, 6. exedra (open veranda), others: living and servants' quarters. Roman
house: 1. vestibulum (entrance), 2. atrium, 3. compluvium, 4. impluvium, 5. peristy-
lum, 6. piscina (pool), 7. exedra, 8. triclinium (dining room), 9. posticum (back
entrance), others: living, sleeping, and servants' quarters.

through"). These H. had no running
water, nor were there toilets. In Hellenistic times, the rich could acquire H. with
shaded back yards surrounded by colonnades (Lat. *peristylum*).

In Italy, the wealthy had H. with an
atrium, a quadrangular court with a *com-*
pluvium, an opening in the tiled roof,
through which rain water fell into the
impluvium, a tank sunk in the floor be-
neath. In Pompeii, this type of house was
combined with the Hellenistic *peristylum.*
The common man had a house with a
workshop at the front and a small living
room and sleeping quarters at the back.
Most of the city dwellers lived in large
apartment houses, *insulae;* many of these
have been found mainly in Ostia. (For
complicated heating systems see HYPO-
CAUST; see also VILLA.)

HUMANISM [Lat. *humanitas,* human
nature]. The term applied to the trend of
thought, which, at the end of the Middle
Ages, stressed interest in man's culture
and man's dignity as opposed to the ab-

stract or supernatural, and strove to revive the teachings of classical antiquity
(Petrarch, Erasmus). The movement was
inspired by the works of Homer, Socrates,
Plato, Cicero, Virgil, and many others,
and was devoted primarily to revive the
literature of classical times.

HUNS. Asiatic horsemen, originally from
China, who later settled in Mongolia. In
the 4th cent. A.D. the westernmost H.
drove the Goths before them; in the 5th
cent. they invaded the West themselves;
see GOTHS; ATTILA.

HYBRIS [Gr. *hubris,* arrogance]. A central concept in Gr. religious thought. A
boundary separates the world of gods
and the world of man. This boundary
cannot be passed by man without punishment. This idea is predominant, particularly in the works of Pindar, Aeschylus,
and Herodotus. There is deliberate H.,
like that of Xerxes in Aeschylus' *The
Persians,* which causes personal guilt, and
there is also involuntary H., like that of
Polycrates in Herodotus III, which does

not convoke personal guilt, but can nevertheless be just as catastrophical in its consequences.

HYDRIA. See VASE FORMS.

HYGINUS. Name of:

—(1) Gaius Julius H., freedman of Augustus who made him librarian of the Palatine library. Under the name of H. we possess two books: the *Fabularum Liber* and the *De Astronomia,* usually called *Poetica Astronomica.* Both are abridgments and their style and elementary mistakes in the rendering of the Gr. originals have led to the belief that they cannot be H.'s work. It is suggested that they are of a later date. They are valuable because the author made use of the works of Gr. tragedians now lost.

—(2) H. Gromaticus (from *gruma,* surveyor's measuring rod). Rom. writer on land surveying. Fragments of a work on geodesy is attributed to him. He worked under Trajan's reign in the 2nd cent. A.D.

HYMETTUS. Mountain ridge in Attica, famous for its honey and its bluish marble.

HYMNS. Songs of praise to a deity; the most famous ones are the thirty-three H. attributed to Homer. A few of them, for example, the one to Demeter (see ELEUSINIAN MYSTERIES) are from the 7th cent. B.C., others were composed later. The H. to Hermes, Apollo, and Dionysus are well-known (see also PAEAN; DITHYRAMB; CLEANTHES; and MUSIC).

HYPERIDES (389-322). One of the ten Attic orators, a supporter of Demosthenes and one of the leaders of the popular party. After the death of Alexander the Great he incited the Athenians to revolt against Macedonia and was the chief instigator of the Lamian War. After its failure, he was executed on Antipater's orders. Of the seventy-seven speeches known to antiquity, only a few fragments were extant until recent times; in 1847 and 1856, in Egypt, additional fragments were found on papyri.

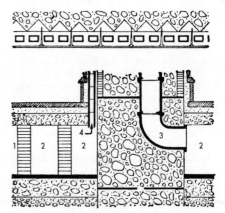

Vertical section of the hypocaust of the thermae of Caracalla. 1. Supporting pillar, 2. Heating chamber, 3. Outlet, 4. Duct. The picture above it shows the view from above of a wall with heating canals in it.

HYPOCAUST. A central heating system for thermae, villas, and mansions of wealthy Romans. Hot air, produced in a heating chamber (supported by pillars and usually located underground) was circulated under the floor and between double walls by means of ducts (hollow tiles).

I

IAMB. See METER.

IAMBLICHUS. Name of:

—(1) Gr. writer, born in Syria, in the 2nd cent. A.D., He wrote a romance in sixteen books, called *Babylonica* from the locale of the greater part of the story. Only an epitome by Photius has survived.

—(2) Neoplatonist philosopher from Syria (c. 250-325), pupil of Porphyry. Infused Plotinus' philosophy with Eastern ideas of theosophy and theurgy. Some of his works are thus a better source for the knowledge of superstitions than for Neoplatonism.

IBERIA.
—(1) See HISPANIA; CELTIBERI.
—(2) Name of a district to the south of the Caucasus.

IBYCUS of Rhegium (6th cent. B.C.). Gr. lyric poet who wrote mainly choral poems and worked at the court of Polycrates on Samos for a long period. In his poems, of which only fragments have survived, love plays an important part; he also has a feeling for the beauties of nature (rare in ancient Gr. authors). According to the legend, made familiar by Schiller's ballad, he was murdered by robbers, who were then betrayed by cranes hovering overhead.

ICTINUS (2nd half of the 5th cent. B.C.). Gr. architect; constructed the Parthenon and the Apollo temple of Bassae. He also designed the plan for the reconstruction of the *Telesterion* (initiation) in Eleusis.

IDA.
—(1) Famous mountain in Asia Minor, southeast of ancient Troy; the location of a sanctuary of Cybele. Actually a mountain range (I. Mountains).
—(2) Highest mountain in Crete; in early times connected with the worship of Zeus.

IDES [Lat. *indus.*] A certain day in the Rom. calendar. The I. fell on the 15th in March, May, July, and October, and on the 13th in the other months (see CALENDAR). The I. were sacred to Jupiter and were also the days when debts became due. It was on the I. of March of 44 B.C. that Caesar was murdered.

IDYL [Gr. *eidyllion,* little scene]. The word *eidyllion* is actually a diminutive of *eidos* (form) and was interpreted to mean "a little piece," that is, a separate poem, not part of the context of a whole work such as epic poems. The I. is a short descriptive poem, mostly on pastoral subjects, giving a charming and often romantic picture of country people and shepherds. Theocritus, and later Virgil and Ansonius, distinguished themselves in this genre.

ILIUM. See TROY.

ILLYRIA. Country on the Adriatic Sea, comprising almost the same area that is now called Yugoslavia. In the 2nd millennium B.C. the Illyrians settled there; a people with an Indo-European language. Herodotus and other Gr. historians described them as resembling the Thracians. From the 6th cent. B.C. onward Gr. colonies were founded on the coast, but commerce with Corcyra was mainly conducted by way of Epirus (see EPIDAMNUS). In the 3rd cent. B.C. a native federation of states was established which was conquered by Rome in 167 B.C. The Romans organized the country into the province Illyricum. Augustus split it into two provinces, Pannonia and Dalmatia (see also DIOCLETIAN).

IMPERATOR [Lat. commander in chief]. The title conferred on a general by acclamation of his soldiers after a great victory. This proclamation then gave him the right to demand a triumph of the senate. As a permanent title, it was first assumed by Caesar, whose adopted son and heir Octavian retained it as a cognomen. It did not become a permanent title for the emperor until Vespasian.

IMPERIUM. Among the Romans, the full power of the king; originally believed to have been a divine gift. (For this reason, in later times, the *magistratus cum imperio* was the only one with the right to consult the *auspicia maxima.*) In practice, however, the king's I. was limited; he was expected to consult the senate before major decisions, for example, before engaging in war. On the king's death the I. passed to the senate, which conferred it on the newly elected king.

In republican times the I. was conferred by the *comitia centuriata* and was transferred to the two consuls, who held power jointly for one year. To avoid disputes over conflicting decisions—either consul could veto the other's ruling—their absolute I. was limited to times of peace, when their decisions were subject to appeal (*provocatio*). Either consul, on the advice of the senate, could appoint a dictator in times of crisis, who then had unrestricted I. Consuls and praetors were able to prolong their I. beyond their year in office by prorogation (*prorogatio*); they were then called proconsuls or propraetors. As such they were employed as provincial governors with their I. bounded within the limits of their province.

In the imperial period the I. again included the highest authority, including the military, usually held by the emperor who had the authority to appoint deputies (for symbol of office with I. see LICTORS; see also INTERREX).

INDIGITES (sing. *indiges*). Primeval Rom. deities, especially Aeneas and the descendants of Aeneas, the fabled ancestors of the Romans (Livy, Virgil). *Indigitamenta* was the name given to a collection of forms of prayer, belonging to the *libri pontificii* (see PONTIFEX). It lists the powers of each god who was invoked to aid in a special situation (see also NOVENSILES).

IN DUBIIS PRO REO. "In things doubtful [be it decided] in favor of the accused," Rom. law term. The principle was also known to the Greeks and founded in myth, by the action of Athena in favor of Orestes before the Areopagus (Aeschylus, *The Eumenides*).

INSCRIPTIONS. See EPIGRAPHY.

INTERREX (intermediary king). The name given by the Romans to a magistrate appointed by the senate who, between the death of one king and the election of another, had the *imperium*. During the republic, an I. was appointed in the absence of both consuls. His term of office was called *interregnum*.

IONIA. The central sector of the west coast of Asia Minor, colonized in about 1100-7000 B.C. (see IONIANS). Some important cities were Miletus, Ephesus, and Smyrna. I. was conquered by Lydia (see also CROESUS) and the Persian empire, against which it revolted in 500 B.C. (see ARISTAGORAS; LADE). After the Persian wars I. was liberated by Athens (see DELIA LEAGUE), but subjected again after the "King's Peace" of Antalcidas (386 B.C.). Alexander the Great put an end to Persian domination for good in 334; I. became a part of the Seleucid empire, the kingdom of Pergamum, and finally the Rom. province of Asia. Point of convergence of current cultures that had come from the East (see Babylonia) and from Egypt (the Saitic empire; see AMASIS), I. was, particularly in the 7th-

6th centuries B.C., the center of a Gr. civilization whose influence made itself felt in all areas of art and literature of antiquity. Ceramic art, the epic poems of Homer, Ionian natural philosophy (see THALES; ANAXIMANDER; ANAXIMENES), geography (see HECATAEUS), all originated in this region. I. was also the original country where the polis (see MILETUS; PHOCAEA) and Gr. colonization developed.

IONIANS. One of the Gr. tribes, which in the 2nd millennium B.C., settled mainly in Attica and the Peloponnesus, probably before the Achaeans. In about 1100 B.C. the I., driven out of the latter region by the Dorians, emigrated partly to Attica and Euboea; the majority went to the islands in the Aegean Sea and to the coast of Asia Minor, where they occupied the country Ionia, named for them. According to certain traditions, this Ionian colonization or migration took place under the aegis of Athens, which called itself the "mother city of the Ionians." This pretension, already opposed in ancient times, has during later centuries also been rejected. During the past few years, however, it has been admitted that Athens played an organizing role, an opinion based on the similarity between the two countries; the same four *phylae* (political, tribal subdivisions) are found among the Athenians and the Ionians, and the Attic dialect is a variation of Ionian. The I. formed a confederation of twelve cities in the 9th cent. The I. held gatherings (Panionia) on Mycale (a promontory) at which Poseidon was worshiped in his temple and political matters were discussed.

IONIAN SEA. Sea from the west of Greece to the south of Italy and Sicily; the islands in it (Corcyra, Ithaca, and Zacynthus) are called the Ionian Islands.

IONIC COLUMN. See ARCHITECTURAL ORDERS; COLUMN.

IPSE DIXIT. "He himself said it"; translation of Gr. *autos epha,* with which the followers of Pythagoras tried to support their statements.

IPSUS. Small city in Phrygia, where Antigonus and Demetrius Poliorcetes were defeated in 301 B.C. by a coalition between the other Diadochsi.

ISAEUS. One of the ten Attic orators; born in Chalcis. He worked in Athens c. 390 (or 377)-353 and was a pupil of Demosthenes. Eleven of his fifty speeches have survived; of a twelfth a fragment only. They are important for our knowledge of Attic laws of succession.

ISIS. Egyptian goddess of fertility, wife of Osiris, the god of vegetation. The service of I. played an important part in the mysteries and spread extensively in Hellenistic times. She was worshiped in the Rom. Empire after the Second Punic War in spite of attempts by the state to suppress her cult which rivaled that of Mithras, who was venerated primarily by men, especially soldiers. Apuleius has given an interesting description of her rite.

ISOCRATES. 436-338. One of the ten Attic orators; pupil of Prodicus, Protagoras and Gorgias, friend of Socrates. His weak voice and his shyness prevented him from appearing as an orator himself, but (like Lysias) he wrote speeches for others and taught elocution. In his speeches (twenty-one have survived) he brought the Attic oratory style to a high degree of perfection by giving it its classical form, although some of his speeches and letters read like political pamphlets. He had great political influence and preached union of the Gr. states against the threat of the Persian empire. This appeal for unity, running counter to the particularism of the polis, foreshadowed the future form of Hellenism. At first he hoped that Sparta and Athens would unite to take the initiative, but was frustrated when Thebes, under the leadership of Epaminondas, realized the old form of hegemony. He then turned to Dionysius I, and finally to Philip II of Macedonia. The Gr. league of states which later came into being under Macedonian hegemony (after the battle of Chaeronea) was actually in consequence of I.'s ideas. However, he did not live to see it established.

ISSUS. City on the coast of Cilicia (Asia Minor), where, in 333 B.C., Alexander the Great first met Darius III on the field of battle and defeated him. Alexander broke the front of the Persian army by outflanking its left center. After the victory, Darius' wife and children fell into Alexander's hands.

ISTER. See DANUVIUS.

ISTHMIAN GAMES. Panhellenic games in honor of Poseidon, held in Corinth in the second and fourth years of each Olympiad. Their inception remains confused—the Corinthians claimed they were founded by Sisyphus, their legendary king; the Athenians attributed their origin to their hero Theseus. One thing is certain; the I.G. were definitely organized after 581 B.C., although they go back to a much earlier date. The Athenians were extremely interested in the games and awarded one hundred drachmae to every citizen who was victorious in the contests.

ISTHMUS [Gr. *isthmos,* neck, narrow passage]. The ancients used the term to designate the I. of Corinth, a strip of land connecting the Peloponnesus with continental Greece. In antiquity a *diolkos* was there, a device (ship camel) by which ships could be raised. Caesar and Nero already planned to dig a canal at the I.'s narrowest point (4 miles), but a canal did not become reality until 1893.

ISYLLUS. See EPIDAURUS.

ITALICI. Collective name for various peoples who, aside from the Romans and Greeks, lived in Italy, (which extended from the Rubicon in the north, to Rhegium in the south before Augustus' time). In a narrower sense, the term also designated the people who spoke a dialect related to Latin, mainly the Umbrians, the Osci, the Samnites, the Sabines, and the Volsci (for other inhabitants of ancient Italy, see ETRUSCANS; LIGURIANS; VENETI; LUCANIA; BRUTTII).

ITHACA. Island in the Ionian Sea, to the south of Leucas. It is possible that this island is identical with the I. of Odysseus; even the ancients were uncertain of this.

ITHOME. Fortress in Messenia, situated on a mountain of the same name; center of defense against Sparta during the First Messenian War from c. 736-716, and again during the revolt of 464 B.C. (see CIMON). In 370 B.C., Epaminondas founded the city of Messana there as a permanent bulwark against the Spartans.

J

JACTA EST ALEA. See ALEA JACTA EST.

JANICULUM HILL. Hill on the right bank of the Tiber, Roman citadel against enemies from the north (Etruria). Gaius Gracchus was killed there.

JANUS. Ancient Rom. deity for whom the month of January (*Januarius*) was named. In Rome the arches (*jani*) which spanned the streets and many doors (*januae*) bore his image—a double head facing in two directions. He was the protector of the archway to the Forum out of which the army marched into battle and by which it returned. The Forum gates remained open during wartime and were closed only in time of peace. J. was also worshiped as the god of entrance into a new division of time and was invoked at the beginning of each day (*pater matutinus*) as well as at the start of each month; his chief festival, however, was celebrated on the first of January with offerings of cakes to him and gifts of sweets by the people to one another.

JASON. Name of:

—(1) The leader of the Argonauts.

—(2) Tyrant of Pherae from c. 380-370. He managed to dominate all of Thessaly, and then wanted to extend his hegemony over all of Greece. Ally of Athens and Thebes, he was called in by them to aid in the conflict with Sparta. His help was not very effective; however, after the battle of Leuctra in 371, he brought about a truce between Thebes and Sparta. In 370, during the Pythian games, he suddenly mobilized the entire Thessalian army, but was murdered before anyone knew what he was planning.

JOSEPHUS, FLAVIUS (37-c. 93). Jewish historian, born in Jerusalem of a family of priests. In 63 he went to Rome but returned to his native land where he at first tried to check the revolt of the Jews against the Romans, but later joined the former and became commander of Galilee. He was imprisoned by Vespasian in 67, but his life was spared by Titus' intercession because J.'s prophecy that Vespasian would become emperor came true. J. remained with Titus at the siege of Jerusalem and afterward returned to Rome where he was given Rom. citizenship. He lived in Rome until his death, devoting himself to his writing. His principal work, written in Aramaic, translated into Greek by Titus' request, is *The Jewish Antiquities,* a history of the Jews from the creation until A.D. 66. Other works are: *The Jewish War;* a treatise against the current misrepresentation of the Jews by a scholar named Apion; and an autobiography.

JOVIANUS, FLAVIUS CLAUDIUS (331-364). Rom. emperor; chosen by the soldiers to succeed Julian in 363. He made a humiliating peace with the Persians and re-established Christianity.

JUDAEA. The Gr.-Rom. name for the land of the Jews. Originally, this name designated all of Palestine; much later it was given to the southern province only. The Greeks made their first contact with J. in the Hellenistic period, when it was part of the Seleucid Empire. Prompted by the pro-Gr. movement among the Jews themselves, Antiochus IV tried to Hellenize it, an action that led to the unification of the Pharisees and resulted in the Maccabean revolt. At the end of this epoch there were two opposing factions: one group, led by the aristocracy, was in favor of Hellenization; the other group, ardently nationalistic, supported the Pharisees. The latter group continued to resist Hellenization, even after 63 B.C., when J. was made a vassal state of Rome by Pompey. Herod the Great and Antipas ruled with the support of Rome. Caligula's injudicious actions provoked a serious revolt but the great rebellion did not break out until 66, in Caesarea. This uprising was quelled by Vespasian; and Titus crushed it completely by destroying Jerusalem in 70. There were several other revolts, of which the one led by Bar Kochbah during Hadrian's reign was the most serious. In spite of the destruction of Jerusalem and its temple, the cultural and spiritual life of the Jews continued in Jewish communities outside Palestine; for example, in Alexandria (see PHILO), Cyrene, and on Cyprus. These communities of the Diaspora (literally: dispersion) were very important in the times that Christianity first began to spread.

JUGURTHA (c. 160-104). King of Numidia, grandson of Masinissa. In 118 he and his two cousins Hiempsal and Adherbal inherited the empire. He had Hiempsal murdered, and banished Adherbal. J. provoked Adherbal into a war of self-defense, and when J. took the embattled city of Cirta (Constantine) and massacred many Italian merchants, the Rom. senate, forced by the people's tribunes, entered the war (111). Several Numidian towns surrendered voluntarily. Bocchus, king of Mauretania and J.'s father-in-law, allied himself to Rome. J. then "bought" a favorable peace from the general in the field. The Rom. tribune Memmius demanded that J. be granted safe conduct to Rome to account for his actions. The Romans set the peace treaty aside and asked J. to leave Rome. It was then that he is said to have exclaimed: "A city for sale, and doomed to perish as soon as it finds a buyer!" (Sall., *B. Jug.*).

The war was renewed, with Metullus in charge of the Rom. army. J., driven out of Numidia by Metullus, then fled to Bocchus. In 106 Marius succeeded Metullus, but it was through the treachery of Bocchus, who handed J. over to Sulla, Marius' quaestor, that the war came to an end. J. was taken to Rome and after being displayed in Marius' triumph, was either strangled or starved to death in the Tullianum.

JULIA (39 B.C.-A.D. 14). Only daughter of Augustus and Scribonia. J. was married three times: at the age of fourteen to her first cousin Marcellus; after his death, without issue, to Agrippa, by whom she had three sons, Gaius and Lucius Caesar and Agrippa Postumus, as well as two daughters Julia and Agrippina; after Agrippa's death, in 12 B.C., to Tiberius Nero. Two of her sons, Gaius and Lucius Caesar, died young; Agrippa Postumus was murdered in A.D. 14. Because of her adulteries, Augustus exiled her to the island of Pandataria in 2 B.C. J.'s daughter, bearing the same name, inherited her mother's licentiousness and was later banished by her grandfather.

JULIAN-CLAUDIAN HOUSE. The imperial dynasty formed by the Rom. Emperors Augustus, Tiberius, Caligula, Claudius, and Nero. Augustus was a member of the Julian house by adoption, the others were Claudians (see CLAUDIAN HOUSE), and also Julians by adoption. It was said that the latter were descendants of Julus (or Ascanius), the son of Aeneas.

JULIANUS, FLAVIUS CLAUDIUS (332-363). Usually called Julian, and surnamed the Apostate. Rom. emperor, nephew of Constantine the Great. On Constantine's death in 337, J. and his brother Gallus were the only members of the imperial family whose lives were spared during a palace revolution. The two brothers were educated in Asia Minor in the Christian religion; during this period J. was introduced to Neoplatonism, and soon abjured Christianity. In 355 he was appointed "Caesar" of the West by Constantius. When the Emperor demanded troops from Gaul for the war against the Persians, the army rebelled and proclaimed J. emperor; the timely death of Constantius in 360 prevented a battle and left J. undisputed absolute ruler. He instituted several political reforms, including one to abolish the corrupt court regime of the eunuchs. He attacked Persia and died on the battle field.

J. became known primarily because he made a final effort to reestablish paganism. He did not persecute the Christians, but did take discriminatory measures against them. However, Christianity had already taken hold too deeply; J.'s effort was doomed to failure from the start. He himself was a firm believer who zealously supported the ideas of Hellenistic

Eastern religion. We owe our knowledge of J. mainly to Ammianus Marcellinus.

JULIANUS, SALVIUS. See SALVIUS JULIANUS.

JUNO. See HERA.

JUPITER [Lat. Iuppiter]. Chief god of the Romans, identical with the Gr. god Zeus in his functions and in the etymology of his name. J. is compounded from *Iovis* (an older form is *Diovis* [root *diu*, bright]) and *pater*. He was the god of the heavenly phenomena, protector of state, society, and the armies. He was venerated as Iuppiter Optimus Maximus (the best and greatest of all Jupiters). His temple was situated on the Capitoline Hill (see CAPITOL).

JUSTINIAN THE GREAT (Flavius Petrus Sabbatius Justinianus or Flavius Anicius Justinianus). Emperor of the East Rom. Empire from 527-565. He diligently kept order in the East and then turned his attention to the West where his generals, Helisarius and Narses, won great successive victories over the Vandals and Ostrogoths. J. was able to establish himself as ruler of the West also, although large areas had been left to the Germans. A major crisis in J.'s reign was the bloody Nika revolt (532) of "Blues and Greens (circus factions). The Empress Theodora refused to flee and thereby saved her husband's crown. J.'s rule is of importance because Rom. law (see CORPUS JURIS) civilis was codified and the last fragments of paganism disappeared during his reign (for example, the Neoplatonist Academy was shut down). J.'s history has been preserved for us in the writings of Procopius.

JUSTINUS. Name of:

—(1) Christian martyr (2nd cent. A.D.); studied various philosophical doctrines before converting to Christianity. He tried to make Christianity understandable for contemporary Platonist intellectuals.

—(2) Marcus Junianus J. (probably 3rd cent. A.D.). Rom. historian. He made an excerpt of the works of Pompeius Trogus.

JUVENAL: Commonly used name of Decimus Junius Juvenalis (c. 62-142). Lat. poet, author of sixteen satires in hexameters, in which he painted a somber picture of his epoch. His pessimism with regard to society can be compared to Tacitus—his first poem sets the keynote: "Why do I write satire?" he asks, "say rather, how could I help it?" Written in a style far different from the amiable, conversational one of Horace, J.'s style is responsible for the modern connotation of the term "satire." His hatred was aimed mainly at the Emperor Domitian, who probably exiled him. That could also explain the poverty which he mentions, as property was confiscated when someone was exiled. He also mocked the immorality of the aristocracy and the hypocrisy of the (Stoic) moralists. Those of his satires written when he began to age show less harshness than does his earlier work. Many of J.'s quotations have become famous (see HOC VOLO; MENS SANA; PANEM ET CIRCENSES; RARA AVIS).

K-L

KALPIS. See VASE FORMS.

KANTHAROS. See VASE FORMS.

KERNOS. See VASE FORMS.

KNOSSOS. See CNOSSUS.

KORE. See PERSEPHONE.

KOTYLE. See VASE FORMS.

KRATER. See VASE FORMS.

KYATHOS. See VASE FORMS.

KYLIX. See VASE FORMS.

LABIENUS, TITUS (c. 100-45). Caesar's second in command; frequently acted as deputy commander in Gaul, and in this capacity often executed commands independently. In 49 he deserted to Pompey and fought against Caesar at Pharsalus. He fell at Munda.

LABRYS. An ax with two cutting edges; religious symbol, particularly of Minoan Crete and of Asia Minor.

LABYRINTH. (The word is probably related to labrys), building with many irregularly built passages which form a maze. The Gr. legend of the L. in which the Minotaur was killed by Theseus is probably based on the irregularly built palace in Cnossus. The funeral temple of Amenemhet III in El Faiyûm in Egypt was also called L. by the Greeks (Hdt. II, 148), as were other complicated buildings. The L. is depicted on coins of Cnossus, Gr. vases, Rom. mosaics, and on a wall in Pompeii on which a maze is drawn with the words: "Here is the L.; the Minotaur lives here."

LACONIA. The district (sometimes called Laconica by the Romans) in which Sparta (Lacedaemon) lay. The city was in the fertile valley of the Eurotas River, the rest of L., was mountainous with a number of small fertile plains, and belonged to the Pericoeci (Gr. *Perioikoi*). The boundaries changed often, as a result of battles with Messenia, Arcadia, and Argos.

LACTANTIUS, L. LUCIUS CAECILIUS FIRMIANUS (c. 250-c. 317). Christian author, pupil of Arnobius. He wrote several works in favor of Christianity in classical Latin; this earned him the nickname of "the Christian Cicero." In his last years of life, he was the tutor of Crispus, the son of Constantine the Great, in Trien (Trèves). It is doubtful whether he was the author of the *"De Mortibus Persecutorum,"* a work about the persecution of the Christians under Diocletian.

LADE. Small island near Miletus, where the Ionian fleet was defeated by the Persians in 494 B.C. That naval battle definitely marked the end of the Ionian revolt.

LAELIUS, GAIUS.
—(1) Friend of Scipio Major, whom he accompanied on his campaigns to Spain. He participated in the conquest of Carthago Nova in 209 B.C., and in 202 in the battle of Zama.
—(2) Son of the preceding, surnamed *Sapiens* (the wise). Friend of Scipio Mi-

nor, whom he accompanied at the taking of Carthage in 146 (see PUNIC WARS). He is known chiefly as the soul of the "Scipioric Circle," a group of Rom. noblemen who encouraged the Hellenization of Rom. society; they sought to conciliate Gr. culture with the best Rom. traditions and were particularly attracted to the ideas of the Stoics. Their group included Greeks also; for instance, Panaetius and Polybius. Cicero, in his dialogue on friendship (*Laelius,* or *De Amicitia*), makes L. the principal interlocutor.

LAGIDI. See PTOLEMY.

LAOCOÖN. According to the saga, a Trojan priest of Apollo who warned the Trojans in vain about the Wooden Horse; he and his two sons were then strangled by two serpents, sent by Athena (Virg. *Aen.* II, 40-56; 199-231). This scene is the theme of one of the most famous examples of Hellenistic sculpture, a masterpiece of the school of Pergamum, now in the Vatican. This L. group is the work of the Rhodian artists Agesander, Polydorus, and Athenodorus (c. 160-130 B.C.). It inspired Lessing to write his famous essay on the relation of poetry to the fine arts. In September 1957 fragments of L. group that may well be the original were found in Italy.

LAODICEA. Name of various cities in the Near East; the most significant one was L. near the Lycus (a tributary of the Maeander), founded in about 225 B.C. by Antiochus II and named after his wife Laodice. Due to its favorable position on an important trade route, it became one of the most famous cities of Asia Minor.

LAPSUS LINGUAE. "A slip of the tongue."

LARES. Rom. tutelary gods of farmlands, worshiped particularly at crossroads. Later, together with the Penates, they became guardians of the home. A small statue of the *lar familiaris,* protector of the family (including servants) stood in the *lararium* (family chapel) with that of the Penates.

LARISSA. The main city of Thessaly; the ruling group was the aristocratic family of the Aleuadae who got a bad name for supporting the Persians during the Persian Wars.

LATIFUNDIA. The Rom. name for large

agricultural estates, in Italy and elsewhere, which originated in the 2nd cent. B.C. During this epoch, Rom. conquests caused a great deal of capital to fall into the hands of a few wealthy men, usually patricians, who acquired this land by purchase or by force. While the landowners remained in Rome, the estates were managed by stewards; the labor was done by slaves imported from the East, who lived under terrible conditions. The free farmers who had been assigned land by the state (see AGER PUBLICUS), not being able to compete with this cheap labor, usually sold their share and moved to Rome where they became proletarians (see GRACCHI). The L. in Italy were used mainly as pasture, the slaves serving as shepherds. Outside Italy—on Sicily and in Egypt especially—the L. were used to grow grain. During the imperial period, slaves were replaced by *coloni* (farmers), serfs who rented a piece of land from a master and cultivated it for their own profit.

LATIUM. A district in western central Italy, in which Rome lay. The prehistoric population called *aborigines* by the Romans and which, according to some accounts, consisted of Siculi (see SICILY) and Ligurians, was subjected in prehistoric times by the Latini. These spoke diverse dialects of an Indo-European language; the Rom. dialect is what we now call Latin. Other tribes beside the Latini settled there, of which the Volsci was one of the strongest. A Lat. league of cities, with Alba Longa as its capital, was formed. After the Etruscan domination (6th cent. B.C.), the league made a pact with Rome against the obtrusive Volsci and Aequi. This treaty was revoked in 338 B.C., and Rome made separate treaties with various cities; in turn, a special right was granted them, the *Ius Latii*. By this authority, they later attained a privileged position with regard to the other Italian communities (see SOCII; DIVIDE ET IMPERA). Later, this Lat. citizen's right was granted to cities outside L. also. At first the territory of L. was fertile, but after 300 B.C. it declined as a result of the increase of *latifundia*.

LATONA. See LETO.

LAUDATOR TEMPORIS ACTI. "A lauder of the time gone by" (Hor. *Ars poet.* 173).

LAURIUM. Mountain in southeast Attica, famous for its silver mines. The mines were state-owned, leased, and worked by slave labor. Their revenues contributed greatly to Athen's commercial and political power (after the battle of Marathon they were used to build Athen's navy). The slaves were the only slaves in Attica who lived under extremely poor conditions; when Sparta occupied Decelea, many of them escaped.

LAVINIUM. City in Latium, founded, according to the saga, by Aeneas, and named L., in honor of his wife Lavinia. This explains why the Romans held L. in high esteem.

LEAGUE. See DELIAN LEAGUE. For the Second Attic League see ATHENS; TIMOTHEUS.

LEBES. See VASE FORMS.

LEGATUS. Rom. term for envoy, ambassador, and, since Caesar's time, also for second in command, usually entrusted with the command of a legion. During imperial times, the term *legati* Augusti was used for governors of imperial provinces (see PROVINCIA).

LEGION. The largest body of troops of the Rom. army, originally consisting of 4,200 men, increased to 6,000 during the time of Marius (their actual strength was often less). A L. was divided into ten cohorts, in each of which there were three maniples, each maniple consisting of two legions. The L. was divided into three groups according to age and experience: the *hastati, principes,* and *triarii* (the last were usually veterans). In the republican period, a L. consisted of heavily armed Rom. citizens, reinforced by lightly armed troops (originally poorer citizens) and cavalry. The *socii* fought in separate formations. Eventually, the cavalry was entirely recruited from the allies. During the imperial period twenty-five to thirty legions formed a standing army, mainly to guard the frontiers. They were each given a number, and often an honorary name. More and more inhabitants of the provinces were now recruited.

LEGISLATORS. In classical times statesmen frequently found it necessary to codify the laws of their people. This need usually arose in periods of social tensions caused by the creation of new means of survival and the resulting redivision of property. This situation occurred in Greece, particularly during the 7th-6th centuries B.C. Some legislators only recorded existing (aristocratic) law, others made an effort to create new principles of justice. (For examples, see CHARONDAS; DRACO; PITTACUS; SOLON; ZALEUCUS; also GORTYNA). The Romans' demand for codification arose during the struggle between the plebs and the patricians (see CLAUDIUS, APPIUS).

LEKANE. See VASE FORMS.

LEKYTHOS. See VASE FORMS.

LELANTIC WAR. War between the cities of Chalcis and Eretria for possession of the fertile Lelantic plain, which lay between them; it is difficult to give a date (somewhere between 750 and 650 B.C.). This conflict became a general Gr. war because Corinth and Samos took sides with Chalcis; Megara and Miletus aided Eretria. Chalcis won, but was exhausted.

LEMNOS. Large island in the northeastern Aegean Sea, very fertile as a result of its volcanic origin (this explains the cult of Hephaestus). Originally inhabited by Pelasgians. In about 500 B.C. it was ruled by Miltiades from the Thracian Chersonesus. Later, it had an Athenian *cleruchia*.

LENAEA. Athenian festival in honor of Dionysus, celebrated in January to February. Performances of comedies and sometimes tragedies were given.

LEOCHARES (4th cent. B.C.). Gr. sculptor, probably of Athens; worked on the Mausoleum at Halicarnassus. A few famous statues are attributed to him, of which Rom. copies have survived. The most famous are the "Apollo Belvedere," "Ganymede and the Eagle" (both in the Vatican), and the "Versailles Artemis."

LEONIDAS. King of Sparta from about 487-480; in 480 he was sent to secure an advance stronghold at the pass of Thermopylae against an attack by the Persians. His army consisted of 4,000 men—Peloponnesians and contingents from central Greece. Their position was strong; ideal to check the Persians' attack. Although the Persians greatly outnumbered them (the remainder of the Gr. army was expected after the Olympic Games), they were unable to break through. L. was aware that a road through the Oeta Mountains existed, by which the Persians could attack; he erred in placing untrustworthy Phocian troops at this strategic point. When the inevitable encirclement occurred and the Phocians fled, L. dismissed most of his army. He himself, however, stayed at his post with 300 Spartans, to cover the flank of the fleet at Artemisium as long as possible. All of them died a hero's death. Simonides and others sang their praises.

LEONTINI. City in the east of Sicily, founded by Naxos in 752 B.C., conquered by Syracuse in the 5th cent. and by Rome in 215 B.C. It was famous for its fertile fields. L. was Gorgias' birthplace.

LEPIDUS, MARCUS AEMILIUS. Name of:

—(1) The conqueror of Gallia Cisalpina to the south of the Po River, consul in 187 and 175 B.C. He built the Basilica Aemilia in the Forum and the Via Aemilia.

—(2) Praetor of Sicily in 81 B.C., elected consul in 78 B.C. He tried to upset Sulla's constitution after the latter's death.

—(3) Son of the preceding; one of the *triumviri* of 43 B.C.; *magister equitum* to Caesar 45-44; after Caesar's death, he supported Antony. The latter and Octavian formed a second triumvirate (43) with him; they needed the troops under his command. After the battle of Philippi, however, they thought it best to send him away and made him governor of Africa and of Numidia. In 36 he was summoned to Sicily to fight in the war against Sextus Pompey. When he attempted to acquire Sicily for himself, he was deprived of his troops by Octavian and forced to withdraw from the triumvirate. He remained *pontifex maximus* until his death in 13 B.C.

LESBOS. The largest Gr. island off the coast of Asia Minor, inhabited by Aeolians. Its political and artistic life flourished in about 600 B.C. (see SAPPHO; ALCAEUS; ARION; PITTACUS; MYTILENE; ERESUS).

LETO [Lat. Latona]. Gr. goddess, the

mother of Apollo and Artemis, who were born on Delos, where she was especially worshiped as the mother of Apollo. Her cult, like that of Apollo, probably originated in Asia Minor.

LEUCAS (White island). Gr. island in the Ionian Sea opposite Acarnania; owes its name to its chalk cliffs. Colonized by Corinth under Cypselus.

LEUCIPPUS of Miletus (5th cent. B.C.). Gr. philosopher, teacher of Democritus. He founded the theory of Atomism, later developed by Democritus.

LEUCTRA. Ancient village in Boeotia, to the southwest of Thebes. Here Epaminondas defeated the Spartans in 371 B.C. by using the so-called slanting phalanx —a revolutionary asymmetrical formation. All the power was concentrated in the left wing, which broke through the Spartan lines, turned right and attacked, from the rear, the left wing of the Spartan army, which had advanced meanwhile. This first defeat in a regular battle in the open field lost Sparta her reputation of being invincible.

LIBANIUS (314-c. 393). Gr. orator from Antioch, friend and fervent admirer of Julian, sixty-eight of his speeches have been preserved, as well as letters, and other writings. He was called "Little Demosthenes."

LIBRI SIBYLLINI. See SIBYL.

LIBRARY. See BOOKS.

LICINIUS. Rom. emperor 308-324 (see also CONSTANTINE THE GREAT).

LICTORS. The attendants of the Rom. magistrates who were invested with the *imperium*. The L. cleared the way for the magistrates and executed sentences of punishment (see FASCES). A dictator had twenty-four, a consul had twelve, the *praetor urbanus* had two (a praetor in a *provincia* had six). Later, the emperors were accompanied by twelve L., since Domitian there were twenty-four.

LIGURIANS. A pre-Indo-European people, who migrated from North Africa over the Pyrenees by way of Spain, and settled on what is now known as the French and Italian Riviera. In about 235 B.C. some of them were conquered by the Romans, the rest in about 180 B.C. Some place names ending in "sc" are reminiscent of them.

LILYBAEUM. Port on the westernmost tip of Sicily, founded by Carthage in 396 B.C. Neither Pyrrhus nor the Romans (during the 1st Punic War) succeeded in conquering it. In 241 B.C. it was ceded to Rome, to Hamilcar's regret. It remained a flourishing port under Rom. rule.

LIMES. Originally, this term signified a strip of land or a path along the Rom. frontiers. Later, particularly during the imperial period, it took on a broader meaning and indicated a frontier fortification, formed by a huge earthen wall, surrounded with palisades, and watch towers (the so-called Wall of Hadrian in Britain is a good example). Usually, the Romans took advantage of natural boundaries, especially big rivers (Rhine, Danube, etc.), but as invasions by barbarian tribes increased and became more threatening, gaps in these natural defenses had to be filled. The famous L. in Germania, for example, curved away from the Rhine south of Bonn and reached the Danube at Regensburg. The feeling of security induced by the L., however, resulted in relaxed vigilance of the Rom. troops (see GERMANIA). Other L. were built in Dacia, Syria, Arabia, and Africa.

LINDOS. City on the east coast of Rhodes. A Danish expedition made significant excavations there and found, among other things, the acropolis containing the remains of the temple of Athena and an inscription of the temple chronicle from mythical times until 99 B.C.

LINEAR B. See SCRIPT.

LION GATE. See MYCENAE.

LIPARI ISLANDS. The modern name for the Aeolian Islands to the north of Sicily, to which the Volcano Stromboli belongs. The island group is named after the main island of Lipari (the ancient Lipara). In 580 B.C. a Gr. colony was founded there; later, there was a Carthaginian naval base, conquered by the Romans in 252 B.C. It was said that Hephaestus and his Cyclopes had a smithy there.

LITURGY [Gr. *leitourgia*]. In Athens, the term L. was applied for a service to the state, compulsory for the wealthier citizens for one year. A way to raise funds for expensive projects had to be found and, as the antique polis had no direct taxation, the L. was instituted as a form of property tax. There were several types of L.: (a) the *choregia* (a person so taxed was called a *choregus*), involving the financing of a chorus for tragedies or comedies during competitions on the occasion of public festivals; (b) the *gymnasiarchia,* maintaining the upkeep of the contestants of public games; (c) the *trierarchia,* bearing the cost of equipping a warship. The latter L. was the most expensive of all, imposed on the wealthiest citizens only. If a citizen felt that a wealthier person should have been chosen instead of himself, he could challenge him to exchange properties. The system of L. existed not only in Greece, but in the empire of the Ptolemies as well. Our meaning for L., public worship, developed from its meaning as "service to the state, to the community."

LIVIA. Third and last wife of Augustus, mother (by a former marriage) of Tiberius and Drusus (3). Extremely beautiful, intelligent and domineering, L. appears to have had great influence on Augustus. On his death, she was able to secure the succession for Tiberius. During his reign too, she wielded great influence behind the scenes, which sometimes led to friction between mother and son. By testamentary disposition, Augustus conferred the honorary title of "Julia Augusta" on her.

LIVIUS, TITUS (59 B.C.-A.D. 17). Commonly called Livy. Rom. historian. Born in Patavium, he spent most of his life there and in Rome, where he became friendly with Augustus. There is practically nothing else known about his life. At the age of thirty he started writing a history, *Ab Urbe Condita libri,* covering the period from the founding of the city until 9 B.C. He completed 142 books; probably his work was interrupted because of his death. The following parts of this enormous work have been preserved: I-X (most ancient history to 293 B.C.), XXI-XXX (Second Punic War) and XXXI-XLV (Macedonian Wars to 167 B.C.). Its tremendous size was fatal; soon the complete works were no longer stud-

ied, and "abridged editions" were made. We have synopses (*periochae*) of the contents of all 142 books (except 136 and 137), and also excerpts in the works of Florus, Eutropius, and others. On the other hand, L.'s great success resulted in the loss of the annalists' works, which were one of his sources.

Even if we take into account that all ancient historians (even Thucydides to a certain degree) strove not only to investigate the past, but especially to give educational examples also, so that to most of them the literary form was more important than a statement of fact, then L. still cannot stand up to the test of reasonable criticism. We must admit, however, that, although he did not strive after objective truth, neither did he consciously falsify history (as did some annalists). L.'s aim was different: he wanted to write a heroic epic in prose. He wanted to show his readers how Rome, originally a small city, became a powerful metropolis, and explain at the same time how it was possible that the Roman people had lapsed into moral decadence in the time of the civil wars. Within the frame of epic composition, we can distinguish three main elements: (a) actual historical research—L. sometimes writes down several accounts and gives the reasons why he prefers one certain narrative; he sometimes looks for causes and motives; (b) rhetoric—he is able to inspire emotion and surprise by means of his refined style; his descriptions are vivid and the speeches expressed by his characters are often miracles of eloquence; (c) drama—his characters become alive; they are either good or evil, and collide with one another in terrible conflicts. All this is realized with a command of language and style that compares with Cicero.

LIVIUS ANDRONICUS (c. 284-c. 204). The first poet of Lat. literature; came to Rome in 242 as a Gr. slave, and was freed by his master Lucius Livius, whose name he bears (his Gr. name was Androneikos). Author of comedies and tragedies after Gr. examples, he paraphrased the *Odyssey* into Italian Saturnian meter. He also composed a hymn for a procession in honor of Juno Regina, on commission from the state (Liv. XXVII, 37).

LIVY. See LIVIUS.

LOCRIS. District in central Greece, comprising: Eastern L., divided into two parts: L. Epicnemidia and L. Opuntia, named after the city of Opus opposite Euboea. Western L., or L. Ozolis, on the Corinthian Gulf. Both sections remained backward and suffered much as a result of the aggression of their neighbors.

LOGOGRAPHERS.

—(1) The first Gr. writers on history and geography. Like early Gr. natural philosophy, the appearance of the L. was a characteristic aspect of Ionian culture in the 7th-6th centuries B.C. Hecataeus, Hellanicus, Pherecydes, and Scylax were famous L. The word L. was also used in a broader sense, meaning prose writers in general, in contrast to epic and lyric poets.

—(2) In Athens in the 5th-4th centuries B.C., L. were lawyers who did not appear in court themselves, but wrote speeches for their clients. Lysias was one of the best known.

LONGINUS, CASSIUS (3rd cent. A.D.). Gr. philosopher, Neoplatonist, and orator; advised Zenobia, queen of Palmyra, and was executed for it by Aurelianus (see MILITARY EMPERORS). A famous work, *On the Sublime,* commonly ascribed to him, is probably by an unknown writer of the 1st cent. A.D. It is a work of particular qualities, written in extremely good taste, which, with the works of Dionysius of Halicarnassus, laid the foundations for all later literary criticism.

LONGUS (probably 3rd cent. A.D.). Gr. novelist; wrote a pastoral novel, *Daphnis and Chloë;* the story takes place on Lesbos, probably L.'s birthplace. It is the only Gr. novel with an Arcadian setting. It enjoyed great popularity in later ages and served as a model for many pastoral novels in the 16th and 17th centuries.

LOUTROPHOROS. See VASE FORMS.

LUCA. City in northern Italy, where the first triumvirate met in 56 B.C. to renew its alliance.

LUCANIA. District in southern Italy, to the north of the Brutti's lands. In the 7th cent. B.C. the Greeks founded several colonies there (Paestum, Velia, and others). In about 400 B.C. they were conquered by the warlike Lucanianis (Osci), who in turn were subjected by Rome in the struggle against Pyrrhus and Hannibal.

LUCANUS, MARCUS ANNAEUS (A.D. 39-65). Commonly called Lucan. Latin epic poet, nephew of Seneca (2) and a friend of Persius. He was born in Corduba and brought to Rome during infancy; there he received the usual schooling in rhetoric and philosophy. At first, he was a favorite of Nero who bestowed offices on him; later he fell into disgrace. When L. got involved in Piso's conspiracy of 65, he was forced to commit suicide. Of his many works, only an epic, *Bellum Civile* (usually called *Pharsalia*), has been preserved. It is about the civil war between Caesar and Pompey. The latter is the hero, the personification of the republican ideals, cherished by the author. Next to Pompey, of course, the Stoic republican idol Cato (2) is eulogized prominently. In spite of the rhetorical, sometimes even bombastic tone, the work has its merits, particularly if we remember how young the author was. His passion for outdated political ideas was certainly sincere. The authority of the gods—so characteristic of the epic—is lacking; instead, L. makes fate the motivation of the action. The play was very popular in the Middle Ages, and had a great influence on later poets like Corneille, Goethe, and Shelley.

LUCIANUS (120-c. 180). Gr. author, commonly called Lucian. He was born in Syria; became a traveling declaimer and teacher of rhetoric. He died in Egypt while holding the office of procurator. He wrote a large number of works, mainly satiric dialogues, in pure Attic. He mocked all possible aspects of the spiritual and social life of his time. His book about a religious charlatan and his *Conversations with the Dead* were famous. Some people also attribute the novel *Lucius or a Donkey* (see APULEIUS) to him. Menippus exercised great influence on his ideas.

LUCILIUS, GAIUS (c. 180-c. 102). The oldest Lat. satiric poet; belonged to the "Scipionic Circle" (see LAELIUS). Of his thirty books of satires almost 1,300 lines have been preserved. He wrote on the most varying subjects: art, literature, morals, customs, etc. His satires are still entertaining; he criticizes social evils, in the genial style of Horace, unlike Juvenal's bitter tones.

LUCRETIA. According to tradition, the wife of Collatinus; she was raped by a son of Tarquinius Superbus, told her husband and father, and, making them take an oath of vengeance, committed suicide. Standing by her body, Lucius Junius Brutus then called upon the people to rebel against Tarquinius. That led to his exile and the proclamation of the Republic. Brutus and Collatinus became the first consuls. The legend inspired Shakespeare to write his poem *The Rape of Lucrece.*

LUCRETIUS, CARUS TITUS (probably 94-55). Lat. didactic poet. We know very little about his life, except that he was a friend or follower of a Rom. aristocrat, C. Memmius, not too prominent a personage (praetor in 58 B.C.). He dedicated his only work to him. The story that he wrote his poem between fits of madness, caused by drinking a love potion, and that he committed suicide during one of these seizures, is purely legendary. All other information about his character and his philosophy, is gleaned from his work, *De Rerum Natura (On the Nature of Things)*, a philosophical poem in six books, written in hexameters (see METER). This poem is considered to be the most beautiful didactic poem of ancient times. It expounds the doctrines of Epicurus: their ethical purport to free man from fear and superstition. L. particularly wants to free man from *religio*. By *religio* he means: (a) the traditional world of gods. That does not stop him from glorifying the goddess Venus in sublime verses in his opening, intended as a poetic image: Venus represents love. (b) the superstitious fear of the irrational, primarily of death: death is something perfectly natural; man dissolves into the atoms of which he was made. The work is not quite complete—especially noticeable in the sixth book—and was published by Cicero after the author's death.

The most interesting thing about L. is that he considered it his vocation to express in verse the doctrine of the Gr. philosopher he honored greatly. He had to overcome two obstacles: (a) Lat. poetry had not yet achieved its refined, artistic form. L. had an example in Ennius, and he used him as an example to a certain degree; however, L. can be considered the pioneer; (b) the subject of philosophy did not lend itself readily to poetic interpretation. Keeping all this in mind, his poem is an extraordinary achievement; some passages attain such polished, poetic expression, that it has not been surpassed even by the great poets of the Augustan period.

LUCULLUS, LUCIUS LICINIUS (c. 117-56) Rom. general; served as a quaestor under Sulla, and went with him to Greece and Asia in 88. In 74 as consul, with Cilicia for his province, he left for the East to fight against Mithridates. He won many battles; Mithridates was driven out of his kingdom and fled to Tigranes, king of Armenia. L. pursued him, took the mountain stronghold of Tigranocerta and followed the enemy farther and farther into the mountains of Armenia. However, he could not follow up his successes; he was forced to cope with his troops, who mutinied. In 66, Pompey superseded him. Actually, he was relieved of his command because of his policy in Asia. He had reduced interest rates in order to free the province of debts, incurred by the exploitation of Sulla and the publicans. This reform so angered the *equites* in Rome, that they delayed his triumph. It was finally granted; L. then retired to a life of luxury, as evidenced in the epicurean taste, for which he has become proverbial. His library was well known; he also was the first to bring the cherry tree from Asia Minor to Europe.

LUDOVISI THRONE. Name of a relief with three sides, on which are depicted: the birth of Aphrodite out of the sea foam in the center and, on the sides, female figures, a naked flute player and a clad incense scatterer, respectively. It was found on the land of the villa belonging to the famous Ludovisi family in Rome, formerly the park of Sallust. It is an original Gr. work of art from about 465 B.C. The great progress in early classical relief art can clearly be seen; the perspective is clearly indicated. It is now in the Terme Museum in Rome.

LUGDUNUM. Important city in Gaul, now Lyons, financial center of the province, where the mint was located. It was made a Rom. colony in 43 B.C., and reached its peak in the 1st-2nd centuries A.D. The Emperor Claudius was born there.

LUSITANIA. The Rom. name for a part of Hispania, corresponding approximately to the greater part of modern Portugal; a separate Rom. province from 27 B.C. until the end of the 4th cent. A.D.

LUSTRUM. Rom. purificatory sacrifice to Mars, made once every five years by the censors; sacred and magical objects were carried (particularly the *suovetaurilia*) in procession. A purification by sacrifice (*lustratio*) could also be held on other occasions, for example, a farmer could protect his land from evil influences by that ceremony, described by Cato in his *De Agri Cultura,* 141.

LUTETIA (or LUTETIA PARISIORUM). Capital of the Gallic tribe of Parisii on an island in the Seine River, the center of what is now Paris. Conquered by Labienus in 52 B.C. (Caes. *B.G.* VII, 57-62); later, it was extended to the southern bank of the Seine. In 360 Julian was proclaimed "Augustus" there.

LYCEUM, [Gr. *lykeion*]. The school of Aristotle; originally, a park adjoining a sanctuary of Apollo Lykeios in Athens. In the Middle ages a school of philosophy was also called L., after the ancient Athenian school of the Peripatetics. Certain European schools also derive their name from the Gr. L.

LYCIA. District in southern Asia Minor; under Persian rule from 546 B.C. to Alexander the Great, with an interruption in the 5th-4th centuries, when it was liberated by Cimon. After that it was ruled by the Diadochi; after 169 B.C. it was a free federal state. It was brought completely under Rom. domination by Vespasian. Curious rock tombs have been found there.

LYCOPHRON of Chalcis (c. 320-c. 250). Gr. poet; worked in the library of Alexandria under Ptolemy II. In addition to fragments of tragedies and a Satyric drama, one of his poems has been preserved, entitled *Alexandra* or *Cassandra,* a drama in 1,474 iambic trimeters (see METER), which attracted commentators of antiquity and the Byzantine epoch by its obscurity; undoubtedly the reason for its preservation. It is certainly difficult to read due to its neologism and disorganized syntax. The story is mainly about Alexandria's (Cassandra) prediction of the catastrophes that will befall the Greeks in retaliation for Troy's suffering. Because L. alludes to the coming of Aeneas to Italy and the future greatness of Rome, the work has also been attributed to a later poet of the same name. If it was created in 273 B.C., then the allusions to Rome stem from Pyrrhus' actions.

LYCURGUS. Name of:

—(1) The legendary legislator of Sparta, who was said to have remodeled the military and civil constitution of Sparta, on the advice of the Delphic oracle. If L. existed, he may have been a political reformer of the 8th-7th centuries B.C.; it is now supposed that he was not a historical figure, but a deity.

—(2) One of the ten Attic orators (c. 390-324), supporter of Demosthenes. After the battle of Chaeronea in 338, he reorganized Athenian finances, saw to improvements in the harbor construction of Piraeus, and had the Dionysus theater completed. He also had an official copy of the texts of the three great tragic poets made, which was loaned to the library of Alexandria at the request of Ptolemy II, and never returned. Only one of his speeches has survived.

LYDIA. Prosperous country in western Asia Minor, very rich in natural resources, and flourishing as a result of trade relations with the hinterland. The capital was Sardes. For a long time L. was a cultural and commercial link between Ionia and the civilizations of the Near East. About 687 B.C. the dynasty of the Mermnadae was founded by Gyges (see also ALYATTES; CROESUS). After 546, L. was one of the most important Persian satrapies; the Satraph's seat was in Sardes. During the Hellenistic period, L. was part of the kingdom of Pergamum; later it was part of the

Rom. province of Asia. L.'s two most important contributions to antique culture were the invention of coining money (see COINAGE) and its influence on Gr. music.

LYSANDER (?-395 B.C.). Spartan general and statesman. Appointed admiral of the Spartan fleet, which had been built with the support of the Persian prince Cyrus the Younger in 408, he defeated the Athenian fleet at Notium on the coast of Asia Minor (407). In 405 he dealt Athens the final blow at Aigospotamoi, forced it to capitulate in 404 and established an oligarchy of the Thirty Tyrants there (see CRITIAS). He traveled through the area formerly encompassing the Delian League, voicing the slogan of "Liberty for the Greeks." Actually, he instituted oligarchic governments everywhere, usually with Spartan supervisors (*harmostae*). His authoritarianism also made him many enemies in Sparta, where he managed to get the throne for Agesilaus in whom he thought to find a supporter. That was his mistake. L. was killed during the Corinthian War (see CORINTH).

LYSIAS (c. 450-c. 370). One of the most important of the ten Attic orators. He was the son of a citizen of Syracuse, who was called to Athens by Pericles. At the age of fifteen, L. joined Athenian colonists at Thurii; in 412 he returned to Athens. In 404, under the rule of the Thirty Tyrants (see CRITIAS), his property was confiscated (he and his brother owned a large shield factory in Piraeus). He was jailed, but escaped and joined Thrasybulus. After the victory of the democrats in 403, he returned to Athens. Because he was a *metoikos* (see METICS), L. could not appear in court himself, but wrote speeches for others (see LOGOGRAPHERS). Written in pure Attic, his speeches show clarity and elegance of style, and his ability to adapt his style to his subject. Particularly splendid examples are the speech *Against Eratosthenes* (his brother's murderer) and the speech

For the Invalid. Thirty-four of L.'s speeches have been preserved in addition to fragments of others.

LYSIMACHUS (c. 360-281). One of the Diadochi. He received Thrace and northwestern Asia Minor on the death of Alexander the Great. L. made an alliance with Seleucus I, Cassander, and Ptolemy I against Antigonus I, which led to the battle of Ipsus (301); in this way he acquired central Asia Minor as well. When he had also taken Macedonia and Thessaly from Demetrius Poliorcetes in 285, he became the most powerful of the Diadochi. But then his former allies turned against him; in 281 he fell during a battle against Seleucus I.

LYSIPPUS of Sicyon (4th cent. B.C.). Gr. sculptor; appointed to the court by Alexander the Great, of whom he made several portraits. Of his works, only Rom. copies remain. The most famous is the "Apoxyomenos" (scraper), an athlete scraping the dirt, mixed with oil, off his arms after the contest (Rome, Vatican). This statue confirms what Pliny the Elder tells us about L., namely that he introduced new proportions, deviating from those set forth in Polycletus' *Canon:* the head was smaller, the body longer and more slender. Another striking feature: the outstretched arms create the impression of depth. Several copies of portraits of Alexander and one of Seleucus I are also attributed to L. Other statues have been deformed by copyists so that the characteristics, typical of L.'s style, have not been respected, as evident, for example, in the "Farnese Hercules" in Naples and the statue of "Agias of Pharsalus" in Delphi. A damaged pedestal of one of L.'s statues has been found in Olympia. The heavily damaged statue on this pedestal may well be the remains of an original work. That L.'s influence extended far into the Hellenistic period can be seen from the "Alexander Sarcophagus." The famous seated "Hermes" found in Herculaneum is attributed to his school.

M

MACEDONIA. District north of Greece, bounded by Thessaly in the south, Epirus in the west, and Thrace in the east. It encompassed two parts, a coastal plain adjoining the sea coast (Thermaic Gulf, Chalcidice), and highlands gradually rising toward the north. In about 1100 B.C. a tribe related to the Greeks settled there during the great migration which resulted, among other things, in the Dorian invasion of Greece. Very little is known about the early history of these people. In the 7th cent. B.C. the royal house of M. was founded by Perdiccas I. In the 5th cent. B.C., M. interfered in Gr. affairs more and more often; Perdiccas II alternately supported Athens and Sparta. The population remained relatively primitive, but the kings wanted to adapt to Gr. culture more and more (see ARCHELAUS). Under Philip II, M. became a world power. (For further history see ALEXANDER THE GREAT; ANTIPATER; CASSANDER; ANTIGONUS; PHILIP V; and PERSEUS.) M. offers an interesting aspect for the study of Gr. government; the old Gr. tribal kingship, which was abolished in Greece itself in the 9th-8th centuries B.C., survived in M.; at the same time, social conditions, which once must have existed in most ancient Greece, can also be seen in M.

MACRINUS. See MILITARY EMPERORS.

MACROBIUS, AMBROSIUS THEODOSIUS (4th cent. A.D.). Rom. scholar and Neoplatonist. He wrote a symposium entitled *Convivia Saturnalia*, following the genre of Athenaeus; it is mainly a commentary on Virgil, with all kinds of valuable data on social conditions. He also wrote a commentary on Cicero's *Dream of Scipio*, the *Somnium Scipionis*. M.'s work had great influence in the Middle Ages.

MAEANDER. Large river in Asia Minor, with its outlet near Miletus. Proverbial for its winding course, its name is applied to the Gr. key pattern originating in the period of geometric art.

MAECENAS, GAIUS CILNIUS (?-8 B.C.). Friend and counselor to Augustus, patron of the arts; he came originally from Etruria. He acted as adviser and mediator during the dispute between Octavian and Antony. When the former was absent from Rome, M. represented him several times, but never officially held office. He preferred to devote his time to the patronage of poets. In his luxurious house and park in Rome, he received the greatest literary talents of his time, among them Horace and Virgil; he encouraged the latter to write his *Georgica*. He willed his estate to Augustus.

MAGIC. Composition of semireligious practices, purporting to influence the powers that are assumed to dominate the world and nature. M. is usually linked to a primitive stage of human thought and emotion; but the "primitive" exists at all times, and it played a strong role in the highly developed Gr. and Rom. cultures. Nevertheless, as the cultural level is raised, the protestations against M. and the revulsion from M. become more intense. Gr. and Rom. legislators also opposed M., without being able to wipe it out.

In theory, there are the following classifications: (a) sympathetic M.: let us take, for example, a person called Germanicus (it is mentioned in Tacitus' *Annales* II, 69, that a Germanicus was under the spell of M.); his name is written on a lead tablet, a hole is pricked in the *a* and the victim gets a stomach ulcer; the same is done to the *G* and he will contract a brain tumor; (b) contagious M.: a piece of clothing or a lock of hair belonging to the victim is burned, and the person will pine away. These are examples of "black magic"; of course these practices are most often found among the lowest social levels, but the line between M. and "official" religion is hard to define, although it is mainly the less asocial practice of "white" M. that is on the border. Many fertility rites are part of these practices (see for example, LUSTRUM). Antique literature is full of M. and pseudo-M., from Homer (where the wounded Odysseus is healed by incantations; *Od.* XIX, 457) to Apuleius, and other writers. In Gr. mythology, Circe and Medea are typical magical characters. In later ancient times, M. also appears in philosophy (see IAMBLICHUS).

MAGISTER EQUITUM. Originally commander of the cavalry, later, the adjutant of a Rom. dictator. Still later, the title was applied generally to the dictator's substitute (for a case of rank at the same level as that of a dictator, see FABIUS).

MAGISTRATUS. A term used by the Romans to designate the public office, also the name of the person who held it. Next to the senate and the people, the magistracy was one of the main elements of the Rom. Republic (see POLYBIUS). The magistrates were classified according to two standards: (a) M. *cum imperio* (dictator, *magister equitum,* consul, praetor) and M. *sine imperio* (quaestor, aedile, censor, tribune): these only had authority (*potestas*) to assist in the administration of the state (see also IMPERIUM); (b) M. *curules* (the same as those with *imperium,* also all censors, and *aediles curules*) and the others (see SELLA CURULIS). The M. curules also wore the toga *praetexta*. Magistrates received no salary; many became deeply indebted, especially the aediles who gave the public big games; they then tried to pay their debts when they became proconsuls or propraetors, by exploiting a province (see, for example, VERRES). A Rom. M. held office for one year only; the magistracy would have been a factor of unstableness in the government, if the senate had not been made up of magistrates and ex-magistrates, thus assuring continuity (see also LICTORS; CURSUS HONORUM).

MAGNA GRAECIA (Great Greece). The Lat. term for southern Italy, where Greece had many colonies. From there, Gr. civilization first expanded in Italy, and then to Rome. It was a center of flourishing cultural life (see ELEATIC SCHOOL; PYTHAGORAS), particulary in the

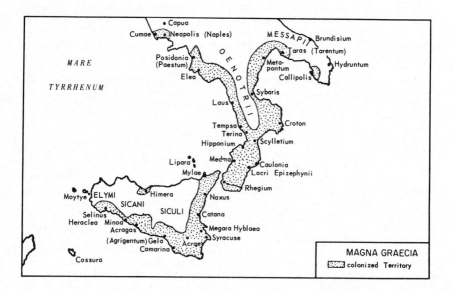

MAGNA GRAECIA
colonized Territory

6th cent. B.C.; after about 500 B.C. it lost significance as a result of internal strife (see SYBARIS; CROTON), and through the invasion of the native inhabitants (see LUCANIA). Only Tarentum remained powerful, until it was subdued by Rome.

MAGNA MATER. See CYBELE.

MAGNESIA. Name of the southeastern part of Thessaly. According to tradition, the founders of two cities in Ionia came from there; both cities bear the same name, one on the Maeander and one in the Hermus valley, at the foot of Mount Sipylus.

MALEA, CAPE OF. The southeastern tip of Peloponnessus opposite Cythera, notorious as a "cape of storms."

MALIS. District in central Greece, near the Pass of Thermopylae.

MAMERTINI. Oscan people from Campania, who had left their country under the protection of the god Mamer or Mars. Mercenaries of Agathocles, they seized Messana after his death, where they founded a robber state. When they were threatened by Hiero II they called in the Carthaginians to help them; the latter took possession of Messana. The M. had also applied to the Romans for help, who took this opportunity to win a foothold in Sicily. Thus Messana was the cause of the First Punic War (264 B.C.).

MANES. Name which the Romans gave the spirits of the dead; therefore also used for (a) the realm of the dead; (b) the gods of that realm; (c) the worshiped ancestors of a family; and (d) the ghost of one individual. Tombstones are often marked D. M. S. that is, *Dis Manibus Saerum* (to the sacred ghost [of the dead person]).

MANETHO. Egyptian priest of Serapis, in the reign of Ptolemy I, who wrote in Greek a history of Egypt which lays the foundation for the classification of Egyptian dynasties. This work was commissioned by Ptolemy II; only fragments of it have survived.

MANILIUS. Name of:

—(1) Gaius M., *tribunus plebis* in 66 B.C., who proposed making Pompey commander in chief against Mithridates and giving him *imperium* over all the magistrates of the East. Cicero supported his suggestion in a famous speech, *De Imperio Gnaeus Pompei.*

—(2) Mareus or Gaius M. (1st cent. A.D.). Lat. poet who wrote a didactic poem, *Astronomica*, in five books, in hexameters (see METER). He discusses astronomy, and particularly astrology after the manner of Aratus. The work is probably incomplete; apparently, the author planned a sixth book.

MANIPLE [Lat. *manipulus*]. Rom. army unit, consisting of two centuries; subdivision of a legion, which had thirty maniples (three in each of the ten cohorts).

MANLIUS. Name of:

—(1) Marcus M. Capitolinus. More or less legendary Rom. commander, consul in 392 B.C. He repelled the attack by the Gauls on the Capitol in 387, after having been awakened by the cackling of the geese; two years later, he tried to lighten the financial burden of the plebeians, imposed on them by the patricians, and is said to have incited the people against Camillus. He was killed in the civil dissension which followed.

—(2) Titus M. Imperiosus Torquatus, also a legendary hero, who is said to have killed a Gaul of huge stature in single combat in 361 B.C.; afterward, he put on the Gaul's necklace (*torques*). It is also said that he had his own son executed because he had fought (and won!) without waiting for a command from the consuls—M. himself was one of the consuls at the time. His victory over the Latini in 340, however, is historical (see LATIUM).

—(3) Gaius M., follower of Catilina; levied an army for him in Etruria; both fell at Pistoria.

MANTINEA. City in southeastern Arcadia, to the north of Tegea with which it was constantly quarreling. It was established in 500 B.C., by synoecism of five villages, and became a moderate democracy in 450. In 420 it turned against Sparta, and was dismantled by the Spartans in 385, after the "King's Peace" (see ANTIALCIDAS). When Sparta's might was broken after the battle of Leuctra, the walls were rebuilt. M. became famous mainly through the last victory of Epaminondas in 362. In 223 B.C. it was destroyed by the Achaean League, rebuilt, and named Antigonia. In A.D. 125 Hadrian gave it its old name back.

MANTUA. City in northern Italy, founded by the Etrurians, became Roman in 219 B.C.; Virgil was born in the neighboring village of Andes.

MANUS MANUM LAVAT. "One hand washes another" (Sen. *Apocol.* 9, 9).

BATTLE OF MARATHON

Marshes

Plataeans

(Vrana)

Persian fleet

Athenians

to Athens

Cynosura (Dog's Tail)

Battle of Marathon

MARATHON. Village on the northeastern coast of Attica, famous mainly for the victory of Miltiades, commander of 10,000 Greeks (mostly Athenians) and a small auxiliary corps from Plataea, over the Persians under Datis and Artaphernes (490 B.C.). The terrain, a coastal plain, was actually more favorable to the Persians than to the Gr. *hoplites,* as the Persian cavalry would have been able to deploy; however, it arrived too late. The Greeks winning on both flanks, pushed toward the center from both sides, and in the ensuing hand-to-hand fighting, the cavalry could do little.

Themistocles and Aeschylus, among others, participated in this battle. After the victory, a runner was sent to Athens —a distance of about 26 miles—with the glorious tidings; he was just able to deliver the message before falling dead of exhaustion. Our M. races commemorate this race. The Spartans had also sent an army, but it was held up for religious reasons and came too late. M. was the native city of Herodes Atticus.

MARCELLUS. Name of:

—(1) Marcus Claudius M. (3rd cent. B.C.). Rom. general. He successfully com-

bated Hannibal during the Second Punic War (Nola 216) and took Syracuse in 211 (see also ARCHIMEDES). He fell in 208, while a consul for the fifth time, after having been lured into a trap by Hannibal.

—(2) Marcus Claudius (42-23 B.C.). Nephew of Augustus and husband of Julia; generally considered as Augustus' successor; he died young, however, to the general sorrow, which is reflected in Virgil, *Aeneid* VI, 883.

MARCOMANNI. German tribe, which participated in the invasion of Gaul by Ariovistus. In about 8 B.C. it migrated to Bohemia, under Rom. pressure; there, the king, Maroboduus, founded a powerful empire, which was a threat to the Rom. Empire. Marcus Aurelius had to campaign heavily against them.

MARCUS AURELIUS (120-180). Rom. emperor and Stoic philosopher; original name Marcus Annius Verus. At an early age, he was already a favorite of Hadrian, and was given an excellent education by him. Hadrian also had him adopted by Antoninus Pius. M.A. married Antoninus' daughter Faustina in 145, and succeeded his father-in-law as Marcus Aurelius Antoninus in 161. He had Lucius Verus appointed his coregent. M.A. was forced to wage constant wars on the frontiers of the Empire. Verus was sent to the East against the Parthians (162-166), but his returning army brought back a dangerous epidemic of pestilence. M.A. himself waged war on the Danube, particularly against the Marcomanni and the Quadi (170-174); after that, against the governor of Syria, Avidius Cassius, who had set himself up as an antiemperor. Then he fought against the Marcomanni again (177); he died soon afterward. His personal tragedy was that he would much rather have devoted himself to study and law; instead, the serious threat to the Empire forced him to campaign again and again. During his lonely expeditions, he wrote his Stoic *Meditations.* This writing is one of the most widely read works from ancient times; it bears witness to his high ideals. But in the meantime, the treasury was emptying, and bureaucracy increasing. M.A.'s most serious mistake was to appoint his own son Commodus to succeed him (see ADOPTIVE EMPERORS).

MARDONIUS. Son-in-law to Darius I; led an expedition to Thrace and Macedonia (see DARIUS) in 492 B.C.; in 480 he commanded the army again, during Xerxes' expedition against the Greeks. When Xerxes left after the battle of Salamis, he left M. behind in Thessaly. In 479 M. invaded Attica for the second time, but was driven back; in September he was defeated and killed at Plataea.

MARIUS, GAIUS (157-86). Rom. general; distinguished himself as a young officer and as a *tribunus plebis* (119) by making an improvement in the voting system, by which even then he bullied the *optimates*. He served as a *legatus* under Metellus against Jugurtha (109), although he was a *homo novus*. He became a consul in 107 and made an end to the war with Jugurtha (see also SULLA). In the meantime, the Cimbri and the Teutons were threatening Italy, and M., in whom the people saw the only savior of the homeland, became a consul four times (104-101). In those years he introduced reforms in the army as well as technical improvements; the most important thing, however, was that he made it a professional army into which mainly proletarians were recruited. The latter saw the army commander as their "master"; they were dependent on him for the allotment of land, and other rewards when they became veterans. This innovation had enormous results for the future; later, especially in the civil wars, the soldiers of the legions no longer fought for their country, but for their generals and their material welfare. After the victory of the barbarians, M. became a consul again in 100, and in order to give his veterans their reward, he allied himself with the *populares;* but when the latter started a revolution, M. acted against them with violence under the *senatus consultum ultimum* (see CAVEANT CONSULES); but now he was in a dilemma, because the *optimates* also remained suspicious of him. In the Social War, Sulla was the better commander. The latter became commander in chief in 88 against Mithridates. In the ensuing turbulence (see SULLA), M. was forced to flee, but returned after Sulla's departure, was welcomed in Rome by Cinna, massacred his opponents, appointed himself consul for the seventh time (for 86), but died a few days after having taken office (January 13th). It is hard to say whether his talent as a general (particularly his talent for organization) should rouse admiration, or his actions as a politician should make us despise (or pity) him.

MARK ANTHONY. See ANTONIUS, MARCUS.

MARRIAGE AND FAMILY. Occupied a different place in antique society than we might think if taking our modern ideas as a starting point. We are used to considering the family as one of the most important, if not the most important and also (at least ideally) the most solid nucleus of society. This family is based on a marriage sanctioned by the community (state and often church). The Greeks and Romans held slightly different views. Of course there was a family tie, as otherwise communal living, education, etc., would be almost nonexistent, but the tendency was to view the family in a larger sense; the tribe was considered the heart of society. When the polis (city-state) and the *res publica* (state) developed further, the situation remained almost unchanged. Marriage was not an institution sanctioned by the state; it was a private contract between families and owed its social security only to traditions (strict monogamy among them). Religious sanction also was not customary with one exception—one certain type of patrician marriage, the *confarreatio,* was performed in the presence of priests, and was, in principle, impossible to dissolve. Aside from this, divorce was very easy in ancient times, and was obtainable by mutual consent or by the decision of one partner, but the man was compelled to pay the bride's dowry back. This again manifests the private nature of marriage. There is practically no evidence that divorce was considered a profoundly tragic occurrence.

All these conventions are closely connected with the position of women in antique society. However, we should not generalize—in the course of the history of ancient times important changes took place, and we can only indicate some main points here. The Greeks invaded the country, like nomads (living in patriarchal family groups), and assimilated there with an agrarian population in which women appear to have held an important position. In early Mycenaean culture, women were also honored, as we can see from the sagas; and as is still the case in Homer's epics; great value is attached to a stable and harmonious marriage (*Od.* VI, 180-185)—characters like Penelope and the queen of the Phaiacians (*Od.* VII) are particularly characteristic. In Sparta this high position of women survived longer, although family life there suffered more than elsewhere because the state took over the education of the children. In classical Athens, however, the position of married women was extremely low. Girls, twelve to fourteen years of age, were often married without knowing their bridegrooms well—love was rarely the prelude to marriage. However, marital fidelity was usually adhered to, mainly because of convention and the severe punishment for adultery (though reprehensible only for a woman).

In 5th cent. Athens women were excluded from public life; they spent their time indoors, occupied with household duties and children (see HOUSES). It was not the same for certain groups of unmarried women, such as the hetaerae, who held a very different position.

In Rome the position of married women was much better, although, according to the law, she was totally dependent. In some forms of marriage (the Romans contracted various types) the bride passed from the jurisdiction (Lat. *manus*) of her father to that of her husband, in other marriages she remained under parental power. However, as seen repeatedly in history, these legal practices were not always strictly observed. The influence of the Rom. mother of the family (*matrona*) was quite extensive. There are also many examples of women who played an influential part (also in politics). In the 1st cent. B.C. marital and family relationships deteriorated drastically. Augustus tried to remedy the situation by enacting moral laws, but the results were hardly

permanent. Christianity brought new conditions, which need not be considered here.

MARS. The most important Italian god next to Jupiter; the Campus Martius is named for him, and the month of March. Besides being a fertility-god (see FRATRES ARVALES; LUSTRUM; SALII) he was also a god of war. He was therefore identified with Ares.

MARTIALIS, MARCUS VALERIUS (c. 40-c. 102). Commonly called Martial. Rom. poet, the most important Rom. epigrammist. Originally from Spain, he came to Rome in 64, where he lived frugally by the favors of important persons to whom he dedicated his poems. Although he never became rich, he was highly esteemed for his topical poems. Pliny the younger, one of the many literators with whom he was friendly, paid for his return to Spain in 98; he also devoted a moving letter to M., after having received notice of his death (*Ep.* III, 21). His 1,561 poems were classified into fifteen books by M. himself. The best known ones are *Xenia* (gifts, book 13) and the *Apophoreta* (mottoes for gifts to be taken home, book 14). He proves to be a sharp observer and a fervent realist; his work reflects the social life under Titus and Nerva. Man, with all his traits is the center of his interest; that is what makes M.'s poetry so vivid to readers of all times.

MARTIANUS CAPELLA (5th cent. A.D.). Lat. author from Carthage; wrote a curious allegorical book called *The Marriage of Philology and Mercurius;* it was greatly admired in the Middle Ages as a manual for the study of language and literature.

MASINISSA (c. 240-149). Ruler of Numidia. He fought on the Carthaginian side in Spain during the Second Punic War, but was won over to the Rom. cause by Scipio Major. When Scipio invaded Africa, M. openly became his ally against Syphax and the Carthaginians (see SOPHONISBA), and played an important part in the battle of Zama. After the peace, he constantly plagued Carthage, which was unable to defend itself against him without permission from Rome; evidently, it was never granted. When the harassed

Carthaginians finally retaliated in 150, it was the cause of the Third Punic War; M. died soon after. One of his grandsons was Jugurtha.

MASK. The stereotyping of the human face. The M. was used to accentuate the individuality of the face and make it permanent, or to give it a superhuman element. Death masks were used by many peoples all over the world during ancient times; for example, the golden masks that were found in Mycenae. These were intended to "conserve" the face of the dead and protect them from harm after death. An example of giving masks a superhuman function can be seen in the use of masks in antique comedy and tragedy; one actor could play several roles. On a more "primitive" level, there is the dance mask, as used during popular festivals. For example, the original function of the Gorgon's head (Medusa) was apotropaic, that is, it was designed to exorcise demons. This function can also be seen in its use by the Etruscans. Their name for the wearer of the mask, *phersu,* is the origin of the Lat. word *persona;* this became the Rom. word for the M. that was used in a drama.

MASSILIA. Now called Marseille, founded in about 600 B.C. by Phocaea. From there, Gr. culture spread to Provence, leaving traces deep in Gaul. M. was friendly with Rome from early times, supported it during the Second Punic War and when the Rom. province in southern Gaul was established. In 49 B.C. it opposed Caesar and lost the whole area as a punishment.

MAURETANIA. District in western North Africa, now Morocco. King Bocchus of M. granted his son-in-law Jugurtha political asylum for a while (see also SULLA). The country was conquered by Rome in A.D. 42.

MAUSOLEUM. Originally, the great monumental tomb erected in 355-345 in Halicarnassus for Mausolus, who ruled Caria in the 4th cent. B.C., by his wife Artemisia. This building, on which the most famous sculptors worked (among whom Scopas and Leochares) was known as one of the Seven Wonders of the World. Some authorities believe that the two large statues found among the remains, now in the British Museum in London, represent Mausolus and Artemisia. The Romans called other large tombs M. also, for example, the one for Augustus on the Campus Martius and the one for Hadrian on the Tiber River, which is now known as the Fortress of the Angels (Castel Sant'angelo).

MAXENTIUS MARCUS AURELIUS VALERIUS. Son of Maximian, Rom. emperor from 306-312. He set himself up as anti-emperor with the support of the Praetorians, because he had been bypassed in favor of Constantius Chlorus, Galerius, and Constantine the Great, successively. M. was able to hold his own against Galerius, but Constantine defeated him in the famous battle of the Pons Milvius, during which he was killed.

MAXIMIANUS, MARCUS AURELIUS VALERIUS. Commonly called Maximian. Father of Maxentius, Rom. emperor from 286-305 (308); was appointed "Caesar" by Diocletian in 285, and "Augustus" of the West in 286; he was constantly forced to fight against the Germanic tribes on the Rhine frontiers. In 305 he and Diocletian abdicated, but in 306 he took up the reins again, in support of his son. After having abdicated again in 308, he led one more revolt against Constantine the Great, was imprisoned and probably committed suicide.

MAXIMINUS. See MILITARY EMPERORS.

MAXIMINUS DAIA. "Caesar" under Galerius; became "Augustus" in 308 (see DIOCLETIAN); in 313 he was defeated by Licinius and died.

MEDES. Indo-European people, first dominated their related tribe, the Persians; in 550 B.C. the situation was reversed. Still, their influence on the Persian empire remained so great, that the Greeks often called the Persians M. (see also CYAXARES; ASTYAGES; ECBATANA).

MEDIOLANUM. Now Milan, was founded in 396 B.C. by the Gallic Insubres. It first became Roman in 222, but not definitely so until 194 B.C. During the imperial period it grew and prospered and even became the residence of the West-Rom. emperors in the 4th cent. A.D.

MEDUSA. See MASK; PERSEUS.

MEGALOPOLIS. City in Arcadia,

founded in about 365 B.C. by Epaminondas as the capital of the Arcadian League; to that end, the inhabitants of forty villages moved to M. (see SYNOECISM); it was meant to be a bulwark against Sparta, and served very well; during the Hellenistic period it played a large part in the Achaean League, under Philopoemen. Polybius was a citizen of M.

MEGARA. Dorian city on the Isthmus of Corinth, on the Attic frontier, at the foot of Mount Cithaeron. Between 730 and 550 B.C. it played an important part in Gr. colonization (among other cities, it founded M. Hyblaea in Sicily, Byzantium, and Chalcedon); during that period, M. had an important wool industry. In about 600 B.C., M. was ruled by the tyrant Theagenes, got into serious internal difficulties, and soon lost its territory to Corinth, and the island of Salamis to Athens. Theognis bore witness to the violent party struggle still raging in 540 B.C. About that time, M. became a member of the Peloponnesian League and took an active part in the Persian Wars. After 460 it became a bone of contention between Athens and Corinth. M. was more and more dependent on Piraeus for its trade relations and when Pericles had the notorious "Megarian Decree" accepted, which excluded M. from trade with the Delian League, it was this fatal blow to M. that became one of the main causes leading to the Peloponnesian War. In the 4th cent. Euclid, a pupil of Socrates, founded a school of philosophy there; these so-called Megarians adopted the theories of the Eleatics and were famous for their dialectical arguments.

MELA, POMPONIUS (1st cent. A.D.) Rom. geographer. He wrote a popular geography textbook about the world as it was then known; his conception of the world is about the same as Strabo's.

MELISSUS of Samos (c. 440 B.C.). Gr. philosopher, pupil of Parmenides; he defended the latter's doctrine against the systems of others (see EMPEDOCLES; ATOMISM; ANAXAGORAS). In contrast to his teacher, he believed the universe to be infinite.

MELITA. Now Malta, colonized by Phoenicians in the 10th cent. B.C. They were succeeded by the Carthaginians. In 218 B.C. it became Roman. Some say that M. is the island Ogygia of Calypso, in the *Odyssey*.

MELOS. Island in the Aegean Sea (one of the Sporades, now considered one of the Cyclades); in prehistoric times, obsidian, a greatly sought-after commodity, was mined in Phylakopi, where important remains from the Minoan period were found. When the Dorians invaded Greece it was colonized from Laconia. Because it remained outside the Delian League it was a thorn in the side of the Athenians; after a first attack under Nicias in 426 B.C. they sent a strong expedition to the island in 416. Thucydides (V, 85, ff.) tells how the Athenian ambassadors first negotiated in a haughty and cynical manner (the so-called Melian Dialogue), and how the Melians refused to knuckle under. All the men were then killed, the women and children dragged away as slaves, and a *cleruchia* was established on the island.

MELPOMENE. See MUSES.

MENANDER (342-291). Gr. poet of comedies, the most important representative of the Attic New Comedy; he was influenced by the philosophical doctrines of Theophrastus and Epicurus, and learned dramatic technique from Alexis, a poet of the Attic Middle Comedy. He spent his life in Athens, where he wrote more than 100 plays, of which the titles of 98 are known. For the characteristics of his dramatic art and the influence of Euripides on it, see COMEDY.

Love is the theme of all his plays. Young couples are always prevented from being happy by social inequality, opposition from parents, etc., until suddenly a coincidental happening or discovery makes the obstacles disappear. The main plot is threaded with little side issues, in which impudent slaves usually produce the comic effects. The sensitively shaded characters of his sketches are striking; M. is a perfect humanist. Until 1905 his work was only known from fragments and through the Rom. editions of his works by Plautus and Terence. Then additional large fragments of four plays were found on papyrus, mainly of his *Epitrepontes*, (*The Arbitration*). In the fifties a papyrus codex of an entire play, *Dyskolos* (*The Grumbler*), an early play, was found in an antiquarian's shop. The discovery of this comedy, which has already been published in many editions, is not only very important for our knowledge of the New Comedy and Gr. literature, but also of the history of the European theater in general.

MENIPPUS of Gadara (Syria) (1st half of the 3rd cent. B.C.). Gr. philosopher, one of the Cynics. He was a slave in Sinope, bought his own freedom and became a citizen of Thebes. He wrote lightly on philosophical subjects in prose interspersed with verse. Later, the Romans called a satire in which prose and verse were mixed "Menippean Satire"; this genre was also represented in works by Varro, Seneca (*Apocolocyntosis*), Petronius, Boethius, and Martianus Cappella.

MENS SANA IN CORPORE SANO. "A healthy spirit in a healthy body" (Juv. *Sat.* X, 356).

MERCURY. See HERMES.

MESSALA (or MESSALLA) CORVINUS, MARCUS VALERIUS (64 B.C.-A.D. 8). Rom. general, author, and patron of literature. In 43 he was proscribed, but escaped to the camp of Brutus and Cassius; later he supported Octavian and Antony. He was appointed consul in place of Antony in 31 and took part in the battle of Actium. His literary circle included Tibullus and the poetess Sulpicia; he was a patron of Ovid. M. was the author of various works, all of which are lost.

MESSALINA, VALERIA (A.D. 24-48) Wife of the Emperor Claudius, mother of Octavia and Britannicus; notorious for her excesses. When she openly lived with her favorite, Silius, during one of the Emperor's tours of duty, she was killed, on the instigation of the freedman Narcissus (Tac. *Ann.* XI, 26-38).

MESSANA. Now Messina in northeastern Sicily, founded under the name of Zancle in about 750 B.C. by Chalcis. In about 493, refugees from Samos settled there, followed by Messenians, who gave it the name of M. It was the native city of Euhemerus (see also MAMERTINI).

MESSENIA. District in the southwestern Peloponnesus, with fertile plains, to the west of Laconia. During the Mycenaean period, Pylos was the most important city. In the 11th cent. B.C. the Dorians settled there. During the First Messenian War, in the 8th cent. B.C., they were subjected to Sparta in spite of their heroic opposition, under the leadership of the legendary Messenian hero Aristodemus (see also ITHOME). In the 7th cent. M. revolted again (the Second Messenian War), under another more or less legendary hero, Aristomenes (see also HOPLITES; TYRTAEUS). After the conquest the inhabitants were made Helots (see SPARTA) and the land was divided among the Spartan noblemen. When a heavy earthquake struck Sparta in 464 B.C., M. revolted again, the Third Messenian War (see also CIMON). Athens caused smaller uprisings after the victory of Sphacteria. In 369 B.C., Epaminondas liberated M., after which *Messana* was established as its capital (as was Megalopolis in Arcadia). In 146 B.C. it was conquered by Rome.

MESSENIANS. The inhabitants of Messenia (see also MESSANA).

METAURUS. River in Umbria, where Hasdrubal (2) was defeated by the Rom. consuls Marcus Livius Salinator and Gaius Claudius Nero in 207 B.C.; the latter had intercepted a message in which Hasdrubal told his brother Hannibal about his plans. He unhesitatingly decided to march north from the south, where his army was camped opposite Hannibal's. That bold operation ensured the Rom. victory.

METELLUS. Name of several Romans of the *Caecillia gens:*

—(1) Quintus Caecilius M. Numidicus. He defeated Jugurtha in 109-107 B.C., but was forced to yield his command to Marius in 107.

—(2) His son, nicknamed Pius, a follower of Sulla, opposed Sertorius in Spain in 79-72.

—(3) Quintus Caecilius M. Creticus. He fought the pirates on Crete (68-66) and opposed Pompey when the latter advocated more humane treatment of the pirates. After Pompey's return from the East (62 B.C.) he was one of the leaders of the opposition to his plans.

METER. The rhythm of the verse of antique poetry (and sometimes of prose). The most important difference from later poetry is that M. is based entirely on a succession of long or short syllables (ancient man had much more of an "ear" for this than modern man); modern poetry in contrast, consists of a succession of accented and unaccented syllables. For this reason we "modernize" when reciting ancient poetry, and usually accent a part of each metrical foot, generally a long syllable. The question of whether or not the Greeks and the Romans accented part of the stanza with some change of tone (Lat. *ictus*, stress) is still debated. Nevertheless, the accent is given here for the modern reader.

The main classifications are: (a) the epic M.; (b) the dramatic M.; (c) the lyric M.; (d) the M. of other genres of poetry; (e) the M. of prose.

(a) The M. in the epic is almost exclusively the dactylic hexameter; only the most ancient Rom. epics are in the ancient Italian Saturnian verse (*Versus Saturnicus*). This hexameter consists of six *dactyls* ($\_\cup\cup$), each of the six feet (except as a rule the fifth) can be replaced by a *spondee* ($\_\_$); the last foot is truncated and thus forms a *trochee* ($\_\cup$), which can also be replaced by a spondee; the rhythmic form is then: $\_\cup\cup|\_\cup\cup|\_\cup\cup|\_\cup\cup|\_\cup$. Each stanza has one (very occasionally two) natural break in the verse, the *caesura*. A line will often have many caesuras, but the principal caesura is the one placed after the long syllable of the third foot, or after the first short one, for example

Arma virumque cano || *Troiae qui primus ab oris*

and:

Sponte sua sine lege || *fidem rectumque colebat.*

(b) The most important M. of the drama is the iambic trimeter, three "measures" of every two *iambs* ($\cup\_\cup\_$), of which the first can again be replaced by a spondee (so: $\_\_\cup\_$). So the rhythmic form is $\cup\_\cup\_\cup\_$. Again, one long can be replaced by two short so that a dactyl ($\_\cup\cup$) or anapest ($\cup\cup\_$) or *tribrachys* ($\cup\cup\cup$) replaces an iamb (or spondee). (c) The lyric M. has many

forms. The hexameter is used with the pentameter in the distichon (see ELEGY); the pentameter consists of twice two and one half feet of the hexameter, so that the rhythmic form of a distichon becomes:

$$\_\cup\cup|\_\cup\cup|\_\cup\cup|\_\cup\cup|\_\cup\cup|\_\cup$$
$$\_\cup\cup|\_\cup\cup|\_||\_\cup\cup|\_\cup\cup|\_$$

Many combinations of iambs were created by lyric poets. Highly complicated rhythmic forms and combinations are found in the lyric chrouses of comedy and tragedy. Certain lyric poets developed their own strophes, for example, Sappho and Alcaeus; these were copied by the Romans, among others by Catullus and Horace.

(d) Among other poetic genres, the satire employed the hexameter most frequently. Aphorisms (gnomic poetry) are often written in iambic M.; for epitaphs, the distichon was often used. The didactic poem (Hesiod, Lucretius, Virgil, *Georgica*) is usually written in hexameters, as is bucolic poetry (Theocritus, Virgil, *Bucolica*).

(e) In antique prose meters are also found, although they did not adhere to a strict rhythm but showed a preference for certain forms; these were applied especially at the end of a sentence (*clausula*). Cicero, for example, shows a marked preference for a limited group of *clausulae;* one which occurs very often is $\_\cup\cup\cup\_\cup$ (*esse videatur*). On the other hand, poetic M. was particularly avoided in prose. That makes it all the more surprising that Tacitus begins his *Annales* with a (slightly archaic) hexameter; this probably constitutes a hidden compliment to his great predecessor Ennius.

METICS [Gr. *metoikos*, foreign settler]. Resident aliens with a special constitutional position. The best known are the Athenian M.; they had to be officially recorded in a deme register, had to pay a special tax (liturgies could also be imposed on them) and serve in the army. Usually they were not permitted to own real estate, nor could they legally marry citizens; however, they did participate in the social life. They had to have a patron (*prostates*), an Athenian citizen. There were almost no political privileges to offset their numerous obligations. Still, the enormous prosperity of 5th-4th cent. Athens attracted thousands of M., particularly to Piraeus (see LYSIAS). Trade and industry provided most of them with a far from frugal livelihood.

METOPE. See ARCHITECTURAL ORDERS.

METROPOLIS. Gr. mother city of a colony (see COLONIZATION).

MICON (5th cent. B.C.). Athenian painter, a contemporary and coworker of Polygnotus. Among other things, he painted the "Amazonomachy" in the Stoa Poikile. We are only familiar with his work through descriptions; we know that he grouped his figures on hilly terrain. Certain vase paintings of that period give us an idea of that kind of composition.

MIDAS. See PHRYGIA.

MILETUS. One of the most important cities of Ionia. The city already existed in Mycenaean times; in the 11th cent. Ionians settled there, according to Athenian tradition, under the leadership of Nestor's descendants from Pylos. It reached its peak of prosperity in the 8th-6th centuries, when M. was the largest center of trade and culture in Ionia (see THALES; ANAXIMANDER; ANAXIMENES; HECATAEUS). During that period, it developed a surprising amount of activity in colonization, particularly in the direction of the Black Sea (see CYZICUS; SINOPE; TRAPEZUS; OLBIA). It remained in a privileged position under the domination of Lydia and Persia. In about 500 it led the Ionian revolt (see HISTIAEUS; ARISTAGORAS); after the battle of Lade the Persians took M. and destroyed it; this created a violent reaction in the whole Gr. world (see also PHYRYNICHUS). Its great prosperity never returned. After 479, M. became a member of the Delian League; during that period, Aspasia, Hippodamus, and others went from there to Athens. Under the Hellenic kingdoms, and Rom. domination, M. again achieved modest prosperity.

MILITARY EMPERORS. The popular name for the Rom. emperors who followed one another in quick succession during the 3rd cent. A.D., and who usually disappeared from the scene again after a few months or years. Many of them came not only from a province, as did Trajan, but were also of barbarian origin. They are called M. E. for two reasons: (a) they depended entirely on the army or the Praetorians and ignored the senate; (b) most of them were hailed as emperor or antiemperor by the legions. For convenience, the few who were proclaimed antiemperor by the senate are also classed with the M. E. There had already been a foretaste of this confusion in A.D. 69, the Year of the Three Emperors. After the death of Commodus, the Praetorians proclaimed Pertinax emperor (193) but replaced him by Didius Julianus after only three months; Clodius Albinus in Britain, Pescennius Niger in Syria, and Septimius Severus now rose against him. Septimius Severus finally won and ruled until 211; his son Caracalla reigned from 211-17. Caracalla was succeeded by Macrinus, his assassin (217-8); then Elagabalus ruled (218-22), followed by a period of calm under Alexander Severus. Then fifty years of anarchy followed. First came the Thracian Maximinus, who rose from the ranks (235-8); the senate proclaimed Gordianus I antiemperor against him in 238 (he appointed his son Gordianus II coregent), then Pupienus and Balbinus; after they had been murdered by the Praetorians, and Maximinus by his own soldiers, Gordianus III was proclaimed by the Praetorians (238-44); he in turn was murdered and succeeded by Philippus Arabus (244-9) who underwent the same fate at the hands of the Illyrian Decius (249-51); during whose reign violent persecutions of the Christians took place. Then came Trebonianus (251-3), Aemilianus (253), and Valerianus (253-60). The chaos was complete. Foreign enemies were invading from every side, the Goths in the Balkans, and the Sassanidae, who even took Valerianus prisoner, in Asia Minor. No less than thirty pretenders arose in various parts of the Empire. But the recovery had begun and was already noticeable under Gallienus (253-68); Claudius II (268-70) drove the Goths back. In the meantime Palmyra had become a buffer state between the Sassinidae and the Rom. Empire, but it turned against Rome under Zenobia. This danger was averted by Aurelianus (270-5), who also recovered Gaul. Again a series of emperors and antiemperors followed, most of whom, however, energetically defended the frontiers of the Empire: Tacitus (275-6), Florianus (276), Probus (276-82), Carus (282-3), Carinus (283-5), and Numerianus (283-4). After the death of the latter, the army chose the commander of the imperial guard, Diocles, to be emperor. With him, who soon received the name of Diocletian, a new period in Rom. history began.

MILTIADES (c. 550-489). Athenian general. He was sent to the Thracian Chersonesus by Hippias in about 524, to continue the domination his uncle, also named M., had established there under Pisistratus. He participated in the Ionian revolt of 500-494 and fled to Athens when it failed, where he was elected as a strategist. He defeated the Persians at Marathon in 490 (see DATIS). After that he led an expedition to Paros, which failed; sentenced to an excessive fine of 50 talents, on a charge of "deceiving the Athenian people," he died in jail, full of bitterness toward the ungrateful people, of a wound received at Paros. His son Cimon later paid the fine.

MIME. Popular play of imitative character, originally in the form of a dance (solo); later, also a farcical play. The genre originated in Sicily, and became popular particularly in the 3rd cent. B.C. (see HERONDAS); some of the *Idyls* of Theocritus are also refined mimes. The M. was especially popular in Rome, and because of its stark realism, it often attracted more spectators than the serious *Fabula;* the *Fabula Atellana* was actually completely absorbed by the M. During the imperial period the M. had won out. Many emperors patronized the performances. The M. was notorious for its obscenity, and the players had questionable reputations. Theodora, the wife of the Emperor Justinian, was originally a M. actress.

MINA. See COINAGE.

MINERMNUS of Colophon (2nd half of the 7th cent. B.C.). Gr. poet. He wrote elegies, warlike and without illusions, having been deeply moved by the con-

quest of Ionia by Gyges. Only a few fragments of poems have survived; their main theme is the resignation of old age abandoned by love and pleasure. His verses are musical, imaginative, and sentimental.

MINERVA. Ancient Italian goddess of handicrafts, therefore, probably under Etruscan influence, identified very early with Athena. She was worshiped with Jupiter and Juno (see CAPITOL); this trinity clearly indicates an Etruscan origin.

MINOAN CULTURE. The civilization of Crete, named after the legendary King Minos of Cnossus. This civilization of the Bronze Age had a great influence on early Gr. culture (see HELLADIC CULTURE; CYCLADES; MYCENAE). Until about 1900 we had only a very vague knowledge of this civilization. Since then, excavations in Cnossus, Phaistos and Hagia Triada have illuminated it. Archaeologists classify the M. C. into Early Minoan (down to 2300), Middle Minoan (2300-1600), and Late Minoan (1600-1100 B.C.). The period from 1600-1400 was the most flourishing one; during the last fifty years of this period, Mycenaean Greeks lived in Cnossus, as proven by the decipherment of Linear B (see CNOSSUS). Crete carried on extensive trade with the Syrian coast (Ugarit, the modern Ras Shamra in northern Syria) and with Egypt. Some of the most beautiful Minoan vases have been found in Egypt. The vases dating from 1600-1400 (for the previous period see CAMARES) are very naturalistic; sea animals are often depicted; later the designs become more stylized; the frescoes from the palaces are also splendid examples of Minoan art. (For religion see MYCAENE.) The M. C. was completely destroyed—after a period of decay—by the invasion of the Dorians. See Appendix.

MINOTAUR. See THESEUS.

MINUCIUS FELIX, MARCUS (3rd cent. A.D.). Lat. writer, converted to Christianity. He wrote a dialogue, *Octavius* (the earliest Lat. Christian work) in defense of the new religion.

MINYAE. Tribe living in Orchomenus and southeastern Thessaly during the Mycenaean period. According to tradition, they are the ancestors of the Argonauts. The vases dating from the 2nd millennium B.C., found in Orchomenus, were called Minyan after this tribe.

MISENUM. Port on the northern headland of the Bay of Naples and, according to the legend, named after Misenus, the trumpeter of Aeneas (Virg. *Aen.* VI, 234). M. was made Rome's main naval base by Agrippa in 31 B.C. (see also RAVENNA). Pliny the Elder was commander there when he was killed in A.D. 79, during the eruption of Mount Vesuvius (Plin. Min. *Ep.* VI, 16 ff.; compare VI, 20). The Emperor Tiberius died in an adjacent villa (Tac. *Ann.* VI, 50). After about 400, the harbor was no longer used.

MITHRAS. Ancient Iranian god. He is already mentioned in the oldest parts of the Persian *Avesta,* which contain the doctrines of Zoroaster (see PERSIAN EMPIRE), but as a minor god of light and sun. In Rom. imperial times he attained great importance; Rom. legions spread his cult over the entire Empire. The worship of M. was a mystery cult and the most important rival of Christianity as the latter spread in the 3rd cent. A.D. Mithrea (temples of M.) were underground; an aperture admitted light. The Dutch excavated a Mithraeum in Rome and discovered ritual texts, among other objects. See also ISIS.

MITHRIDATES VI (132-63). Surnamed Eupator (the Great), king of Pontus. He dreamed of founding a great Hellenistic empire in and around Asia Minor, in which the traditions of the Achaemenidae would be revived. In order to emphasize his ideology, he had himself proclaimed the "New Dionysus." The expansion of his kingdom brought him into conflict with Bithynia, which was supported by Rome. This was the cause of the First Mithridatic War (88-84). M. occupied almost all of Asia Minor, and was hailed as a liberator, particularly in the Rom. province of Asia. More than 80,000 Romans and Italians were killed on his orders. When he crossed to Greece, Sulla opposed him (see also ARCHELAUS) and defeated him, forcing him to withdraw to Pontus. Later, M. successfully engaged Sulla's second in command, Murena (83-81: the Second Mithridatic War); he

even made a treaty with Sertorius in 75. After renewed preparations, M. started fighting again when Rome annexed Bithynia (74-63: the Third Mithridatic War). Lucullus defeated him again and again (see also TIGRANES); when the latter was replaced by Pompey, M. was able to make a temporary recovery, but it was Pompey who finally ended the war. M. fled to the Crimea, and when his subjects there revolted under Pharnaces, he tried to poison himself; however that failed because he had become immune by prolonged use of antitoxic preparations; for this reason he ordered a slave to kill him. M. was archenemy of Rome in the East in the 1st cent. B.C.

MNESICLES (5th cent. B.C.), Gr. architect who built the Propylaea.

MODUS VIVENDI. "A mode of living"; that is (in international law), a temporary arrangement.

MOESIA. Rom. province on the lower course of the Danube, about what is now Serbia and Bulgaria; first part of Macedonia or Illyria. It did not become a separate province until A.D. 44, and was split into two sections under Domitian. After Trajan it was intensively Romanized (compare DACIA).

MOIRA. See FATE.

MONUMENTUM ANCYRANUM. An inscription found in Ancyra in 1555, containing a personal report by Augustus of his deeds as a ruler, written in Latin and Greek. It is a copy of the inscription that was engraved on bronze plates on his mausoleum, on his own orders. Other fragmentary copies of the text were found in two places in Asia Minor. It is a historic document of the first order (see also EPIGRAPHY). It was certainly written by Augustus himself; its tone is very apologetic; the Emperor wants to make it very clear that he did not want to be a dictator and that he respected the institutions of the Republic.

MORITURI TE SALUTAMUS. We who are about to die salute you. The phrase with which gladiators saluted the Rom. emperor (compare Suet. *Claud.* 21: *"Ave, Imperator! morituri te salutant!"*).

MOSCHUS of Syracuse (c. 150 B.C.). Gr. poet; wrote bucolic poetry (see

THEOCRITUS); three of his pastoral poems have been preserved in the works of Stobaeus; three epyllia (see EPIC) are also attributed to him, of which the *Rape of Europa* may be authentic.

MOSAIC. Floor or wall decoration of inlayed small colored stones. The technique originated in the Near East. On a small scale, M. existed in Minoan art. M. floors dating from about 400 B.C. were found during excavations in Olynthus. During the Hellenistic period mosaics were more generally used, but still remained a great luxury. It was not until Rom. imperial times that M. floors were in general use, in the farthest corners of the Empire. In Byzantine art, M. reached its peak (see also RAVENNA). Because it is so durable, M. compensates to some degree for the loss of antique monumental painting. A famous M. is the one depicting the battle of Issus (Pompeii).

MUCIANUS. Governor of Syria from A.D. 67-69. He supported Vespasian when he was proclaimed emperor in 69. He led the latter's army to Rome and, although Antonius Primus (see YEAR OF THE THREE EMPERORS) was there before him, M. substituted for Vespasian until he arrived. M. was an elegant man who was also an author. His character was described astutely by Tacitus (*Hist.* II, 10).

MULTUM, NON MULTA. "Much, not many" (Plin. *Ep.* VII, 9; Quint. X, 1).

MUMMIUS, LUCIUS. Rom. consul in 146; attacked the Achaean League, plundered and destroyed Corinth. He transported the art works of that city to Italy; the Achaean League was disbanded; Greece was made a Rom. province of Achaea.

MUNDA. City in Spain, where Caesar defeated the last followers of Pompey (among them Labienus) who still opposed him after the battle of Thapsus, in 45 B.C. It was one of Caesar's most heavily bought victories.

MUNICIPIUM. Originally the term for towns in Italy whose inhabitants had Rom. citizenship without the right to vote (*sine suffragio*). Like the *socii*, they had self-government, without the right to an independent foreign policy; they were, however, obligated to send troops to

Rome. They also had private rights: the *ius conubii et comercii*, that is, the privilege of making lawful Rom. marriages and trade contracts. The status of a M. was between that of the *coloniae Latinae* (see LATIUM) and the *socii* (see also DIVIDE ET IMPERA). After the Social War, every M. was granted complete Rom. citizenship. In the imperial period, many cities outside Italy were put into the position of *municipia*.

MUSES. Gr. goddesses of song, music, the dance, and the sciences; daughters of Zeus and Mnemosyne (goddess of memory). They were said to have dwelled on Mount Helicon and Mount Parnassus, where they made music under the leadership of Apollo (in Homer, they also add luster to the meals of the gods on Mount Olympus, *Il.* I, 604). Hesiod already mentions the number of muses and their names, but the classification of their functions does not antedate Rom. times. That classification is usually as follows: Clio (history), Euterpe (lyric poetry), Thalia (comedy), Melpomene (tragedy), Terpsichore (dance), Erato (love poetry), Polyhymnia (hymns, later also mime), Urania (astronomy), and Calliope (epic poetry). The poetess Sappho was sometimes called the Tenth Muse (see also MUSEUM; HERODOTUS).

MUSEUM. Originally, temple of the Muses, later, the place where art (and science) was practiced. The most famous M. was the one in Alexandria, founded by Ptolemy I on the advice of Demetrius of Phaleron; scholars came there from far and near. There they could study quietly; they were paid by the Ptolemies, later by the Rom. emperors. The M. was mainly a center of philosophic and scientific study, the adjoining library (see BOOKS) was mainly the center of literary study.

MUSIC. Played a very large part in the Gr. world; it was a focal point of education; it enhanced religious festivals, banquets, and dramatic performances. Our knowledge of lyric poetry is limited and one-sided, because we do not know the music that accompanied their recitation; the same holds true for the choruses in drama. From the beginning, one of the various contests in the Pythian Games was a music contest. The Romans were much more reserved toward music; at best, they considered it as a secondary art form; there was no native Rom. music at all; they simply adopted the Gr. genres. See Appendix.

Actually, what we know about Gr. music, we owe to its significant role in Gr. culture. We have a number of writings on musical theory, of which the book of Aristoxenus (4th cent. B.C.) is the oldest, also some of the works of Aristotle, Plutarch, the astronomer Ptolemy, and others. We also have descriptions and pictures of the most important instruments (lyre, zither, flute, pipe of Pan, horn, and percussion instruments). We also know that Pythagoras discovered the mathematical relationship between pitch of the tone and the length of the string, and that Plato (who only allowed serious music in his ideal state) and other philosophers placed a high value on musical education. We know that the ancients distinguished between the serious Dorian scale, the effeminate Lydian (variant: Ionian) and the ecstatic Phrygian scale. But we lack the most important thing: we can no longer *hear* their music. A few fragments of texts with musical notes have been found. Next to a few small fragments on papyrus they were rediscovered mainly in inscriptions: two Delphic hymns and the epitaph of Seicilus found in Asia Minor; and in the texts named above, a hymn to the Sun God and one to Nemesis (goddess of avenging justice). Impressive efforts have been made to transcribe these bits of music into modern notes, to perform them, and to record them. Still, the results remain hypothetical.

MUSONIUS RUFUS, GAIUS (1st cent. A.D.). Rom. Stoic philosopher; exiled from Rome twice (by Nero and Vespasian); his proverbs were preserved by his pupils. He taught Epictetus, among others.

MUTINA. City in northern Italy, now Modena; in 43 B.C., Decimus Brutus and Mark Antony fought about it violently (the so-called *Bellum Mutinense*).

MYCALE. Promontory to the north of Miletus, where the Persians were defeated both on land and on the sea in 479 B.C.; that Gr. victory crowned the work of Salamis and Plataea.

MYCENAE. City in Argolis (see AR-GOS), the most important political and cultural center of Mycenaean culture (1600-1100 B.C.); in Homer, the city of Agamemnon. M. was excavated after 1874; first by H. Schliemann, later in a more systematic manner by several other expeditions. M. was first inhabited by a pre-Gr. population (the name is therefore pre-Hellenic); in about 2100-1600, successive waves of Gr. tribes came to settle there. In about 1600-1400, M. rose to great power under a royal house; shaft graves have been found which yielded a tremendous amount of gold and other treasures. These kings were definitely not the same type of ruler as the legendary Gr. tribal kings (see MACEDONIA), but absolute monarchs. The monumental beehive tombs, the heavy citadel walls, and the Lion Gate belong to the period of 1400-1100. With the Dorian invasion Mycenaean culture ended. After that, M. was only a small city; after about 470 B.C. it was subjected to Argos.

Mycenaean culture was greatly influenced by Minoan Crete. Still, there are striking differences: (a) the art of M. is much more inclined to be monumental; the most impressive example of this is the well-known Lion Gate; (b) the palaces of M. were fortified by heavy walls; the kings appear to have felt less secure than those of Crete (see CNOSSUS); (c) the architecture of M. is much more systematic and surveyable; a Mycenaean palace is no "labyrinth." The Minoan and Mycenaean religion, in contrast, are closely related. Minoan religion was a typical nature religion, with a tree cult and the worship of a nature-goddess, in whom we can later recognize Demeter; she has a male partner. In the Mycenaean religion there is also a cult of a mountain-goddess who reminds us of Cybele, and of a snake-goddess who may be a precursor of Athena. It is striking that both cults use the labrys as a religious symbol, as well as the "sacred horns," probably connected with a bull cult (see also HAGIA TRIADA; ELYSIUM). The recently deciphered Mycenaean documents (see CNOSSUS, PYLOS) do give the names of Athena, Demeter and, especially often, the word *Potnia* (Mistress); several other names of Gr. gods already appear, among them Dionysus; but the ecstatic element was not represented particularly by that god, but by a "Zeus" figure, who was worshiped there as *kouros* (young man) with ecstatic dances (for other centers of Mycenaean culture see TIRYNS; PYLOS; ORCHOMENUS).

MYRON (5th cent. B.C.). Gr. sculptor from Eleutherae in Boeotia; pupil of Ageladas, and contemporary of Phidias and Polycletus. M. worked mainly in bronze; his most famous works are the "Discobolus" (the best of several Rom. copies is now at Rome), and the statue of "Marsyas" (also at Rome). The latter was one of a pair, "Athena and Marsyas." A copy of the "Athena" is at Frankfurt. A work, greatly admired by the ancients, and celebrated in several extant epigrams, is a realistic animal figure, "Cow in the Marketplace at Athens."

MYSTERIES. Secret initiation rites (for the most important Gr. M. see ELEUSINIAN MYSTERIES; CABIRI; ORPHISM). Many of the rites in honor of Dionysus were also M. These were not connected with any special place (see also BACCHANALIA). During the Hellenistic period and Rom. imperial times many M. of Eastern gods like Isis and Mithras became popular.

MYTILENE. Capital of Lesbos. When, as a member of the Delian League, it rebelled in 428 B.C., it narrowly escaped a massacre; Thucydides (III, 2, ff.) tells about this in an exciting narrative.

N-O

NABIS. Last king of Sparta, reigned from 207-192; was the first to build walls around the city; continued the revolutionary policy of Cleomenes III, notably by giving the Helots citizenship. He was defeated by Philopoemen and Flamininus. After he had been murdered (192 B.C.), Sparta lost its independence.

NAEVIUS, GNAEUS (c. 270-c. 200). Lat. poet; was exiled from Rome for attacking leading politicians (Scipio Major and members of the Metellus family); he then lived in Utica until his death. His comedies had a great influence on Rom. drama (especially Plautus); he created the *Fabula praetexta,* and also practiced the genres of the *Fabula palliata* and *Fabula togata.* However his most important work is an epic on the First Punic War, written in the ancient Italian Saturnian meter; it had great influence on Ennius and Virgil. Only fragments of his work remain extant.

NAIADS. See NYMPHS.

NAMATIANUS, RUTILIUS CLAU-DIUS (c. 400 A.D.). The last Rom. poet; he came from Toulouse, and was the city prefect of Rome in 414. N. was a fervent follower of paganism and of the ancient Rom. tradition. His poem, *De Reditu Suo (My Return)*, an elegy, is an autobiographical work. It is written in beautiful Latin, and describes a trip from Rome to his estates in Gaul; the fragment about the sea voyage along the coast of Italy has been preserved.

NARBO. Now Narbonne, the capital of the Rom. province Narbonensis (see GALLIA). It was a city of the Celtiberi, even before the Rom. conquest, mentioned by Hecataeus (about 500 B.C.).

NAUCRATIS. Gr. commercial city, to the west of the Nile Delta. Founded in about 610 B.C. by Miletus, N. was the main point of contact between Greece and Egypt under the Saitic dynasty (see AMASIS). Traders from various Gr. (especially Ionian) cities settled there. During the Hellenistic period, Alexandria became the trade center.

NAVIGARE NECESSE EST, VIVERE NON NECESSE EST. "Navigation is necessary, but living is not," saying attributed to Pompey when he was surprised by a storm while transporting wheat to Rome.

NAVIGATION. Played a very important part in antiquity; ancient civilization developed primarily in the coastal areas around the Mediterranean Sea, and N. was the principal medium of communication. During their migrations the Greeks became acquainted with the Aegean Sea and considered it a *pontos* (that is, channel of communication); they soon built ships to make use of it. Just how much they learned from the Minoan Cretans about N. is problematical. Until recently we believed in the *thalassocracy* (maritime supremacy) of Minos, mentioned by Thucydides; now, however, we know that during this same period of Minoan supremacy, the Achaeans ruled in Cnossus. During the 9th-6th centuries, Chalcis, Corinth, and Aegina controlled N.; in the 5th cent. B.C. they were supplanted by Athens. Merchant ships were broad abeam, were propelled by oars in case of need; they had one mast and a square sail. War ships (and pirate ships, see PIRACY) needed to be much narrower and faster, of course; they were manned by oars, with auxiliary sails. There were several types of ships: the *pentekontoros,* a vessel with fifty rowers with two banks of twenty-five oarsmen. This type of ship was replaced in the 6th-5th centuries B.C. by the trireme (in the Hellenistic period by the quinquereme). In contrast to the merchant ships these were more vulnerable in storms (see for example ARGINUSAE); nevertheless the merchantmen preferred to set their course along the coast also, because they were rather small (80-90 tons; there are a few examples of much larger ships); it is almost unbelievable that such small vessels were able to maintain the intensive traffic which, for example, took place during colonization, but one must consider that even in the period of great discoveries (Columbus) ships were still small. The Romans were entirely dependent on N. for their food supplies, as early as the 2nd cent. B.C. The long and vulnerable coast-line of Italy necessitated a naval force, but the Romans detested N. (see NAVIGARE NECESSE EST), causing them to neglect their fleet again and again, unless it became indispensable (see PUNIC WARS; PIRACY; POMPEY; MISENUM).

NAXOS. Name of:

—(1) The largest island of the Cyclades; it supported the Ionian uprising in 500 B.C. and was then destroyed in 490, by a Persian punitive expedition led by Datis. It was later a recalcitrant member of both Attic Leagues. N. was famous for its wine and the cult of Dionysus.

—(2) The oldest Gr. colony on Sicily, founded in 757 B.C. by Chalcis; the arch-enemy of Syracuse. Dionysius I destroyed it in 403 and gave the land to the native Siculi, who afterward founded Tauromenium near it.

NEAPOLIS. Now Naples, founded by Cumae on the site of ancient Parthenope (hence N., literally: new city) in about 600 B.C. Eventually, it overshadowed the mother city and became the most important Gr. city of Campania. In 327 B.C. it was conquered by Rome, to which it remained loyal against Pyrrhus and Hannibal. Puteoli surpassed it as a port, but it remained popular as a resort, and preserved the Gr. traditions until late into the imperial period. Virgil liked to stay in N., and was entombed there; it was the native city of Statius.

NEARCHUS. Admiral of Alexander the Great; he conducted his fleet from the Indus to the Persian Gulf, and so opened the seaway between India and the West (325 B.C.). N. wrote an account of this expedition, which was rich in geographical and scientific discoveries. The work was used by Arrianus for his book about India.

NEC LUSISSE PUDET, SED NON INCIDERE LUDUM. "It is not shameful to play, but it is [shameful] not to finish the game" (*Hor. Ep.* I, 4, 36).

NEMEAN GAMES. Games, held every two years, in the Nemean Valley, to the southwest of Corinth. The games were a Panhellenic festival since 573 B.C., held in honor of Zeus; fragments of his temple have been found, as have remains of the gymnasium and the palaestra.

NEMESIANUS, MARCUS AURELIUS

OLYMPIUS (2nd half of the 3rd cent. A.D.). Lat. poet from Carthage; wrote bucolic poetry after the example of Calpurnius Siculus and Virgil; his most famous work is his *Cynegetica* (about hounds and preparations for the chase), inspired by the poem of Grattius.

NEMO ANTE MORTEM BEATUS. "No man [can] [be called] happy before his death"; Lat. translation of the philosophy that, according to tradition, Solon expressed to Croesus.

NEOPLATONISM. The most important philosophical school during the late Rom. imperial period; it was based mainly on the doctrines of Plato, but also contained elements adopted from Pythagoras, Aristotle, and the Stoics; in addition it had a strong mystical character. After a period of preparation in the 1st cent. A.D., N. reached its culminating point in the 3rd cent. with Plotinus and Porphyry. Then came a time when N. was completely intermingled with Eastern mystico-religious attributes (see IAMBLICHUS; SALLUSTIUS) in the schools of Syria and Pergamum (the latter influenced Julian); it flourished again in the 4th-5th centuries.

NEPOS, CORNELIUS (c. 100-c. 25). Lat. biographer; friend of Cicero, Atticus, and Catullus. His work, *De Viris Illustribus* (*Famous Men*) used to be favorite literature for beginners in Latin at school, and is still sometimes used as such. It has little historical value, except for the life of his friend Atticus. It is interesting to note that he was the first biographer to compare Romans with non-Romans. Some of his works have been lost, including a history of the world.

NEPTUNE. See POSEIDON.

NE QUID NIMIS. "Avoid excess"; translation of an ancient Gr. proverb *mèden agan* (Ter. *And.* 61).

NEREIDS. See NEREUS.

NEREUS. The most important of the Gr. "lesser gods of the sea," father of the fifty Nereids, of whom Amphitrite, the wife of Poseidon, and Thetis, the mother of Achilles, are the most famous. N. was pictured as "the old man of the sea," a graybeard, who could foretell the future, and was as capricious as the sea itself, as were the other lesser sea-gods, Triton, Proteus, etc. They often guided great heroes. Whether or not they were originally one figure, is problematical, but it has been established that they, especially N., are pre-Hellenic.

NERO CLAUDIUS CAESAR DRUSUS GERMANICUS. (37-68). Rom. emperor, the last of the Claudian-Julian house; son of Gnaeus Domitius Ahenobarbus and Agrippina the Younger, who had him adopted by her second husband Claudius and proclaimed emperor by the Praetorians on the latter's death (54). The first few years of his reign were good, particularly as far as the government of the provinces was concerned. N.'s governors Burrus and Seneca (2) had a moderating influence on him (Tac. *Ann.* XIII, 2). But the relationship between N. and his mother became more and more tense. When, as a result, she started favoring Britannicus, N. first poisoned him (55), and then had his mother killed (59) on the instigation of Poppaea, the wife of Otho. Then Burrus died (it was rumored by poison); and Seneca retired (62). Now N. divorced Claudius' daughter Octavia and married Poppaea. In the meantime he had been devoting more and more time to his passions, especially to art. He devised new games and appeared at them himself, as a performer, allowing himself to be loudly acclaimed, particularly by the Gr. public. Still, the provinces were ruled well, because energetic governors were sent there (Mucianus, Vespasian, Corbulo). But in Rome things were less pleasant; the treasury was depleted and had to be refilled through devaluation and confiscation of the fortunes of the notables, who were gotten rid of on the mere suspicion of *lèse majesté*. In 64 an enormous fire laid waste half of Rome. N. blamed the Christians; they were persecuted horribly (Tac. *Ann.* XV, 44). The people accused N.—without proof—of setting the fire himself. He did take advantage of the fire to rebuild the city more spaciously, and to have an enormous palace, the Golden House, built for himself. In 65 a serious conspiracy against N. was discovered, of which Piso (4) was the leader. His accomplices were persecuted ruthlessly; Seneca and Lucanus were among the victims. In 66, N. forced others to commit suicide, among them Paetus Thrasea, Petronius, and a little later, Corbulo. The following year, N. took a trip to Greece to study art. In 68, Vindex rebelled against him in Gaul; shortly afterward, Galba did the same in Spain. N., deserted by the Praetorians, fled from Rome and had himself killed by a slave while crying, *"qualis artifex pereo!"* (what an artist is being lost in me).

NERVA, MARCUS COCCEIUS (30-98). Rom. emperor, the first of the adoptive emperors; held office under Vespasian and Domitian (consul in 71 and in 90); the senate proclaimed him emperor after the murder of the latter in 96. His reign was a relief after the tyranny of his predecessor; he applied himself to social politics, particularly by furnishing state aid for the education of poor children (*alimenta*). However, he did not have enough authority over the Praetorians and the army. After ruling for only sixteen months he died, and was succeeded by his adopted son Trajan.

NERVII. The strongest tribe (half Celtic, half German) in northern Gaul, lived in what is now Flanders and Hainaut; conquered by Caesar in 57 B.C.; after that they took part in the revolt of Ambiorix.

NERVUS RERUM. "The tendon, that is, tensile force of the things" (compare Cic. *Phil.* V, 2, 5; *nervus belli pecuniam infinitam* "the sinews of war [are] unlimited money").

NESTOR. Oldest Gr. hero in the Trojan war (see PYLOS).

NE VARIETUR. "Let it not be changed"; superscription on a document, especially with a signature.

NICANDER of Colophon (2nd cent. B.C.) Gr. poet; wrote two didactic poems in hexameters (see METER), the *Theriaca* (about poisonous snakes) and *Alexipharmaca* (about poisons and antidotes).

NICIAS (c. 470-413). Athenian statesman and general, leader of the moderate democratic party (mainly substantial farmers), who strove for an honorable peace with Sparta during the Peloponnesian War. This brought him into conflict with Cleon, whose death left him a free hand; N. negotiated the peace named after him in 421. When Alcibiades later suggested the expedition to Syracuse, N. opposed him violently in the ecclesia, with the only result that still more men and troops were voted. He himself became a commander, with Alcibiades and Lamachus. The expedition failed, and N. postponed the urgent retreat because of a superstitious fear of an unfavorable omen, until it was too late. He was taken prisoner by the Syracusans and executed. N. was a noble man; too levelheaded to inspire others; indecision at the critical moment was fatal to him.

NICOMEDES. Name of several kings of Bithynia.

NIKE TEMPLE. Small Ionic temple (see ARCHITECTURAL ORDERS) on the Acropolis in Athens, devoted to Nike Athena, a combination of Athena and Nike, the goddess of victory. The relief of Nike loosening her sandal, a fragment of the balustrade of the temple, is well known.

NIL (or NIHIL) **NOVI SUB SOLE.** "Nothing new under the sun"; Lat. translation of Ecclesiases I: 9.

NOBILES. The highest Rom. senatorial families, especially those whose ancestors had been praetors or consuls. They formed a closed caste (see HOMO NOVUS); in the civil strife of the 1st cent. B.C., the N. were often identified with the *optimates,* although the latter were actually a much broader circle.

NOLA. City in Campania, famous for Hannibal's first defeat at the hands of the Romans (under Marcellus) in 216 B.C., and because the Emperor Augustus died there (A.D. 14).

NOLI ME TANGERE. "Touch me not"; Lat. translation of Christ's words (John 20:17).

NOLI TURBARE CIRCULOS MEOS. "Do not disturb my circles," said Archimedes, while bending over the figures he had drawn in the sand. He was addressing a Rom. soldier who had come to stab him during the conquest of Syracuse by Marcellus (212 B.C.). Freely after Valerius Maximus VIII, 7.

NOMEN EST OMEN. "The name is an omen," that is, the name is rightly his (for example, Verres literally means pig); compare Plaut. *Persa,* 625.

NOMOS [Gr.]. Originally, "law," "usage," "custom." The Greeks always had a deep respect for the laws of their polis; they considered them their only sovereign (see also LEGISLATORS).

NONES. The Rom. name for the 7th of March, May, July, and October. In other months they fell on the 5th. The word means "the ninth" (that is, the 9th day before, and including, the ides (see CALENDAR).

NON LIQUET. "It [the case] is not clear," "I reserve judgment" (Cic., *Par. Stoic.* VI, 3, 49).

NONNUS (5th cent. A.D.). Gr. poet from the Egyptian city Panopolis; wrote an epic poem *Dionysiaca* about the triumphal voyage Dionysus made to India, in forty-eight books; he also paraphrased the Gospel of St. John, in hexameters. N. had perfect mastery of the hexameter, but the transition to the accented meter of the Middle Ages is noticeable.

NON PLUS ULTRA (also: *nec plus ultra*). "[Until here and] no farther"; Lat. translation of Job 38:11; also used for: "no longer possible" or "unsurpassed."

NON SCHOLAE, SED VITAE (DISCIMUS). "[We learn] not for school, but for life"; compare Seneca (*Ep.* 106, 11), who remarks that the opposite happened in his day.

NON TALI AUXILIO ."[This crisis does] not [call for] such assistance" (Virg. *Aen.* II, 521). This quotation refers to the fall of Troy and help from the aged Priam.

NORICUM. Rom. province in the Alps, comprising the modern Austria, east of the Inn River. The oldest element of the population is Illyrian; after 300 B.C., Celts settled there and founded quite an important federal state with the capital of Noreia; N. probably became a Rom. province in 16 B.C.

NOSCE TE IPSUM. "Know thyself" [acquire insight into yourself]; translation of the famous Gr. saying *gnothi seauton* (compare Cic. *Tusc.* I, 22, 52).

NOVEL. Fictional prose narrative. In contrast to modern literature, in which the N. takes first place, ancient literature produced hardly any novels; still this genre is not entirely absent. There are prototypes of the historical N. in classical literature, when the author does not write with complete freedom as, for example, the *Cyropaedia* of Xenophon. The entirely fictional N., with the history of a pair of lovers as its theme, can also be found. Romantic narratives originated in Miletus during Hellenistic times, and were later adopted by the Romans. One of the most important Gr. writers of novels whose work has survived is Longus. The most important of the Rom. novelists were Petronius and Apuleius.

NOVENSILES. Group of Rom. gods; often explained as being gods whose worship had been introduced from foreign countries (see INDIGETES).

NOVIOMAGUS. A Batavian settlement near the modern Nijmegen. Under Trajan, it received the status of *colonia* and the name *Ulpia N.;* it developed into an important commercial town.

NUMANTIA. Celtiberian city in Spain, a center of resistance against Rom. imperialism for many years; after many vain efforts by other Rom. generals, it was finally taken by Scipio Minor in 133 B.C. Extensive excavations were made there.

NUMA POMPILIUS (715-673). According to tradition, the second Rom. king and founder of the official Rom. religious worship. He was said to have come from the land of the Sabines. The oldest Rom. calendar was also attributed to him (it also had a religious significance). His daughter Pompilia was said to have been the mother of Rome's fourth king, Ancus Marcius.

NUMEN [Lat.] The term is derived from *nuo,* a nodding, beckoning; a nod, as a sign of command, *a command.* The Romans applied the word for the divine will, divine command. Later, it referred to the divine spirit itself.

NUMERIANUS. See MILITARY EMPERORS.

NUMIDIA. Country in North Africa, its territory nearly that of modern Algeria; bounded in the east by Carthaginian lands (the later Rom. province, Africa), in the west by Mauretania. The Numidians were known as excellent horsemen, and formed the cavalry for Hannibal. Famous Numidian rulers were Masinissa and Jugurtha. In 46 B.C., N. became a Rom. province. In the 5th cent. A.D. the Vandals ruled it. There are many ruins from Rom. times (see also TIMGAD).

NUMISMATICS. See COINAGE.

NYMPHIDIUS SABINUS. *Praefectus praetorio* (see PRAETORIANS) under Nero. In A.D. 68 he allied himself with Galba and forced his collegue Tigellinus to retire; afterward, he wanted to have himself proclaimed emperor. However, the Praetorians killed him.

NYMPHS. Nature-goddesses, particularly protectors of springs, rivers, mountains, and trees; each had its own N. They often were companions of Artemis. *Nymphaea* —buildings dedicated to N.—were erected especially at springs. In Rom. times, these sometimes became luxurious buildings. In mythology, they were regarded as daughters of Zeus.

OBOLUS. See COINAGE.

OCEANUS. In mythology, the river encircling the whole world. Out of and into this river the sun and the stars were believed to rise and set. In earliest times, the Greeks, in contrast to the Phoenicians, did not venture outside the Strait of Gibraltar, and were not acquainted with the areas east of the Red Sea and the Persian Gulf. It was not until about 600 B.C. that the Greeks first made voyages of discovery and found out that the O. was a large, salt water sea. High and low tides, phenomena that are of course unknown in the Mediterranean, remained wondrous to them.

OCTAVIA. Name of:

—(1) Half sister of Augustus.

—(2) Sister of Augustus, and wife of Mark Antony. Several times she played the role of mediator between her husband and her brother, when there was a threat of dissension among the triumviri. After the marriage between Antony and Cleopatra she earned the general approval for her loyalty to her stepchildren. She died in 11 B.C.

—(3) Claudia O. (c. A.D. 40-62), the daughter of the Emperor Claudius and Messalina; she married Nero in 53. He became emperor a year later. The marriage was purely political, designed to secure Nero's succession to his father-in-law. In 62, Nero divorced her in order

to marry Poppaea; he soon had O. exiled on a fictitious charge and later killed. Her adventures are the subject of the only preserved *Fabula praetexta, Octavia,* attributed to Seneca, but possibly written after his death.

OCTAVIAN. See AUGUSTUS.

ODENATHUS (c. A.D. 260). King of Palmyra who ruled his empire on condition of formally recognizing the supreme authority of the Emperor Gallienus (see MILITARY EMPERORS). He drove back the Persians and ensured the safety of the Rom. Empire's eastern frontier.

ODERINT DUM METUANT. "Let them hate [me], provided they fear [me]"; motto of Caligula (Accius *Atreus,* quoted by Cic. *Off.* I, 28, 97).

ODEUM [Gr. *oideion*] Theater for musical performances (see also HERODES ATTICUS).

ODI PROFANUM VULGUS ET ARCEO. "I hate the common rabble and keep it at a distance" (Hor. *Carm.* III, 1, 1).

ODOACER (c. 433-493). German army commander who overthrew the West Rom. Empire. In 476 he led the revolt of the German auxiliaries and brought about the abdication of Romulus Augustulus. After that he became king of Italy; he was tolerant toward Catholics—and the Romans. However, in 493 he was forced to surrender to the Ostrogoths in Ravenna, and was killed by their king Theodoric.

ODYSSEUS. See HOMER.

OEDIPUS [Gr. *Oidipous,* swollen foot]. The most famous hero of the Theban sagas. According to Homer, the king of Thebes, who kills his father and marries his mother. In the 8th-6th centuries the saga was the subject of poems of the Epic Cycle, and was depicted on vases; but it is known mainly through 5th cent. B.C. tragedy, namely the plays of Sophocles, *Oedipus Coloneus,* and *Oedipus Tyrranus,* and *Seven Against Thebes* by Aeschylus.

OENOCHOE. See VASE FORMS.

OETA. A mountain range in central Greece, on the Thessalian frontier; the valley of the Spercheos River lay below it, as did the pass of Thermopylae. According to the legend, Heracles burned himself to death on the O; this story has its origin in a fire cult, of which clear traces have been found on top of the mountain.

OLBIA. Colony of Miletus in southern Russia, founded in 645 B.C. A flourishing city, especially in the 6th and 5th centuries B.C. This prosperity was due to the export of grain from the Ukraine to the Mediterranean area. In Rom. imperial times, O. experienced a second era of wealth. Russian scholars have made important excavations there.

OLEUM ET OPERAM PERDERE. "To lose oil [time] and trouble"; that is, to take trouble fruitlessly (compare Cic. *Ad fam.* VII, 1, 3; Plaut. *Poen.* 332).

OLIGARCHY [Gr. *oligarchia,* from *oligos* few, little and *archein* to rule]. Form of government in a Gr. polis, by which the political power was in the hands of a minority of the citizens, usually the rich. Their wealth was usually based on property ownership, so that it is sometimes difficult to distinguish between O. and an aristocracy. Famous examples are the O. of the Bacchiadae in Corinth, the one in Athens of 411 B.C. (see PISANDER) and of 404-3 (see CRITIAS). Sparta usually favored O. in Greece, although it had its own form of government, with inherent characteristics, and could not really be called an O. In the 2nd-1st centuries B.C., Rome was also an O., through the government of the *nobiles.*

OLYMPIA. Place in Elis on the Alpheios River, where the most famous temples of Zeus were located. It was in his honor that, every four years, the Olympic Games were held. Kronos Hill rises above the *Altis* (the place where the festival was celebrated), and the athletic fields are adjacent. There are traces of prehistoric inhabitants in O., but the town did not flourish or become famous until the games were founded in the 9th cent. B.C., possibly earlier. Almost all the objects of art found in O., among them the sculptured façades and the metopes of the Zeus temple, Praxiteles' "Hermes," and Paionius' "Victory," are in the local museum. Phidias' huge statue of Zeus has been lost. The *Altis,* fragments of the Doric temples of Zeus and Hera can still be seen; the temple of Hera predates the temple of Zeus. After the Emperor Theodosius had closed the sanctuary of O. in A.D. 394—and all other pagan temples—and had forbidden the games, the prosperity of O. declined. German scholars have been excavating the area since 1874 (with several interruptions). During the past few years these excavations have been crowned with renewed success. Among other things, the stadium was laid bare in its successive phases (see OLYMPIC GAMES), the studio of Phidias has been discovered; the matrices he had used for the statue of Zeus and a piece of pottery, inscribed on the bottom with: "I belong to Phidias," were found. The treasure houses (see DELPHI) can be seen there, as well as other remains.

OLYMPIAD. An interval of four years between two successive Olympic Games, by which the Greeks reckoned time from 776 B.C. until A.D. 394.

OLYMPIAS. Molossian princess from Epirus, wife of Philip II of Macedonia, and mother of Alexander the Great. She was unjustly accused of having planned the murder of Philip. After the death of Alexander she fought stubbornly for the rights of his descendants, but finally had to give way to Cassander. She was killed in Pydna.

OLYMPIC GAMES. The most important Panhellenic games, for which athletes came not only from Greece, but also from all the Hellenic states outside of Greece. Besides the sporting events and the cults, there was also a fair, recitations, and other manifestations. Originally, the only events were jumping, sprinting, discus and spear throwing, and wrestling. Later the spectacular chariot races and other events were added. In Olympia, the victor was only given a laurel wreath, but was later honored in the grand manner in his native city. A regular and continuous list of the victors was recorded from 776 B.C.; with this year begins the division of time into Olympiads. The O.G. were closely connected with religion. The same holds true for the Pythian, Isthmian, and Nemean Games, as well as for the Panathenaea. All Gr. games originated in the funeral games that were part of the ritual of

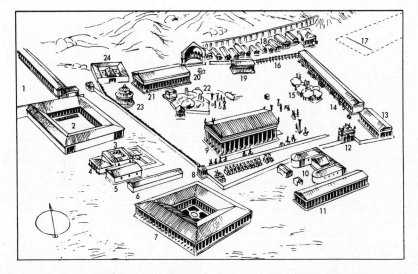

Olympia. Of the collection of buildings and temples called Olympia, the Altis, a partly walled-in domain of temples at the foot of Kronos Hill, was the consecrated focal point. Outside the Altis there were mainly profane buildings and terrains used for the Olympic Games. 1. Gymnasium, room for gymnastics practice and for the classic pentathlon. 2. Palaestra or wrestling arena. 3. The so-called Theocoleum, where the priests lived. 4. The Heroön, a sanctuary for Pelops or his wife Hippodamea. 5. Megaron, rectangular little building which was once the studio of the sculptor Phidias, who made, among other thing, the colossal statue of Zeus for the main temple. 6. Long, narrow shed; ancient studio of Phidias. 7. Leonidaeum, guests' quarters; during Roman imperial times important guests were quartered there. 8. Entrance gate to the Altis, from Roman times. 9. Temple of Zeus, in Doric style, from ca. 465-450 B.C. 10. Bouleuterion or council house. 11. Stoa or hall of columns. 12. Roman triumphal arch, entrance to the Altis. 13. Stoa or hall of columns. 14. The so-called Hall of Echoes. 15. The great altar of Zeus. 16. Bases of votive offerings. 17. The stadium of the Olympic Games. 18. 12 Treasure houses. 19. Metroum, or temple of the mother-goddess Rhea. 20. Exedra of Herodes Atticus. 21. Temple of Hera from the end of the 7th cent. B.C. 22. Pelopium, rectangular enclosed court, sanctuary and grave of Pelops. 23. Philippeum, temple of Philip of Macedonia. 24. Prytaneum, seat of government of Olympia and the Games.

death, particularly the hero cult. In classical Greece, the athlete believed that he was serving the gods by his achievements. The "sacredness" of the contests was maintained by separating the Altis from the athletic fields by a wall ascribed to Heracles (see also OLYMPIA).

OLYMPUS. Mountain in northern Thessaly, highest peak 9,570 ft.; considered as early as Homer to be the abode of the gods (see particularly *Od.* VI, 42-46), because the peak was usually invisible. Mount O. was also strategically impor-

tant; it dominated the Vale of Tempe. A mountain of the same name is in Mysia, Asia Minor.

OLYNTHUS. Capital of Chalcidice; during the Peloponnesian War it remained neutral, but was forced to recognize Sparta's supreme authority in 379 B.C. After that it participated in the second Attic League. Philip II of Macedonia first made a pact with O., but later attacked it. In spite of unsuccessful appeals to Athens and the Olynthiac orations of **Demosthenes** to support O., Philip took and destroyed the town in 348 B.C. The excavations of O. greatly increased our knowledge about the construction of houses (see Houses; Mosaic).

OMNE ANIMAL. "Every living creature"; expression often used in classical literature in various combinations (for example, Cic. *De Deor. Nat.* III, 33).

OMNIA MEA PORTO MECUM. "I carry all mine [all my spiritual property] with me" (Cic. *Par. Stoic.* I, 8; translation of a saying of Bias, one of the Seven Sages).

OMNIA VINCIT AMOR. "Love conquers all" (Virg. *Ecl.* X, 69).

ONESICRITUS. Gr. historian, sent on a voyage by Alexander the Great; the author of a not very veracious biography of Alexander, which has contributed to the many legends and anecdotes about him.

OPTIMATES. The conservative aristocracy in the later Rom. Republic. Although it was no hereditary nobility or a specific political party, the O. held the reins of government for a long time. Their opponents were called *populares* (see also Nobiles).

ORACLE. An institution or means of gauging the will or intention of superhuman powers. The answer these powers give to questions asked, usually through their priests, is also called O. The main types in Greece are: (a) the O. of the dead or heroes, for example, the O. of Amphiaraus in Oropus (often consulted for healing); (b) the O. from natural phenomena, for example, that of Zeus in Dodona; (c) the ecstatic O., for example, that of Delphi, where the Pythia, seated on a tripod, pronounced oracles while in a trance. The oracles were then interpreted by the priests. Among the Romans, the haruspices foretold the future from the entrails of the sacrificial animals, among other things, and the augurs interpreted the flight of the birds.

The Oracle of Delphi was the most famous one of ancient times. It had the greatest influence in the 7th-6th centuries B.C., when not only the Greeks, but also many foreigners (for example, Croesus) came to consult it and enrich it with gifts. It also played an advisory role in colonization. During the Persian Wars, its prestige declined through the unpatriotic attitude of the priests. Later, it recovered—the Romans also consulted it more than once. The O. by dreams of Asklepios in Epidaurus, where revelations were granted during ritual sleep is also worthy of mention.

ORATIO PRO DOMO. "Speech on behalf of one's [own] house"; title of Cicero's speech for the reconstruction of his home after his return from exile.

ORBILIUS, LUCIUS. Rom. schoolmaster. Horace, one of his pupils, nicknamed him *plagosus* (slapper), because he often slapped dull pupils (Hor. *Ep.* II, 1, 69).

ORCHESTRA [Gr. *orchestra,* from *orcheisthai,* to dance]. The circular area in a Gr. theater, where all the action of a drama originally took place. There was an altar (for Athens, the *thymele* or altar of Dionysus) in the center, around which the players and the members of the chorus were grouped. It was much later before a *skènè* (literally: tent) was added from which the actors entered the stage, and still later (about 300 B.C.), the *proskènè* (proscenium), the area in front of the *skènè* (comparable to our stage) was added. In the Rom. theater, where there was no chorus, the O. was used for the seats of honor of senators and other important persons; the Rom. O. was smaller and usually in the form of a semicircle.

ORCHOMENUS. City in Boeotia, to the north of Lake Copais; it flourished in the Mycenaean Age. Excavations have revealed important remains from this period (palace, beehive tomb). O. was one of the most powerful cities of Boeotia at that time. According to tradition, it was inhabited by the Minyae. Later it was completely overshadowed by Thebes, and in 364 B.C. it was destroyed by the army of the Boeotian League, which was led by Thebes.

ORGIES. See Bacchanalia.

ORIGENES (c. 185-c. 255). Usually called Origen. Gr. christian author, born in Alexandria. He was given a Christian education by his parents, which was continued in the catechetical school of Alexandria under Clement and others; later O. himself became the head of the school. He also took lectures from the Neoplatonist philosopher Ammonius

Saccas, in order to improve his understanding of paganism. He offended his own bishop, Demetrius, by giving public instruction in the Scriptures, and was forced to leave Alexandria in about 230. He went to Caesarea Palestinae, where he founded a school. He died in Tyre after having been tortured during the persecution of the Christians in 250-1 under the Emperor Decius (see MILITARY EMPERORS). His works include the *Hexapla,* six versions of the Old Testament.

ORONTES. River in Syria; since the most ancient times, terminal stop for caravan trails, and therefore an important point of contact between Mycenaean Greece and the empires of the Near East. In 300 B.C. Antioch was founded on the O.

OROSIUS (4th cent. A.D.). Christian theologian and historian. He wrote a history of the world on the suggestion of Augustine, which may be compared to the latter's *De Civitate Dei;* although O.'s work is more concise and clearer, it is inferior to Augustine's. It has some value as a source of history, but only for O.'s own times; O. also used some passages from Livy and from the *Historiae* of Tacitus.

ORPHISM. Religious movement which spread through Greece in the 7th-6th centuries B.C., and which, according to legend, was founded by the famous Thracian singer Orpheus (O. probably did originate in Thrace). The doctrine won supporters mainly in Magna Graecia and Attica. O. had its sacred writs, hymns, and mythological poetry. But the ancient texts have been entirely lost, and so we have to depend on later writings: an Orphic saga about the Argonauts, hymns from Rom. times, and sayings on golden platelets, placed mainly in graves in southern Italy during Hellenistic times; also on allusions made by more ancient authors, particularly Pindar and Plato. There is a difference of opinion on the question of what may be attributed to the original O. A few things are certain: O. taught a cosmogony (a theory regarding the creation of the universe) derived mainly from Hesiod's *Theogony;* the teachings on the creation of man, however, were separate; man originated in the ashes of the Titans, who were pulver-

ized by Zeus for tearing young Zagreus (Dionysus) to pieces. As a result, man has a sinful nature, particularly in his body, where the soul is shut up as in a prison. In order to be liberated, he must experience a cycle of rebirths; only when he is purified, is he allowed to enter Elysium. These doctrines were stated to the initiates in the Orphic mysteries. The followers of O. led an ascetic life (vegetarianism, among other things). By preaching the impurity of the body and rejecting the traditional image of Hades, O. ran counter to traditional Gr. concepts. It never became very popular with the people. However, thinkers like Pythagoras and Plato were deeply influenced by it, so that, nevertheless, O. had some influence on young Christianity. The sixth book of Virgil's *Aeneid* also clearly shows traces of O.

OSCI. The inhabitants of Campania, who spoke in a dialect which, together with Umbrian (see UMBRIA), forms one of the two groups of the so-called Italic languages (the Lat. dialects were the other group). Long after Campania had been Romanized, the language was still spoken. Many inscriptions written in Oscan have been preserved.

OSIRIS. Egyptian fertility-god; after his resurrection, ruler of the hereafter (see also ISIS).

OSSA. Mountain range in Thessaly that, with Mount Pelion, separates the Thessalian plain from the sea.

OSTIA. The port of Rome, at the mouth of the Tiber. According to tradition (completely legendary), it was founded by Ancus Marcius; the oldest known settlement dates from the 4th cent. B.C. During republican times, O. aquired its great importance as the place where the grain for Rome was transhipped. It flourished most during the imperial period, particularly under Trajan and Hadrian, when the ladge apartment buildings which are characteristic of O. were built. In about A.D. 200 it began to decline; during the big invasions it was plundered repeatedly. The cosmopolitan nature of the port is apparent from the great variety of native and foreign gods worshiped there.

OSTRACISM. In Athens, a method of removing people dangerous to the state for ten years (in practice usually less), without, however, dishonoring them in any way. Originally instituted by Clisthenes in 509 B.C. in order to remove possible future tyrants. In Athens, O. eventually became an instrument for rendering political opponents harmless. If the ecclesia decided to hold an O. in a given year, the population was assembled and each citizen wrote upon a potsherd (*ostrakon*) the name of a person whose exile he deemed desirable. A total of 6,000 votes against one person was necessary. Many of these potsherds (*ostraka*) have been found, bearing the names of Themistocles, Cimon, Aristides (who really were exiled), and Pericles, among others. In Syracuse, there was an institution of the same sort in the 5th cent. B.C., called *petalismos,* in which the names were written on leaves from trees.

O TEMPORA! O MORES! "What times! What morals!" (Cic. *In Cat.* I, 1, 2).

OTHO, MARCUS SALVIUS (32-69). Rom. emperor in A.D. 69. Favorite of Nero, husband of Poppaea. When Nero wanted to marry her himself, he sent O. to govern Lusitania; from there, after Nero's death (68), O. and Galba returned to Rome. O. was soon proclaimed emperor by the Praetorians because of the general discontent about Galba's government. However, he was defeated by Vitellius, near Bedriacum and Cremona (see YEAR OF THE THREE EMPERORS) and committed suicide.

OTHRYS. Mountain range in southern Thessaly.

OTIUM CUM DIGNITATE. "Leisure with dignity" (Cic. *Pro Sexto,* 45). Cicero's order of words is *cum dignitate odium.*

OVID. See OVIDIUS.

OVIDIUS NASO, PUBLIUS (43 B.C.-c. A.D. 17). Commonly called Ovid. Rom. poet; born in Sulmo in Middle Italy, of a well-to-do family, of the *equite* class. He was first educated for a career as a government official and studied rhetoric, but he soon devoted all his time to poetry, to his father's anger. He had a natural talent for poetry; because he had money he did not need the protection of Maecenas. He became friendly with Tibullus and Propertius. His early work *Amores* (love

elegies, about 25 B.C.) already brought him fame. Temporarily, he remained faithful to the erotic elegy; he wrote *Heroides* (feigned love letters of heroines), *Medicamina Faciei* (about cosmetics) *Ars Amatoria* (art of love, 1 B.C.), and as a counterpart *Remedia Amoris* (cures for love). A tragedy that has been lost, *Medea,* also written during the early period, was highly praised in ancient times. Then followed his most important works: *Fasti* (an elegiac description of the calendar of Rom. festivals). Only the first half (January to June, six books) was completed; the *Metamorphoses* in fifteen books in hexameters (see METER), a colorful collection of sagas, mainly Greek, all ending in metamorphoses, from the creation of the world to the apotheosis of Caesar. When this work was nearly finished, in 8 B.C., O. was struck an unbelievable blow: Augustus ordered him to be banished (*relegatio,* exile without confiscation of fortune) to Tomi on the Black Sea. For this man—so much at home in Rom. society—this must have seemed like a death sentence. O. gives two causes for his exile, his *Ars Amatoria* and an actual offense (*Tristia* II, 207); Augustus felt that the *Ars Amatoria* undermined his program of moral reforms. The poet does not state the nature of the actual offense; it is believed that it may have been connected with the scandal involving Augustus' granddaughter Julia. In spite of the natives' friendliness, O. could never get used to Tomi; he tried to have his sentence revoked, by what sometimes became the most servile flattery, but both Augustus and his successor Tiberius remained implacable. O. died in exile. There he wrote the elegiac *Tristia* (*Songs of Lament*) and *Epistulae ex Ponto* (*Letters from the Black Sea*) as well as a few smaller and less significant works.

O. was the grand master of the Lat. poets; he employed hexameters and elegies with surprising ease; he knew Greek, and was particularly familiar with Alexandrine literature in all its detail; although his style is fluent and brilliant, it nevertheless lacks depth, and rarely, as for example in his description of his departure from Rome (*Tristia* I, 3), does O. arouse deep emotion.

OXYRHYNCHUS. Small town in Egypt, where many papyri were found, most of them dating from Rom. and Byzantine times; some of historical and some of literary value. In 1906 a large fragment of a lost Gr. historical work, a history of the years 396-395 B.C., was found there, the so-called *Hellenica Oxyrhynchia.*

P

PACUVIUS, MARCUS (c. 220-c. 130). Lat. tragic poet from Brundisium, nephew and pupil of Ennius. Titles of twelve plays after Gr. examples and of one *Fabula praetexta* are known; about 400 lines of his work have been preserved.

PADUS. The Rom. name for the Po, the largest river in Italy, called Eridanos by the Greeks. Prehistoric lake dwellings have been found in the Po valley.

PAEAN. Originally the epithet of Apollo, particularly in his function as a healer. From Apollo himself the name was applied for the song of praise to him, and to other gods and even people (Lysander, for example); the P. was often sung as a war song.

PAEONIUS (2nd half of the 5th cent. B.C.). Gr. sculptor from Mende in Thrace. His most famous work is the "Victory" in the museum of Olympia, a votive offer from the Messenians, probably after the battle of Sphacteria (424 B.C.); he also worked on the temple of Zeus in Olympia.

PAESTUM [Gr. Poseidonia]. Colony of Sybaris in Lucania, founded in about 600 B.C.; famous for its beautifully preserved city walls and three Doric temples. After a period of prosperity in the 6th-5th centuries B.C., it was dominated first by the Lucanians and then by the Romans. It remained loyal to Rome against Hannibal, in contrast to most of the cities in the south of Italy. During imperial times it was abandoned because of the increasing health hazard of the near-by marshes.

PAETE, NON DOLET. "Paetus, it doesn't hurt," the words spoken by the Rom. woman Arria, while stabbing herself, to encourage her husband, Caecina Paetus, to commit suicide after an unsuccessful conspiracy against the Emperor Claudius in A.D. 42 (Plin. *Ep.* III, 16, 6; Mart. I, 13).

PAINTING. See VASE PAINTING; PINAX; PORTRAITURE; POMPEII; POLYGNOTUS; MICON; PARRHASIUS; ZEUXIS; APELLES; ETRUSCANS; and PALATINE HILL.

PALAESTRA. Gr. wrestling arena, usually adjacent to a gymnasium.

PALATINE HILL. The most important one of the seven hills of Rome, and the site of the oldest Rom. settlements. The palace (Lat. *palatium*) of the Rom. emperors was situated there; also temples, which were, however, less important than those on the Capitoline Hill. Renewed investigations were recently undertaken, which shed new light on Rom. painting, among other things.

PALEOGRAPHY. An ancient manner of writing; ancient writings, collectively, and the science of studying ancient manuscripts. (For writings on durable material see EPIGRAPHY.) Thus, P. includes the study of ancient manuscripts on parchment (see BOOKS), whereas writing on papyrus is confined to papyrology. We do not possess any authentic ancient manuscripts of ancient authors. (Timothy's papyrus comes closest to it)—the expensive parchment codex was rarely used before the 4th cent. B.C. Practically all extant manuscripts date from the Middle Ages, because they were copied time after time in the monasteries. It is extraordinary that we do have fragments of Virgil's manuscripts from the 3rd-2nd centuries B.C.

PALIMPSEST. A piece of parchment (see BOOKS) which has been used twice or three times, the original text having been erased. This was usually done in order to make the costly material usable more than once. By using ultraviolet rays, the original text, which is often of more interest to us than the later one, can be made to appear. Examples of works which came to light on palimpsests are: fragments of Cicero's *De Re Publica* and Plautus' best manuscript. A papyrus which has been washed to erase the original text in order to make it usable again, is also called a P.

PALLADIUM. Archaic image of Pallas Athena.

PALLAS ATHENA. See ATHENA.

PALMYRA. City in eastern Syria, important center for caravan traders in the 3rd cent. A.D., capital of an independent empire almost as big as the ancient Assyrian empire. After the Nabataei (see ARABIA) had lost their power, P. flourished under Odenathus and his widow Zenobia. In 273 Aurelianus (see MILITARY EMPERORS) conquered P. There are imposing ruins, among them the great temple of Baal.

PALUDAMENTUM. Purple cape for Rom. officers, and particularly for generals; fastened on the right shoulder.

PAMPHYLLA [Gr. land of all tribes]. District in southern Asia Minor between the Mediterranean Sea and the Taurus Mountains, irrigated by the river Eurymedon. Beside the original inhabitants, Cilicians (notorious pirates in Rom. times) and Greeks settled there, who spoke an ancient dialect derived from the Achaean and related to Arcadian. At present, attention is focused on the area because of the recent deciphering of Mycenaean script (see CNOSSUS). P. was dominated consecutively by the Persians, the Seleucids, and (since 189, definitely since 63 B.C.) the Romans who incorporated it successively with several provinces.

PANAETIUS OF RHODES (c. 185-110). Gr. Stoic philosopher; came to Rome in about 144 B.C. where he moved in the circle of Scipio Minor (see LAELIUS). He became the leader of the Stoa in Athens in 129, and tried to adapt its doctrines to the traditional Rom. virtues. In connection with this he also introduced ideas adopted from Plato and Peripatetics. Even at Rhodes, many young Rom. aristocrats came to listen to him. P. played an important part in the Hellenization of Rom. culture; he had great influence on Cicero, whose *De Officiis* is an adaptation of one of P.'s writings.

PANATHENAEA. Annual festival in Athens in honor of Athena. Every four years (July-August) it was celebrated more splendidly; games were held, with a beautiful amphora (see VASE FORMS) filled with oil from the sacred olive trees of the state for a prize. These amphorae, showpieces of many museums, are all painted in the black-figure style, even those from the red-figured vase painting epoch. A procession was also held during the P., at which Athena was offered a new peplos. This procession is depicted on the Parthenon frieze.

PANEGYRIST. Gr. and Rom. laudatory orators, originally appearing during a Gr. festival (*panegyris*), as, for example, Isocrates who wrote his *Panathenaicus* for the Panathenaea, and his *Panegyricus* for the Olympic Games. The Romans had the custom of making a laudatory speech at important burials, much as we do today. From this, a separate literary genre, the *Panegyrici Latini,* developed; twelve laudatory speeches on Rom. emperors are preserved, most of them dating from about 300 B.C.; the oldest and most famous speech is the one of Trajan, delivered by Pliny the Younger, thanking the emperor for the consulate he had been granted (A.D. 100).

PANEM ET CIRCENSES. "Bread and the circus"; food and amusement (Juv. *Sat.* X, 81).

PANHELLENISM. The idea or movement for all Greeks to form one nation and unite politically as well. This idea is in striking contrast to the particularism innate in the Gr. polis, and P. was not carried through decisively until the city-state was a thing of the past. The beginnings of P. can be seen during the early clashes between Hellenes and the *bar-*

baroi (barbarians) and when members of the same tribe formed associations, such as the Ionian Confederation of Twelve Cities, and in the Panhellenic games. Pericles tried to create a Panhellenic movement in about 450 B.C. to restore the temples the Persians had destroyed and to found a communal colony in southern Italy (Thurii). In about 380-350, P. was again actively propagated by Isocrates, and finally realized by Philip II, although it was for the purpose of revenge against Persia, and the realization of Macedonian imperialism. Later, the idea was again brought into existence in the East Rom. Empire (see BYZANTIUM). It reappeared in the 18th cent., especially during the Gr. war of liberation (1821-29). It was encompassed in the motto *Henosis* (unity) in the struggle for the freedom of Cyprus.

PANNONIA. Rom. province to the south and west of the Danube, embracing part of modern Hungary and Yugoslavia. Originally it was inhabited by Illyrians. After partial conquests by Rome and a violent revolt, P. was definitely annexed by Tiberius in 9 B.C.; later it was divided into P. Inferior and P. Superior. The province was abandoned by the Romans in the 4th cent. and overrun by barbarians.

PANORMUS. City in Sicily, now Palermo. In spite of its Gr. name, it was first a Phoenician and later a Carthaginian colony. It was conquered by the Romans during the First Punic War (254 B.C.); later, they founded a colony there. In A.D. 440 it was conquered by the Vandals; in 535 reconquered by the East-Rom. general Belisarius (see JUSTINIAN).

PANTA RHEI. See HERACLITUS.

PANTHEON [Gr. *pantheion*, from *pantheios* of all the gods; Lat. *pantheum*]. The term is applied to the aggregate gods of a people and to the temple dedicated to all the gods. In the latter meaning it refers especially to the temple in the Campus Martius in Rome, built by Agrippa in 27-25 B.C. It was twice destroyed by fire and restored by Domitian, Hadrian, and Septimius Severus. It has an enormous cupola (142 ft. and 6 in. in height and inner diameter) with a portico of Corinthian columns (see COL-

UMN). We know that the seven principal niches of the interior once held statues of the gods. The walls and arches of the P. have been completely preserved. The P. is now used as a Christian church.

PANTOMIME [Gr. *pantomimos*]. The performance of a dramatic subject where the actions are expressed by gestures alone, accompanied by music and dancing. Among the Romans, the term *pantomimus* was applied to the actor himself. The genre was introduced in Rome in 22 B.C. and soon became enormously popular with the people. The emperors sometimes prohibited pantomimes because of their indecent character. Nevertheless, the genre was more refined than the bucolic mime. For example, tragic subjects were also chosen, and mental acuteness was demanded of actors and spectators alike.

PAPHLAGONIA. District in northern Asia Minor, with many Gr. colonies along the coast (Sinope, among others); it was an almost independent country under the Persians; later it became part of Bithynia and Pontus. It was annexed to the Rom. Empire in the 6th cent. B.C.

PAPHOS. City on Cyprus, colonized in Mycenaean times by the Greeks; famous for its cult of an Eastern queen of the heavens, identified with Aphrodite; she was said to have been born out of the sea foam (Tac. *Hist.* II, 2-3).

PAPINIANUS, AEMILIANUS (c. 146-212). One of the greatest Rom. jurists. He held high office under Septimius Severus; was executed by Caracalla in 212 for disapproving of the murder of Geta. Many of his sentences and decisions have been preserved in the *Corpus juris*. He was a lawyer with a very independent mind. Later, his opinions were given the form of law and were applied to decide cases where there was an equal number of lawyers on either side.

PAPYROLOGY. The science of studying the writings (usually Greek) found on Egyptian papyrus. It serves as an auxiliary science for several fields, for example jurisprudence and theology, but particularly for: (a) philology and the history of literature; various lost writings have been found on papyrus (for example, Sappho, Menander, Bacchylides, Aristotle, and *Athenaeum Politeia*). The textual criticism of many known works (especially Homer) is also supported by papyrus fragments, because these are, as a rule, centuries older than the oldest parchment manuscripts; (b) history, because now we possess extremely detailed information about the daily life in one country (Egypt) during the Hellenistic and Roman period (see also OXYRHYNCHUS).

PAPYRUS. The writing material used most often in ancient times, made from the marrow of the P. plant, which grew profusely in the valley of the Nile. In modern times, it is still found in Sicily. In contrast to parchment, P. is perishable; with rare exceptions (Dura-Europos, Herculaneum, and others, see PHILODEMUS) papyri were only preserved in the extremely dry climate of Egypt.

PARCAE. See FATUM.

PARIS. See TROJAN WAR.

PARMENIDES of Elea, 1st half of the 5th cent. B.C. The most prominent philosopher of the Eleatic School. Various large fragments of his didactic poem in hexameters (see METER) have been preserved. In the first part, P. explains the true doctrine (see ELEATICS), the second part is about the world of illusion; that is, the "opinions" (*doxai*) formed by the people about the illusions of a world of the senses.

PARMENION (c. 400-330). General of Philip II and Alexander the Great. During the expedition against the Persians, he was regularly in command of the left (defensive) wing. His cautious attitude is illustrated by the following anecdote: after the battle of Issus Darius III offered peace, and renunciation of his claim to the entire Western part of his empire. Parmenion, asked for his advice by Alexander, said: "I would accept, if I were you," to which Alexander replied: "So would I, if I were Parmenion." P. was sent to Ecbatana to guard the treasures left behind when Alexander moved East. P. was murdered there on Alexander's orders, after his son Philotas had been put to death for alleged high treason. Although this was certainly a dastardly deed, it is nevertheless understandable that Alexander should be afraid to leave

—in a strategic position behind him— the father of the man he had executed.

PARNASSUS. Mountain in Phocis, according to legend, sacred to Apollo, the Muses, and Dionysus. On the southern slope lay Delphi.

PAROS. One of the Cyclades, famous for its white marble, widely used in ancient times by sculptors. As a result of its ambiguous attitude during the Persian Wars, it was subjected by Athens, and treated quite harshly. A marble tablet, known as the *Parian Chronicle,* giving an outline of Gr. history from the reign of Cecrops to about 264 B.C., was found at P. Now one of the Arundel Marbles at Oxford University.

PARRHASIUS (2nd half of the 5th cent. B.C.). Gr. painter, contemporary and rival of Zeuxis. None of his work has been preserved. It is said that his figures were very sculptoral in form; his style can be seen in certain lekythi (see VASE FORMS) from that period. He also wrote about the art of painting, and appears as a character in Xenophon's *Memorabilia.*

PARTHENON. The famous temple of Athena Parthenos (the virgin goddess) on the Athenian Acropolis, the greatest masterpiece of Gr. architecture. The temple is peripteral, of the Doric order (see ARCHITECTURAL ORDERS; TEMPLE), with a number of Ionic elements, among them the frieze around the cella. The P. was built in 447-432 by the architects Ictinus and Callicrates; the sculpture was completed under the direction of Phidias, who himself took part in the work. The pediments represent the birth of Athena and her contest with Poseidon; the metopes the battle between the Lapithae and Centaurs (see also PANATHENAEA). In the Middle Ages, the P. served as a Christian church and a mosque, successively, and remained in good preservation until 1687. In that year, during a siege of Athens by the Venetians, the building was blown up by an explosion of a Turkish powder magazine, and seriously damaged it. Since then it has been restored as well as possible. In 1800-03 Lord Elgin took most of the sculptures to England, where they have been placed in the British Museum (the Elgin Marbles).

PARTHIANS. A Middle Eastern people,

who formed an empire under the dynasty of the Arsacidae, the only power able to brave the Rom. Empire until about A.D. 200. The Parthians believed themselves to be the descendants of the Achaemenidae; their language and their religion were Iranian; however, the upper class of the population was greatly Hellenized. Their cataphracts (cavalry clad in armor) and mounted archers were greatly feared. In 20 B.C., after concluding negotiations, they returned the Rom. prisoners and standards taken at Carrhae in 53 B.C. to Augustus. The later emperors fought the P. with varying success. Their empire was finally overthrown by the Sassanidae. Their art, which resembles that of the Greeks, had a widespread influence.

PATAVIUM. Now Padua in northern Italy, originally the capital of the Veneti; later (c. 180 B.C.), subjected to Rome while keeping a certain measure of internal independence. It prospered as a result of its wool industry and became the wealthiest city in northern Italy until Mediolanum and Aquileia eclipsed it. Paetus Thrasea and Livy were born there.

PATER FAMILIAS. The term applied by the Romans to the head of the house (including servants), and also to a Rom. citizen not under the guardianship of his father.

PATER PATRIAE. "Father of the fatherland," honorary title given to Augustus, Cicero, Caesar, and certain other emperors including Trajan, Hadrian. Tiberius was one of those who expressly refused the title.

PATRAE. Now Patras in the northwestern Peloponnesus, built like an amphitheater against the mountainside. P. played quite an important part in the Achaean League. The harbor was already used for traffic with Italy in ancient times.

PATRES. Name for the Rom. senators. The term is based on the fact that the senate consisted of the heads of the patrician families during Rom. regal times. Later, the senators were called *patres conscripti;* this probably indicated the plebeian senators who had entered it. The authority of the senators (probably only the patrician ones) to ratify popular decisions was called *patrum auctoritas.*

PATRICIANS. The highest Rom. class, originally holding all the political power. The origins of the separation between P.'s and plebeians (see PLEBS) cannot be ascertained, but it has been determined that, from very ancient times, newly arrived citizens could only become plebeians. Thus the P. were a closed caste; a plebeian could only be admitted into a family by their cooptation. On the other hand, P. were able to become members of the plebs voluntarily (see CLODIUS PULCHER). At the end of the republican period only twelve patrician families were left; Caesar and Octavian named new ones. In the 5th and 4th centuries B.C. a very persistent struggle between the two groups took place, during which the P. had to give up most of their privileges one by one, and in 287 B.C. they finally had to grant the plebs complete equality. They retained a number of the more formal privileges (for example, the priesthoods). Under Constantine the Great, "Patrician" became a personal honorary title.

PAULUS, JULIUS (c. A.D. 200). Rom. jurist, contemporary of Papinianus and Ulpianus. His career ran parallel to that of Ulpianus; both became *praefectus praetorio* (see PRAETORIANS) at the same time under Alexander Severus. However, his theories seem to have differed radically from those of Ulpianus; at any rate, neither of the two scholars ever cited the other. P. was productive as a legal author; about a sixth part of the *Digesta* (see CORPUS JURIS) was his.

PAUSANIAS Name of:
—(1) Regent of Sparta from 480-468; decisively defeated the Persians at Plataea in 479, but later entered into traitorous relations with Persia. When he sought asylum in the temple of Athena in Sparta, he was starved to death there on the orders of the ephors, who justly suspected him of planning a coup against them.
—(2) Author of a *Periegesis* or Itinerary of Greece. He traveled extensively, and then, in the second half of the 2nd cent. A.D., settled in Rome. His work is an inexhaustible source for the study of the history of art; it enables us to identify many works that have survived, and accu-

rately describes many that were lost. The *Periegesis* is also useful for the knowledge about Gr. religion and folklore; P. describes numerous customs and religious festivals.

PAX ROMANA. The peace the Romans imposed on their whole Empire; it was often no more than a cover for icy imperialism, sometimes imposed with cruel despotism, and coupled with the most egoistical exploitation. Idealistic Romans like Virgil (*Aen.* VI, 851-3) for example, postulated that it was Rome's moral vocation to impose peace on the countries it subjected, and that they benefited by it. Seen in historical perspective, the P.R. certainly did permit the spread of antique culture throughout Europe. Another form of the P.R. was the *Pax Augusta,* the peace that prevailed in Augustus' time; it was in his honor that the senate built the Ara Pacis.

PECUNIA NON OLET. "Money does not smell." Vespasian used only the words *non olet* to Titus, when the latter reproached him for imposing taxes on sewers (Suet. *Vespasian,* 23).

PELASGIANS. Pre-Rom. tribe whose descendants lived near Cyzicus and in Chalcidice in historical times and preserved traces of a non-Gr. language. The Greeks regularly used the name *Pelasgos* for any pre-Gr. inhabitant of the country; Homer mentions *Pelasgoi* in Thessaly. The origins of some Gr. place names ending in—nthos and—ssos are sought in their language.

PELIKE. See VASE FORMS.

PELION. Mountain in Thessaly where, according to legend the wise centaur Chiron had his cave. Mount P. and Mount Ossa separated the Thessalian plain from the Aegean Sea.

PELLA. Capital of Macedonia from about 400 to 167 B.C.; chosen as the capital by King Archelaus because he wanted to develop Macedonia economically and politically, and P. was in a more favorable position than the former royal residence Aegae.

PELOPIDAS (c. 410-364). Statesman and general of Thebes. He and Epaminondas ruled the state during Thebes' short period of hegemony. In 379, in a courageous attack, he drove the Spartan occupation out of the fortress of Thebes. He fought at Epaminondas' side at Leuctra and ultimately during the Peloponnesian expeditions against Sparta. After that, he led operations against Alexander of Pherae in Thessaly, and fell at Cynoscephalae.

PELOPONNESIAN WAR. The struggle between Athens and Sparta, supported by their respective allies, and lasting from 431-404 B.C. This war is authoritatively described by Thucydides (until 411); the rest by Xenophon in his *Hellenica.* Motives: Sparta's fear at the growth of Athens' supremacy; the jealousy, particularly of Corinth, of Athens' westward expansion; the general bitterness about Athens' tyranny in the Delian League. Causes: (a) Corcyra sought the support of Athens in a conflict with Corinth; (b) Potidaea sought the help of Corinth while trying to revolt against Athens; (c) Athens barred Megara from Attic ports and markets. Corinth declared war.

Sparta was superior on land, and Athens on the sea. The conflict became more and more of an ideological struggle between oligarchy and democracy, pursued even in the different cities and families (see CORCYRA). There were three phases of the war: (a) The Archidamian War, named after King Archidamus II. Pericles' strategy embraced a passive attitude toward the Spartan invasion of Attica: the population was to retreat inside the Long Walls of the Piraeus, the fleet would be able to block the Peloponnesian coast. This plan was thwarted because an epidemic of the plague broke out in the overcrowded town (430-29); the plan was not strictly adhered to after Pericles' death. After the battle of Sphacteria, Sparta sued for peace in vain. The death of the most fervent warmongers, Cleon and Brasidas, was followed by the peace of Nicias: *status quo ante bellum* (421). (b) The expedition against Sicily. Alcibiades suggested a large expedition against Syracuse, which ended in a catastrophe (see also GYLIPPUS; DEMOSTHENES). (c) The Decelean War (413-404), named after Decelea, occupied by the Spartans. An oligarchical revolution took place in Athens in 411 (see THERAMENES; PISANDER), ending in the restoration of democracy and the recall of Alcibiades, who, however, was exiled again in 406. The Persians (see CYRUS) supported Sparta financially, enabling it to build a fleet commanded by Lysander (see also ARGINUSAE; AEGOSPOTAMI). Athens capitulated in April 404. It was forced to surrender the rest of its fleet, pull down the Long Walls, and disband the Delian League. Athens now had to recognize the hegemony of Sparta.

PELOPONNESUS. The peninsula to the south of the Isthmus of Corinth, embracing the regions of Argolis (see ARGOS), Laconia, Messenia, Elis, Achaea, and Arcadia. Originally the most powerful city was Mycenae, later Sparta, which conquered all of Messenia, and made successive treaties with the cities of the other districts (only Argos remained neutral). That was the origin of the Peloponnesian League, the first large military alliance in Greece.

PELTASTS. Lightly armed Gr. soldiers who carried a small round shield (peltè) of Thracian origin. At first P. were only used for supporting the hoplites; however, the commander of the mercenaries, Iphicrates (4th cent. B.C.), made improvements in their weapons and tactics, so that the P. were able to fight more independently.

PENATES. Rom. household-gods, literally the protectors of the pantry, worshiped in every Rom. home, together with the Lares and Vesta. The Rom. state also had its P.; their origin goes back to the household-gods of the Rom. kings. According to tradition, Aeneas had removed them from burning Troy (Virg. *Aen.*). They were sometimes identified with the Cabiri of Samothrace.

PENTAMETER. See METER.

PENTATHLON. In Gr. gymnastics, five sporting events, originally jumping, running, discus and javelin throwing, and wrestling.

PENTECONTAËTIA. The period of approximately fifty years between the Persian Wars and the Peloponnesian War, when Gr. culture flourished most greatly, especially in Athens (see PERICLES).

PENTELIKON. Mountain in Attica, 10 mi. northeast of Athens; famous for its marble, which was used for the Parthenon and other buildings.

PENTHEUS. See DIONYSUS.

PEPLOS. A Gr. woman's garment, mentioned already in Homer. The P. was a rectangular piece of woolen cloth, draped around the body, fastened on one or both shoulders (with a pin, for example) and held together below the breasts with a girdle.

PER ASPERA AD ASTRA. "Along crude [roads] to the stars"; to victory in spite of difficulties.

PERDICCAS. Name of:

—(1) P. I, the founder of the Macedonian monarchy (c. 640 B.C.).

—(2) P. II, king of Macedonia from c. 450-413; repeatedly played Athens against Sparta in order to weaken the Gr. influence on the sea coast (especially Chalcidice).

—(3) Distinguished general of Alexander the Great. After Alexander's death (323 B.C.), P. had the chief authority entrusted to him and ruled the empire until he was murdered in 321 because he was hated by the other Diadochi (Seleucus, among others).

PEREGRINUS. See PRAETOR.

PERGAMUM. City in Mysia (Asia Minor), made the capital of a Hellenic empire in the 3rd cent. B.C. by the Attalidae (see ATTALUS; EUMENS), which embraced the largest part of Asia Minor. It had enormous natural resources and flourishing industries (among others, parchment; see BOOKS). In the field of culture, it was also well able to compete with other Hellenic empires. German excavations laid bare some large public buildings, including the big temple of Zeus with the frieze depicting the combat between gods and giants. The statue of the "Dying Gaul" is also one of the masterpieces of P. In 133 B.C., Attalus III willed the empire to Rome, by testamentary disposition, and Rome made it the new province of Asia.

PERIANDER. Son of Cypselus, tyrant of Corinth from c. 625-585 (40 years later, according to some). His reign was a period of economic prosperity and political expansion for the city. He reestablished the ties with Corcyra and

Reconstruction of the fortress and altar of Zeus in Pergamum. 1. Altar of Zeus, 2. fortress wall with theater below it, 3. Temple of Athena, 4. Hall of columns with library.

entered into overseas relations. He was succeeded by his nephew, who was soon murdered, and with whom the tyrants in Corinth died out. P. was reckoned among the Seven Sages.

PERICLES (c. 495-429). Athenian statesman, member of the family of the Alcaeonidae, son of Xanthippus, political leader of Athens during that city's most flourishing period. In 472 he was *choregus* (see LITURGY) when Aeschylus' *The Persians* was produced. He suddenly became prominent as the leader of the democratic forces, because his older associate Ephialtes was murdered (c. 456). He immediately began to extend Athens' power by strict organization of the Delian League, well aware of risking the enmity of Sparta. He was not afraid to wage war on Persia (until 448; see CALLIAS) and Sparta (until 446) at the same time. In internal politics, he democratized the state by instituting, among other things, payment for services rendered to the state. In the field of culture, he took the initiative of building the Parthenon and other public structures, and supported artists and scholars, of whom several were his personal friends (Anaxagoras, Herodotus, Sophocles, Phidias, and others). The attacks of P.'s political opponents, who did not dare oppose the great man himself, were often aimed at them, or at Aspasia. After his most violent opponent, Thucydides, the son of Melesias, had been ostracized, P. was elected strategist year after year; under his regime, this office became more and more political in character. P. was so influential at that time, that the historian Thucydides said: "It was a democracy in name, but actually it was dominated by the first citizen." Still, his power, year after year, was based on the choice of the Athenian people: he was certainly no tyrant. His rule was a blessing for Athens, which could call itself "the Hellas of Hellas." But there were negative sides to it too: (a) the political, cultural, and economic expansion really made a larger number of citizens necessary; but P. introduced a law which gave Athenian citizenship only to those born to parents who both were Athenian citizens. This gave some inhabitants the status of metics. P. was nevertheless egoistical enough to have his own son by Aspasia naturalized specially; (b) the allies were treated tyranically; they were degraded to the position of subjects. P. personally took part in the punitive expedition against rebellious Samos (439).

P. also took the initiative of expanding toward the West, particularly Sicily, which had to lead to conflict with Corinth. When he realized that the Peloponnesian War was unavoidable, he hastened the outbreak by boycotting Megara. He decided on the strategy for the war himself. When Attica was destroyed by Archidamus, P. was reproached for his policy of war; he was dismissed as a strategist and fined for embezzling state funds. But it was soon found that his leadership was needed; he was reelected, but died soon afterward of the plague.

Next to Themistocles, P. is the greatest Athenian statesman of the 5th cent. B.C. Themistocles was more ingenious, but P. was more tactful. In that respect, they might be compared to Caesar and Augustus, respectively. Themistocles was certainly a clever diplomat, but P. understood the art of persuading and leading the Athenian masses like no one else. They were both democrats. P. had the advantage in finding democracy nearly accomplished at the beginning of his career. He did not seem destined to become a popular leader, either through descent or through character (he was haughty, an "Olympian" as the mocking comic poets called him). Still, in his role as a politician, he acquired a democratic ethos; he was responsible for making Athenian democracy reach its peak.

PERIOIKOI. See SPARTA.

PERIPATETICS. The followers of Aristotle. *Peripatos* (from *peripatein,* to walk about) was the name of the hall in the Lyceum where Aristotle taught. The building finally became the property of the school as a gift from Demetrius of Phaleron. The history of the school can be divided into two periods: the first, from Theophrastus to Strato, emphasized particularly the study of the professional sciences, and neglected theoretical philosophy, especially metaphysics; the second period, starting with Andronicus (1st cent. B.C.), stressed mainly metaphysics and logic. During this period the many hitherto unpublished manuscripts of Aristotle were published, and commentaries were written. These later P. had a great influence on Neoplatonism.

PERSEPHONE. The wife of Hades, queen of the underworld. A pre-hellenic figure of the underworld, the Greeks identified her with Kore (girl), the daughter of Demeter. In the Eleusinian mysteries, she was, as Kore, the symbol of death and rebirth of nature. Orphism identified her with the mother of Zagreus. The Romans called her Proserpina.

PERSEPOLIS. Capital of the Persian empire. In contrast to the other capitals, Susa and Ecbatana, it was not a political center for the more ancient states, but was especially founded as a residence by Darius I. He had the palaces, ornamented with beautiful Persian reliefs, built around a throne room (*apadana*). Xerxes completed the buildings. Nearby are the rock tombs of the Achaemenidae. Enormous amounts of precious metals, the tributes of subjected peoples, were kept in the treasure chambers. In 331 B.C. the palaces were burned down by Alexander the Great, in reprisal. The gold and silver then found were brought into circulation, disastrously devaluating money in early Hellenistic times.

PERSEUS. Name of:

—(1) One of the most important Gr. heroes, son of Zeus and Danaë. P. was said to be the ancestor of many heroes, including Heracles, and it is possible that he was the historical founder of Mycenae, where a cult existed in his honor. He was also worshiped as a hero or demigod on the island of Seriphos, in Argos, and at Athens.

—(2). The last king of Macedonia (212-166, ruled from 179-168), son of Philip V. Having come to the throne by removing his younger brother Demetrius, who enjoyed the support of Rome, P. tried to consolidate the position of Macedonia by entering into alliances with other Hellenic rulers, and by intervening in the politics of Thessaly and central Greece. The Romans alleged that all this was only leading up to war against the Rom. Empire—this was probably their one-sided Rom. version. Eumenes II of Pergamum incited Rome to war (Third Macedonian War, 171-168). Lucius Aemilius Paullus defeated P. at Pydna, after which he was taken prisoner and walked in Aemilius' triumph. He died in prison.

PERSIAN EMPIRE. The empire founded by Persians—a people who spoke an Indo-European language—in the 6th cent. B.C., with the Iranian plateau as its center. The sides entirely to the fight for the Ionian cities in Asia Minor. After Persia's military defeat, she nevertheless reached her goal by diplomacy and cleverly playing the divided Gr. cities off against one another. This supremacy was of short duration: Alexander the Great destroyed the empire of the Achaemenidae 55 years after the notorious "King's Peace." The

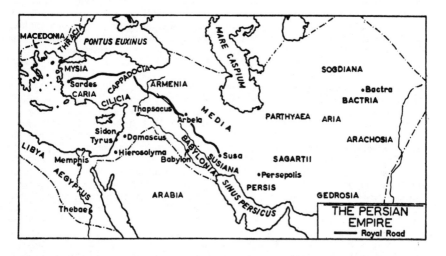

empire's political history can be divided into five periods: (a) the empire of the Achaemenidae (see ACHAEMENIDAE; SUSA; PERSEPOLIS; SATRAP); (b) the conquest by Alexander the Great; (c) the Seleucid empire; (d) the empire of the Parthians; (e) that of the Sassanidae. After 500 B.C., the Greeks and Romans almost always found a political opponent, usually an adversary in the P.E. The great conflict between Greece and the P. E., known as the Persian Wars, are—in a narrower sense—the happenings between 490-479 B.C.; in a broader sense—those from 500 to the so-called King's Peace of 387 B.C. (For details see IONIA; MARDONIUS; DATIS; MARATHON; THERMOPYLAE; SALAMIS; PLATAEA; MYCALE; EURYMEDON; CALLIAS; CYRUS; AGESILAUS; ANTALCIDAS). The wars began with the Ionian uprising in 500, but the real motives were the P.E.'s struggle for domination of the Aegean Sea, and the Greeks' desire for liberty. The conflict was limited on both

Greeks generally represented the conflict as a struggle between Hellenes and *barbaroi* (this word originally designated all "strangers," but slowly acquired a derogatory meaning). The struggle of 480-479 was symbolized by the battle between the Lapithae and Centaurs, depicted on the temple of Zeus at Olympia. We could be inclined to see the Persians as enemies of Gr. culture; this certainly is not the case; the "barbaric" conduct of Xerxes (destruction of sanctuaries) was contrary to the tradition of the Achaemenidae; the P.E. generally allowed subjected peoples to keep their own institutions and customs. But the Gr. victory of 479 was a guarantee for the freedom of the Gr. polis; and without that freedom it would have been impossible for Gr. civilization to develop the way it did in the 5th-4th centuries.

The influence of the P.E. on Gr. and Rom. culture was great. The three most important points are: (a) the P.E.'s excellent organization made it possible for many Greeks to travel in the Near East, especially in the 6th cent. B.C.; this resulted in fruitful contact between Greece and its Eastern neighbors; (b) during the reign of the Diadochi (as the successors of the Achaemenidae); the civilizing influence of the East was again channeled to give Hellenistic culture its own characteristics; (c) the Persian religion, established by Zoroaster (principal god, Ahura Mazda) influenced the religious currents in the Rom. Empire deeply, particularly the worship of Mithras.

PERSIUS, FLACCUS, AULUS (A.D. 34-62). Lat. poet; follower of the Stoa. His teacher, the Stoic philosopher Annaeus Cornutus, published P.'s poems after his death. There were six satires, written in obscure language, and often containing mixed metaphors. They are much less true to life than the satires of Lucilius and Horace, who were his examples.

PERTINAX. See MILITARY EMPERORS.

PERUSIA. Ancient city in Etruria, now Perugia; conquered by Rome in 295 B.C., and always loyal to Rome thereafter, even against Hannibal. In 41 B.C. the consul Lucius Antonius, the brother of Mark Antony, used P. as his base when he opposed Octavian (Augustus), who took it after a long siege (the Perusian War). The city was forced to surrender, and was burnt to the ground. However, the city walls and some Etruscan graves are well preserved.

PERVIGILIUM [literally: a nightwatch]. A nocturnal festival in honor of a divinity. Such a festival is referred to in a beautiful anonymous Lat. poem, probably dating from the 4th cent. A.D. It is called *Pervigilium Veneris,* and describes a spring festival in Sicily in honor of Venus. One of the typical characteristics is its recurring refrain: *cras amet qui numquam amavit, quique amavit cras amet,* "let him who has never loved, love tomorrow, and he who has loved, let him [also] love tomorrow."

PESCENNIUS NIGER. See MILITARY EMPERORS.

PETILLIUS CEREALIS. See CEREALIS.

PETRA [Gr. rock]. Capital of the Nabataean empire in Arabia; after A.D. 105 it was only a religious center. P. was the central point for the caravan trade routes. Surrounded by rock temples and graves, it exhibits a great variety of architectural styles; the ruins resemble those of Palmyra.

PETRONIUS ARBITER, GAIUS. Author and master of ceremonies at the luxurious court of Nero. He was accused by Tigellinus of being a member of Piso's conspiracy against Nero, and committed suicide in just as curious a way as he had lived (Tac. *Ann.* XVI, 18, 19.). In addition to other works, now lost, he wrote a strange novel in the form of a Menippean satire (see MENIPPUS); the *Banquet of Trimalchio* is the most important extant fragment. Three young men from the fringes of the half-Gr., half-Rom. society of southern Italy find themselves at the banquet of a parvenu called Trimalchio; the most fantastic stunts are exhibited and the most fantastic stories are told here. The fragment is one of the most important sources for Vulgar Latin (colloquial form).

PEUTINGER TABLET. Ancient map of the Rom. world, named after its former owner, Konrad Peutinger (1465-1547). It is a copy of the original dating from the 3rd-4th centuries A.D., which in turn was based on a map of Marcus Agrippa. It is important for the identification of otherwise unknown Rom. place names. Now at Vienna.

PHAEDRUS (1st cent. A.D.). Lat. poet of fables, Macedonian slave, later freed by Augustus. He introduced the Gr. fable in Rom. literature; he adapted most of them from Aesop, supplemented them with other examples. About the 10th cent. an author calling himself Romulus, published a prose adaptation, which became very popular in the Middle Ages. P.'s poems contain an element of satire in addition to the usual tendency to moralize.

PHAISTOS [Lat. Phaestus]. Place in southern Crete, where a Minoan palace, built according to the same plan as the palace of Cnossus, was found; it differs in one feature: there is a peristyle around the courtyard. It fell into ruin in about 1400 B.C.

PHALARIS. Tyrant of Akragas (Agrigentum) from c. 570-554, notorious for his cruelty. According to trustworthy data, he burned his victims in a bronze steer, so that their cries would create the illusion that the animal was lowing.

PHALERON. Town, an early port of Athens, superseded by Piraeus in the 5th cent. B.C.

PHARNACES. Name of:

—(1) P. King of Pontus from c. 185-169, grandfather of Mithridates. He laid the foundation for the expansion of Pontus by conquering Sinope, among other places.

—(2) P. II. Son of Mithridates, led the revolt against his father, whom he drove to suicide. Later, during the civil war between Caesar and Pompey, he reinstated himself in his father's dominions, but in 47 B.C. he was quickly defeated at Zela by Caesar, coming from Egypt. The battle was so easily won that Caesar was able to write to Rome: *Veni, vidi, vici.*

PHAROS. Small island off the Egyptian coast near Alexandria, famous for its lighthouse, which was one of the Seven Wonders of the World. Later, the name of the island was used in the meaning of lighthouse by the Romans (compare French: *phare*).

PHARSALUS. City in Thessaly, after 300 B.C. the most important city of that region. The decisive battle between Caesar and Pompey was fought at P. in 48 B.C. Cynoscephalae, nearby, was the scene of several historical battles.

PHEIDIAS. See PHIDIAS.

PHEIDON (beginning of the 7th cent. B.C.). King of Argos. He dominated the entire northeastern Peloponnesus and deprived the Eleans of their control of the Olympic Games. The (probably correct) story was handed down, that P. was the first to have Gr. coins minted (see COINAGE).

PHERAE. City in southern Thessaly, in mythology, the most important city of that region. It became a political power in the 1st half of the 4th cent. B.C. under the tyrants Lycophron, Alexander, and Jason. It was robbed of its influence by Philip II of Macedonia.

PHERECYDES of Syros (6th cent. B.C.). The first Gr. prose writer. He wrote a book about myths on creation and the origin of the world, of which only frag-

ments have survived; even in ancient times, he was confused with P. of Athens (5th cent. B.C.), who wrote genealogies.

PHIALE. See VASE FORMS.

PHIDIAS [Gr. Pheidias]. (5th cent. B.C., period of greatest activity, around 440). Gr. sculptor, contemporary of Myron, Polyclitus, and Cresilas, friend of Pericles. Even the ancients considered him to be the greatest master of classical sculpture. In 448 he directed the decoration of the Parthenon and was commissioned to make the chryselephantine cult statue of Athena Parthenos. In 432 he was accused of stealing ivory and gold intended for the statue and, probably as a result of the trial, was exiled (an indirect attack on his friend Pericles). However, he proved his innocence by having the adornments of the statue removed and weighed. Afterward, he worked on the statue of Zeus at Olympia.

P.'s artistry and his method of working can most clearly be seen in the sculptures of the Parthenon, which were executed under his direction by his pupils. The frieze is the best preserved. Only copies of the other statues have survived. Those of the "Athena Parthenos" are mediocre. Portrayals on coins permit us to recreate the attitude of the "Zeus." We are in a better position with regard to the "Athena Lemnia," because a copy of the head has been preserved in Bologna, and one of the torso in Dresden. All we have of the huge "Athena Promachos" which stood in the Acropolis, is a small bronze figurine and pictures on vases. One of the Amazons (see CRESILAS) of which copies have been preserved, is attributed to P.

The development of sculpture in the 2nd half of the 5th cent. B.C. can be seen clearly in P.'s work. In the sculptures of the Parthenon alone, there is evidence of a definite evolution; the metopes, among the earliest works, are still in a somewhat severe style (best represented in the sculptures of the temple of Zeus in Olympia). The frieze shows the blossoming of the classical style. The pediments with the skillful portrayal of diaphanous drapery, show a more elaborate style. The classical authors already praised the ethos, the spiritual content, which gives the figures in P.'s work their character and his groups their mood. The ancients also noticed the resemblance between his work and that of the painter Polygnotus.

PHIGALIA. City in southwestern Arcadia, adjacent to the Village of Bassae.

PHILIP. Name of:

—(1) P. II. King of Macedonia (c. 382-336), founder of the Macedonian empire; came to Thebes as a hostage in 368 where he met Epaminondas. He received a Gr. education. After the death of his brother Perdiccas III in 359, he obtained the government of Macedonia, at first acting as the guardian of his young nephew Amyntas; after a short time, P. took the title of king. He soon turned Macedonia's old tribal kingship into a powerful autocracy; his first aim was to acquire an outlet to the sea, and for this reason he expanded his territory toward Chalcidice; furthermore, he undertook the exploitation of the gold mines in Thrace (see PHILIPPI) and made the Macedonian army into what was then an invincible force by adopting and improving the tactics of the slanting phalanx (see LEUCTRA). He also saw to it that the fleet was strong. He now began to intervene, with increasing success, in the affairs of the Greeks who were divided among themselves. In Athens, Demosthenes attacked him violently, but Isocrates welcomed him as the leader of a Gr. league of states (see AESCHINES). By intervening in the so-called Holy War (see AMPHICTYONS), he penetrated further and further into central Greece. In 338 he defeated the united Thebans and Athenians at Chaeronea. The Greeks united in the Corinthian League under the personal hegemony of P., with the aim of undertaking a retaliatory expedition against Persia. However, during the preparations P. was murdered at a court festivity (see OLYMPIAS). He was succeeded by Alexander the Great.

—(2) P. V. King of Macedonia (238-179), adopted son of Antigonus III, whom he succeeded in 221. He waged war against Rome as an ally of Hannibal (215-205), which ended in a peace that was quite advantageous to P.; then he turned against Egypt and met with rebel-

lion from Rhodes and Pergamum, who persuaded Rome to undertake the Second Macedonian War (200-197). P. was defeated at Cynoscephalae by Flamininus and limited to Macedonia proper, which had in reality now become a vassal state of Rome. P. strove for consolidation of the remaining empire, through expeditions in the North, among others. Of his sons, one, Demetrius, wanted friendship with Rome; for this reason, the other, Perseus, had him killed (180). P. died soon afterward and was succeeded by Perseus.

PHILIPPI. City in Macedonia, founded in 358-7 by Philip II in connection with his exploitation of the gold mines in the Pangaion Mountains. In 42 B.C., Brutus and Cassius were decisively beaten here by Mark Antony. The battle consisted of two phases: after the first phase, things seemed to go well for the republicans; nevertheless, Cassius, whose camp was captured, committed suicide too hastily. The second phase definitely gave the victory to Antony. Octavian (Augustus), who felt ill, only played a minor part.

PHILIPPUS ARABUS. See MILITARY EMPERORS.

PHILO of Alexandria (c. 25 B.C.-c. A.D. 50). Surnamed Judaeus. Principal representative of Jewish-Hellenistic philosophy; leader of the Jewish community in Alexandria. In A.D. 40 he went to Rome as an emissary to Caligula to ask for help against the persecution of the Jews and to plead for exemption from worshiping the Emperor. In his writings, P. tried to reconcile Hellenism with Judaism; he was greatly influenced by the philosophy of Plato and Posidonius.

PHILODEMUS of Gadara (1st cent. B.C.). Gr. poet and Epicurean philosopher. He had a school of philosophy in Neapolis, where he came in contact with Horace and Virgil. Several of his epigrams have been preserved in the *Anthologia Palatina;* large fragments of his philosophical writings were found in 1752 on half-charred rolls of papyrus in the villa of Piso (Rom. aristocrat whose protégé P. was) in Herculaneum.

PHILOLAUS of Croton (c. 400 B.C.). Gr. philosopher of the school of Pythagoras. Attributed to him is the theory of a cosmic system in which ten spheres of astral bodies revolve around a central fire (the "hearth of the universe"): earth, a conception he called "counter-earth," moon, sun, five planets, and the sphere of the fixed stars.

PHILOPOEMEN of Megalopolis (253-183). General and statesman of the Achaean League. In 223 he drove back Cleomenes III of Sparta, who had occupied his native city; for the next ten years he was a commander of mercenaries on Crete; then he succeeded Aratus as the leader of the Achaean League, and became commander in chief in 208. After the death of Nabis of Sparta (192), whom he had defeated several times, he annexed Sparta into the League; in 188 he demilitarized it and became the uncrowned king of the entire Peloponnesus. In 183 he was taken prisoner by rebellious Messenians and compelled to drink poison. Although he was a fervent patriot, and was honored by all Greeks, in reality he was too much a figurehead of Flamininus and of the Rom. senate to be a true national figure. Plutarch wrote his biography.

PHILOSOPHY. For pre-Socratic P. (natural philosophy) see ATOMISM and the philosophers referred to there. For Socrates and his period see also ETHICS; PLATO; ACADEMY; ARISTOTLE; PERIPATETICS; MEGARA; CYRENAIC SCHOOL; CYNICS; STOICS; EPICURUS; SKEPTICS; and NEOPLATONISM.

PHILOSTRATUS. Name of four members of a family from Lemnos of the 2nd-3rd centuries A.D., to whom a number of literary works have been attributed. Flavius P. the Elder (c. A.D. 200), protégé of the wife of Septimius Severus, wrote the romantic *Life of Apollonius of Tyana;* the biography of an ascetic, prophet, and miracle worker of the 1st cent. A.D. Another of his more important works is *Lives of the Sophists.* His *Eikones* is a description of paintings in a collection at Neapolis. P. the Younger (d. c. A.D. 264) followed his grandfather's example and wrote a work also entitled *Eikones.*

PHOCAEA. The northernmost Ionian city on the coast of Asia Minor. P. founded colonies in the western Mediterranean region, among them Massilia, and maintained trade relations with Tartessus. In 540 B.C., when the Persians conquered P., most of the inhabitants emigrated to Elea in southern Italy.

PHOCION (4th cent. B.C.). Athenian general and statesman adversary of radical democracy. Although he did not really have much political and military ambition, he was generally esteemed for his honesty, vigor, and incorruptibility, and was elected strategist forty-five times. In about 350 he and Aeschines led the pro-Macedonian party in opposition to Demosthenes and his followers, and welcomed Philip II and later Alexander the Great. When democracy was restored in Athens in 318, during the war with the Diadochi, he was sentenced to death.

PHOCIS. District in Central Greece, where Delphi, Mount Helicon, and Mount Parnassus are located; it waged several wars against its neighbors about the possession of Delphi; the third war, called the Phocian or Sacred War, in which almost all of Greece became involved (355-45), and during which the Phocians Philomelus and Onomarchus were defeated after initial successes, is the most famous. The war was brought to a close by the victory of Philip II; P. was razed and lost its importance. Under the Romans it became part of the province of Achaea.

PHOCYLIDES of Miletus (6th cent. B.C.). Gr. poet who wrote in hexameters and distichs. Of his maxims a few fragments have survived. A long moralizing poem bearing his name, the so-called *Pseudo-Phocylides,* incorporating many Eastern-Hellenistic ideas, is now considered to be the work of an Alexandrian Jewish Christian of the 1st–2nd centuries A.D.

PHOENICIANS. People who spoke a Semitic language and inhabited a number of cities on the Syrian coast, mainly in what is now Lebanon. The most important ones were Ugarit (Ras Shamra), Sidon, and Tyre. Their name is derived from the Greek *phoinix* (red) probably with reference to their copper-colored skin. Although the Mycenaean world did have many trade connections with Ugarit, the P. did not play any part in

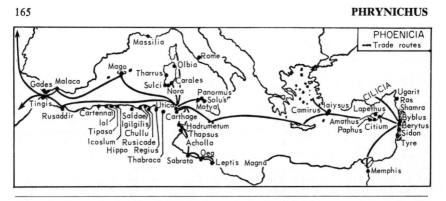

Distribution area of the Phoenicians, along with their land of origin in what is now Lebanon and colonies in the Mediterranean area.

Gr. history until about 1000 B.C.; the "P." of the Gr. sagas (Cadmus and others) probably were Minoan Cretans. The period from 1200-800 marked the time of their greatest prosperity and expansion; they founded many trade stations [among them Cyprus, Utica, and Gades (Cadiz)], one of which, Carthage, developed into a great city. Many contacts with the Greeks originated at that time, especially with Corinth. The fantastic descriptions of places in the western Mediterranean region in Homer's *Odyssey,* are often attributed to the stories of the P. In the Persian empire the P. furnished the fleet, which played an important part during the Ionian revolt and at Salamis, among other places. Still, during all the years of war between Greece and Persia, Phoenician trade with Greece continued, at that time usually by way of Piraeus. The main export articles of the P. were purple dye and glass. Alexander the Great conquered Tyre in 332 B.C. after a siege of seven months. After that, Phoenicia became part of the Seleucid empire; in 64 B.C. it was annexed to the Rom. province of Syria. The most important cultural asset the Greeks adopted from the P. was the alphabet (see SCRIPT).

PHORMIO. Athenian general who subjected recalcitrant Samos (see PERICLES) in 440 B.C. He also distinguished himself during the Peloponnesian War by his operations in the Gulf of Corinth.

PHOTIUS (9th cent. A.D.). Patriarch,

scholar of Byzantium, the greatest scientist of his time. His literary work the *Bibliotheca* contain excerpts and criticism of 280 Gr. works of classical authors, the originals of which are now to a great extent lost. This work is of special value to the student of Gr. literature of antiquity. His second book, the *Lexicon,* is a glossary of Gr. literature and the Bible. A large part of this work (*Ap-Ep*) was lost until recently; the missing section was found in a Macedonian monastery a very short time ago.

PHRYGIA. A region in central and northwestern Asia Minor, invaded by European tribes in the 2nd millennium B.C., who founded a kingdom of which Gordius and Midas in the 8th cent. B.C. were the best known kings. Later, P. only embraced the western central section of Asia Minor; the epithet Phrygians for the Trojans, used by Rom. poets, is a reminder of the earlier northern expansion. P. was conquered by Lydia, the Persian and the Seleucide empires in succession, and then by Pergamum. In 133 B.C. the Romans annexed it to the province of Asia. Because of trade relations, P. was strongly influenced by Greece; Greece in turn benefited from P. influence in the fields of music and religion (see CYBELE).

PHRYNICHUS (c. 500 B.C.). The most important Athenian tragic poet before Aeschylus. He was the first to write plays on not only mythological but also historical subjects. In 494 he presented the *Fall of Miletus;* the play made such a devastating impression that all further performances were prohibited and the poet was heavily fined for reminding the people of "their own catastrophes" (Hdt. VI, 21). Public reaction to the play can be explained in two ways: Miletus was considered by Athenians to be a daughter city (see also IONIANS); also, they were ashamed of giving too little support to the Ionian revolt. It was the first time in the history of the European theater that the government decided to take steps against a play. In 476, P. produced the *Phoenissae,* with Themistocles as the *choregus* (see LITURGY). This play was about the Persian Wars; it served as the model of Aeschylus' *The Persians.*

PHYLAE. The largest tribal subdivisions among the ancient Athenians. The Dorians had three P., the Ionians four; if the original population was assimilated during a settlement or colonization, one or more new P. were sometimes created (see also CLISTHENES).

PILATE. See PONTIUS PILATE.

PINAX [Gr.]. Painting on wood (literally: board) or terra cotta; a few ancient ones have been found. The word *pinacotheca,* meaning museum of paintings, is derived from P.

PINDAR (518-438). The greatest Gr. lyric poet from Cynoscephalae near Thebes. He wrote choral songs in the artificial Dorian dialect of that genre. Among them were hymns, paeans, and dithyrambs, of which fragments have survived. His *Epinikia,* forty-five laudatory songs for the victors at the great Panhellenic Games, classified as "Olympian," "Pythian," "Nemean," and "Isthmian Odes," have all been preserved. They were written on commission; many are dedicated to the tyrants of Sicily (P. himself spent some time after 476 at the court of Hiero I in Syracuse) and the king of Cyrene. P. had a certain natural sympathy for the nobility; he himself was of aristocratic descent and did not have much respect for Athenian democracy. He forgave Thebes her neutrality during the Persian Wars, but afterward he could not resist praising Athens for her courageous resistance.

P. starts his *Odes* with praise of the victor himself; a myth or saga relating to one of the hero's ancestors follows; he finishes with a hymn to the gods. Written in endlessly varied meter, the *Odes* bear witness to his deep, almost monotheistic religious feeling, and to firmly founded, elevated moral thought. The influence of Orphism and the Eleusinian mysteries can be seen here. His language and style are profound and difficult. P. has to be "conquered," the "conqueror" being richly rewarded.

PIRACY. One of the constant practices of ancient times. Merchant ships were slow, and thus easy prey for quick and experienced pirates, who were not only interested in the cargo, but also in the people on board, because selling slaves was a lucrative business. In Homeric times, P. was certainly a feared, but not a disdained occupation (Thuc. I, 5); people newly arrived from overseas are simply asked if they happen to be pirates (*Od.* III, 71-74). The exploits of Polycrates' fleet were nothing but official piracy. Only during periods in which there was a strong naval power, for example, the Delian League, could this evil be suppressed, but this relative security was of short duration. The coasts of Illyria, Crete, Cilicia, and Pamphylia were notorious pirates' nests, especially during the Hellenistic period, when chaos reigned on the seas as a result of the wars of the Diadochi, and the slave market on Delos willingly accepted the victims. The fleet of Rhodes put an end to this state of affairs for a time. Occasionally, the Romans went into action against the pirates along their own coasts (see ANTIUM; ROSTRA), but usually neglected their fleet completely, so that, during the 1st cent. B.C., P. flourished as never before. Mithridates and Sertorius became allies of the pirates. Pompey finally stopped P. in 67 B.C. During imperial times, after Augustus had established permanent naval bases at Misenum and Ravenna, peace prevailed on the ocean until the widespread migrations (especially by the Vandals) caused a revival of P.

PIRAEUS [Gr. Piraieus]. The main port of Athens; fortified by Themistocles. Between the years 461 and 456 B.C., the P. and Phaleron were connected with Athens by the Long Walls, making the city and her harbors into one fortress. In 450, the P. was rebuilt according to a rectangular city plan of Hippodamus. The inhabitants were the most radical element of the Attic population; many metics also lived there (see also THRASYBULUS). Sulla destroyed P. completely in 86 B.C.

PISA. The district surrounding Olympia. The inhabitants presided over the Olympic Games after Pheidon's time.

PISAE. City in Etruria, now Pisa. Under Rom. rule since 182 B.C.; used as a frontier fortress against the Ligurians. It was a prosperous Rom. colony under Augustus.

PISANDER [Gr. Peisandros]. Athenian politician who played an important part in the Athenian revolution of 411 B.C. (see OLIGARCHY; THERAMENES). He suggested limiting the number of voting citizens to 5,000, and entrusting the executive power to a Council of Four Hundred.

PISISTRATUS (560-527). The first tyrant of Athens. As a nobleman he led the *diakrioi* (party of the poor mountain dwellers) and usurped power with the help of a bodyguard. He was exiled twice, but returned both times. He retained the broad outlines of Solon's constitution; and under his regime Athens experienced a period of economic and cultural prosperity. Among other things, he arranged for the recitation of Homer's poetry by the state, to enhance the Panathenaea. Only a few prominent families (among them the Alcmaeonidae) continued to oppose him. He died a natural death; there was no tyranny in the modern sense in Athens, until his son Hippias succeeded him.

PISO. Name of various members of the Rom. *Calpurnia gens;* the most famous are:

—(1) Lucius Calpurnius P. Caesoninus, Caesar's father-in-law, consul in 58 B.C. He supported Clodius in his measures against Cicero and was in turn attacked by Cicero in 55 for maladministration in the province of Macedonia.

—(2) Gnaeus Calpurnius P., consul in 7 B.C. with Tiberius, was appointed governor of Syria in A.D. 17 (see also GERMANICUS).

—(3) Lucius Calpurnius P. Frugi, grandson of the last, was adopted by Galba in A.D. 69 and appointed his successor (see also GALBA; OTHO).

—(4) Gaius Calpurnius P., a rich man, patron of literature; in spite of his reputation, he was the main conspirator against Nero in A.D. 65. When at the last moment the plot was betrayed, P. and his followers were forced to commit suicide (see also SENECA; LUCANUS).

PISTORIA. City in Northern Etruria, where Catilina fell in 63 B.C.

PITHOS. Large earthenware jars, sometimes taller than a man, used as a storage place for liquids, grain or other provisions. The jar was set half in the ground and lifted with ropes. Many of these jars have been found in the storage rooms of the palace of Cnossus.

PITTACUS (c. 650-570). Statesman of Mytilene. He was elected legislator with absolute power in about 600. His laws, like those of Solon in Athens, were moderately democratic. He abdicated after ten years (see also ALCAEUS). One of his laws doubled the punishment for any crime committed under the influence of alcohol. P. was one of the Seven Sages.

PLATAEA. City in Boeotia, on the northern slope of Mount Cithaeron. Ally of Athens since 519 B.C., it sent an auxiliary corps to Marathon in 490. In 479, Pausanias defeated the Persians under Mardonius there; this victory was commemorated in P. at the festival of freedom (*Eleutheria*). During the Peloponnesian War P. was besieged by the Thebans and Spartans; captured and destroyed by the latter; in 386 the Spartans rebuilt it. It was destroyed again by Thebes (373 B.C.) for being loyal to Athens. Philip II and Alexander the Great supported its restoration, but it never regained its former prosperity.

PLATO (427?-347). Gr. philosopher whose ideas were of fundamental importance to European philosophy. He was born of a noble Athenian family; he is said to have written tragic poems in his youth, but after he had met Socrates, whose most gifted pupil he was to become, and had witnessed his death, he devoted the rest of his life to philosophy. He traveled through Magna Graecia where he became friendly with Archytas and other Pythagorians. After that he visited the court of Dionysius I in Sicily where he is said to have fallen into disgrace; he ended up in a slave market on Aegina; a friend bought his freedom. Twice he traveled to Egypt and then twice to Syracuse (see DIONYSIUS II; DION). In 387 he founded the Academy in Athens, where he taught until his death.

P. was not only a great creative thinker, but also a marvelous stylist. His works comprise, outside of a number of letters (most of which are probably authentic; the seventh, autobiographical one is particularly famous), some epigrams, and a large number of dialogues—philosophical conversations, usually led by Socrates. These may be divided into three groups: (a) the early dialogues, real "Socratic conversations"—short, lively, acuminated to one subject. Examples: *Crito* (obedience to the laws); *Laches* (courage); *Ion* (artistry); *Euthyphro* (piousness); (b) the larger works of his middle period. Socrates is still the main character, but the conversation is no longer scintillating, and more frequently Plato's own philosophy predominates. The most famous works are: *Phaedo* (immortality of the soul); *Symposium* (Eros); *Politeia* (the idea of justice embodied in the ideal state); (c) the works of his old age; Socrates and the characteristics of the dialogue are relegated to the background. Some of his more famous works are: *Timaeus* (creation and the universe) and *Laws* (again the ideal state, but now more realistic and dogmatic). Each category is just indicated by a few works above, however, the others are also important. His *Apology* (speech of defense by Socrates) is the most widely read, with *Protagoras, Gorgias, Hippias I-II, Meno* (about *anamnesis,* see below). The essence of P.'s thinking is the so-called doctrine of ideas. Socrates was already looking for definitions of generally accepted ideas. P. went further. For example, everyone knows that there are specific trees—the oak, lime tree, etc., and all of them have something in common, namely what we call "tree"; we also know different kinds of just acts; however, they

have something in common, namely, "justice," because, says P., they are all part of the *idea* (literally "form," "shape") of Justice. This "idea" exists on its own somewhere, in the world of ideas: the soul has beheld the ideas in an earlier stage of existence and still remember them *(amamnesis).* The goal of the philosophy is to free the soul from the ties of the body, and to bring it to this world of ideas. His theory of the ideal state, expounded in *Politeia,* is connected with this doctrine. The idea of Justice must be realized in the State. There are three elements in the soul: greed, aspiration to power and to honors, and reason. Three groups in the State correspond to these elements: tradesmen, soldiers, and regents. The latter must abstain from all personal pleasures and prepare themselves for their task by years of hard training, particularly in mathematics and philosophy.

The most important heritage left to European ideology by P. is the doctrine that a Being on earth is no more than a reflection of the Being in a higher world; that in thought, the general must precede the specific. After the Academy, his ideas were disseminated primarily by Neoplatonism. Since the Renaissance the influence of Platonism has never died out.

PLAUTUS, TITUS MACCEIUS (before 250-184). Lat. comic poet from Sarsina in Umbria. At an early age, he earned his living as an itinerant actor, but later became destitute and was forced to do menial work at a flour mill. During these years he wrote his first plays; they quickly became a great success. Because P. was often imitated, 130 plays were attributed to him; Varro recognized 21 as being undisputedly authentic; all of these have survived. They belong to the genre of the *Fabula palliata;* P. drew his plots from the plays of the Attic New Comedy, completely adapted them to Rom. life, although their locale and the characters were Greek. P. permitted himself quite a lot of freedom in adapting them; his dialogue is perfectly original and his use of language is our main source for the knowledge of archaic Latin. Large sections have been turned into songs *(cantica);* only one quarter of the text is spoken. P. often combined the plots of two or more Gr. plays. In ancient times, and also in later centuries, P. was less highly esteemed than Terentius; now we value him more highly, particularly for his genuine comic effects. He does not shrink from crude jokes. Several of his plays have been adapted and copied in later European literature.

PLEBS. The term probably means "multitude" and designated the unprivileged class in Rom. society. Several theories exist about the origin of the distinction between P. and patricians; none can be proved with any degree of certitude. The most probable explanation is the social one, which presupposes an increasing difference in wealth and influence. From the beginning of the Rom. republic, the patricians were a closed caste and new citizens were admitted to the P. only. The class struggle of the 5th-4th centuries B.C. began, according to tradition, with the secession of the P. to the so-called *Mons Sacer* (sacred mountain) outside Rome. The patricians, needing the P. for their military campaign, compromised and granted the P. its own magistrates (tribunes and aediles), and an assembly of its own, the *concilium plebis* (eventually no longer distinguishable from the *comitia tributa*). The originally purely patrician offices, that is, consulship through the *Lex Licinia Sextia* (Licinian Rogations) of 367 (see CONSUL), and membership of the senate were opened to the P. in 287 B.C. Complete political equality followed. Later, the union of patricians and prosperous plebians produced the new nobility, the *optimates* (see also CLIENT).

PLINY.
—(1) Gaius Plinius Secundus, commonly called Pliny the Elder (23-79). Rom. author of encyclopedic works. He was a cavalry officer in Germany 47-57; devoted his time to literary studies under Nero; under Vespasian he held several governorships; finally he was commander of the Rom. fleet stationed at Misenum. On August 24, 79, his interest in the eruption of Mount Vesuvius aroused, he sailed to Stabiae, where he perished. His works embraced 102 books, of which only the *Naturalis Historia* has survived (37 books). Next to the natural sciences in the modern sense, the work covers geography, ethnology, anthropology, and history of art. Although the book is not sufficiently critical to be of any scientific value, still it is a rich source of information on all sorts of natural phenomena and geographical particularities in ancient times. His history of Germany, actually lost, was used by Tacitus, among others.
—(2) Gaius Plinius Caecilius Secundus, commonly called Pliny the Younger (62-before 114). Nephew of the preceding and author of an extensive collection of letters. Pupil of Quintilianus; consul in 100 with Trajan; imperial delegate for government and financial control in Bithynia in about 112. The *Epistulae*, ten books, were written expressly for publication. The first nine books are directed at several people, among them Tacitus and Seutonius; the tenth contains his correspondence with Trajan in Bithynia. P. wrote in a pleasant style and appears to have been interested in diverse subjects. His letters VI, 16 and 20 (about the death of his uncle) and X, 96-97 (about the Christians) are famous (see also COMUM; BOOKS; PANEGYRICS).

PLOTINUS (204-270). The principal representative of Neoplatonism, the most important Gr. philosopher of Rom. imperial times. He was born in Egypt; studied under the Neoplatonist philosopher Ammonius Saccas in Alexandria; accompanied the Emperor Gordianus on a campaign to the East, in order to acquire firsthand knowledge of the Eastern religions; settled in Rome in about 244, where he remained until 269; the following year he visited Campania, where he died. His writings were published after his death by Porphyry in six *Enneads* (sets of nine books). They cover the whole field of ancient philosophy with the exception of politics. According to P., the center of the cosmos is the "One" (compare ELEATICS): it is from this center that concentric circles emanate that are interdependent on the planes of existing things, in order of their creative force: the Spirit (also embracing the ideas of Plato), the Soul (the intuitive element), Nature (approximately the "world soul" of the Stoics) and finally noncreative material. All these elements are potentially united in man. The mystical and religious element found in all philosophy of these times is represented by *ekstasis:* man can lift himself out of his bond with lower circles and be unified with the One. However, this is not a condition of blessedness, but a moment of ecstasy to be achieved by free will.

PLUTARCH of Chaeronea (c. 46-c. 120). Gr. writer of biographies, works on philosophy, pedagogy, and miscellaneous subjects. He held high office in his native city and a priesthood in Delphi. P. gathered a circle of young men around him and conducted their education; this gave birth to a philosophical circle, which lasted until the 3rd cent. P. had influential friends in Rome. He ignored the existence of young Christianity, did not belong to any definite school of philosophy, but had a preference for Plato. His extensive works are of two kinds: (a) *Vitae,* the parallel life stories of Greeks and Romans, ending with a comparative view. Twenty-three "pairs" and four separate biographies have survived (for example, "Theseus and Romulus," "Alexander and Caesar," "Demosthenes and Cicero"). (b) *Moralia,* about seventy-five articles on the most divergent subjects, usually on philosophy, theology, and natural history.

P. was not an original thinker. He was not very critical, but well-read; he owes his reputation to his harmonious and humane character, which earned him the epithet "the sage of Chaeronea." In his historical works, he looks for instructive examples of political and social virtues; in his philosophical writings, for good natured worldly wisdom. His language is *koinē,* the literary dialect based on the Attic of the Hellenistic world. Since the Renaissance, the *Parallel Lives* particularly have had a great influence on European literature. Shakespeare, for example, took most of the data for his plays based on antiquity from an English translation of P. The works were very popular during the French Revolution and also had a certain influence on Napoleon.

PLUTO. See HADES.

PNYX. Hill in Athens with a semicircular slope, where the ecclesia met.

POLIS. The Gr. city-state, the pre-eminent political and social community in Greece; also realized in the Rom. Republic, and still retained there even after it had become a fiction. In later European history, this form of state is only found incidentally, for example, in the Venetian Republic and the German free cities. That the same word could serve the Greeks for "city" and "state," implies several things: the P. was by definition no territorial conception, nor was it a national one. It was not an abstract idea (see RES PUBLICA), but something very concrete; the P. was the community of the citizens; in principle, it was small: only Athens and Sparta, comprising Attica and Laconia, respectively, were exceptions. As a rule, people knew each other, and the officials were known personally to everyone.

The origin of the P. is slightly obscure, because it was formed in the period between 1000 and 800 B.C., sometimes called the "Dark Ages." Homer was already familiar with the P., but it must be taken into account that in the epic not only the P. is described, which had certainly already originated in the 8th cent. with the downfall of Gr. monarchy, but that the royal and lordly fortress of Mycenaean times (much later called the Acropolis), was also called P. during those times. It is usually assumed that the Greeks, during the Ionian migration (see IONIANS), concentrated more than formerly around a fortress in the new and still hostile territory of Asia Minor. By enclosing this settlement with walls they formed the classical P., which in turn became the type of community used in the homeland. Others have pointed out that the Dorians had a different type of P., not surrounding a fortress, but originally consisting of scattered groups of villages (synoecism); this type of P. is said to have been brought specially from Crete by way of the Peloponnesus, and to have produced the classical P. more than the Ionian type. In any case, the Gr. P. was perfected in the 7th cent. B.C. It was a city, with or without walls, usually surrounded by some land. The people lived in the city, and, if their homes were in the country, they exercised their rights and duties as citizens in the city. The ideal of the P. was freedom, autonomy, and (as far as was practicable) autarchy, "self-sufficient independence." This ambition to be one's "own master" is also called particularism; it was facilitated by the mountainous Gr. terrain, by the division of the people into tribes, and by the worship of the gods which varied greatly from place to place. Because the P. was also the center of a cult, and there was no "state church"—churches were unknown—a priest was a citizen, elected to serve the gods and to lead his fellow citizens in doing so.

The political organs were usually a popular assembly, a council, and magistrates (archons). The division of power among them varied according to the form of government: an aristocracy (oligarchy) or a democracy. But even in a democracy the citizens were still in the minority, due to the great number of metics and slaves. That is why some people have deridingly spoken about a pseudodemocracy, even as it existed in the Athens of the 5th-4th centuries. Unjustly, because the objection named is easily compensated for by the direct nature of antique democracy, now only found in a very limited way, for example, in the Swiss cantons. In our society a much smaller group has direct influence on the everyday government of the state. For the Greeks, the slaves were a separate problem and most of the metics chose to live in a strange P. voluntarily for economic reasons. Nevertheless, it was an error not to gradually assimilate them politically (see PERICLES). However, being charged directly to assume political responsibility—alternately ruling and being ruled by one's neighbor—was a training school of the greatest importance in the development of political consciousness in Europe.

The spread of Panhellenism was the antithesis of particularism of the P. When, during and after the Peloponnesian War, the cities became more and more enmeshed in struggles among themselves and in civil strife, the idea of the P. flagged and other forms of political life were sought. Eventually this led to the Hellenistic form of government, but the P. survived during Hellenistic times nevertheless, although its characteristics were altered, and, in the Eastern countries, it acquired an entirely new significance as a Gr. community.

POLLUX, JULIUS, of Naucratis (2nd cent. A.D.). Gr. lexicographer, teacher of the Emperor Commodus. He wrote an *Onomasticon*, a systematic list of Attic words and technical terms; an excerpt of it has survived. It has some value because it gives us several quotations from lost works and, for example, an article on music. Mainly, however, it is just a list of words. The thirty-three strong words to use when swearing at a tax collector are interesting.

POLYAENUS (2nd cent. A.D.). Author of a small book entitled *Strategemata* (a collection of military stratagems). This work is interesting for the history of ancient wars.

POLYBIUS (c. 203-120). Gr. historian of Rome; held high offices in the Achaean League and was deported to Italy with 1,000 Achaeans after the battle of Pydna. There he was able to associate freely with influential Romans and was made a member of the "Scipioric Circle" (see Laelius). He wrote a history of the world in forty books, embracing the period from 266-144. Books I-V have survived complete; we possess epitomes of the others made by later historians. In P.'s opinion, History reached its apogee with Rome's domination of the world: the Rom. constitution had achieved the ideal combination of monarchy (the consuls), aristocracy (the senate), and democracy (the comitia). P. was no scholarly recluse, but a man of practical ideas. He strove for objectivity; for example, he also used a pro-Carthaginian source when writing his history of the First Punic War. His relations with Rom. notables enabled him to get firsthand information for his history of his own time; he also had access to the state archives. P. is considered to be the greatest Gr. historian after Thucydides.

POLYCLITUS [Gr. Polycleitos] of Argos (2nd half of the 5th cent. B.C.). Gr. sculptor; with Phidias, the most important sculptor in the classic style. His most famous work was the chryselephantine statue for the temple of Hera in Argos, of which neither traces nor copies remain extant (only pictures on Rom. coins, and one description by Pausanias. Three of P.'s statues are known to us through good Rom. copies: (a) "Doryphorus" (spear holder), a statue completely embodying the ideals of 5th cent. sculpture: a naked figure of a young man with a perfectly harmonious physique; his weight is supported by the right leg, the left is free. This attitude, which gives the impression of continuous but controlled movement, is called *contrapposto* as opposed to the frontality of archaic sculpture (see also CANON). Best copy: National Museum in Naples, identified from the description of Pliny the Elder; (b) "Diadumenus" (headband binder), statue of a young man who has been victorious at the games; the best of all the copies is of this work (Athens, National Museum); the attitude is more supple than that of the "Doryphorus"; (c) "Wounded Amazon," executed for a contest (see CRESILAS); copies in Berlin and New York's Metropolitan Museum. P. was also well known for his statues of Olympic victories. Three signed pedestals of his statues have been found in Olympia. It is assumed that an athlete, a Rom. copy of which is in the British Museum, is a reproduction of one of these statues.

POLYCRATES. Tyrant of Samos from c. 540-522, held a powerful position in the Aegean Sea with the help of a strong fleet, and made treaties with Amasis of Egypt and with Cyrene. Great public works (including the temple of Hera and an aqueduct) were executed during his reign; artists and poets stayed at his court. In 522 he was lured into a trap by the Persian satrap Oroetes and killed. The story about the ring that was found in the belly of the fish, is told of him (Hdt. III, 39 ff.); the German poet Schiller based his poem *Der Ring des Polykrates* on Herodotus' tale.

POLYGNOTUS of Thasos (5th cent. B.C.). Gr. painter. He came to Athens, where he became a friend of Cimon and probably Sophocles, and where he was granted honorary citizenship (*honoris causa*). His most famous frescoes depicted a battle with the Amazons and one with the Centaurs, in the sanctuary of Theseus in Athens (probably c. 470); the fall of Troy, in the Stoa Poecile in Athens (c. 460), and the same subject in the Lesche (public hall) of Delphi (c. 450), where he also painted Odysseus' descent to the underworld. None of his work has survived; our only information is given us by ancient authors. Pausanias describes the attitude and the grouping of the figures; Aristotle praises the ethos of his statues, that is, their elevation above the temporary—the real greatness of being and action; Pliny the Elder writes of the subtle execution of draperies and faces. P. was considered just as much the pioneer in painting as Phidias in sculpture. On the basis of Pausanias' descriptions, P.'s influence on several vase paintings can be clearly discerned.

POLYHYMNIA. See MUSES.

POMERIUM. The name given by the Romans to the space they considered sacred, originally along both sides of the city wall. Sulla, Caesar, Augustus, and several later emperors extended the P. The area was marked off by stones; armed troops were only allowed inside the P. for a triumph, because only the *imperium domi* (civil authority) was valid there. In respect to the auspices the P. defined the boundary between city and country.

POMPEII. Ancient seaport in Campania near Mount Vesuvius. Originally inhabited by the Osci, who were strongly influenced by the Greeks during the 8th cent. B.C., and by the Etruscans during the 7th cent.; the native Italian culture was predominant until about 350 B.C., when it gave way to Hellenistic civilization. P.'s great prosperity, based on agriculture and trade relations, reached its height during the Hellenistic period; beautiful houses and public buildings were erected during that time. After the Social War, it was quickly Romanized; the Oscan language was soon replaced by Latin. In A.D. 63, P. was largely destroyed by an earthquake, and in 79 it was buried entirely by an eruption of Mount Vesuvius. In 1748 it was rediscovered and partially excavated; archaeological work still goes on at the present time. The discoveries are important for our knowledge of ancient houses and for an insight into the daily life of the Romans. Several villas have yielded mosaics and murals. Four different styles of murals have been found which serve as a yardstick for the classification of Hellenistic-Rom. paintings found elsewhere.

POMPEIUS. Name of:

—(1) Gnaeus P. Magnus, known as Pompey the Great (106-48). Rom. general and statesman. He served under his father Gnaeus P. Strabo in the Social War, and then as a general under Sulla, who, after taking Italy, sent P. to Africa to fight the remaining followers of Marius. After Sulla's death (78) he was sent to Spain to combat Sertorius; when he returned he finished the war against Spartacus (71) with Crassus; both became consuls in 70, in spite of the senate's opposition. Both went over to the *populares* party from the *optimates* and abolished most of Sulla's laws. In 67, P. was entrusted with absolute *imperium* to put an end to piracy; he succeeded in three months. In 66 he was given the same unlimited *imperium* against Mithridates, on Manilius' suggestion (see also LUCULLUS); after his successful campaign against this king, he subjected almost the entire Near East to Rome. When he came home in 62 he demobilized his army—this was constitutional, but lost him most of his power. When the senate dared to defy him by refusing to ratify his measures in the East and to grant land for his veterans, P. was forced to seek the support of Crassus and Caesar. They formed the first triumvirate in 60; Caesar became consul in 59 and approved P.'s demands without consulting the senate. Caesar left for Gaul soon afterward. After P.'s second consulship with Crassus in 55, he was given Spain as his province. However, he preferred to stay in Rome and had the province governed by *legati*. He sought the support of the *optimates* more and more, and in 52 they appointed him *consul sine collega,* although the triumvirate was maintained (see LUCA). (For the Civil War in 49 see CAESAR.) After the battle of Pharsalus, P. fled to Egypt, where he was murdered on landing.

In spite of his revolutionary actions at the beginning of his career, P., in contrast to most of his significant contemporaries, was an honest man who respected the law; he also had high private standards. He was known as the greatest general of his period. His political ideas have often been compared with those of Augustus. That he finally had to yield to the more ingenious but also crueler and more cynical Caesar is not to his dishonor.

—(2) Sextus P., son of the preceding. He continued the struggle against Caesar, and fled to Africa and Spain after Caesar's death. In 43 B.C. he was proscribed by the triumvirate; he put himself at the head of a large fleet and used it to combat the second triumvirate. He occupied Sicily, blockaded Italy, and was a constant threat to Augustus. P. was finally defeated by Agrippa during the naval battle of Naulochus (36) and killed in Asia Minor.

POMPEY. See POMPEIUS.

PONTIFEX. [Lat., literally: bridge builder, by extension "expert" in magic and in relations with supernatural powers.] A member of the highest priestly college in Rome. At first it consisted of three, later of more, and finally of sixteen members, who advised the magistrates on religious questions and supervised the other priests. The college also saw to the calendar (see ANNALES). The head of this college (and of the entire priesthood) was the P. *maximus,* an office always held by the emperor since Augustus. P. *maximus* is still the title of the popes.

PONTIUS PILATE. Procurator of Judaea from A.D. 26-36; Jesus was crucified during his term of office. He often provoked the Jews to rebellion and was sent to Rome in 37 by the governor of Syria, Vitellius, after a massacre among the Samaritans.

PONTUS. Empire in Asia Minor; so named during the reign of Mithridates I (281 B.C.) After Mithridates VI had been defeated by Pompey, the latter annexed most of P. and Bithynia to the Rom. Empire. Several Gr. colonies were established in P., among them Trapezus (see also PHARNACES).

PONTUS EUXINUS. The Black Sea; the

name (literally: hospitable sea) is explained in two ways: (a) the Greeks who founded many colonies there, particularly the inhabitants of Miletus, felt welcome in this familiar environment; (b) the first Greeks to explore this sea found it inhospitable and gave it a flattering name to escape its anger (so-called apotropaic naming). The best antique description of its coasts was written by Arrianus (see also SINOPE; TRAPEZUS; OLBIA; COLCHIS; and TOMI).

POPPAEA, SABINA. See SABINA.

POPULARES. The "peoples' party" in Rome during the civil strife (c. 130-30 B.C.); the term is deceptive—the leaders of the P. were oligarchs like those of their opponents the *optimates;* however, they agitated among the masses for their supporters.

POROS. Tuff; rock composed of the finer kinds of volcanic material. Found in Attica, P. it was used there and elsewhere for temples and statues before marble came into use.

PORPHYRIUS of Tyre (232-305). Usually called Porphyry. Gr. philosopher of Syrian origin; pupil of Plotius, whose works he published, commented on, and supplied with an introduction and a biography of the master. He also wrote commentaries on various other philosophers (particularly Aristotle) and works on the most diverse scientific subjects. Many of his works have survived. A polemic work against Christianity was publicly burned in 448.

PORSENNA. Legendary Etruscan king, who, according to tradition (Livy, II), tried to restore Tarquinius Superbus as the king of Rome. Actually, P. is a title given to Etruscan kings.

PORTRAITURE. Because all the monumental antique paintings have been lost, with important exceptions of the Egyptian mummy portraits, we have to rely mainly on sculpture for ancient portraits (see also GEMS). Several portrait heads from classical Greece have survived in copies; for example, the famous head of Pericles by Cresilas, the Alexander portraits by Lysippus, the expressive head of the statue of Demosthenes in Rome. It was characteristic of Gr. P. that the artist wanted to give an idealized portrayal; the artist strove to express the inner strength of the subject. As early as Hellenistic times realistic portraits were found next to the idealized (for example, the head of Homer). Realism did not occur extensively until Rom. times; the portrait was the most prevalent form of Rom. sculpture. This was so for many reasons: (a) the highly realistic mummy portraits of Hellenistic-Rom. times, which continued in the native Egyptian tradition; (b) the gallery of ancestors of the Rom. patricians; these portraits of ancestors were carried during burials; (c) the highly realistic heads on Etruscan funeral urns. Although these influences—connected among themselves—all originated in the ritual of death, they nevertheless influenced the portraits of the living. The idealized portraits in the Gr. style revived, particularly under Augustus, and yet we also have beautifully realistic heads of the later emperors. It is significant to note that almost all the artists were Greeks or Easterners. The style, therefore, appeared to have been determined by the people who gave the commissions.

POSEIDON. The Gr. god of the sea; originally god of rivers and wells, and thus related to the earth (the name P. or one of his surnames, probably Greek, means "husband of the goddess of the earth"). He caused earthquakes, and one of his titles is "earth shaker." In mythology, P. is a son of Cronos and Rhea, brother of Zeus and Hades. In the *Odyssey,* he appears hostile to Odysseus, who had blinded his son Polyphemus (Hom. *Od.* I, 68-75); the myth about his contest with Athena for dominion over the city of Athens is well known (see PARTHENON). P.'s symbol of power is a trident. The Romans identified him with Neptune.

POSIDONIUS (c. 135 B.C.). Gr. Stoic philosopher and historian from Apamea, pupil of Panaetius. He founded a school on Rhodes, where Cicero, among others, studied. His historical and geographical work was a continuation of Polybius and had the same ideological purport; according to P., Rome's world domination was intended by the gods to unify all peoples. His philosophical work also had a religious tendency; although it was chiefly

Stoical, it had an eclectic character. P. also wrote on many other subjects; he can, for this reason, be compared with Aristotle. His importance for the penetration of Hellenistic civilization to Rome can hardly be overestimated. Only fragments of his works have survived.

POTIDAEA. Colony of Corinth in Chalcidice, founded in about 600 B.C.; deserted from the Delian League in 432 B.C., and sought the support of its mother city when it was besieged by Athens; P.'s revolt against Athens was one of the causes of the Second Peloponnesian War. In 356 B.C. it was destroyed by Philip II.

PRAEFECTUS. See PRAETORIANS.

PRAENESTE. City in Latium about 23 mi. southeast of Rome, famous for its silver-and-goldsmiths' work; after it had been conquered by Rome (4th cent. B.C.) it had certain privileges and fought loyally for Rome against Pyrrhus and Hannibal. Later, it fought against Rome and was plundered by Sulla in 82 B.C. During Rom. imperial times it was a colony with luxurious country houses and a famous oracle. A particular Latin dialect was spoken there.

PRAETOR. Holder of the most important judiciary office in Rome. Originally it was the title of the consuls, and thus the function of the P. was military. Praetor is derived from *praeitor* one who goes before (commander); the original application has been retained in the words Praetorians, *praetorium,* etc. Rom. tradition does not cite this previous history but mentions that the first P. was elected in 366 B.C. as a chief judge with *imperium,* and was accompanied by six lictors (the P. *urbanus,* who always remained the most important). In 242 B.C. the office of the P. *peregrinus* was instituted; to judge matters concerning foreigners. Later the praetors were also entrusted with governing the provinces; their number was augmented as the number of provinces increased. Sulla restored the exclusively judiciary function and appointed propraetors and proconsuls to govern the provinces. On taking office, the P. published an edict, indicating the policy his administration of justice would follow (see CORPUS JURIS).

PRAETORIANS. The body guard of the Rom. emperor, originating from the *cohors praetoria,* the body guard of an army commander of republican times. Augustus formed nine cohorts of P. as a permanent guard. Sejanus concentrated them right near Rome in A.D. 23. Since then, they were a greatly feared power; many emperors were proclaimed and dethroned by them. The commanders were called *praefectus praetorio;* famous examples are Sejanus, Burrus, Tigellinus, and Ulpianus. In 312 the P. were disbanded by Constantine the Great.

PRAETORIUM. The general's tent (headquarters) in a Rom. army camp, sometimes also the residence of a provincial governor.

PRAETORIUM AGRIPPINAE. Rom. fort near Leyden, The Netherlands, dating from the times of the Emperor Claudius, and named after his second wife Agrippina.

PRAXITELES (4th cent. B.C.). Athenian sculptor to whom a large number of works can be attributed, so that the evolution of his style can be easily followed. One statue among his works is almost certainly an original—the "Hermes," found in the temple of Hera in Olympia. This may be the only monumental statue by a recognized Gr. master of which the original has survived; however, some archaeologists still believe it to be an excellent copy; a few others claim that it is an original by a sculptor of the same name of the 2nd cent. B.C. The most famous statues of P., known to us from Rom. copies, are: the "Apollo Sauroctonus" (lizard slayer, c. 350); the "Aphrodite of Arles" (c. 354, like the "Hermes"); the "Aphrodite of Cnidus" (the first statue of a naked female figure, and easily his most famous); and the "Artemis of Gabii" (c. 335). A pedestal found in Mantinea, representing Apollo, Marsyas, and the Muses, is often considered an original by P. The statue called "Resting Satyr" is attributed to his school. P. was the most classical master of the 4th cent., and carried on the work of Polyclitus. Still there is a big difference between the ethos of his figures and those of the 5th cent. Divinity is not longer reflected in unapproachable sublimity, as for example in the "Zeus" of Phidias, but by supernatural beauty.

PRIAM. See TROJAN WAR.

PRIENE. Ionian city, exceedingly well-preserved, in the valley of the Maeander opposite Miletus, rebuilt in the 4th cent. B.C. according to a plan of the architect Hippodamus. German excavations have laid bare many public buildings (among them a temple of Athena) in beautiful Ionic architecture, and a section of the city walls almost intact.

PRIMUS INTER PARES. "The first among his peers"; the name fitted the old Gr. tribal kingship wonderfully well, as we know it for example, through the figure of Alcinous, the father of Nausicaa in the *Odyssey*. It continued to exist in Macedonia, among other places.

PRINCEPS [Lat. the chief, the most distinguished]. Title already known in Rome during the republican times, for example, in the form of P. *senatus,* the senior member of the senate, who was usually a patrician ex-censor, and whose opinion was asked first. It became the particular title of the Rom. emperors until Diocletian (for later developments see DOMINATE). The title was assumed by Augustus to show that he did not want to be a monarch, but only the leader of the government. We therefore call that type of emperorship "principate."

PRINCIPIIS OBSTA. "Withstand beginnings" (Ov. *Rem. Am.* 91).

PROBUS. See MILITARY EMPERORS.

PROCONSUL. Rom. consul whose *imperium* was prolonged after his term of office; the proconsuls were generally governors of provinces (see also PRAETOR; PROPRAETOR). During imperial times every governor of a senatorial province was called P., even if he had not been a consul previously. The emperors also saw to it that the *imperium proconsulare* was granted to them permanently.

PROCOPIUS of Caesarea (c. 490-565). Gr. historian. He wrote the history of Justinian's reign, and he was the secretary general of Justinian's general, Belisarius (527-542). In 562 he became prefect of the city of Constantinople. His history, mainly on the war with the Vandals and the Goths, is written in pure Attic prose and is of great historical value. He also published a book on archi-

tecture. A curious writing *Anecdota,* a chronicle of the scandals of the court of the day, was published after the author's death. Some scholars refuse to believe that this work was really written by a man of P.'s level.

PROCRUSTES. See THESEUS.

PROCURATOR. Fiscal agent during Rom. imperial times, usually appointed from the ranks of the *equites* or freedmen. A. P. was appointed specially, next to the governor of a province, to collect the imperial revenues; less important provinces were ruled by the P. himself (see PONTIUS PILATE).

PRODICUS (5th cent. B.C.). Gr. sophist, contemporary of Socrates, a famed itinerant teacher. He was particularly interested in the correct usage of words and the differences between synonyms. We find one of P.'s myths about Heracles in Xenophon (*Memor.* II, 1): Heracles had to decide in his youth between enjoyment and virtue, and chose the latter.

PRODIGIA. See DECEMVIRI.

PROLETARIANS. Among the Romans, the P. were the poorer class of citizens and were, literally "producers of offspring" (*proles*). They were also called *capite censi* from their status as citizens (*caput*) in the list of the census. Since originally each Rom. soldier paid for his own equipment (compare HOPLITES), they could not serve in the legions. Nevertheless, Marius received them into his army, which had been reformed into a professional military force. There were already many P. in Rome at the time of the First Punic War; they, like the *socii,* served as oarsmen in the fleet. Their number increased enormously when the expansion of the *latifundia* in the 2nd-1st centuries B.C. impoverished many farmers and forced them to settle in Rome. They lived mainly on the distributions of wheat and by selling their votes at elections.

PROMETHEUS [Gr. the man of forethought]. Gr. demigod, one of the Titans, benefactor of mankind. During a sacrifice to Zeus, he concealed the edible parts of the sacrificial animal for the people. Zeus retaliated and forbade them the use of fire. In disobedience to him, P. stole fire from Mount Olympus and brought it back to earth. As punishment he was chained to a rock, where an eagle daily ate his liver; Zeus caused it to grow again during the night. Heracles killed the eagle and P. and Zeus were reconciled. P. was also said to create human beings; he was worshiped, especially in Athens, by craftsmen who worked with clay and fire.

PROPERTIUS, SEXTUS (c. 50-15). Lat. poet; along with Tibullus and Ovid, one of the most important elegiac Lat. poets. His life is similar to Virgil's: he too was hit by the confiscation of land under Octavian (Augustus) and Mark Antony; he too found a protector in Maecenas; on the other hand, with Catullus he shared the experience of an unfaithful mistress, his beloved Cynthia of whom he sang (her name was actually Hostia). In his last four books Cynthia remains in the background; P. discusses national subjects. His last poem is a masterpiece —it treats of the death of Cornelia, a noble Rom. lady, and paints an idealized picture of the Rom. *matrona* in an unforgettable way.

PROPONTIS. Now the Sea of Marmora, connected with the Pontus Euxinus by the Bosporus and with the Aegean Sea by the Hellespont. The most important city was Cyzicus.

PROPRAETOR. Rom. praetor whose *imperium* was prolonged after his term of office; during the latter part of the Rom. Republic propraetors as well as proconsuls were governors of provinces.

PROPYLAEA. The monumental roofed gateway on the western side of the Athenian Acropolis; started by the architect Mnesicles in 435 B.C.; built chiefly in the Doric style, although the interior colonnade is Ionic (see ARCHITECTURAL ORDERS). The construction of the wings was interrupted due to the Peloponnesian War; the work could have been resumed after the peace of Nicias, but the enemies of Pericles prevented its completion according to the plan by building the temple of Nike. The north wing contained murals by Polygnotus.

PROSCRIPTIO [Lat.] Declaration of outlawry with confiscation of property; procedure often used by Sulla and the second triumvirate to rid themselves of their enemies.

PROSERPINA. See PERSEPHONE.

PROTAGORAS of Abdera (c. 485-415). The most important Gr. Sophist. He taught mainly in Athens, where he became a friend of Pericles who requested him to make laws for Thurii (444); there is a story (probably invented) that he fled after being accused of atheism (*asebeia*) and died in a shipwreck on his way to Sicily. His most famous saying is: "Man is the measure of all things: of those which are, that they are; of those which are not, that they are not." The latter part of this statement is usually not quoted, but from it may assume that P. confined his skepticism to the theory of knowledge; he rejected the absolute truth concerning "being"; his skepticism did not extend to the doctrine of good and evil which became the dogma of the latter Sophists. He did adopt an agnostic view toward the existence of the gods.

PROTEUS. One of the lesser Gr. gods of the sea who had the ability to take all kinds of shapes (see also NEREUS).

PROTO-CORINTHIAN POTTERY. The ceramics of Corinth of the 7th cent. B.C. (the times of the Bacchiadae). Their most striking characteristic is the oriental influence; Corinth was then the biggest trade center of Greece, especially for the Near East. Vases depicted animal friezes with griffins, sphinxes, and other figures adopted from the East; palmettos also appeared frequently.

PROTOGEOMETRICAL POTTERY. The vases, made after about 1000 B.C. when Mycenaean culture disappeared, and that were a transition to the geometrical art form.

PROVINCIA. Originally meant the jurisdiction of a Rom. magistrate with *imperium;* later it was applied to a territory conquered by the Romans. The first P. was Sicily (241 B.C., definitely after 227), then Sardinia with Corsica (231), Hispania (197); numerous other regions followed. (For government and administration see PRAETOR; PROPRAETOR; PROCONSUL; PUBLICANI; and PROCURATOR.) During imperial times the government of the P. was greatly improved; there were two kinds of provinces then: (a) imperial provinces, usually the areas in which strong concentrations of troops were camped. In theory the emperor governed these provinces in person, but actually he delegated the task to a *legatus* (sometimes a procurator); (b) senatorial provinces, over which proconsuls ruled, as of old.

PROVOCATIO. The right of every Rom. citizen who had been sentenced to physical punishment by a magistrate to appeal to the popular assembly. The P. could only be suspended by a dictator or (but this is disputed) by the *senatus consultum ultimum* (see CAVEANT CONSULES). During imperial times the P. was superseded by the *appellatio* (right of appeal to the emperor).

PRUDENTIUS, Aurelius Clemens (348-after 405). The most important among the Christian Lat. poets. He came from Spain where he held high offices before retiring to a monastery. In 405 he published his collections of sacred poems, the *Cathemerinon,* hymns for daily prayer, and the *Peristephanon,* a martyrology, written in epic and lyric meters.

PRUSIAS. See BITHYNIA.

PRYTANEUM [Gr. from prytanis, a president]. The building where the *prytaneis,* the members of the executive council of a Gr. polis met. In Athens these were the fifty members of the council, belonging to one *phylae* (see CLISTHENES), who daily chose by lot one among themselves as president of the council and ecclesia. The P. contained the sacred hearth; it was the place of refuge for all those who sought the protection of the state. Foreign ambassadors, Athenian envoys, victors in the Panhellenic Games, and deserving citizens were entertained and given public banquets in the P.

PSYKTER. See VASE FORMS.

PTOLEMAEUS CLAUDIUS (c. 85-161). Commonly called Ptolemy. Gr. astronomer and geographer from Alexandria. His most important astronomical work was the *Great Syntaxis of Astronomy,* also known as the *Almagest,* from the Arabian translation, *Tabrir al Maghesthi,* through which it became famous in the Middle Ages. It is an impressive creation, in which Hipparchus' (see ASTRONOMY) geocentric system took definite form. The work also had great influence because the theory of the heliocentric sys-

tem, which had already been discovered before P., had been forgotten (see ARISTARCHUS). Next to other, smaller works on astronomy and physics, P. also wrote the *Geographice Hyphegesis,* the most complete ancient geographical work; it remained the standard work in its field until the 16th cent. It gives the principles of mathematical geography and the drawing of maps, the calculation of the degrees of longitudes and latitudes of places in the then known world. This work is one of our main sources of knowledge of ancient geography; the errors it contains can be attributed, among other things, to a miscalculation of the measurement of the circumference of the world—more correctly estimated to be longer by Eratosthenes.

PTOLEMIES. The Macedonian royal house of Egypt, also called Lagidae. The most important kings, named Ptolemy, are:

—(1) P. I (c. 367-283), surnamed Soter (preserver) son of Lagus. He was one of Alexander the Great's favorite generals and author of the best history of the latter's expedition (used by Arrianus); satrap of Egypt 323-304. At that time he assumed the title of king; waged several wars against Antigonus I and Demetrius Poliorcetes. P. laid the foundation for Hellenistic administration in Egypt, founded the cult of Serapis in Alexandria, invited scholars and artists to his court, and founded the famous library and the Museum in Alexandria. He conquered Cyprus and Palestine. After 285 the co-regent was his son:

—(2) P. II (309-246), surnamed Philadelphus. He too expanded the empire and directed his efforts to the internal administration of his kingdom. He is famous for instituting the ruler cult, for increasing the library, and building the lighthouse on Pharos.

—(3) P. III (c. 282-221), surnamed Euergetes (benefactor), king since 247; son of the preceding. Under his rule Egypt expanded to the greatest size.

—(4) P. IV (c. 244-203), surnamed Philopater (loving his father). His reign was the beginning of Egypt's political decline, increasing Rom. influence, and the growing nationalism of the native population, which was expressed in sometimes violent revolts.

—(5) P. V (c. 210-181), surnamed Epiphanes, son of P. IV. He was only five years old when he succeeded his father. He was declared of age in 196. Betrothed to Cleopatra I, daughter of Antiochus.

—(6) P. VI (c. 186-145), surnamed Philometer (loving his mother), son of P. V. He married his own sister Cleopatra I. During his minority, the country was ruled by his mother.

—(7) P. VII (c. 184-116), surnamed Phycson (fat paunch), brother of P. VI. He married his own sister Cleopatra II, widow of P. VI. He ruled jointly with his brother. He is said to have improved the library at Alexandria and to have restored many Egyptian temples.

—(8) P. VIII (d. 81 B.C.), surnamed Soter II, also Lathyrus, son of P. the VII. He ruled jointly with his mother from 116-108. Twice married to his own sisters, Cleopatra IV and Cleopatra V Selene. After being expelled by his mother, he fled to Cyprus, where he reigned from 88-80.

—(9) P. IX (d. 88 B.C.), surnamed Alexander I, brother of P. VIII, he ruled from 108-88. He caused his mother's death (101).

—(10) P. X (c. 105-80), surnamed Alexander II, son of P. IX. He married his stepmother Berenice and murdered her after twenty days' reign. He was killed by the populace.

—(11) P. XI (c. 95-51), surnamed Philopater Neos Dionysus, and nicknamed Auletes (the piper), son of P. VIII. He married his own sister Cleopatra VI Tryphaena. He willed his kingdom to his eldest son, P. XII and his daughter Cleopatra VII.

—(12) P. XII (61-48). He married his sister Cleopatra VII. King from 51-48, he ruled jointly with her from 51-49. Defeated by Caesar and drowned in the Nile during his flight.

—(13) P. XIII (c. 58-44), younger brother and husband of Cleopatra VII. He was king from 47-44 and ruled jointly with her from 51-49. Killed on her orders to make room for her son Caesarion.

—(14) P. XIV (47-30), surnamed Philopater Philometor Caesar, or commonly called Caesarion. Son of Cleopatra the VII by Julius Caesar. He ruled with his mother from c. 44-30. He was put to death by Octavian. Papyrology enables us to have a thorough knowledge of the government and the social relationships in Egypt under the Ptolemics. It was the most centralized bureaucracy of the entire Hellenistic world. There was extreme segregation between the caste of the Gr.-Macedonian rulers and the native population (including the large Jewish community of Alexandria). The Ptolemies, who assumed the function of the pharaohs in the eyes of the natives, did take over some of the customs of the ancient rulers of Egypt, for example—by marrying their sisters. But, for their Macedonian-Gr. subjects they were the bearers of the Hellenistic conception of monarchy (see HELLENISM).

PUBLICANI. The tax collectors in the Rom. Republic. During the Second Punic War they were already in existence, as men who became contractors for public buildings and supplies. Later they devoted all their time to collecting taxes in the provinces, where their assistants (publicans of the New Testament) made themselves hated everywhere by their exactions. The P. came from the *equites;* they organized in societies (*societates*). During imperial times their influence declined quickly; they then increasingly became state officials.

PUNIC WARS. The three wars waged against Carthage by Rome. Motive: Rome's desire to expand toward western Mediterranean region, after having subjected all of Italy. (a) First P. W. 264-241. Cause: the Mamertines asked for help from Rome—this Carthage could not tolerate. The Romans won a naval battle at Mylae (near Sicily) by using mobile boarding bridges, nullifying Carthage's naval supremacy. The struggle for the possession of Sicily did not start until then. First the Romans tried to force a quick decision by invading Africa (see REGULUS); then they tried a systematic blockade of the Carthaginian bases on Sicily, Panormus, Lilybaeum, and Drepanum. Panormus fell (254), but not the other bases (see HAMILCAR).

Finally Catulus Lutatius defeated the Carthaginian fleet decisively near the Aegadian Islands (241). Carthage yielded Sicily and sought compensation in Spain (see HAMILCAR; HASDRUBAL; HANNIBAL); (b) Second P. W. 218-201. (For the cause of the war see SAGUNTUM; for the war's development see HANNIBAL; TREBIA; TRASIMENUS; FABIUS; CANNAE; CAPUA; TARENTUS; NOLA; MARCELLUS; SCIPIO; HASDRUBAL; METAURUS; SCIPIO MAJOR; MASSINISSA; SYPHAX.) In the beginning of the war Hannibal held the initiative, however, the Rom. senate was able to keep the situation in hand. Rome then organized a counteroffensive on several fronts at once, in Italy, in Spain, and even in Greece, where Philip V of Macedonia had turned against Rome. A decisive factor was that Rome's army was composed of citizens, while Carthage fought with mercenaries; moreover, the *socii* in central Italy remained steadfastly loyal to Rome, and the "home front" did not give Hannibal sufficient support. He was finally beaten at Zama. When peace was made, Carthage was forbidden to wage war without Rome's permission. This led, almost in itself (but see also CATO MAJOR), to (c) the Third P. W. 149-146. (For the cause of the war see MASINISSA.) Scipio Minor destroyed Carthage completely after a bitter struggle.

PUPIENUS. See MILITARY EMPERORS.

PUTEOLI. Port in Campania, competed in importance with Ostia as harbor for commercial trade.

PYDNA. Town in Macedonia where King Perseus was defeated by Aemilius Paullus in 168 B.C.; this battle terminated Macedonian independence.

PYLOS. The name of three places in the western Peloponnesus. For a long time it has been debated which P. was the one where Nestor resided (*Od.* III), but now it has been determined that it was P. in Messenia opposite Sphacteria. A Mycenaean palace and a beehive tomb have been found there, and recently many clay tablets inscribed with Mycenaean characters have come to light; they are in the same Linear B script as that found in Cnossus; these documents, however, are about 200 years younger, dating from c. 1200 B.C.

PYRRHO (or PYRRHON) OF ELIS (c. 360-c. 270). Gr. philosopher, the founder of the philosophical school of Skepticism whose aim was a state of imperturbable calmness and balance of the mind; according to P., this is achieved by being aware of the impossibility of arriving at the absolute truth. P. himself did not write down his doctrines; they are known to us through fragments of works of his pupil Timon.

PYRRHUS (319-272). The first Gr. ruler with whom Rome came into conflict; king of the Molossi, the strongest tribe in Epirus, first from 307-303, later exiled and recalled by Ptolemy II in 297. He then founded a monarchy of the Hellenistic type in Epirus, which was completely different from the old Molossian tribal kingship (the *primus inter pares* type). Several times he fought for the domination of Macedonia with Demetrius Poliorcetes and Antigonus II. In 280 Tarentum asked for his help against Rome. P. dreamed of realizing the expedition to the West which Alexander the Great had probably intended; he crossed over to Italy with an expeditionary force and twenty elephants and defeated the Romans at Heraclea (280) and Asculum (279); these were inconclusive, but costly triumphs (hence "Pyrrhic victories")— Rome did not yield. Afterwards he helped the Greeks of Sicily fight the Carthaginians, but lost his popularity because of his arrogance and his failure in an attempt upon Lilybaeum. His position in Sicily became dangerous and he returned to Italy where he again gave battle to Romans and was defeated at Beneventum (275). Later, he was killed by a tile hurled from a roof during street riots in Argos.

PYTHAGORAS (6th cent. B.C.). Gr. philosopher and mathematician, born on Samos. In about 531, during the reign of Polycrates, he emigrated to Croton in southern Italy, where he founded a philosophico-religious school, which was influential in many areas, including the field of politics. Exiled from Croton, he settled in nearby Metapontum, where he died. Later, his followers, the Pythagoreans, signed his name to their writings (see IPSE DIXIT) which makes it very difficult to ascertain which of the precepts are P.'s own, and which are by his disciples. We do know the great interest P. had in music and we can attribute to him the mathematical theory of music (measuring intervals by the length of the string). The adoption of several ideas from Orphism (metempsychosis, asceticism) is also probably his. P. did develop certain astronomical theories, although the famous doctrine of "harmony of the spheres" (music, caused by friction between the orbits in which the celestial bodies circle) probably originated a century later. The Pythagorean Theorem can be found in Euclid; it can be assumed that this is P.'s, in one form or another. From a historical point of view, P. is important mainly because he represents a religiously oriented school in the midst of preponderately materialistic pre-Socratic natural philosophy. The school, suspect because of its aristocratic nature, disappeared in the 5th cent. Pythagoreans were still found later mainly in Thebes and Tarentum. The doctrine had a profound influence on Plato and Empedocles, among others. In the 1st cent. A.D. a Neo-Pythagoreanism originated, which later merged with Neoplatonism (see also ALCMAEON; ARCHYTAS; and PHILOLAUS).

PYTHEAS of Massilia (c. 350-300). Navigator of Gr. origin who wrote an interesting account of a voyage, known to us through a few fragments. He appears to have visited Britain and "Thule," probably not as a tin trader, but purely from curiosity. Avienus incorporates P.'s data in his *Ora Maritima.*

PYTHIA. The priestess of Apollo at Delphi (she also bore the more ancient name of Pytho) who gave oracles while in ecstasy.

PYTHIAN GAMES. The most important Gr. games after the Olympics, held in honor of Apollo in Delphi every four years, that is, in the autumn of the third year of every Olympiad. A Panhellenic festival since 582 B.C.

PYTHON. See DELPHI.

PYXIS. See VASE FORMS.

Q

QUAESTIO. See QUAESTOR.

QUAESTOR. Rom. magistrate in charge of finance. Originally the quaestors had a juridical function; the term is related to *quaestio,* a court of inquiry. The office was established at the beginning of republican times. First there were two, then four, and finally twenty questions. The most important ones, the *quaestores urbani,* controlled the state finances, the others were paymasters for generals and governors. The office was the first step in the *cursus honorum.*

QUINQUEREME. [Gr. *pentērēs*]. The war ship of the Hellenistic kingdoms, also used during the Punic Wars; propelled by five banks of oars (see also TRIREME).

QUINTILIANUS, MARCUS FABIUS (c. 35-c. 95). Commonly called Quintilian. Rom. orator and writer on rhetoric; originally from Hispania. He practiced law in Rome and was appointed the first paid teacher of rhetoric by Vespasian. Among his pupils were Pliny the Younger and Hadrian. After twenty years in practice, he retired in about 90 to write a textbook on the training of an orator, *De Institutione Oratoria.* In this work he defends Cicero's language, style, and educational principles; in doing so he went against the contemporary style which sanctioned short, concise phrases. The work consists of twelve books, of which book 10 contains a short Gr. and Lat. history of literature. The twelfth is a study of oratory. Other works of Q. have been lost. *Declamationes,* hypothetical trials in the style of Seneca, have been incorrectly attributed to him.

QUINTUS SMYRNAEUS (4th cent. A.D.). Gr. epic poet. He wrote *Posthomerica*, a continuation of the *Iliad* in the style of the epic cycle. The poem ends as the Greeks return home. It does not have much poetical merit.

QUIRINAL HILL. The northernmost hill of Rome; originally the Sabines had a settlement there. Several famous temples stood on this hill.

QUIRINUS. Rom. god of war, according to tradition, of Sabine origin (his temple was on the Quirinal Hill). He was often worshiped with Jupiter and Mars, and like them, had a *flamen for a priest* (see FLAMINES). The deified Romulus was identified with him (see also SALII).

QUIRITES. Term usually used when addressing peaceable Rom. citizens, or civilians, as opposed to soldiers. A well-known anecdote relates how Caesar subdued a dangerous mutiny among his soldiers, who demanded their release from the army in 47 B.C., by addressing them as *quirites*, instead of the usual *commilitones* (fellow soldiers).

QUOD ERAT DEMONSTRANDUM. "Which was to be proved"; abbreviated Q.E.D.

QUOS EGO. . . . "But I shall . . ." (Virg. *Aen.* I, 135).

QUOT HOMINES TOT SENTENTIAE. "Many men, many minds"; there are as many opinions as men. The ancient saying actually is: *quot capita, tot sensus* (Ter., *Phorm.* II, IV, 14).

QUOUSQUE TANDEM. "For how much longer," Cicero's opening words in *Orationes in Catilinam* (in full, *quousque tandem abutere, Catilina, patientia nostra*, "Pray, how much longer will you abuse our patience, Catilina?").

R

RAETIA. Rom. province, embracing parts of what is now Bavaria, Tirol, and Switzerland, inhabited by Illyrians and Celts. R. was conquered in 16 B.C. by Drusus and Tiberius. The Rom. governor lived in Augusta Vindelicorum (Augsburg).

RARA AVIS IN TERRIS. "Rare bird on earth"; prodigy (Juv. *Sat.* VI, 165, where it refers to a black swan).

RAVENNA. City in northern Italy on the Adriatic Sea, originally inhabited by Umbrians and Etruscans. Augustus made it his second naval base next to Misenum; it was the residence of the West-Rom. emperors since A.D. 404. The lovely mosaics, to which R. owes most of its fame, date from this period.

REGULUS, MARCUS ATILIUS. Rom. consul twice: in 267 B.C., when he took Brundisium, and in 256, when he crossed to Africa with an expeditionary army to force a quick decision in the First Punic War. The undertaking failed, and R. died in Carthaginian imprisonment. Tradition (usually considered incorrect) claims that he was allowed to go to Rome with a Carthaginian offer of peace on the promise that he would return to Carthage if the proposal were declined, nevertheless he advised the Rom. senate to reject it.

RES PUBLICA. The name for the Rom. "State." In order to understand this term, one must keep in mind that the words mean literally "public affairs," "public interest." In Latin one could say: "to conduct the R.P.," "promote the R.P."; the conception of R.P. (from which our *republic* is derived) was not something concrete, like the Gr. polis. However, the Romans certainly had an equivalent of the Gr. idea of polis, in *civitas,* which is often translated as "state," but which the Romans used for the Gr. city-states. In Rome itself, *civitas* meant "the citizenry"; the constitutional term is R. P., which thus actually embraces an *abstract* idea, determined by the mutual cooperation of a number of "powers." These are: in first place, the *imperium*, usually held by consuls and praetors in republican Rome; the *potestas*, held by the other magistrates, especially by the *tribuni plebis;* the *potentia*, an "unofficial" power in regard to the constitution; it included the personal influence of certain leading figures; nevertheless it was very important in the political relationships, particularly in the period starting with the Gracchi. There was also *auctoritas*, "authority," "prestige" of the senate, whose reflections and decisions had a dominating influence—rooted in tradition—through the experience of its members. Finally, the power of the people (impossible to express in one word) exercised in the various comitia. The people were formally sovereign in legislation and made vital decisions such as declarations of war or peace. *Senatus censet, populus iubet,* "the senate is of an opinion, the people command," was the formula. The comitia were called together by the magistrates, who, having heard the advice of the senate and the "command" of the people, executed the measures. This mutual cooperation was studied and admired by Polybius, a Greek, who saw the ideal realization of the "mixed constitution"; it was also recommended by Gr. theorists who attributed Rome's greatness and success to it. Polybius was partially misled, namely in the sense that he spoke with admiration about the balance of power. Only partially, because who can deny that this born politician, who associated with the leading Rom. statesmen of the 2nd cent. B.C., had excellent insight into the rapport between Rom. powers? But viewed from a greater distance, and considered more objectively, the balance proves to have been all too precarious. Sovereignty of the people particularly was a fiction. The "democratic" element, formed by the popular assemblies, was far from having the amount of power that a Gr. ecclesia possessed (not even under a moderate oligarchy). This was not only due to an organization in which the classification into income groups was considered undemocratic, but also to the curtailment

of their functions. In the comitia there was no debate, no right of interpellation, and no right of amendment. In Livy XXXI, 6-7 (at the occasion of the declaration of war against Macedonia), it can be read just how close the "command" of the people came to being a ridiculous performance. The "monarchal" element among the magistrates was in a different position. The latter had much more freedom, and were able to take some initiative, especially as commanders in the field. But in the end—and this held true particularly for the internal government —they were bound hand and foot to the "aristocratic" element, the senate. The *senatus consultum,* advice in name, was in fact a decision, which could not be ignored without ensuing punishment.

If we come to the conclusion that the Rom. state, particularly in the 3rd-1st centuries B.C., was an oligarchy, it does not necessarily express disapproval. It must be recognized that the senate enabled the Rom. Republic to survive through the dangers of struggles with Pyrrhus, Carthage, and the Hellenistic empires; the senate had the same kind of backbone that a democratic assembly such as the British House of Commons demonstrated during the critical years of the Second World War. And undermining the authority of the senate in the 1st cent. B.C. did not lead to the founding of a democratic republic, but to monarchy, the principate of Augustus.

REX [Lat. king]. It is certain that Rome was ruled by kings (seven, according to tradition) until the 6th cent. B.C. They were absolute rulers and also held the offices of high priest, supreme judge, and commander in chief of the army. Kingship was not hereditary. The king was chosen by the *comitia curiata.* After Tarquinius Superbus was driven away, the term R. was odious to the Romans, unless applied to foreign kings. For the Romans themselves, *regnum* was just about synonymous with tyranny. A trace of the high priest's office remained in republican times in the *rex sacrorum,* or high priest's office (see also INTERREX; SELLA CURULIS; PATRES; PENATES; VESTA).

RHAPSODOI [Gr.]. Reciters of epic poetry. Originally the poet recited his work himself, later this task fell to the professional R. Since Pisistratus' time (Solon's, according to some sources), Homer's poems were recited publicly, in Athens. The R. often inserted passages of their own among the poet's work; this is our main source for the interpolations discovered in the epic poems by the Alexandrine critics (see ARISTARCHUS). A rhapsodist himself and his performance are described humorously in Plato's *Ion*.

RHEA. See CYBELE.

RHEGIUM. Now Reggio di Calabria on the southernmost tip of Italy opposite Messana; founded in about 743 B.C. by Chalcis. In about 600 new colonists arrived from Messenia. Dionysius I of Syracuse destroyed it in 387; after it had been rebuilt it withstood Pyrrhus and Hannibal as a loyal ally of Rome. Ibycus was born there.

RHENUS. The Rhine River (see also GERMANIA; LIMES).

RHETORIC. The art and technique of eloquence, having fixed rules that had to be learned. It was first practiced as a "profession" in Sicily, during the 5th cent. B.C.; from there Gorgias introduced it to Athens (see ATTIC ORATORS). The later Sophists used it exclusively for the service of "the art of having one's words find acceptance" (*peithein*). In the meantime an argument had broken out about what is more important: *what* one says, or *how* one says it. Plato was convinced of the former, Aristotle took the middle road in his *Rhetoric*. He demanded technical mastery of this discipline as well as philosophical knowledge. He also determined the three genres for good oratory: political (or deliberative), forensic, and laudatory (panegyrical). During Hellenistic regal times R. in the popular assembly was nonexistent and it became more and more a scholastic subject. At that time two competing schools originated: the Asiatic (bombastic) and the Neo-Attic (serious). In the 2nd cent. B.C., R. appeared in Rome. Cato Major tried to retain the ancient Rom. traditions in this field, but Asiatic R. quickly spread there also (see HORTENSIUS). The oldest surviving Lat. book on the theory of R. is the *Rhetorica ad Herennium* (c. 68

B.C.), handed down among the works of Cicero, which seeks to adapt Gr. theories to Rom. practice. Cicero was the greatest Rom. orator, in theory as well as in practice; in the rivalry between the schools he was able to find a true "golden" mean. In the struggle between "what" and "how" he also chose the middle road—already indicated by Aristotle. He acquainted the Romans with the ideal of Demosthenes. During imperial times—with the disappearance of political freedom—R. was no longer an instrument of political power—again it became merely a "school subject" (see SENECA). Too late Quintilian took up the defense for Cicero's ideals. During the same period the Greeks Dionysius of Halicarnassus and Pseudo-Longinus devoted themselves to R. In the 2nd cent. A.D. the "Second Sophistic" appeared (see HERODES ATTICUS; ARISTIDES, PUBLIUS). In about 170 Hermogenes in his textbook gave the theory of R. its definite form. This book remained the standard work in the Middle Ages (see also ELOQUENCE).

RHODES. Large island off the coast of Caria, colonized by Dorians in about 1100 B.C., who founded the cities Lindos, Ialysus, and Camirus. These in turn founded the city of R. by synoecism in 411-407 B.C. During Hellenistic times R. was a powerful commercial republic with a strong fleet; it profited from good trade relations with Rome and became an important center of arts and sciences (the "Laocoön" group was created there). R. had a school of rhetors and philosophers where many Romans studied (see PANAETIUS; POSIDONIUS). Vespasian annexed R. to the province of Asia.

RHYTON. See VASE FORMS.

RIDENTEM DICERE VERUM, QUID VETAT? "What forbids one's telling the truth gaily?" (Hor. *Sat.* I, 1, 24). This quotation characterizes the style of Horace's satire (see also JUVENAL).

ROME. City on the Tiber founded, according to tradition, in 753 B.C. by Romulus and Remus. The site was inhabited long before the traditional date of the legendary founding (see PALATINE HILL; QUIRINAL HILL). The old settlements merged gradually and became a city-state, first ruled by kings, later a

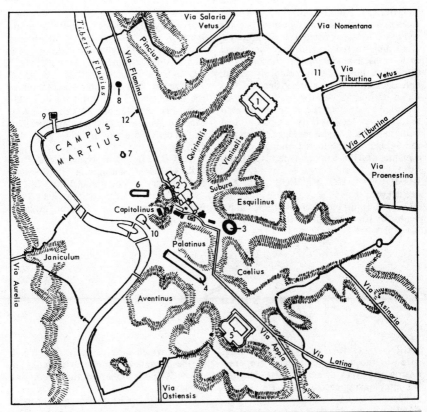

Rome during imperial times. 1. *Diocletian's Thermae,* 2. *Fora,* 3. *Colosseum,* 4. *Circus Maximus,* 5. *Caracalla's Thermae,* 6. *Circus Flaminius,* 7. *Pantheon,* 8. *Mausoleum of Augustus,* 9. *Mausoleum of Hadrian,* 10. *Marcellus' Theater,* 11. *Castra Praetoria,* 12. *Ara Pacis.*

peasant republic, extending its domination progressively to Latium, and then to the entire peninsula of Italy. The fiction of the primitive city-state was still maintained, until it was given up, much too late, during the Social War (90-88). During this period R. became the capital of a country, soon of a world empire. Rom. citizenship, once the proud possession of a minority, became a national civil right for all of Italy, was gradually bestowed on larger and larger groups within the Empire, and finally (see CARACALLA) on all free subjects.

For details on republican times see REX; BRUTUS; CAMILLUS; SAMNITES; ETRUSCANS; LATIUM; PLEBS; PYRRHUS; PUNIC WARS; PHILIP V; PERSEUS; ANTIOCHUS III; FLAMININUS; MITHRIDATES; OPTIMATES; GRACCHI; MARIUS; SULLA; CICERO; TRIUMVIRI. For imperial times see PRINCEPS; DOMINATE; JULIAN-CLAUDIAN HOUSE; ADOPTIVE EMPERORS; MILITARY EMPERORS; DIOCLETIAN; CONSTANTINE THE GREAT; JULIAN; WEST ROMAN EMPIRE. For state institutions see RES PUBLICA. For law see CORPUS JURIS. For art see ARCHITECTURAL ORDERS; PAINTING, and in particular POMPEII, PORTRAITURE.

ROMULUS. The legendary founder of Rome; he and his twin brother Remus were said to have come from Alba Longa. According to the legend they were said to have been abandoned at the banks of the Tiber, but were miraculously saved, and suckled by a wolf. After he had killed Remus, R. became the first king of Rome. To populate the town, he offered asylum to exiles. The city was soon filled with men; but, there being no women, the inhabitants abducted the wives and daughters of the Sabines (see also QUIRINUS).

ROMULUS AUGUSTULUS. See AUGUSTULUS.

ROSTRA [plural of Lat. *rostrum*, ship's beak]. In Rom. antiquity, the curved end of a ship's prow, especially the beak of a war galley. The orators' platform in the Rom. Forum was called R. because it was embellished with the bronze prows of the ships captured at Antium in 338.

ROXANA. Princess from Sogdiana (northeast Persia), married Alexander the Great in 327 B.C. After his death she took her small son Alexander IV to Macedonia, where she was murdered on Cassander's orders in 311 (see also OLYMPIAS).

RUBICON. Boundary river between Italy and Gallia Cisalpina in northeastern Italy, emptying into the Adriatic Sea. In 49 B.C., Caesar crossed it to fight Pompey after writing his famous exclamation: *Alea jacta est!*

S

SABINA, POPPAEA (?-A.D. 65). First wife of Otho, who later became emperor, mistress of Nero after 58. Nero married her after having cast off his wife Octavia in 62.

SABINES. Ancient tribe in the northeastern section of Rome. They were part of the oldest population of Rome (see QUIRINAL HILL; ROMULUS). Numerous Rom. religious customs can be traced to them (Numa Pompilius is said to have been of Sabine origin) as well as one of the most important Rom. families, namely the *Claudia gens*. The independent lands of the S. were conquered in 290 B.C. by Manius Curius Dentatus. In 268 B.C. the S. were granted complete Rom. citizenship.

SAGES, THE SEVEN. Name for a group of Gr. historical characters of the 6th cent. B.C., famous as propagators of practical worldly wisdom; several lists of them have been handed down; a few names occur on all the lists, including Solon, Thales, and Pittacus. Short aphorisms (*gnomes*) are attributed to them such as "know thyself," "avoid excess," some of which were hewn into the façade of the Temple of Apollo at Delphi. The only real philosopher of this group was Thales.

SAGUNTUM. City on the east coast of Spain, allied with Rome when the Ebro treaty was signed by Hasdrubal so that the city was under Rom. protection although it was south of the Ebro. Nevertheless it was attacked by Hannibal in 219 B.C., which precipitated the Second Punic War. Traces of Iberian and Rom. remains have been found there.

SALAMIS. Name of:
—(1) Island in the Saronic Gulf opposite Eleusis. In mythology, the residence of Telamon and his son Ajax. Solon advocated its annexation by Athens. In 480 B.C. the Persian fleet was overwhelmingly defeated here, before Xerxes' very eyes (see also THEMISTOCLES). In 318 B.C. the island was conquered by Macedonia, but in about 230 B.C. it came under Athenian rule again.
—(2) City on the east coast of Cyprus, successor to the Mycenaean settlement in Encomi. In 449 B.C. the Athenian fleet

was victorious over the Persians here, and in 306 B.C., Demetrius Poliorcetes defeated Ptolemy I. During Rom. times the majority of the population was Jewish; in 117 the Jews revolted and S. was destroyed; it was rebuilt by Constantine II and proclaimed the capital of Cyprus, under the name of Constantia.

SALII (dancers). College of priests in Rome and other Italian cities, usually in the service of the god of war. In Rome there were S. of Mars and of Quirinus; they performed war dances usually in March, the onset of the campaigning season. During these rites they beat holy shields (*ancilia*) with their spears or staves and sang the *Carmen Saliare*, a song that was incomprehensible to the priests themselves because it was written in archaic Saturnian verse in a primitive language.

SALLUST. See SALLUSTIUS.

SALLUSTIUS. Name of:

—(1) Gaius S. Crispus (86-35 B.C.). Commonly called Sallust. Rom. historian. He was *tribunus plebis* in 52, and, as such, made a violent attack on Cicero and supported Clodius. In 50 he was expelled from the senate by the censors, ostensibly for immoral behavior, but actually for political reasons: his activities in favor of the *populares*. He was appointed quaestor by Caesar in 49, and thereby reinstated in his senatorial rank. Afterward he became praetor and governor of Numidia under Caesar's protection. He enriched himself immeasurably in this province and with the money built a country house and also gardens (the *Horti Sallustiani*) in Rome that later became a pleasure spot of the Rom. emperors. He spent the last years of his life there. After Caesar was murdered, S. retired from politics for good and devoted himself to the writing of history. He modeled his literary form after Thucydides, and his language closely imitated the style of Cato Major. He wrote two historical monographs, *Bellum Catilinae* (43, on the Catilinarian conspiracy) and *Bellum Jugurthinum* (about 41, on the Jugurthine War). Of his history in five books (after 39) only fragments have survived, among them a few complete speeches and letters. A few other letters and speeches are also attributed to him. In order to form an opinion on his works, we must rely mainly on the two monographs; there he shows himself to be a competent writer of history. He is not satisfied with reporting events, but, in the manner of Thucydides, he also searches for causes and motives. Insofar as these are of a political nature, he sees them clearly. The more or less philosophical introductions to the two works are too moralizing, particularly from the pen of a follower of Caesar. S. is not entirely impartial; his work is strongly anti-*nobiles*. His style is terse and resembles that of Tacitus; his use of language is consciously archaic.

—(2) S. (4th cent. A.D.). Author of a curious writing called *On the Gods and the Universe*, a treatise on antique paganism, embracing Neoplatonist ideas and influenced by mystico-religious trends (see IAMBLICHUS). The author is probably the same S. who was a friend and adviser of Julian.

SALONA. City in Dalmatia near contemporary Split, capital of the province of Illyrium (see ILLYRIA). Birthplace of Diocletian, who had an enormous palace built there. Its ruins as well as other Rom. monuments have been found there. Diocletian retired to S. after his abdication in A.D. 305.

SALVIUS JULIANUS (c. 100-c. 169). Rom. jurist. He was commanded by Hadrian to revise the *edictum perpetuum* (see CORPUS JURIS). Under that emperor and Antoninus Pius he held high offices (consul 148) and was a member of their advisory council. His most important work can be found in the *Digesta*, large sections of which have survived in the *Corpus Juris* and other Rom. juridical works.

SAMNITES. Tribe of central Italy, originally inhabiting the Apennines; they soon came to rule parts of Lucania and Bruttium and all of Campania (5th cent. B.C.; see also OSCI). Rome combated them in the three Samnite Wars, of which the first (343-1 B.C.) is partly legendary; the second (328-04) has become famous through the Rom. defeat in the Caudine Forks; the third (298-90) brought about a coalition of all of central

Italy against Rome. This war was decided by the battle of Sentinum (see also DECIUS). The S. resisted the longest during the Social War of 90-88. Sulla had many of them killed. The survivors were Romanized. The weakness of the S., although a warlike people, was due to their very lax federal government.

SAMNIUM. The lands of the Samnites in the Apennines.

SAMOS. Fertile island off the coast of Asia Minor, already in ancient times famous for its wine. It was colonized in the 11th cent. B.C. by Ionians. In the 7th and 6th centuries B.C. it participated intensively in the colonization of the Mediterranean Sea coasts. S. produced explorers, artists, poets, and famous craftsmen (Pythagoras was born there). It reached its peak of prosperity under Polycrates' reign; in the 5th cent. it became a member of the Delian League; Pericles curbed an attempt by S. to secede in 440-39. In 411 B.C. it was the base from which the Athenian oligarchy was overthrown (see PISANDER). During Hellenistic times it was completely eclipsed by Rhodes. The main cult on S. was of Hera.

SAMOTHRACE. Island in the Aegean Sea off the coast of Thrace; the Gr. population originally came from Samos. S. was mainly known for the mystery cult of the Cabiri. The famous statue "Nike of S." was found there. It is now one of the showpieces of the Louvre.

SAPPHO (c. 600 B.C.). Gr. poetess, born in Eresus on Lesbos, compatriot and contemporary of Alcaeus. Among the Greeks the only really great poetess (see also CORINNA) and also one of the most important, if not the most important representative of the lyric style. As a young girl she was forced to flee to Sicily in consequence of political disturbances on Lesbos (see PITTACUS), but returned to Mytilene, where she founded a school of music among the girls of Lesbos. The poems she addressed to them show her passionate affection for these girls. She herself was married and had a daughter, Cleïs, to whom she dedicated a charming poem. In another poem she chides her brother Charaxus for falling in love with Rhodopis, a hetaerae whose freedom he had bought in Naucratis. Nothing else is known with certainty about her life; the story that she refused an offer of marriage from Alcaeus is dubious; Ovid (*Her.* XV) alludes to her flight from Mytilene to Sicily. The legend that she threw herself into the sea from a cliff on Leucas—out of despair over her unrequited love for a sea captain named Phaon—seems to have been invented by the Attic comedians.

Of her poems, only one has survived completely (cited by Dionysius of Halicarnassus), the "Ode to Aphrodite." However, many fragments have been found on papyrus. No poet of ancient times expressed in verse the range of emotions the way S. did: love, hate, irony, happiness, love of nature, jealousy—all can be found in her work. Her meter is very varied; she developed also one strophe of her own, which is imitated to this day. Of the Romans, Horace and particularly Catullus copied her. S.'s poems are also important for our knowledge of the Gr. language, as she and Alcaeus are our main sources for Aeolian dialect (see AEOLIANS).

SARAPIS. See SERAPIS.

SARCOPHAGUS [Gr. *Sarkophagos,* eating flesh]. Monumental coffin made of stone, terra cotta, or wood, often painted or decorated with reliefs. The most famous are the archaic terra cotta sarcophagi from Clazomenae and the stone sarcophagi made by Greeks in Phoenicia; the Alexander S. belongs among the latter group. Several wooden sarcophagi of Gr. origin have been found in southern Russia. The sarcophagi of the Etruscans, on which one sees a man and a woman supine, are also well known. During Rom. imperial times Sarcophagi were in widespread use and were often made of marble and decorated with lovely reliefs. The ancient Christian sarcophagi are of special interest, with their biblical scenes, influenced by classical art.

SARDES. Capital of Lydia (see also CROESUS). Residence of the Persian satraps, it was the political center of Asia Minor until 300 B.C. and the first city where coins were minted (see COINAGE). In 499 the Ionians burned it down during their revolt against the Persians. Later it was ruled by Hellenists and Romans,

successively. Diocletian made it the capital of the province of Lydia once more.
SARDINIA. The largest island in the western Mediterranean region. The prehistoric inhabitants built megalithic monuments there, of which the so-called *muraghi,* conical defense towers of stone, are the most impressive. In about 550 B.C., S. was annexed by Carthage, and in 328 B.C. by Rome, which made it into a province—at the same time as Corsica —in 277. The inhabitants often revolted, and Rome did not grant them freedom. S. did not enjoy prosperity until imperial times.
SARMATAE. Indo-European tribe, related to the Scythians, split into two groups, the Roxolani and Iazyges. Both groups were subjected to Rome in the 1st cent. A.D. Later, under the pressure of the German migration, they were displaced from their territory.
SASSANIDAE. The royal house of the Neo-Persian empire (226-651), successors to the Arsacidae, they traced their descent from the Achaemenidae. They led a strongly centralized government from their capital Ctesiphon (see SELEUCIA). The priests of the Persian god Ahura Mazda were very influential. The S. empire waged constant war against Rome for the possession of Asia Minor, under its most important kings, Sapor I (241-272) and Sapor II (310-379). Sapor I took the Emperor Valerianus prisoner; Julian fell while opposing Sapor II.
SATIRE [Lat. *satira,* a poetic medley, from the older form *satura,* a dish of various fruit.] The word S., properly denoting a medley of heterogeneous things, was applied in particular to a dramatical farce which was a form of poetry, interspersed with prose, song, music, and dancing. It was the only literary genre the Romans could claim as "all theirs" (Quint. X, 1, 93). Various subjects were discussed, either in a friendly, chatty manner, or with biting sarcasm—social evils were criticized and human weaknesses exposed. Although the first satirists were certainly Roman (Ennius, Lucilius), there are nevertheless traces of Gr. influence in this genre: the "street sermons" of the Cynics, the Attic Old Comedy, and the philosophical polemics of Men-

ippus. Lucilius wrote all of his satires in hexameters and was the first to employ the S. as a form of expression of social criticism; he was initialed by numerous poets, for instance, HORACE, PERSIUS, JUVENAL, and CLAUDIANUS, who was the last of this series; his S. became veritable lampoons against enemies of the court. A second series, in which poetry and prose are mingled in Menippus' style, began with Varro and was continued by Seneca in his *Apocolocyntosis,* and by Petronius; with Boethius this type of S. returned to its Menippean origin.
SATRAP. Title of the governors of districts in the Persian empire since Darius I. There were twenty of them (Hdt. III, 89-94); of these, many were actually independent rulers. Alexander the Great conserved this system; it was also maintained under the Arsacidae and partly under the Sassanidae.
SATURN [Lat. Saturnus]. Italian god whose name is usually connected with the Lat. word for "sowing"; however it is not certain whether his function of an agricultural god is really of Italian origin, or whether he only acquired it through his identification with Cronus. S.'s most important festival was the Saturnalia.
SATURNALIA. Rom. festival in honor of Saturn, celebrated on December 17th-19th (end of the autumn sowing). The S. was perhaps a native Rom. custom or was brought from Greece by the Etruscans. For the duration of the festival, slaves were free and were sometimes served by their masters. A mock king was elected and the people gave gifts (in particular clay figurines and wax candles) to one another. The Christian Church opposed the festival, yet the influence of many pagan customs can still be seen in our New Year's celebrations.
SATYRS. Gr. spirits of the woods, members of Dionysus' retinue. S. were half man and half animal, with shaggy hair, goat's feet, and a tail. They personified coarse, sensual desires. In ancient times, the S. were often confused with the Sileni, the latter originally were part horse. In mythology there is a particular Silenus, a companion of Dionysus, who is brought back to his master by

Midas (Ov. *Met.* XI, 85 ff.) S. formed the chorus in Satyric drama, a play that treated its theme in a half-comic manner, presented in Athens as the fourth play following three tragedies. We possess one example in its entirety: Euripides' *Cyclops.* Large fragments of Sophocles' *Ichneutai* have been found on papyrus.

SCAEVOLA. Name of:

—(1) Gaius Mucius S. Legendary Rom. hero. He entered the camp of Porsenna in 507 B.C., in order to kill him; after he had been captured and threatened with torture, he thrust his right hand into the sacrificial fire to show his lack of fear. Porsenna, full of admiration for his courage, let him go free. Mucius received his surname of S. (left hand, from *scaevus,* left) from this action.

—(2) Publius Mucius S. Rom. lawyer; descendant of the above. Consul in 133 B.C.

—(3) Quintus Mucius S.; famous for his knowledge of the law. Consul in 117 B.C.

—(4) Quintus Mucius S., son of the latter. He was the first to make a systematic summary of Rom. law. Consul in 95 B.C.

SCHOLIA. Antique commentaries on classical authors, written in the margins of manuscripts, embracing explanations of both the language and the contents. Usually they are excerpts from more extensive commentaries, which can often be traced back to valuable work of Alexandrine scholars. In addition to insignificant comments, they often contain very good explanations of the text, as well as many data on antique culture taken from writings actually lost. The S. on Apollonius Rhodius, for example, are a first-rate source of information on Gr. mythology.

SCIPIO. The most famous family of the Rom. patrician *Cornelia gens.* The most famous members are:

—(1) Publius Cornelius S. Africanus, commonly known as S. Major (236-184). He conquered Hannibal and saved the life of his father during the battle against Hannibal at Ticinus in 218. After the death of his father and his uncle Gnaeus during a battle against Hasdru-

bal in Spain, he was made commander of the forces there, despite his youth (210). He took Carthago Nova (see also LAELIUS) and defeated the Carthaginians time and again by using new tactics. When he had driven them entirely out of Spain, he returned to Rome in 206 and was elected consul the following year. Then he decided to cross to Africa although Hannibal was still in Italy and carried out his plan in spite of the senate's opposition (see FABIUS). First he gained victories over Syphax and Hasdrubal, so that Carthage was compelled to sign an armistice; but after Hannibal returned to Africa the batle raged again; S. defeated Hannibal at Zama with the help of Masinissa, thereby ending the Second Punic War. S. returned to Rome in triumph. In 199 he was censor, in 194 he was consul for the second time. In 190 he went as legate to Greece to serve under his brother Lucius, and to Asia Minor in the war against Antiochus the Great. Here S. reveals himself as a philhellenist and later was to influence prominent Romans and especially S. Minor (see FLAMININUS). A bitter opposition under the leadership of Cato Major now was directed against both brothers; S., offended, retired to his estate and died soon afterward. His daughter Cornelia was the mother of the Gracchi.

—(2) Publius Cornelius S. Aemilianus Africanus Numantinus, commonly known as S. Minor (185-129), son of Aemilius Paullus and adopted by the eldest son of S. Major. He was consul in 147 and destroyed Carthage in 146 (Third Punic War); in 134 he was again consul and conquered Numantia in 133. In spite of his military exploits, he was always interested in art, philosophy, and science. A circle of admirers of Gr. civilization gathered around him, some of them prominent Romans (see LAELIUS), some of them Greeks (see POLYBIUS; PANAETIUS). However, his social insight was too limited; he was too much the traditionalist to understand the reforms of his cousins, the Gracchi.

—(3) Publius Cornelius S. Nasica Corculum; opposed Cato Major's fanaticism in 155 B.C. to destroy Carthage because he believed that the existence of a rival was a stimulus for Rome.

—(4) Publius Cornelius S. Nasica Serapio, consul in 138 B.C., son of the preceding, leader of the group of senators who murdered Tiberius Gracchus.

SCOPAS of Paros (4th cent. B.C.). Gr. sculptor. He took part in decorating the Mausoleum at Halicarnassus in c. 355. His "Pothos" (desire), a statue of a youth, dates from his first period; the casual attitude of this figure was often adopted in vase paintings of that epoch. After the Mausoleum, S. worked on the temple of Athena Alea in Tegea. We know positively that he worked as an architect on this temple; but the heads of the façade sculptures that have been preserved have the powerful plastic, the pathetic expression, and deep-set eyes typical of S.'s sculptures. A Maenad, a Heracles, and a Meleager date from later periods. S.'s style is also recognized in reliefs on one of the columns of the Artemis temple in Ephesus. The attributions of several works to S., however, remains dubious; it is based mainly on reports furnished by Pausanias, Pliny the Elder, and through gems from Rom. times. As opposed to the art of Praxiteles (and also that of Lysippus), which is a continuation of the classical style of the 5th cent., S.'s art brings to sculpture something entirely new. His figures are not static—not even restrainedly dynamic—but passionately moving: an effect produced by the pathetic look and the attitude of the entire figure (for example, the "Maenad" with her head thrown back). All this heralded a school which was to reach its climax in Hellenistic times (in the "Laocoön," for example).

SCRIPT is usually classified into: (a) pictographic S. (ideographs, for example, the Egyptian hieroglyphics in their original function); (b) syllabic S., for example, cuneiform S. which developed from type (a); (c) phonetic S. (alphabet). In the 2nd millennium B.C. a type (a) S. is found on Crete, followed by a linear S.; these symbols have not yet been deciphered, particularly as the language of the Minoan Cretans is unknown. About 1400 the so-called Linear B, a type (b) S., appeared which has recently been deciphered. This S. also occurred on the Gr. mainland and was used to render Mycenaean Greek (see Cnossus). Syllabic S., which was later used on Cyprus, was derived from Linear B. After the decline of Mycenaean culture, the Greeks did not know a S. during a long period until they adopted the Phoenician alphabet, probably in the 9th cent. B.C. Thus the ideal medium for expressing language was found because only type (c) makes it possible to reproduce all sounds with twenty-two to twenty-six symbols. However, there was one difficulty: the Semitic languages (of which Phoenician is one), used consonants only, whereas vowels are especially essential for the Greek language. Luckily, the Phoenicians had certain sounds the Greeks did not need; these signs and a few new letters were used to represent the Gr. vowels. There was various types of Gr. alphabets, of which the Ionian (introduced in Athens in 403 B.C., see EUCLID) eventually became the standard alphabet. The alphabet of western Greece was adopted by the Etruscans, and from them by the Romans. This also presented certain problems: the Etruscans made no distinction between *k* and *g;* the abbreviation "C." for Gaius can be attributed to this. The Romans also needed a symbol for their *f;* they took the Gr. *digamma,* which still survives in some Gr. dialects, and which approximates the English *w.*

SCRIPTORES HISTORIAE AUGUSTAE. The name given to the six authors of biographies of the Rom. emperors from A.D. 117-284. The work was united into a single collection, the *Historia Augusta,* probably in the 4th cent. The work has some value, in spite of deficiencies in style; the authors of the first part (before Caracalla) are far superior to the rest.

SCULPTURE. For Gr. S. in the 7th-6th centuries B.C. see ARCHAIC ART. For the 5th cent. B.C. see MYRON; PHIDIAS; POLYCLITUS; and the cross references cited there; also, particularly, STELE. For the 4th cent. see PRAXITELES; LYSIPPUS; SCOPAS. For Hellenistic art see PERGAMUM; LAOCOÖN; APHRODITE; and HELLENISM. For Etruscan art see ETRUSCANS.

CONSONANT	VOWEL 1		VOWEL 2		VOWEL 3		VOWEL 4		VOWEL 5	
(H-)	A AI		E		I		O		U	
D-	DA		DE		DI		DO		DU	
J-	JA		JE				JO			
K-G-CH-	KA		KE KWE?		KI		KO		KU	
M-	MA		ME		MI		MO			
N-	NA NWA?		NE NEKO?		NJ		NO		NU	
B-P-PH-	PA		PE PTE		PI		PO		PU	
QU-GU-			QE		QI?		QO			
R-L-	RA RJA		RE		RJ		RO RJO		RU	
S-	SA		SE		SI		SO		SU	
T-TH-	TA TJA?		TE		TI		TO		TU	
W-	WA		WE		WI		WO			
Z-			ZE				ZO		ZU?	

Survey of the probable phonetic sounds for 68 of the 88 signs of linear B script.

For Rom. S. see ARA; PORTRAITURE; and SARCOPHAGUS.

SCYLAX (6th cent. B.C.). Gr. geographer. At the command of Darius I, he made an expedition to what is now India. A geographical work is attributed to him which, however, was written in the 4th cent. B.C.; Hecataeus and Herodotus used S.'s data as a source for their knowledge of the Persian and Arabian coastal areas.

SCYTHIANS. People in southern Russia, probably of Iranian origin and speaking an Iranian dialect, but mingled with other tribes. They were nomads, and feared as mounted archers. In about the 7th cent. B.C. they conquered the country and subjected the prehistoric population; some of them even penetrated into Mesopotamia. Darius I undertook an expedition against them in 513 B.C., but was unsuccessful. The S. who lived along the seacoast traded extensively with the Greeks and came under their influence; on the other hand, the Greeks had some customs and ideas (especially ecstatic aspects of religion) that can be attributed to the influence of the S. After 330 B.C. they were driven out first by the Celts and then by the Sarmatae. In Athens, Scythian slaves (archers) served as policemen.

SECUNDUM NATURAM VIVERE. "To live according to nature (inspired by the universe and the gods); fundamental tenet of the Stoic doctrine, formulated by Cleanthes (Cic. *De Fin.* IV, 10, 36; Sen. *Ep.* V, 4).

SEGESTA [Gr. Egesta or Aegesta]. Elymean city in western Sicily, founded, according to tradition, by the Trojans. The city asked for help from Athens in 426 and 416 B.C., in order to combat the hereditary enemy of S., Selinus. This led to the Athenian expedition against Sicily (see PELOPONNESIAN WAR); later S. was supported by Carthage. During the First Punic War it came under Rom. rule, then prospered. There are important ancient monuments, among them a beautiful Doric temple.

SEJANUS, LUCIUS AELIUS (?-A.D. 31). Held the office of *praefectus praetorio* (see PRAETORIANS) under Tiberius; he brought all the cohorts of the guards together in one barracks near Rome. In the hope of becoming emperor himself, he put one member of the imperial family after another out of the way to achieve that end. When he was about to perpetrate his great coup in 31, he was unmasked and executed. He had a great and sinister influence on Tiberius, especially after the latter had retired to Capreae in 27 (Tac. *Ann.* IV-VI).

SELEUCIA. City on the Tigris River, founded in 312 B.C. by Seleucus I; soon eclipsed Babylon as a commercial center, and became an important focal point of Hellenism in Asia. S. remained a flourishing trade city under the Arsacidae, but its administrative function was taken over by Ctesiphon, on the other side of the Tigris. After the destruction of S. in A.D. 164, Ctesiphon definitely became the more important city; the present-day Baghdad was founded there.

SELEUCIDS. The Macedonian rulers of the Hellenistic kingdom of Syria from 312-64 B.C. (see SELEUCUS; ANTIOCHUS).

SELEUCUS. Name of:

—(1) S. I. Nicator (c. 358-280). The first of the Seleucids, son of Antiochus, one of the generals of Philip II. He accompanied Alexander the Great on his expedition into Asia and, after the battle of the Diadochi against Antigonus I and the battle of Ipsus (301), he became king of the greater part of the former Persian empire. He was the only one of Alexander's generals who did not repudiate his Eastern wife after Alexander's death. He founded many Gr. cities, thereby expanding Hellenistic civilization in the East. He was killed by a son of Ptolemy I while trying to conquer Macedonia too. His son was Antiochus I.

—(2) S. II Callinicus (265-226). King of Syria, son of Antiochus II. He ruled from 247 on; his empire lost its importance during his reign. The provinces of Bactria and Parthia revolted and when S. undertook an expedition to the east to quell these disturbances, he was defeated by the king of Parthia in a great battle. The Parthians considered this victory the foundation of their empire. His son was Antiochus III.

SELINUS. City on the southern coast of Sicily, founded in 650 or 627 B.C. by Megara Hyblaea (see MEGARA). In the 5th cent. B.C. it flourished; it was destroyed in 409 and 250 B.C. by the Carthaginians, allies of Segesta. Nowhere outside of continental Greece can one find so many Gr. temples as in S. The metopes on some of them have been well preserved.

SELLA CURULIS. The Lat. term for the chair of office belonging to the curule magistrates (see MAGISTRATUS), and also to the emperors. The chair was made of ivory and could be folded; its seat was constructed of woven leather straps. The magistrates with *imperium* sat on this chair while conducting official business, and even took it with them during military campaigns.

SEMONIDES (2nd half of the 7th cent. B.C.) Gr. lyric poet; born on Samos, he later worked at Amorgos, a colony of Samos. He wrote iambic and elegiac poems (see METER; ELEGY), among these a history of Samos. The longest of the surviving fragments (118 lines) is a comparison of various types of women with various animals.

SENATE. Originally the advisory council of the Rom. kings, consisting of 100 members of patrician houses (see PATRES); during republican times there were 300 members (including plebeians). Under Sulla they were increased to 600 and under Caesar to 900; Augustus reduced their number to 600. From 312 B.C. on, the senators were elected from ex-magistrates by the censors, who also had authority to expel unworthy members. The S. was summoned by a *magistratus cum imperio* (see IMPERIUM), and always met in a temple (usually the Curia); later it could also be summoned by a *tribunus plebis*. Theoretically the S. only had an advisory capacity, but in practice it assumed all power. This power was based, among other things, on: (a) the life tenure of the senators; (b) administration of finances; (c) control of foreign relations; (d) allocation of provincial and military commands; (e) supervision of the state cult. The S. was especially powerful in the 3rd-2nd centuries B.C., while Rome was laying the foundations for her Empire. Membership was limited to a closed caste (see OPTIMATES; HOMO NOVUS). The election of magistrates was delegated to the S. by Tiberius, therefore it actually supplemented itself; however, Tiberius asserted his personal influence, so that, in practice the senators were appointed by him. Some people have tried to prove that the principate was based on a dyarchy, that is, on a dual form of government with the *princeps* and the S. exercising equal power. This may possibly have been true, but only in theory. Nevertheless, the S. occasionally asserted its power, for instance, when a new emperor had to be chosen (see NERVA); under the dominate the S. lost its political influence entirely.

SENATUS POPULUSQUE ROMANUS. "Senate and people of Rome." Abbreviated S.P.Q.R.

SENECA. Name of:
—(1) Marcus (or Lucius) Annaeus S. (c. 55 B.C.-A.D. 39), Rom. rhetorician, born in Corduba. In A.D. 37, at the request of his sons, he wrote a collection of declamations (oratory exercises) for use of schools of rethoric. The work was entitled *Oratorum et Rhetorum Sententiae; Divisiones; Colores,* and consisted of one book, the *Suasoriae* (deliberations of difficult decisions), and ten books, the *Controversiae* (imaginary legal cases and methods of presenting them). Of these, five books have been preserved. S. is not very favorably disposed toward the kind of oratory, which, after the disappearance of political freedom, filled the musty schoolrooms instead of the Forum with an avalanche of words. Cicero was his ideal. The work is a very important source for the history of Rom. rhetoric in early imperial times.
—(2) Lucius Annaeus S. (4 B.C.-A.D. 65). Son of the preceding, Rom. moralistic writer, author of tragic poems, and statesman. He was born in Corduba and educated in Rome; lawyer, quaestor, senator; was exiled to Corsica (41-49) by the Emperor Claudius on the instigation of Messalina, but recalled by Agrippina the Younger, who appointed him Nero's tutor. When the latter had become emperor (54), S. and Burrus really ruled the Empire at first, but later Nero freed himself from S.'s influence; S. then retired from court as much as possible. In 65, Nero used Piso's conspiracy, in which S. was not involved, as an excuse to force him to commit suicide.

S.'s works can be divided into five groups: (a) Philosophical-moralistic treatises; twelve of the fourteen are called *dialogi,* although they are not dialogues. Among those most often read are: *De Providentia* (on providence); *De Ira* (on anger); *De Constantia Sapientis* (on the constancy of the wise man); *De Tranquillitate Animi* (on combating inner restlessness and lack of peace). (b) *Quaestiones Naturales* (on natural philosophy, but with moral overtones). (c) *Letters to Lucilius* (124 preserved), each being a brilliant little treatise on ethics. (d) Nine tragedies, not written as plays to be performed, but possibly for public recitation; these tragedies were adapted from plays by Sophocles and Euripides, but with a tendency toward the pathetic and the macabre (we also have the play *Octavia,* incorrectly attributed to him). (e) A Menippean satire on the death and deification of Claudius, named *Apocolo-*

cyntosis by S. himself or possibly later by others (the title probably means "punishment by the gods").

S.'s personality had many facets. In some ways he was a great man; witness his statesmanship during the years after 54 and the truly Stoic manner in which he met his death (Tac. *Ann.* XV, 60 ff.); but on the other hand, he had many weaknesses; to name only the gravest: from his exile in Corsica, S. addressed Claudius in the most abasingly flattering terms, but as soon as the Emperor was interred, he mocked him. He also wrote the speech Nero delivered to justify his matricide to the senate. In short, as Dio Cassius writes: "He was noted for doing everything in the opposite way from what he preached as a philosopher." In order to appreciate his works fully, one must disregard the character of the historical S. (although this is difficult, especially for a moralist); one will then find S. to be a charming guide to life's problems, which are the same then as now. His doctrine is that of the so-called Neo-Stoicism, mixed with practical wisdom drawn from other schools, among them the Epicurean. His doctrine of divine providence, that of a sublime spirit in man, and the moral tone of his writings, gave rise in the Middle Ages to the legend that S. was a Christian. A feigned correspondence with the Apostle Paul was even circulated. His tragedies greatly influenced classical drama in France, and in England before Shakespeare.

S. wrote in a very affected style, usually with short and sharp sentences—the style of his epoch. In this style, quaintly compared with "loose sand" in ancient times, he is certainly an unsurpassed master.

SENTINUM. Town in Umbria, where the Rom. consul Publius Decius Mus gained the victory that terminated the Third. Samnite War (see SAMNITES) in 295 B.C.; this victory brought all of central Italy, including Umbria, under Rom. domination.

SEQUANA. The Rom. name for the Seine River.

SEQUANI. Gallic tribe west of the Jura Mountains, capital Vesontio (now Besançon). The S. called in Ariovistus to help them combat the Aedui, which led to Caesar's action in Gaul in 58 B.C.

SERAPIS (or SARAPIS). The imperial god of the Ptolemies. His cult was established by Ptolemy I—this dynasty's most important experiment—in order to draw Gr. civilization and native culture together. According to tradition, Ptolemy had the statue of S. brought from Sinope (Tac. *Hist.* IV. 81. ff.). According to other stories, however, the cult originated in Babylonia. His temple in Alexandria was called the Serapeum; his cult statue was said to have been created by Bryaxis. This new cult (together with the cult of Isis) spread through the entire Greco-Rom. world.

SERENUS. Name of:

—(1) Quintus S. (3rd cent. A.D.). Author of a Lat. medical didactic poem in 1,107 hexameters; obviously more of a "medicine man" than a physician.

—(2) Gr. mathematician (probably 4th cent. A.D.); wrote two works on cylindric and conic sections.

SERIPHOS. Island in the Cyclades where iron was mined. A large part of the story of Perseus was enacted here.

SERTORIUS, QUINTUS (c. 122-72). Rom. general, follower of Marius; escaped Sulla's proscription and continued to wage war on him in Spain, where he was supported by the native population and where he established an antisenate. When Pompey was sent to oppose him, he made a treaty with Mithridates. However, he lost control of his revolt and was murdered by one of his officers, Perperna. A man of great political ability, S. was one of the most capable commanders of his period. Unfortunately, he found an even more talented (and unscrupulous) opponent in Sulla; his plan to gain control over Rome and Italy from one of the provinces was well thought out, but the time was not yet ripe for the realization of such a plan.

SERVIUS (2nd half of the 4th cent. A.D.). Full name S. Marius (or Maurus) Honoratus. Rom. grammarian. In addition to some lesser works, he wrote an elaborate commentary on Virgil, for which he used Aelius Donatus' work. An abridged version of S.'s work is extant as well as a longer one, first published in 1600 by Pierre Daniel, and called *Servius Danielis*. This longer version probably embraced those portions of Donatus' work that S. had not used. S. discusses grammar and content expertly. Important variants of texts and valuable elucidations are sometimes found in his works.

SERVIUS TULLIUS (578-535). According to tradition, the sixth Rom. king. His mother was a slave; a miraculous sign is said to have informed him that he would become king. The fortifications of Rome and the constitution are attributed to him, although both date from a later period. However, a treaty he made with the Lat. League (see LATIUM) is probably historical.

SESKLO. Village in Thessaly, with Dimini, one of the main settlements of a tribe that came from the north in the 3rd millennium B.C.; although they were not yet Greeks, they were already acquainted with the *megaron* type of houses (see HOUSES).

SESTERTIUS. See COINAGE.

SESTOS. City on the Hellespont with an excellent harbor; the place where Darius I and Xerxes crossed the straits. It was the first city to be liberated after the Persian Wars (478 B.C.); later it became an Athenian naval base.

SEVEN AGAINST THEBES. The aftermath of the saga of Oedipus, whose sons fought for the mastery of Thebes. Polynices, with his father-in-law Andrastus, king of Argos, and five other heroes, marched on his native city, but he and his brother Eteocles are killed in battle (Aeschylus, *Septem contra Thebas*). The regent Creon, Oedipus' brother-in-law, forbade Polynices' burial, but Antigone, Oedipus' eldest daughter, resolved to bury him despite this order, putting the laws of the gods above those of man; she maintained her proud conviction unto death (Sophocles, *Antigone*).

SEVEN SAGES. See SAGES.

SEVERUS. Name of:

—(1) Marcus Aurelius Alexander S. (209-235). Rom. emperor, coregent of Elagabalus and after his death (222) absolute monarch under the regency of his mother, with Ulpianus as an influential adviser. The senate was given more power, and an active social policy was followed. He waged war against the Persians and the Germans successively, and then started negotiating with the latter for peace. His soldiers, thinking this an act of cowardice, murdered him and his mother.

—(2) Lucius Septimius S. (146-211). Rom. emperor, proclaimed by his troops in Pannonia in 193; after having defeated several rivals, he was generally recognized. He won Mesopotamia from the Parthians. During an expedition to Britain he died in Eboracum (now York), embittered by the conduct of his son Caracalla, whom he had appointed his successor with Geta. He was the first and the most powerful of the military emperors; he relied completely on the army, which was privileged at the expense of the civilian population. The *praefectus praetorio* (see *Praetorians*) had even more power than formerly; he also had the highest authority in criminal cases. Therefore, prominent lawyers were appointed to that office: Papinianus, Ulpianus. The *fiscus* completely superseded the *aerarium*. The senate was robbed of all its power. The preparations for the assimilation of the provinces with Rome, later officially sealed by Caracalla, were made by S. The triumphal arch that bears his name is one of the most impressive ancient monuments in Rome.

SEXTUS EMPIRICUS (c. A.D. 200). Gr. philosopher. Although he had no original ideas, he is important because he committed the theories of the Skeptics to paper. His works on medicine have been lost.

SHIPS. SEE NAVIGATION; TRIREME; QUINQUEREME.

SIBYL. Gr. woman who, inspired by Apollo, made prophecies while in ecstasy. Originally there was only one S., but she appears in several places. Later, the number varies, as many as ten or twelve are mentioned. The most famous one is the S. of Cumae, who guided Aeneas to the underworld (Virg. *Aen.* VI; lines 77-102 describe her ecstasy matchlessly). According to tradition, she had nine books of prophecies that Tarquinius Priscus wanted to buy for Rome. The S. named a price; Tarquinius thought it was too high; she then threw three books onto the fire and doubled the price for the rest; the same thing happened with the next three, so that the king finally left for Rome with the last three books at four times the price of the original nine. These were the *Libri Sibyllini*, consulted in times of need by the *decemviri sacris faciundis*. The books were lost in a fire in 83 B.C.; a new collection of sayings was assembled, but definitely destroyed by Stilicho in about A.D. 400. There is no connection between these and the still existing Sibylline Books of oracles. The latter are compiled from Jewish and Christian sources, originating in the Near East. For this reason they hold an important position in Christian literature and art (for example, the ceiling of the Sistine Chapel in Rome and the role of the S. in the "Messianic" *Fourth Eclogue* by Virgil).

SICILY. Large island to the south of Italy, in ancient times a point of convergence of various cultures. The prehistoric population can be divided into several groups: Elymeans (see SEGESTA), Sicani (in the center), and Siculi (the most important group; archaeologically, almost impossible to distinguish from the Sicani; their language was probably related to Latin, see also LATIUM). Greeks settled on S. from the 8th cent. B.C. on; main cities: Syracuse, Gela, Agrigentum, Selinus (Dorian), Zancle (Messana), Leontini, Naxos, Himera (Ionian). Carthaginians settled in the western part of the island. The natives were driven inland, and later Hellenized. Most of the cities had an aristocratic form of government; there were also tyrants (see PHALARIS; THERON; HIERO). One of them, Gelon, made Syracuse the most powerful city of S. and, in 480, defeated the obtrusive Carthaginians at Himera. In the 5th cent., Athens became increasingly interested in S.; this finally led to the expedition against Syracuse (see PELOPONNESIAN WAR; SEGESTA; ALCIBIADES); Carthage especially profited by the failure of this undertaking by making great conquests. (For the opposition to Carthage see DIONYSIUS; AGATHOCLES; PYRRHUS; HIERO II.) S. became a Rom. province as a result of the First Punic War; later it served as a granary; violent slave revolts occurred on the *latifundia*. S. was often scandalously plundered (see VERRES). Imperial times brought great relief to S. and to all the other conquered countries. In the 5th cent. A.D. it was dominated by the Vandals. S. produced great men in ancient times (see EMPEDOCLES; GORGIAS; ARCHIMEDES; THEOCRITUS). Pindar and Plato visited there; Aeschylus died there (see also COMEDY; RHETORIC).

SICYON. City in the northern Peloponnesus, founded by Argos. S. flourished in the 7th-6th centuries B.C. when it was ruled by tyrants. In the 3rd cent. B.C. it was an important member of the Achaean League (see ARATUS). It became a famous center of the arts; Lysippus was a citizen of S.

SIDON. See PHOENICIANS.

SIGNUM. The Rom. name for a military standard carried by legions, maniples, and cohorts. It was a pole, decorated with various ornaments and emblems; the standard-bearer (*signifer*) received the commands for tactical maneuvers.

SILENUS. See SATYRS.

SILIUS ITALICUS, TIBERIUS CATIUS (c. 25-101). Lat. epic poet. He was consul in 68, the year Nero died; governor of Asia in about 77. He withdrew from public life and led a luxurious life on his many country estates, one of which had belonged to Virgil and one to Cicero. To put an end to an incurable illness, he starved himself to death with Stoical resignation (Plin. *Ep.* III, 7). He wrote the longest Lat. poem that has been preserved, an epic in seventeen books (about 12,200 verses) on the Second Punic War, *Punica*. He derived his material from Livy, and older annalists; his style was copied from Virgil. Pliny the Younger claimed that he wrote "with more devotion than talent."

SIMONIDES of Ceos (c. 556-468). Gr. lyric poet; principal author of choral lyric poetry next to Pindar and Bacchylides. He traveled extensively; from Ceos he went to Athens, where he stayed at the court of Hipparchus; then into Thessaly, where he lived under the patronage of the Scopadae, a notable family. A famous anecdote dates from this period (c. 514): S. had celebrated the Dioscuri and Scopas in the same song, so the latter advised him to ask the Dioscuri for half of his payment. Soon afterward, servants announced that two young men were at the door, demanding to speak with S. No sooner had he gone outside, when the whole hall collapsed behind him, burying all members of the Scopadae (Cic. *De Or.* II, 86). In about 478, S. was back in Athens; there he became the friend of Themistocles. Then he settled in Syracuse at the court of Hiero I. He was buried at Akragas (Agrigentum). S. wrote not only songs of victory (especially for the rulers named) and choral songs, but also elegies. His epitaphs were particularly famous (for example, the one for those who fell at Thermopylae, and the one for those who fell at Marathon, which was preferred to Aeschylus' poem). The lament of Danaë floating around on the ocean with small Perseus, is well known. Because S. was renowned for his fluent style, his exquisite choice of words, and his conciseness, many epigrams were soon attributed to him.

SINOPE. Colony of Miletus on the south coast of the Black Sea, founded in the 7th cent. B.C., destroyed by the Cimmerians and reconstructed in about 600. An important trade center, S. founded many other colonies. Later, it was the capital of Pontus until it became a Rom. colony.

SKEPTICS. The followers of a school of philosophy who believed that one cannot attain absolute knowledge concerning the essence of things; by being aware of this and by abstaining from all judgment, one can find peace of mind. The Sophists (see particularly PROTAGORAS) already outlined this theory; with Pyrrhon it took the form of a real philosophical school. His doctrine and that of his disciple Timon was revived in the 1st cent. B.C. by Aenesidemus (see also SEXTUS EMPIRICUS). The Middle Academy constituted another center of Skepticism, particularly with Carneades, who, through his doctrine of "probability verging on certainty" was able to apply the Theory of the Skeptics to daily life.

SKYPHOS. See VASE FORMS.

SLAVERY. Throughout ancient times S. existed in different degrees and under extremely varying circumstances. There was a vast difference between the relatively small number of slaves in Homeric Greece and the enormous groups on the Rom. *latifundia;* between the slaves serving as policemen in Athens (see SCYTHIANS) or as private physicians or tutors in Rom. patrician families; and between those who worked in the mines at Laurium and the laborers on the Sicilian plantations under Rom. rule. The principal sources of slaves were: (a) the children of female slaves (during some periods the children were free if the master was the father); (b) prisoners of war; (c) piracy; (d) foundlings. Originally it was also possible to become a slave through indebtedness; in Attica this legislation was abolished by Solon, and in Rome in early republican times.

The slaves did a very large part (but not the majority) of the manual work in ancient times, and an important part of the specialized work (including intellectual tasks). This is the basis for the opinion that the entire antique economy was a system based on the exploitation of slaves. But "exploitation" only exists if slave labor yields a significantly higher profit than free labor. Now we know—from an inscription—that free citizens and metics worked side by side for the same wages on the construction of the Erechtheum in Athens, and that foremen also received the same amount; a foreman who was a slave is also mentioned. The slaves handed over a greater part of their wages to their masters; some slaves saved the amount they kept for themselves with a view to buying freedom; some slaves had their own shops and gave a percentage of their earnings to their masters. Reliable calculations have been made that show that in Rom. republican times the labor of one slave working the fields cost about half what a married free laborer's work would cost. However, not considered in these calculations were the costs incurred to raise the slave children born in the master's house—and the most important point—the productivity, which must have been significantly higher in the case of free laborers. All these factors reduce the difference considerably, so that the "exploitation" proves to be a figment of the imagination—except in the case of some groups, for example, such as those on the *latifundia* and at Laurium, mentioned earlier.

The above is meant to disprove the economic theory, not to excuse S. Socially, any kind of S. remains a curse and a violation of human dignity (but "free" labor relations can be that too, as was the case at the start of the Industrial Revolution). The presence of a large minority of slaves (estimated at one-third of the population for Attica and Italy, slightly more in the cities of Athens and Rome) also led to a social evil: some circles considered manual labor, even craftsmanship, to be inferior. In Italy the great influx of Eastern slaves also had significant influence on the national character.

These remarks lead to the conclusion that economically slavery was hardly or not at all remunerative; socially it was an absurdity. That makes it all the more surprising that the antique philosophers and moralists never attacked the root of the evil. Many of them advocated good treatment of the slaves (this was, especially in the case of a schooled slave, the most profitable thing to do); some of them were even irritated by the boldness of the slaves and by the similarity in their clothing and appearance; a few moralists advocated social intercourse with them and spoke up for their moral betterment (Sen. *Ep.* 47; after all, the Stoics did preach the brotherhood of man). But everyone accepted the institution of S. itself as a natural thing, even young Christianity. Aristotle, for example, considered slaves to be living tools, without personalities. And yet the same slaves were suddenly seen as perfect equals once they became free, a thing that often occurred; in Athens they then became metics, in Rome usually Rom. citizens in the second generation. In any case, this liberation (which was seldom if ever disdained) proved that the slaves themselves preferred the life of a free laborer, which was often difficult, to enslavement, however bearable.

SMYRNA. Ionian city on the west coast of Asia Minor, near the mouth of the Hermus River, an ideal place for trading with the East. In 627 B.C. it was destroyed by Alyattes and rebuilt in its present place by Alexander the Great. It flourished again in Rom. times.

SOCIAL WAR. A war of more or less subjugated allies against the leading state. The allies of the second Attic League (see ATHENS) waged such a war from 357-355. The best known of these wars was the so-called Marsic War of the Italians against Rome, in 90-88. The *socii* were embittered by the delay in solving the problem of the *ager publicus* and by the fact that only Rom. citizens shared in the division of the spoils of war. The assassination of Marcus Livius Drusus, who had attempted to extend Rom. citizenship to the *socii*, precipitated the war. The *socii* chose Corfinium as their capital. After vain efforts to subdue them, Rome first bestowed citizenship on those who had remained loyal, and then on all those who were willing to make peace within sixty days. Only the Samnites persevered. These were defeated by Sulla, but not until 82. After that, the ethnic and linguistic differences quickly disappeared, and Italy became, in fact, one state with Rome as its capital —a development which had been delayed much too long.

SOCII [Lat. allies]. Cities in Italy and other countries who had made a special treaty with Rome. They were autonomous in matters of internal politics, but had to give Rome troops and had no foreign policy of their own. The S. in Italy were granted Rom. citizenship after a prolonged struggle, the Social War of 90-89 B.C. The S. outside Rome always remained more loosely connected with Rome.

SOCRATES (469-399). Gr. philosopher whose life is the dividing line between the pre-Socratics, who occupied themselves almost exclusively with natural philosophy, and the later philosophers, all of whom indirectly underwent his influence and who occupied themselves with ethics. S. was the son of a stonemason; his mother was said to have been a midwife

(S. himself said that his method was a "midwife's technique": he helped people to bring the truth, hidden in themselves, to the surface). On principle, S. wrote no treatises and made no long speeches; he accosted all kinds of people on the streets of Athens and held conversations with them; by preference he chose people who were supposed to be "experts" in some field, and pretended to know nothing himself (Socratic irony); he then destroyed their prepossessed wisdom entirely, in order to build up a new insight in the vacuum of knowledge that he had created. He deliberately irritated his fellow citizens in this manner; and although he remained in Athens all his life (except when he was on military campaigns) and served his country as a good citizen and a brave soldier, many people began to consider him an underminer of society and a supporter of the Sophists, although it was S.'s whole aim to oppose them and their relativism. Also, among S.'s followers, there were people like Alcibiades and Critias, whose names were anathema after the restoration of democracy in 403 (see THRASYBULUS). That explains the accusation brought against him in 399 of not honoring the state gods, of trying to introduce strange deities (an accusation founded upon his belief in *daemon,* his conscience), and of corrupting youth. When the *Heliaea* had declared S. guilty and his punishment had to be decided on, S. asked for the honor of being allowed to eat in the Prytaneum every day. Then a large majority pronounced for the death sentence. It would still have been easy for S. to escape, but he chose to drink the hemlock calmly and with dignity; for "it is better to suffer injustice than to inflict it."

There are four main sources for our knowledge concerning S.'s "doctrine": (a) Plato (advantage: the most brilliant pupil; disadvantage: attributes his own opinions to S.); (b) Xenophon (advantage: not a profound thinker with personal ideas; disadvantage: could not follow S.'s transcendent thought); (c) Aristophanes in his play *The Clouds* (advantage: gives the ideas held by the average Athenian; disadvantage: gives a caricature); (d) Aristotle (advantage:

greater distance, unprejudiced criticism; disadvantage: did not know S. personally). In spite of the fact that they sometimes contradict each other, these four sources give us quite a clear picture. Aristotle says that S. taught two things in particular: general definitions and inductive reasoning. That these are connected can be seen from the early dialogues of Plato. For example, S. first sought instances of courageous or pious deeds, and then reasoned to a general conception of "courage" or "piety." These always concerned *aretè* (virtue); for a Greek this always embraces a conception of "soundness," "command of a matter or a subject"; therefore it is not surprising that S. taught his "victims" that "virtue" can be learned. "Nobody sins consciously" was his great theorem. This intellectualistic ethic is the grandeur, but also the weakness of S.'s ideas. This teachable virtue is based on objective possible knowledge; this was his great answer to the Sophists.

SOLINUS GAIUS JULIUS (c. A.D. 200). Author of the *Collectanea Rerum Memorabilium,* a geography textbook containing all kinds of interesting facts based on Pliny the Elder. He was the first to employ the words *Mare Mediterraneum.*

SOLON (c. 640-c. 560). Athenian statesman, legislator, poet, and pioneer of democracy; considered one of the Seven Sages; born of a noble family. In about 600 he roused the Athenians to recover the island of Salamis from Megara by his patriotic poems. In the meantime, the social evils in Attica had caused a crisis. The nobility owned all the land and had all the political rights. People who had become prosperous through the new means of support, trade and small industries, were nevertheless politically inferior to the rich landowners. But the worst thing was, that the small farmers, who could not keep up in the social struggle, got into debt and for this reason sometimes even became slaves. In 594, S. was appointed archon with unlimited power to resolve the problems and to create new laws (Draco's laws were completely unsatisfactory). He reformed the legislature and took social, economic, and political measures. Among S.'s economic reforms was the *Seisachtheia* (shifting of burdens): all current debts secured by the person of the debtor or by his land were canceled. He made all such further loans illegal. He also revised the economy by converting the standard of currency, regulating interest rates, attracting skilled immigrants, encouraging commerce, and placing an embargo on the export of Athenian commodities, with the exception of olive oil. He promoted the cultivation of olives in order to improve the quality of this export product. A limit was placed on vast accumulation of lands, and laws such as the *Seisachtheia* that affected the wealthy and did not entirely satisfy the poorer classes, made political reforms imperative.

S. divided the citizens into four classes according to income—in place of the existing four divisions based on capital wealth. Members of the highest class could become archons; other offices were open only to the first three groups. The lowest class, the *thetes*, who were generally without property (laborers, rowers in the triremes, etc.), were given the right to vote in the assembly and the popular law courts (see ECCELESIA; HELIAEA). The establishment of the Council of Four Hundred decreased the power of the Areopagus, the old court of the aristocrats.

S.'s constitution laid the foundation for complete and true democracy. He is said to have refused to become tyrant of Athens and to have extracted oaths from the citizens to preserve his laws without change for ten years; but the struggle among the classes continued after his retirement and Athens was next ruled by a tyrant (see PISISTRATUS). Still, S.'s work was not done in vain—later, Clisthenes succeeded in setting up a democratic government based on the features of S.'s constitution.

SOPHISTS. A Gr. word which meant originally any man of wisdom or skill. In the 2nd half of the 5th cent. B.C. the S. traveled through Greece as teachers of practical worldly wisdom, particularly of methods to attain success in politics and society; they often criticized current religious, moralistic, and social views. (For the mainsprings of their actions and

the reasons for their success, see ETHICS.) The first S. were respectable men; some of them (Pythagoras) focused their teachings on ethical and philosophical matters, others (Gorgias) on rhetoric, and again others (Hippias) on professional skill. Everywhere they found groups of youths of good family, who paid them a stipend for their teachings. The younger S. carried their criticism of conventional morals further and no longer recognized any objective standard of good and evil, of justice and injustice; nature, says Thrasymachus in Plato's *Politeia*, knows only the rights of the strongest; the rights of the polis were only established by the weak in order to protect themselves against the might of the strong, the only ones of any value. Their specious reasoning led to our expressions "sophistry" and "sophism" (that is, deceptive argument). In the 2nd cent. A.D. a movement originated which was called the "Second Sophistic"; however, this movement was not rooted in philosophy, but in rhetoric.

SOPHOCLES (c. 496-406). The second of the three great Athenian tragic poets, born in Colonus near Athens. He received an education in music, gymnastics, and dancing, and is said to have led the paean sung by the chorus of boys after the victory of the battle of Salamis in 480. In 468 he achieved his first victory (over Aeschylus) in the *agon* (contest) for tragedy. He took an active part in public life and held high offices: in 443/2 he was the treasurer of the Delian League, in 440 the strategist with Pericles during the expedition against Samos. He was also a priest of a god of healing and, when the cult of Asklepios was introduced to Athens, S. allowed his home to be used for the God's worship until the temple be completed (he also composed a paean to this god). S. was greatly admired in his ripe old age; he retained his poetic gifts to the last. He was enormously successful; he won first prize 24 times, that is, with 96 of his 123 plays. Seven of his tragedies have survived and a fragment of a Satyric drama, *Ichneutai* (trackers), on papyrus. The extant plays are (probably in chronological order): 1) *Ajax*—his madness and suicide after he has been offended by the Atridae; 2) *Antigone* (probably 441); 3) *Oedipus Tyrannus* (c. 430); 4) *Trachiniae*—the last adventures and the death of Heracles (see TRACHIS); 5) *Electra* (c. 415-412); 6) *Philoctetes* (409)—the hero is brought back to Troy with the bow and arrows of Heracles ("happy ending" through a *deus ex machina*); 7) *Oedipus Coloneus* (performed posthumously in 401).

Just which philosophy S. wanted to disseminate is a matter of controversy; it is certain that he wanted to prophesy and not present the philosophical questions of the day to the public as problems, as Euripides did; but that is all that is certain. There are two opposed points of view: (a) S. was a traditionalist, a pious man; he preached submission to the will of the gods and to fate; (b) S. was a humanist; he was only interested in man and his personal experiences, to him the world of the gods was no more than a traditional institution, with little or no significance for the drama. Many variegations exist between these two views. One of the greatest difficulties in judging S. is that the chorus is not the spokesman of the poet. In the plays in which the poet sympathizes with the hero, the chorus is but the voice of mediocrity and conformism; the "moral" of the play is woven into the action and makes all kinds of subjective interpretations possible. The plot is subtly constructed and its development is less obvious than it is in Aeschylus' plots; in particular, the "reversal" (*peripeteia*, praised especially by Aristotle) of still hopeful expectations into total collapse (or the opposite, as in *Philoctetes*). S.'s heroes are truly heroic: they have a supernatural dimension. Whatever we may think about these differences of opinion—the meaning of S.'s dramas for present-day people lies in the manner in which heroic man reacts to the important problems of life and society; of human laws and those of the conscience; of suppression, freedom, and revolt; of acceptance of fate or rebellion against it; of egoism or altruism. In some ways S.'s plays are less "dramatic" than those of Aeschylus, and perhaps also less so than those of Euripides; but in other

ways they convey more to us (see also TRAGEDY; DRAMA).

SOPHONISBA. Daughter of Hasdrubal (3) and wife of Syphax, whom she won over to Carthage. When he was defeated by the Romans, she committed suicide in order not to fall into their hands (Liv. XXX, 12-15).

SORANUS of Ephesus (2nd cent. A.D.). Gr. physician. He practiced in Rome under Trajan and Hadrian and was the greatest methodologist of his period. Two treatises by him are extant: *On Fractures* and *On Midwifery and the Diseases of Women*, translated into Latin (6th cent.) and commonly used in the Middle Ages, and *The Life of Hippocrates*. Of his most important work *On Acute and Chronic Diseases* only a few fragments in Greek have survived, but we possess a complete Lat. translation (5th cent.).

SPAIN. See HISPANIA.

SPARTA. Capital of Laconia, situated at the foot of Mount Taygetus on the right bank of the Eurotas, the city was for a long time the main political and military power of Greece and leader of the Peloponnesian League. The site has been excavated by the British, and the fortress with the temple of Athena Chalkioikos, the agora, and the temple of Artemis Orthia have been identified. S. came into existence through synoecism of four or five villages, and was not enclosed by walls until the 2nd cent. B.C. "The men are the walls of S." was the customary saying. The Dorians who settled there, the remains of the original inhabitants of Laconia, living in Amyclae, Vaphio, and other places, were reduced in status to form the two lowest classes of society: the *perioikoi* (literally: those that dwell round and about or near) and the *heilotes*. The *perioikoi* were free inhabitants of the country towns and lived mainly by trade and industry; they enjoyed civil but not political privileges. The *heilotes* (Helots) were state slaves, lived in the country and worked the fields. In Laconia they were almost certainly descendants of the original Achaeans. The ruling class was formed by the Dorian *Spartiatai*, who called themselves "equals" and had all the political rights. At first they lived partly on the labor of the Helots, later entirely so. Kingship, abolished elsewhere in Greece, was retained here, namely a double kingship with two dynasties, the Agiadae and the Euripontidae. There was also a *gerousia* (a council of elders) and an *apella* (a military assembly) without much actual power. The authority was vested mainly in the five ephors (overseers), magistrates controlled all foreign relations, etc. The form of government is attributed to Lycurgus, and is said to have been modeled on that of Crete. In any case, it must have been revised at some time afterward, the power of the ephors, for example, was probably greatly increased in the 8th cent. B.C.

Until about 550 B.C., S. was a city with important commercial relations and a flourishing cultural life. Land for the growing population was sought in Messenia whose inhabitants were made Helots, although they were also Dorians. S. founded only one colony, Tarentum. In the 6th cent. the war against Tegea took place; eventually the Spartans concluded an alliance with this city. This was the beginning of the Peloponnesian League, of which only Argos did not become a member, It was this period that produced the social dogmatism that turned S. into the nation of soldiers described by tradition. The children were educated by the state; the men lived in community tents and took part in extensive military drills. S. possessed a certain supremacy during the Peloponnesian War of 480-79, even as far as the fleet was concerned (see EURYBIADES; PAUSANIAS), but was surpassed in many ways by Athens (see also THEMISTOCLES), S.'s rival in the Pentecontaëtia. The Peloponnesian War ended in a victory for S. through the intervention of Persia (see ANTALCIDAS). S.'s prestige rested entirely on figures like Lysander and Agesilaus. The number of *Spartiatai* declined disastrously due to the rigid social system, and efforts at reform (for example, by the kings) were constantly being prevented by the ephors. S.'s reputation as being invincible was lost for good at Leuctra (371); after this defeat the Peloponnesian League quickly dissolved (see EPAMINONDAS). During the Hellenistic period, Agis IV and Cleomenes III tried in vain to institute reforms. The latter was defeated by Antigonus III in 222. Finally S. was forced to become a member of the Achaean League and was incorporated into the Rom. province of Achaea after 146. It was destroyed by Alaric in A.D. 395; in the Middle Ages, Mistra arose on the site of S.

SPARTACUS. Gladiator from Thrace who, in Capua in 73-71 B.C., started a revolt of gladiators and slaves against Rome. Eventually he was at the head of 90,000 men whom he wanted to take back to their own countries, but they preferred to plunder Italy. S. was defeated by Crassus and the rest of his troops by Pompey. S. was a tragic figure who invoked powers he could eventually no longer control.

SPECTATUM VENIUNT, VENIUNT SPECTENTUR UT IPSAE. "They [the ladies] come to look [in the theater], [but especially] to be looked at" (Ov. *Ars. Am.* I, 99).

SPERCHEOS, River on the frontier of Thessaly and central Greece, emptying into the Malian Gulf near the Pass of Thermopylae.

SPEUSIPPUS. Pupil and nephew of Plato; his successor as the head of the Academy (347-339). Only a few fragments of his many writings have survived.

SPHACTERIA. Small island near Pylos in Messenia where in 425 B.C. a Spartan army (comprising 120 *Spartiatai,* among others) was trapped by the Athenians under Demosthenes (the general). Sparta sued for peace at once, but this was refused on the advice of Cleon. The occupation troops of S. were then imprisoned. This was the crisis of the Archidamian War for Athens (see PELOPONNESIAN WAR).

SPONDEE. See METER.

S.P.Q.R. *Senatus populusque Romanus.* "Senate and people of Rome."

STABIAE. Rom. coastal resort in Campania, buried in A.D. 79 when Mount Vesuvius erupted, rebuilt on another site.

STADIUM [Gr. *stadion*].

—(1) Gr. linear measure, approximately 197 yards.

—(2) The course for footraces amongst the Greeks. The stadia at Delphi, Athens,

Epidaurus, and especially Olympia are well known.

STAGIRUS (or STAGIRA). Gr. city in Chalcidice; Philip II destroyed it in 348 B.C., but rebuilt it to show his respect for Aristotle, whose birthplace it was.

STAMNOS. See VASE FORMS.

STATIUS, PUBLIUS PAPINIUS. (c. 40-96). Rom. poet from Neapolis, where his father was a school teacher and also a poet. S. became very popular in Rome as a competitor in poetry contests; his amiability won him many friends; his health was not very good. His extant works are an epic *Thebais* (twelve books), about the expedition of the Seven against Thebes, and an unfinished epic *Achilleis* (two books), about Achilles' youth. Also *Silvae,* thirty-two occasional poems, very polished; these show his ingenious style and give many interesting facts about his life. Once in a while he addresses Domitian with servile flattery, but this was probably inevitable during that period. The most famous of these poems is the one on Sleep. S. was still very famous in the Middle Ages, and, strangely enough, some considered him, to have been a Christian. Dante refers to him thus in his *Purgatorio.*

STAT SUA CUIQUE DIES. "Everyone's day [of death] is determined" (Virg. *Aen.* X, 467).

STATUS QUO. "The state in which"; the state existing. *Status quo ante bellum.* "State existing before the war."

STELE [Gr.]. An upright tablet or slab of stone (for example a boundary stone), in particular, tombstone, usually square, often tapering toward the top and sometimes with an ornament of flowers or leaves. The surface was usually decorated with a painting or relief. Among the archaic steles of elongated form, Aristion's is the most famous (National Museum, Athens); a somewhat older, originally almost square S. from Sparta, on which the deceased couple is depicted as heroes (see HEROES) should also be mentioned; figures, greatly reduced in size, offer sacrifices to the dead (Berlin, Altes Museum). In classical times, especially fine steles were produced in Attica; this type is broader and lower, so that more figures could be shown on it (example: the

S. of Hegeso). Steles were also made in higher and higher relief, so that the S. becomes a little "house," as it were, with almost free-standing figures. The scenes are often moving ones from everyday life; the handshake that unites the dead with members of the family is notable. According to some opinions, this is only a last farewell; according to others, it is a symbol of communion beyond the grave. These reliefs are of great significance for the history of art because the original sculptures of the great masters of that period have almost all been lost. These works, although executed by lesser artists and commissioned by private citizens, are nevertheless original Gr. works—the characteristics of style of a Phidias, a Polycletus, or a Lysippus, which were copied, are discernible. In about 315 B.C., Demetrius of Phaleron found it necessary to issue a decree against luxurious burials; this interrupted the creation of these elaborate steles. However, beautiful steles from other places, particularly Asia Minor, produced in later periods, have been found. See Appendix.

STENTOR. A Greek who participated in the Trojan war and whose voice was equivalent to that of fifty others. (Hom. *Il.* V, 785 ff.); hence, stentorian, extremely loud.

STESICHORUS (c. 640-c. 555). Gr. lyric poet; originally called Tisias, he received the name of S., actually a title meaning "marshal of choruses" from his office of directing choruses. He lived in Himera and wrote twenty-six books of poetry, of which only about fifty lines are extant. S. rendered epic subjects in lyric form, and thus influenced tragedy, perhaps even Virgil's *Aeneid.* His two poems on Helen were famous. In the first he tells the well-known story of her infidelity; this poem was said to have been a sacrilege because Helen was considered a goddess, particularly in Sparta. S. was stricken with blindness and his sight was not restored until he had written the poem *Palinodia,* a retraction. In this poem he declares that Helen had never been in Troy (as Euripides did later in his *Helena*). In another poem he tells of the unhappy love affair of the shepherd

Daphnis; this story can be found in later times, particularly among the bucolic poets (see THEOCRITUS).

STILICHO, FLAVIUS (c. 360-408). Statesman and general of the West Rom. Empire. S., a Vandal by birth, had a successful career under Theodosius whose son-in-law he became; later he became Honorius' father-in-law. He drove Alaric out of Greece in 397 and out of Italy in 401-2 and defeated the Germanic general Radagaisus at Faesulae in 406. When his position was no longer strong, he negotiated with Alaric and was put to death for treason.

STIPENDIUM. Among the Romans, a soldiers pay for one year of service; hence, stipend, settled pay or compensation for services.

STOA. Gr. portico; the S. Poecile in Athens, north of the Agora, decorated with murals by Polygnotus and others, is famous. In about 308 B.C. Zeno of Citium taught philosophy there; his adherents accordingly obtained the name of Stoics.

STOBAEUS, JOANNES (about A.D. 500). Gr. author, named after his native city Stobi (Macedonia). He wrote an anthology of poetry and prose, classified by subjects, for the instruction of his sons; fragments of Gr. works now lost have thus been preserved.

STOICS. Members of the school of philosophy established by Zeno of Citium in about 308 B.C. The history of this school can be divided into three periods: (a) Early Stoicism, represented by Zeno, Cleanthes, and Chrysippus. They were preoccupied mainly with ethics, but also with logic and the doctrine of knowledge. (b) Stoicism of the intermediate period, represented by Panaetius and Posidonius. Their interest in natural philosophy was revived, but this phase is important primarily because they began to put ethics into practice. This was also the period (1st-2nd cent. B.C.) in which the Romans became acquainted with Stoicism and in which Stoic ideas first penetrated the "Scipionic Circle" (see LAELIUS) and deeply influenced Cicero and others (Cato Minor, for example); the revised Stoic doctrine (now also embracing certain ideas of the Peripa-

tetics and the Academy) fitted in remarkably well with the ancient Rom. social virtues: self-control, intrepidity, devotion to duty; true republican virtues, personified in Cato Minor. (c) Late Stoicism: in the Rom. senate it was Stoics like Paetus Thrasea and Barea Soranus who opposed the emperors (particularly Nero) in the 1st cent. A.D., but courtiers like Lucius Annaeus Seneca also belonged to the S.; of the Greeks, Epictetus is particularly well known; in the 2nd cent. a Stoic, Marcus Aurelius, ascended the throne. During this phase the S. were interested almost exclusively in ethics. In the 3rd cent. the school disappeared, but having influenced Neoplatonism and some fathers of the church, the stoic doctrine remained influential for many centuries. The main principle of the Stoic doctrine is that only virtue can make man happy (compare ANTISTHENES); this virtue is based on knowledge (compare SOCRATES). The blows of fate are not dependent on our will, therefore we are "indifferent" to them (compare CYNICS); one must submit to them with apathy (*apatheia*); nevertheless, if it is possible to evade illness, death, etc., the wise man will choose more pleasant things (health, life, etc.); this in contrast to the Cynics. Nature is dominated by Reason (compare HERACLITUS) which is identical with God and Providence, and which reveals itself in Fate (*Fatum*). This gives nature its harmony and its meaning. Man's task is to live according to nature (see SECUNDUM NATURAM). Materially, Reason (*logos*) consists of fire, into which the cosmos is periodically absorbed, to re-emerge from it (this doctrine had already been attributed to Heraclitus).

STOLA. Long outer garment worn above the *tunica* by Rom. matrons; a long piece of material, with wide sleeves, worn hanging to the feet, gathered up below the breast by a girdle.

STRABO (64 B.C.-after A.D. 20). Gr. historian and geographer, follower of the principles of the Stoics. He came from Pontus, lived in Rome and Egypt for many years and undertook many journeys. All but a few fragments of his history, a continuation of Polybius has been lost. However, his *Geographica* in seventeen books is extant. Although it has little scientific value, it is an inexhaustible source of various topographical data, institutions, customs, etc.

STRATEGIST [Gr. from stratos, army and *agein,* to lead]. Commander of a military unit or a fleet in Greece. In Athens, in about 500 B.C., there was already a college of ten strategists, later presided over by a chief S. The strategists were annually elected in the public assembly. Only those were chosen for this high and influential office who were landowners in Attica. In the Hellenistic leagues of Greece, S. was also the title of the highest military and political leaders (see ACHAEA; AETOLIA).

STRATON of Lampsacus (on the Hellespont). Gr. philosopher, pupil of Theophrastus, leader of the school of Peripatetics from 287 until his death in about 270. He specialized in physics and transformed the Aristotelian philosophy into a materialistic science.

STYLOBATE. See ARCHITECTURAL ORDERS.

STYX. Actually a river in northern Arcadia that plunged down a rock to a wild gorge. The ancients considered this orifice the entrance to Hades and, as a result, soon made this river one of the most important of the underworld (Hdt. VI, 74).

SUB JUDICE. See ADHUC SUB JUDICE.

SUETONIUS TRANQUILLUS, GAIUS (c. 70-c. 140). Rom. historian. At first he was a lawyer, later he became the secretary of Hadrian. After he had been dismissed from this office (121), he devoted his time to literature. He was first of all a biographer. Only sections of his *De Viris Illustribus* are extant; *De Vita Caesarum* (the lives of the emperors from Caesar to Domitian) has surived almost complete. There is great disparity in this work: serious data alternate with scandalous stories. His work greatly influenced later biographers.

SUIDAS (c. A.D. 970). A Gr. lexicographer who compiled a most important lexicon from the works of ancient writers. It contains explanations of words, accounts of history, biographical data, scriptural and pagan subjects. The work

is put together inexpertly; nevertheless it is valuable because much of the information given is not being found elsewhere.

SULLA, LUCIUS CORNELIUS (138-78). Rom. general, dictator, political reformer; born of an obscure branch of the *Cornelia gens* (see SCIPIO; GRACCHI). Quaestor under Marius (107), he managed to take Jugurtha prisoner. S.'s senatorial career was not extraordinary; it was only during the Social War of 90-89 that he distinguished himself considerably. For this reason he was entrusted with the command of the army opposing Mithridates in 88. No sooner had S. left Rome than one of the *tribuni plebis* had this command transferred to Marius. As a consequence, S. marched on Rome at the head of his army. That was the beginning of the Civil War between Marius and S. It was the first time a Rom. army had marched on the city. The *populares* did not stay to fight it out; Marius fled, S. invaded the city, massacred many of Marius' followers, carried through emergency legislation, and then left for Greece to do battle with Mithridates. He had hardly left before his fellow consul Cinna recalled Marius. Now the *optimates* were annihilated, but many were able to flee and joined S. in Greece, where an anti-senate was established. In his war against Mithridates, S. had all the disadvantages: he had fewer troops, no fleet, and no funds; not only did Rome fail to support him, the city actively opposed him; nevertheless he managed to gain victory after victory, but the news from Italy was so alarming that he granted Mithridates fairly favorable terms of peace and, in 83, returned to Italy. Cinna was waiting for him with strong troops, but his power was diminished by the reversal of Pompey who became his adversary. Still, S. had a hard struggle before he was able to enter Rome as the victor; the Samnites in particular resisted determinedly; their resistance was broken during the horrible battle before the Colline Gate in Rome. The prisoners were mercilessly slain. S. now became dictator for an unspecified period. He officially assumed the surname "Felix" (blessed; the Gr. equivalent was *epaphroditos,* darling of Aphrodite, a surname chosen to counteract Mithridates' Dionysus ideology). All his opponents were killed and their property confiscated by means of ruthless proscriptions (see also CATILINA; CRASSUS). Then S. pushed through his program of reforms, which purported to give the senate absolute power again, and to strengthen the position of the *optimates* as a class; however, the individual optimates were not satisfied at all because an extensive system of guarantees made it impossible for one strong man to defy the will of the senate. The censors lost their power. The senate was to be automatically supplemented by ex-quaestors (then numbering twenty). Consuls and praetors were forced to remain in Italy during their term of office; a permanent system of proconsuls and propraetors was created for governing the provinces. Because the *tribuni plebis* (whose powers were also limited) were no longer allowed to hold senatorial office later in their careers, the tribunate lost all its attraction. Most of these laws were later abolished. The institution of the permanent law courts was the most lasting one. In 79, to everyone's surprise, S. suddenly gave up the dictatorship and retired to his estate, where he wrote his memoirs. He died the following year.

S. is one of the most problematical figures in the troubled history of the late Rom. Republic. He was in part a typical Rom. *nobilis,* in part a man inspired by a sort of Hellenistic ideology, in part a prototype of the monarchal aspirations of Caesar. His sudden abdication, unique in the history of the great tyrants, remains, in spite of many guesses, an enigma.

SUNIUM. The southeastern promontory of Attica, with a town of the same name upon it, containing ruins of an ancient temple. Many Egyptian articles found there, bear witness to the extensive overseas trade of Athens.

SUOVETAURILLA. Rom. sacrifice comprising a swine (*sus*), a sheep (*ovis*), and a bull (*taurus*), offered to ensure fertility (see LUSTRUM). Among other things, a S. is depicted on the Rom. altar, the Ara Pacis.

SUSA. Capital of the Persian empire with a huge palace built by Darius I. In 331

B.C., Alexander the Great conquered S. It was renamed Seleucia under the Seleucids. Under the Parthians it was still an autonomous Gr. city.

SUUM CUIQUE. "To teach one his own" (Cic. *De Leg.* I, 6, 19; compare Tac. *Ann.* IV, 35).

SYBARIS. Gr. city in Lucania, founded by Achaeans in about 720 B.C.; the luxuriance of the inhabitants was proverbial. S. was destroyed by the neighboring Croton in 510 B.C. Thurii was founded near S. in 443 B.C. (see also PANHELLENISM).

SYMMACHUS, QUINTUS AURELIUS (c. 345-402). Rom. orator and politician. He held high office (consul in 391); defended decaying paganism against Christianity; his published letters (to Ausonius, among others), divided into ten books on the same plan as those of Pliny the Younger, consist of nine books of personal and one book of official correspondence. The letters are carefully composed, and afford much information about the author's life and times.

SYMPOSIUM. In ancient Greece, a drinking-party, usually following the banquet proper, with music, singing, and conversation. A master of the feast (*symposiarchos*), chosen by the casting of dice, presided at the table and led the conversation. Both Plato and Xenophon wrote dialogues entitled *Symposium;* as a result the S.'s form became a literary genre (see also ATHENAEUS; PETRONIUS).

SYNOECISM [Gr. *synoikismos*]. The joining of several small communities (villages or towns) into one polis either because the population went to live there, or because one city became the political center (see also MEGALOPOLIS).

SYPHAX. The most powerful Numidian ruler in about 210 B.C. During the Second Punic War he tried to retain the friendship of both adversaries, but finally took Carthage's side (see also SOPHONISBA); defeated and taken prisoner by Laelius and Masinissa in 203 B.C. He died in Rom. imprisonment.

SYRACUSE. Colony of Corinth, founded in 734 B.C.; it soon became the largest city of the Gr. world, partly due to its favorable location with a beautiful natural harbor. The town of S. was originally confined to the island of Ortygia, where the fountain of one of the Nereids, Arethusa, was situated. Soon a new part of the city, Achradina, was built opposite the island and was connected with it by a dam; later other districts were added. At first, S. had an aristocratic form of government; in about 485 Gelon became tyrant and made Syracuse the most powerful city of Sicily. He defeated the Carthaginians at Himera (480). His brother Hiero I continued his policies; after his death in 467, S. became democratic. It had to share the power with Agrigentum; a revolt of the native Siculi, led by Ducetius, was suppressed. In the meantime, Athens was giving the Ionian Sicilian cities more and more support against S.; but the large expedition of 415-13 was repulsed (see PELOPONNESIAN WAR; NICIAS; ALCIBIADES; HERMOCRATES; GYLIPPUS). Renewed pressure by Carthage led to the rise of another tyrant, Dionysius I (see also DIONYSIUS II; DION). Timoleon repulsed the Carthaginians again, but his democratic reforms were soon eliminated by Agathocles. After that, S.'s power declined quickly; even Pyrrhus could not help indefinitely.

In reality, S. became a puppet state of Rome under Hiero II, and after his death, S. became the ally of Carthage. It was conquered by the Rom. general Marcellus in 212 and then became the capital of the Rom. province of Sicilia. Several Gr. temples, a Gr. theater, and a Rom. amphitheater have survived on the site of S. The coins of S. are perhaps the most beautiful ones minted in ancient times.

SYRIA. District bounded by Asia Minor to the north, Mesopotamia to the east, and Palestine to the south, center of commercial relations with the East, and terminal point for overseas trade, with Mycenaean Greece, among other places. In the 2nd millennium B.C., S. was part of the Hittite empire. From about 550-333 it was a Persian satrapy (see SATRAP); after Alexander the Great conquered it in 333, its possession became a bone of contention between the Diadochi. After 301 it was the nucleus of the Seleucid empire. In 83 it was conquered by Tigranes; when he fell (63 B.C.) Pompey conquered it for Rome. S. became an important province during imperial times, protected by a large army.

T-U-V

TABULARIUM. See CAPITOL.
TACITUS, CORNELIUS (c. 55-after 115). The most abstruse Rom. historian; pursued his official career under Vespasian, Titus, and Domitian; married a daughter of Agricola in 77; consul in 97; proconsul of Asia in about 112.

One of his earliest works was the *Dialogus de Oratoribus* (dialogue about orators). It treats of the reasons for the decay of eloquence in imperial times and the conclusion is reached that the loss of political freedom is responsible. It is sometimes assumed that this small book was already written in about 80, but was prudently concealed from the tyrant

Domitian, and published only after his death in 96. This assumption is made because its style is very different from that of T.'s other works. It is also possible that it was written in about 101, and then, the difference in style can be attributed to the difference in genre. Like Sallust, T. commenced his historical works by writing two historical monographs, written in short succession in 98: a biography of his father-in-law Agricola, *De Vita et Moribus Iulii Agricolae*, important for its history of Britain during that period; and *De Situ, Moribus, ac Populis Germaniae*, a description of Germany at that time, a work originally intended as part of the *Historiae,* already planned by T. His two main works (c. 105-115) followed: (a) *Historiae,* probably in fourteen books, of which I-IV and the first half of V remain extant, comprising the history of the Year of the Three Emperors and its aftermath (see BATAVI; JUDAEA; his fabulous narrative on ancient Jewish history is interesting); the complete work covers the period to the death of Domitian in 96; the letters of Pliny the Younger about the eruption of Mount Vesuvius were written for this work. Ammianus Marcellinus later wrote a sequel. (b) *Ab Excessu Divi Augusti,* usually called *Annales* (by T. himself in IV, 32), the history, in sixteen books, of the Julian-Claudian house, beginning with the death of Augustus. Books I-IV are complete, the end of V and the beginning of VI are lost (the reign of Tiberius) as well as VII, VIII, IX, and X. The second half of XI, all of XII-XIV (the reign of Claudius to the last years of Nero) are extant. Although the *Historiae* is probably the most balanced work from a literary point of view, the last is certainly the most profound. T. also planned to write a book about his own period.

T. claims to write without prejudice and prepossession (*sine ira et studio*), but actually he is full of rancor toward a regime that he detests; still, he understands that the old Republic is gone forever. According to him, the best form of government that can be achieved is an enlightened principate like that of Trajan (see PRINCEPS). His point of view is typical of a Rom. senator. The occurrences and the social development in the provinces only interest him in so far as they serve as a background for the exploits of the Rom. aristocracy and members of the imperial family (for example, Germanicus). His style is terse and sometimes difficult to fathom. He often terminates a dissertation with an opinion (*sententia*) of general significance; some of these may be enigmatic to the reader. Although he distorted some character (Tiberius, Claudius), his insight into the motivation for human actions is so profound that his work is nevertheless a monument of the art of writing history.

TACITUS, MARCUS CLAUDIUS. See MILITARY EMPERORS.

TAENARUM. The southernmost tip of the Peloponnesus; of three peninsulas, T. is the one in the center. A temple of Poseidon stood near the south cape. Adjacent to the temple is a natural cave into which Heracles was said to have descended to drag Cerberus up from Hades.

TALENT. See COINAGE.

TANAGRA. Town in Boeotia near the frontier of Attica, native city of Corinna; numerous terra cotta statues, placed in graves as funerary offerings, and dating from the 4th-3rd centuries B.C., have been found there.

TANAIS. The Gr. name for the river Don and for the city at its estuary. An important trade route to the interior of what is now Russia, followed the Tanais valley.

TAORMINA. See TAUROMENIUM.

TARENTUM [Gr. *Taras*]. The most powerful city in southern Italy; trade relations between the native population and Greece were maintained as early as Mycenaean times and the 10th-8th centuries B.C. The Spartans founded a permanent Gr. settlement there in about 700 B.C. In the 5th cent., T. became a democracy. T.'s prosperity reached a peak in the 4th cent. B.C. The city sent for Pyrrhus to come to Italy (280); after his retreat Rome conquered it; it deserted to Hannibal in 213 and was reconquered and sacked by Rome in 209 B.C. After that it declined.

TARPEIAN ROCK. See CAPITOL.

TARQUINII. Capital of the Confederation of Twelve Cities of Etruria, near what is now Corneto. Beautiful painted tombs have been found there.

TARQUINIUS PRISCUS. According to tradition, the fifth king of Rome, reigned from 616-579. Of Gr. origin, he came to Rome by way of Etruria. The last is reliable; it is known that the Etruscans ruled Rome during that period. The construction of the temple of Jupiter Capitolinus (see CAPITOL) and other public buildings was attributed to him.

TARQUINIUS SUPERBUS. According to tradition, the seventh and last king of Rome, reigned from 534-510. He is considered to be a historical (Etruscan) figure, although he may have been confused with Tarquinius Priscus in many ways. Tradition says that the people revolted, led by Lucius Junius Brutus, to avenge the rape of Lucretia, perpetrated by T.'s son. This rebellion put an end to T.'s reign, and Rom. kingship (see REX; PORSENNA).

TARSUS. City in Cilicia, residence of the kings and the Persian satraps; renamed "Antiochia on the Cydnus" by the Seleucids; the birthplace of the Apostle Paul (the Jewish community of T. was greatly Hellenized). Julianus the Apostate was buried there. The city's main source of income was the linen industry.

TARTESSUS. A region and a city in southwest Spain (probably the Tarshish of the Old Testament); center of trade in tin and silver with Britain and Phoenicia. In about 650 B.C. it was visited by the Greek Colaeus from Samos and in about 600 by traders from Phocaea. Excavations at this site (the mouth of the Guadalquivir) failed to give results, probably because the coastline or the riverbed has shifted. T. was later confused with Cadiz.

TAUROMENIUM. Now called Taormina. Gr. city in eastern Sicily, founded by Siculi (see SICILY) in about 400 B.C. They were expelled by the soldiers of Dionysius I. Remains of a Gr. theater are preserved there.

TAYGETUS. Mountain range in the south Peloponnesus (highest peak 7,904 ft.), the western boundary of the territory of Sparta.

TEGEA. City in southeastern Arcadia on the route between Sparta, Argos, and Corinth. In about 550, T. became the first member of the Peloponnesian League, having been besieged by Sparta for a long period. The city's greatest monument, the temple of Athena Alea, burned down in 395 B.C. and was rebuilt with work by the sculptor Scopas.

TEMPE, VALE OF. Valley of the Peneus River in northern Thessaly. As a result of its strategic position it served as the front line during the defense against Xerxes in 480 B.C., but it had to be abandoned because of the actions of the Thessalians (see LARISSA). T. is known as one of the most charming of the vallies of Greece.

TEMPLE. Among the Greeks and Romans, solely the house of the god; this is the most fundamental difference between a T. and a church or synagogue; the latter are also the houses of the community (for example, the French *église,* church, is derived from the Gr. *ekklēsia,* popular assembly); the service did not take place *in* the T. but *in front of* it. Originally, neither the Greeks nor the Romans had temples. The Greeks worshiped the gods in a sacred wood or a grotto. The temples mentioned in Homer refer to arbors dedicated to the gods. In Latin, *templum* literally means "space," the holy space in the sky or on the earth marked out by the augurs for the purpose of taking auspices. The first real Gr. temples originated in the 8th cent. B.C. They were built of wood, later of stone. The oldest Gr. temple extant is the Heraeum, or temple of Hera, in Olympia (6th cent. B.C.). The concept of a temple being a "house of the god" can be seen in the temple configuration: The central enclosure (cella) as well as the front vestibule (*pronaos*) were already known in Mycenaean homes (see HOUSES); in addition, there is often a rear vestibule (*opisthodomos*) and a colonnade (*peripteros*) around the cella; sometimes this is a double colonnade (*dipteros*). Smaller temples (the temple of Nike in Athens and the treasure houses in Delphi) have no colonnade (temple *in antis*). The main temple entrance always faces east. (For the various architectural styles see ARCHITECTURAL ORDERS.) The most perfectly preserved Gr. temples are the Hephaesteum, or so-called Theseum in Athens and the T. of Poseidon in Paestum. Rom. temples were influenced by those of Greece and Etruria. The Romans adopted the well-known Gr. types, but developed a separate Corinthian order (see COLUMN). From the Etruscans they adopted a more elevated type of construction with the emphasis on frontal architecture, high pediments, and three connected *cellae* (for example the Capitol).

TERENTIUS AFER, PUBLIUS (c. 190-159). Commonly called Terence. Rom. comic poet from Carthage, of African origin. He came to Rome as a slave, was

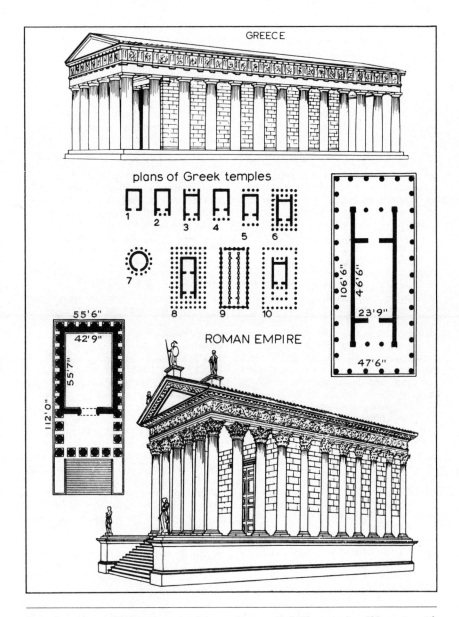

Temples. Above: Hephaesteum in Athens, the so-called Theseum (c. 403 B.C.), with the ground plan below it on the right; center: types of Greek temples: 1. *Megaron,* 2. *Temple with front vestibule,* 3. *Temple with front and back vestibules,* 4. *Prostylos,* 5. *Amphiprostylos,* 6. *Peripteros,* 7. *Tholos,* 8. *Dipteros,* 9. *Pseudoperipteros,* 10. *Pseudodipteros; below: the so-called Maison Carré in Nîmes (16 B.C.), one of the best preserved Roman temples extant, with the ground plan at the left.*

freed by his master Terentius Lucanus, and soon became a member of the "Scipionic Circle" (see LAELIUS). In 166-160 he wrote six comedies modeled after the Attic New Comedy (particularly Menander). They are much more refined and humane than Plautus' plays, but many thought them less humorous. Caesar called T. "half a Menander." Not all the plays met the public approval. For example, during the first performance of *Hecyra* (mother-in-law), the spectators left to watch ropedancers in the vicinity. In later centuries T.'s plays were enjoyed as reading matter, especially for the many sayings they contained (see, for example, QUOT HOMINES; HOMO SUM). But unlike Plautus' plays, they were not imitated by later poets. His apologetic prologues are interesting: T. refutes the critics and defends his practice of constructing plots by combining those of several earlier plays. A commentary on T. by Donatus is extant.

TERPANDER of Lesbos (7th cent. B.C.). Gr. poet and musician; said to have added three strings to the original lyre of four strings. He was the first to compose hymns for solo with lyre accompaniment and established a school of music in Sparta. Only a few fragments of his lyric poetry are extant.

TERPSICHORE. See MUSES.

TERRA COTTA. Unglazed decorative pottery, used particularly in Greece for small figurines, already found in Minoan art, and generally since the 7th cent. B.C. The T. C. statuettes of Tanagra are famous. The archaic Gr. temples had T. C. roofing tiles. Beautiful sarcophagi from this period have also been found. The Etruscans liked to use T. C. for temple sculpture.

TERRA SIGILLATA. Pottery bearing the maker's seal (*sigillum*), modern name for the red-glazed pottery made in Italy in about 30 B.C. and especially in Gaul and the Rhineland after about 20 B.C., probably modeled after examples from Asia Minor. Originally this pottery was not made on a wheel, but poured into a mould. The seals tell us the various places in which the pottery was produced, some of the main ones were to be found in Gaul.

TERTULLIANUS, QUINTUS SEPTIMIUS FLORENS (c. 160-c. 230). The first important Christian Lat. author; a Carthaginian lawyer who converted to Christianity in about 195. He wrote a defense of Christianity against paganism, the *Apologia,* papers against the heretics (especially the adherents to Gnosticism), and other dogmatic works; he also attacked luxury and immortality, which prompted him to join the ascetic sect of Montanists. More than thirty of his works in Latin have survived; his Gr. writings have been lost. His language is very difficult to read; he created a style of his own and, by using many neologisms, laid the foundation for Lat. Christian terminology. He was obviously well-read in antique literature, but sharply opposed the influence of classic civilization on Christianity.

TEUTOBURGER WALD. The range of hills in Germany where a Rom. army under the command of Varus was destroyed by Arminius in A.D. 9. The identification with the present T.W. is very uncertain.

TEUTONS. See CIMBRI.

TEXTUAL CRITICISM. The science of classifying the texts handed down and of restoring them to their original form as far as possible. This demands, above all, preparatory work in the field of Paleography. T. C. itself is an attempt to arrange the manuscripts into genealogical order (*recensio*) by means of comparison; sometimes it will be discovered that all of them are derived from one existing manuscript. As a rule, the common "ancestor" will have to be reconstructed; it is known as the archetype; between this manuscript and the original one by the author, there are always a few lost copies in which errors may have been made during transcription, so that an attempt at criticizing the archetype can also be made (*emendatio*). During the 19th cent. especially, scholars went to great lengths in this field, but their findings were largely superseded by the results obtained by papyrology—it was found that the texts on papyrus generally predated the oldest manuscripts considerably, thus rendering useless the so-called conjectures found earlier. Since then, T. C. has become much more conservative.

THALES of Miletus (1st half of the 6th cent. B.C.). The first Gr. philosopher, founder of Ionian natural philosophy (see also ANAXIMANDER; ANAXIMENES), counted among the Seven Sages. He was also a statesman, and advised the Ionians to unite against Persia. However, long before that, he had made use of the strong ties existing between Ionia and the hinterland by traveling through the Near East. He was said to have studied astronomy in Egypt, and the science of the Chaldeans either in Babylonia itself, or at home. Armed with this knowledge, he was able to predict the eclipse of the sun that took place on May 28, 585 in Asia Minor. This is the only actual fact we know about his life. He wrote no books; he was only known through his pronouncements. He established Gr. natural philosophy by methodically asking the question: "From what did the world originate?" His answer was: Water (the fluid element); this is the *archè* (primordial matter) of the universe. A very plausible postulation, for no life is possible without water, moreover, the life of the Ionians was completely dominated by the ocean, the liquid element, the gateway to their sources of prosperity. Seeking an *archè* was to preoccupy his successors constantly; Heraclitus, although he was also an Ionian, was the first to posit the problem in a different way. Tradition also say that T. generalized Egyptian methods of mensuration and attributed the periodical Nile floods to a natural cause (but to the wrong one).

T. is primarily important because he was the first to seek a definite theoretic principle, that would govern the constant changes in matter. This marks the beginning of the history of European philosophy.

THALIA. See MUSES.

THAPSUS. City on the African coast, where Caesar conquered the remains of Pompey's army in 46 B.C.

THASOS. Island in the north Aegean Sea, colonized by Paros in about 680 B.C., famous for its gold mines, which were exploited by the inhabitants and by those on the opposite coast of Thrace. A member of both Attic Leagues; dominated by Macedonia from 340 and by Rome after 190 B.C.

THEATER [Gr. *theatron*]. In Greece and Rome, the place where dramatic performances were given out of doors. The T. originally consisted of two sections: the orchestra and seats for the audience (the *theatron* proper). The seats were often cut from the natural rock of a hill in semicircular, concentric tiers, one above another, then covered with wooden seats. The third section, the *skènè*, which is the forerunner of our stage, did not appear

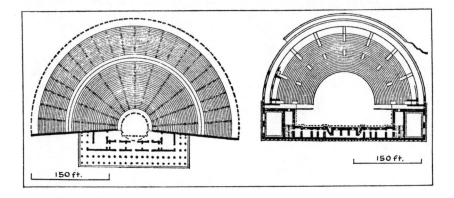

Ground plans of the Greek theater at Epidaurus (left) and the Roman theater at Arausio (Orange).

until later (see ORCHESTRA). In Rom. theaters, all three sections were present. Later, some of the theaters were built of marble, replacing wooden scaffolding erected for the spectators. The natural acoustics are sometimes amazing, particularly, keeping in mind just how large the auditorium could be (for example, the T. in Megalopolis seated 20,000). The T. of Dionysus in Athens, in its present (rather damaged) shape, dates from about 330 B.C.; there are well-preserved Gr. theaters in Epidaurus, Syracuse, Tauromenium, and other places; Rom. theatres in Arausio and Athens (Odeum of Herodes Atticus).

THEBES. The biggest city in Boeotia; already powerful during the Mycenaean period, as can be deduced from the sagas (Oedipus). In the 7th-6th centuries B.C. it led the Boeotian League, but lost this position temporarily by collaborating with the Persians in 480-79. Its aristocratic government and society are reflected in the poems of Pindar. Because of its hereditary enmity to Plataea, which was allied with Athens, it fought on the Spartan side during the Peloponnesian War. However, in the Corinthian War (see CORINTH) it turned against Sparta. The Spartan occupation, encamped in the citadel since 382, was expelled in 379 (see PELOPIDAS). Following this, especially after the battle of Leuctra (371), T. had the hegemony in Greece for a brief period (see EPAMINONDAS). Then it became violently anti-Macedonian, joined Athens in resisting Philip II at Chaeronea, and also revolted against Alexander the Great; this ended in its destruction in 335 B.C. It was never again a great city.

THEMIS. Gr. goddess of law and order, protectress of popular assemblies. according to Hesiod, she was the second consort of Zeus. As the daughter of Earth she was also a guardian of oaths and a prophetess. Ovid (*Met.* I, 321) describes her as the goddess of Delphi before the advent of Apollo. The Romans identified her with Justitia (she is pictured with a blindfold and scales).

THEMISTOCLES (c. 528-459). Athenian statesman, established the Athenian navy; born of a noble but not rich family. In 493/2 he became archon and con-

tinued with the fortification of the Piraeus. Even then he advocated checking the dangerous naval forces of Persia, but for the time being the policy of Miltiades, who pinned his faith on the hoplite army, prevailed. During the crisis of Marathon, T. supported Miltiades' policy loyally, but after 490 he made his plans for a fleet known again. He succeeded in having the revenues of the silver mines of Laurium used to build up a fleet (483). Aristides, who opposed him in this, was banished (see OSTRACISM). When Xerxes attacked, Athens had the most powerful fleet in continental Greece (see also GELOX). Half of the fleet was employed at Artemisium; the other half was used to cover the evacuation of Athens. Until recently it was assumed that the evacuation was an emergency measure, taken after the fall of Thermopylae. However, an inscription found recently at Troezen makes it clear that T. had foreseen the outcome of the battles of Artemisium and Thermopylae, and had ordered the city evacuated in advance as a precautionary measure. The exiles (including Aristides) were recalled, and the battle of Salamis became T.'s "finest hour." According to Herodotus, T. hastened Xerxes' defeat and precipitous retreat by sending two misleading messages; some people consider these stories to be anecdotes, but, in any case, the first message is already mentioned in 472 in *The Persians*, written by the eye witness Aeschylus. After the victory, T. advocated a severe policy with regard to Persia and Sparta. He built walls around Athens in a hurry—to the fury of Sparta, which could only interpret this measure as being aimed at her, since Persia had just been defeated. The fight against Persia, under the combined leadership of T. and Aristides, was also continued forcefully and the Delian League was established. Now Athens was just as powerful as Sparta. The fact that this Athenian power was based mainly on the fleet, had political repercussions within Athens too, because the poorest of her citizens were the ones who had served as oarsmen and had protected the country. Now they were able to demand more political influence. However, eventually, the moderate conservatives under Cimon, who wanted friendship with Sparta, prevailed. T. was ostracized and went to Argos. He kept on agitating against Sparta from there; when the Spartans accused him of being a party to Pausanias' treachery in Athens, he was outlawed (468). After an adventurous flight by way of Corcyra, Epirus, and Macedonia, he went to Persia, where Artaxerxes I appointed him overlord of Magnesia. He lived there for years, a local potentate. Magnesian coins of the period, bearing his likeness, have been found (see also end of PERICLES' article).

THEOCRITUS of Syracuse (1st half of the 3rd cent. B.C.). Gr. poet, main representative of the bucolic genre (Arcadian poetry). T. lived at the court of Hiero II in Syracuse, later on Cos and with Ptolemy II in Alexandria. At first he devoted himself to lyric poetry in general. Possibly he was attracted to the bucolic genre by Stesichorus' portrayal of the shepherd Daphnis. He became a pastoralist on Cos, and continued to use this genre in Alexandria. His poetry combines realism with romanticism, and exhibits typical Alexandrine scholarliness and a true appreciation of nature with fine character drawing. He also practiced the epyllion (see EPIC) and mime. In addition to the colloquial language of his times, Attic koinē, T. used several Gr. dialects, especially a literary Doric dialect (see also IDYL).

THEODORIC the Great (456-526). King of the Ostrogoths; was educated in an atmosphere of ancient culture in Byzantium; sent to conquer Italy by the East-Rom. emperor. At Ravenna, T. killed Odoacer (493) and then founded an almost independent kingdom of the Ostrogoths in Italy. Toward the end of his reign several revolts against him broke out (see BOETHIUS). These put an end to his policy of reconciliation, aimed at a combining Germanic domination with ancient Rom. political ideals. His mausoleum in Ravenna has survived. He lived on in the sagas as Dietrich von Bern (that is, T. of Verona).

THEODOSIUS. Name of:
—T. I (346-395). Surnamed the Great. Rom. emperor. He became emperor in the East in 379, and, after two civil wars, managed to restore the unity of the Rom. Empire once more. Threatened by an invasion of Goths, T., in an act of diplomacy, introduced many of them into the Rom. army. However, as a result, the army lost its Rom. characteristics. He placed his sons Arcadius and Honorius under the guardianship of Stilicho. He ordered many pagan temples destroyed, and terminated the Olympic Games (see OLYMPIA).

—T. II. (401-450). Son of Arcadius. East-Rom. emperor, reigned from 408. During his rule, wars with Persia were waged and Attila also was a source of trouble, but was pacified as much as possible. In 438 the Codex Theodosianus was published—the first official imperial code of law.

THEOGNIS of Megara (c. 540 B.C.). Gr. elegiac poet. We possess under his name an elegy of 1,389 lines; the poem consists mainly of admonitions to a certain Cyrnus. It is evident that it was edited and lengthened during a later period, so that it is exceedingly difficult to ascertain just what T. wrote himself. T., a confirmed aristocrat, violently attacked the rising tide of democracy. His outspokenness during the political struggle probably resulted in his exile. T. is an excellent source of knowledge for social tensions of his epoch.

THEOPHRASTUS of Eresus (372-287). Gr. philosopher whose real name was Tyrtanus. Originally, a pupil of Plato in Athens, he later studied under Aristotle, who is said to have given him the surname of T. (divine speaker). When Aristotle left Athens in 323, T. succeeded him in the leadership of the Peripatetic school, during which period it flourished and reached its peak of expansion. Although T. did not have the originality of thought of Aristotle, nor that of the founders of the Stoa, or Epicurus, he nevertheless was master of the entire range of Aristotle's learnedness: he also had the gift of being able to work out and sytematize the master's doctrine. Under his leadership the Lyceum became a center of professional sciences, while the Epicureans and the Stoics took over the practice of the actual philosophy. Of his many works on the most divergent subjects, we still possess

On the History of Plants, part of *On the Origin of Plants,* and *Characters,* lively descriptions of human types; this kind of writing was often copied in later centuries.

THEOPOMPUS of Chios (4th B.C.). Gr. historian, pupil of Socrates. He and Ephorus were the two most important Gr. historians of the rhetorical school. Only fragments remain his two large histories: *Hellenica,* a continuation of Thucydides, covering the period from 411-394; *Philippica,* treating of the life and times of Philip II. His slandering of well-known politicians was so notorious that he was forced to flee, taking refuge with Ptolemy I in Alexandria. There, however, he was not favorably received and was almost executed by Ptolemy. Only fragments of T.'s works have survived. The so-called *Hellenica Oxyrhynchia* (see OXYRHYNCHUS) is sometimes (probably incorrectly) attributed to him.

THERA. Island in the south Aegean Sea, later called Santorin, or part of the crater of an ancient volcano. Inhabitants of T. founded Cyrene in about 630 B.C. German archaeologists have found many remains from Hellenistic and Rom. times there.

THERAMENES (c. 455-404). Athenian politician who played an important part as the leader of the moderated oligarchic party in the revolution of 411 (see also PISANDER). He negotiated for peace with Sparta in 405/4 (see PELOPONNESIAN WAR). After the peace he was elected to the oligarchy of the Thirty Tyrants, but soon came into conflict with the extremist Critias and was executed (Xen. *Hell.* II, 3, 23 ff.).

THERMAE [Lat. hot springs, warm baths, from Gr. *thermai,* plural of *thermē,* heat]. Among the Romans, the name for monumental public baths; the first were built by Agrippa in 33 B.C., in combination with a gymnasium. The more recent T. were often much more ostentatious; the largest were built by Caracalla and Diocletian. Outside of Rome, T. were also built, for example, the ones in Trier (Trèves, ancient Augusta Trevirorum). Recent excavations have led to the belief that these are the biggest ever built by the Romans. Sometimes it was possible to make use of natural warm springs, as in Bath in western England. During imperial times, the T. were social and cultural meeting places for all classes of the population, as were the Gr. gymnasia. The focal point was always the actual baths, embracing a

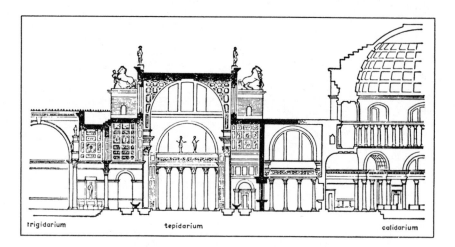

frigidarium   tepidarium   calidarium

Reconstruction of a section of the thermae of Caracalla

swimming pool, a cold bath (*frigidarium*), a sudatorium, or sweating room (*laconicum*), a lukewarm bath (*tepidarium*), and a hot bath (*caldarium*). There were also rooms for physicians and masseurs, lounges, gymnasia, and sometimes museums and libraries.

THERMOPYLAE [Gr. hot gates]. Narrow pass between Mount Oeta and the Malian Gulf in central Greece, source of hot springs. Although it was an ideal strategic position—according to Herodotus (VII, 176), only one wagon at a time could pass the narrowest point—still it was forced several times by outflanking movements, in 480 B.C. by Xerxes (see LEONIDAS), in 279 by Brennus (2), and in 191 B.C. by Manius Acilius Glabrio fighting against Antiochus III. The mountain pass of T. has over the course of the centuries become a broad stretch of land due to silt deposits of the Spercheos River

THERON (c. 530-472). Tyrant of Akragas (Agrigentum), reigned from 488. He was the father-in-law of Gelon, with whom he defeated the Carthaginians at Himera in 480. T., a great lover of art and culture, made Akragas one of the most beautiful Gr. cities. Pindar lived at his court and dedicated two Olympian odes to him.

THESAURUS [from Gr. *thesauros*, a store laid up, treasure]. Term used (already by Pausanias) for the treasure houses maintained by the various Gr. cities at sanctuaries such as Delphi and Olympia. At Delphi, the Siphnian (see CARYATIDS) and the Athenian one have survived. The thesauri served not only as store houses for the votive offerings given to the god by the citizens, but also as lodgings for official delegations to the Panhellenic games (see also TEMPLE).

THESEUS. The national hero of Greece. According to legend, he was a son of a princess from Troezen and the Athenian king Aegeus (or, according to another story, Poseidon). Legend tells of his delivering Athens from its tribute of nine youths and nine maidens to the Cretan Minotaur; his capture of the Marathonian bull; his killing of evil characters such as Sinis, who tore travelers asunder between two pine trees, Siron,

who threw wayfarers from a cliff into the ocean, and Procrustes, who tortured them on his two proverbial beds. Further legends make T. take part in the journey of the Argonauts, rescue Persephone from the underworld, join the Calydonian hunt, and help Pirithous and the Lapithae against the Centaurs. T. is said to have united Attica by synoecism, reorganized the Panathenaea, and founded the Isthmian Games.

T.'s adventures are depicted on the metopes of the best preserved temple in Athens. For this reason it is still called the Theseum, although it is actually a temple of Hephaestus. In Gr. drama, T. is represented as the champion of Athenian ideals of freedom.

THESMOPHORIA. An autumn festival in honor of Demeter, celebrated in many parts of Greece, but especially in Athens. Only married women were chosen to preside over the sacred functions. The most interesting rite consisted of throwing piglets into subterranean caves; the putrified remains of these animals were later laid on an altar and mixed with seed grain. One of Aristophanes' plays is called *Thesmophoriazousae* (women celebrating T.).

THESPIS. See TRAGEDY.

THESSALONICA. City in Macedonia, founded in about 315 B.C. by Cassander (the present-day Salonika). The city soon became the most important Macedonian port and later the capital of the Rom. province. In Rom. times it had a large Jewish community, from which sprang one of the earliest Christian communities, mentioned in the epistles of the Apostle Paul. After Constantinople, it was the second city of the Byzantine Empire; many Byzantine objects of art have been found there.

THESSALY. A district of northern Greece, consisting mainly of plains; as a result T. was richer in wheat and cattle than other parts of Greece. When the Gr. tribes entered the district, they made use of existing elevations to build their citadels; several cities originated in this manner, including Larissa, Pherae, and Pharsalus. T. supported Athens in the struggle against Sparta, but not very effectually. In the 4th cent., a battle took place between the tyrants of Pherae (Lycophron and Alexander) and the Aleuadae of Larissa that devastated the country. Alone, Jason of Pherae restored the country's unity and power temporarily, but in about 350 B.C., T. was taken by Macedonia, and, in 148 B.C., by Rome. Important prehistoric remains have been found in Dimini and Sesklo among other places.

THETIS. See NEREUS.

THOLOS (or BEEHIVE) TOMBS. See MYCENAE.

THRACE. District east of Macedonia and north of the Aegean Sea. The prehistoric population had a significant culture of its own. After 700 B.C., Greeks settled on the the coast, establishing important trade relations. Darius I conquered it; it was also temporarily subjected to Persia under Xerxes. During the 5th cent. B.C., a Thracian empire was established under Sitalces, while the Greeks (especially the Athenians) constantly showed their interest in the coastal regions due to the gold mines of Mount Pangaeus. These mines later attracted Philip II of Macedonia, who conquered the southern part of T. In about 300 B.C., Lysimachus ruled in T. During Rom. times, T. remained independent for a long period, but in 46 B.C. the Emperor Claudius annexed it for good.

THRACIANS. An Indo-European people, inhabitants of Thrace, comprising the Getae, the Bessi, and the Odrysians; it was a warlike people (Ares was said to have been a Thracian) and they had a barbarian and ecstatic religion, of which the Greeks adopted several elements (see ORPHISM). Dionysus also had Thracian affinities.

THRASEA, PUBLIUS PAETUS. Rom. senator and Stoic philosopher; consul in A.D. and leader of the senate opposition to Nero. In 66 he and Soranus Barea were accused and forced to commit suicide by Nero, during which his courageous attitude aroused general admiration (Tac. *Ann.* XVI, 21-35).

THRASYBULUS. Name of:
—(1) Tyrant of Miletus in about 600 B.C., who defended Miletus' independence against Alyattes of Lydia.
—(2) Athenian statesman and general, leader of the democratic opposition to

the oligarchic revolution of 411 B.C. (see PISANDER), and the revolution of 404 (see CRITIAS). He conquered the Piraeus in 403, and then restored democracy in Athens with the approval of Sparta; he also played a part during the Corinthian War (see CORINTH).

THROCHEE. See METER.

THUCYDIDES. Name of:
—(1) The son of Melesias, Athenian oligarchic politician, successor to Cimon as the leader of the conservatives. In 443 he was ostracized; as a result Pericles definitely became the first citizen of Athens.
—(2) The first scientific, historical writer (c. 456-c. 400); born of a prominent Athenian family. He contracted the plague in 430/29 (see PELOPONNESIAN WAR). In 424 he was a strategist and led an expedition to relieve Amphipolis; he failed, and was exiled for this reason. During his period in exile (which did not end until 404) he wrote his (unfinished) history of the Peloponnesian War. Following an introduction of early Gr. history, the part he finished (eight books) covers the years 431-411. The events are reported year by year, and each year is divided into summer and winter campaigns. The narrative is constantly interrupted by speeches; these are among the most difficult, but also the most grandiose parts of the book; for example, Pericles' speech commemorating the fallen warriors (II, 35-46); for other brilliant discourses see CORCYRA; MELOS). T. tried to be objective, and searched into the connection of causes and events (so-called pragmatic history). He himself states at the beginning of his work that he wanted to produce a "possession for all time," (*ktèma es aei*), not only "an essay to win the applause of the moment." His rigorous historical criticism, his profound analysis, his objectivity, and his insight into human nature make T. the greatest ancient historical writer. He was often copied—no doubt successfully—especially by the Romans Sallust and Tacitus, but they were unable to attain his objectivity.

THULE. A land north of Britain, first described by Pytheas, who said that there the sun shone at night in midsummer; it is probably Norway or Iceland. Later, it was believed to be one of the Shetland Islands.

THURII. City founded by Pericles in 443 B.C., near the site of ancient Sybaris. Herodotus lived there in his old age. It became a Rom. colony in 193 B.C., and was renamed Copia (see also PANHELLENISM).

TIBER. Largest river of central Italy, rising in the Apennines at Arretium (Arezzo), and entering the Tyrrhenian Sea at Ostia. In ancient times the T was navigable as far as Narnia (about 62 mi.), but the large amount of silt it carried to the sea, continuously choked up the harbors. Tiber floods caused great damage in Rome several times. The river-god Tiberinus was worshiped zealously.

TIBERIUS, CLAUDIUS NERO (42 B.C.-A.D. 37). Rom. emperor, ruled from A.D. 14; adopted son and successor of Augustus, who, in 38 B.C., married T's mother Livia. T. had a brilliant military career, and fought against the Parthians in Pannonia and in Germany, among other places. The Emperor Augustus compelled him to divorce Vipsania Agrippina and marry his daughter Julia. T.'s unhappiness prompted him, after having suffered additional affronts, to retire to the island of Rhodes from 6 B.C.-A.D. 2. When almost all pretenders had died, Augustus appointed him as his successor, pressed to do so by Livia. He followed Augustus' policy and consulted the senate as often as possible, but did not get along well with the senators because of mutual suspicion. He was just as unfortunate with regard to his relations with his family and entourage (see AGRIPPINA THE ELDER; GERMANICUS). Sejanus, who encouraged T.'s departure for Capreae (Capri) in 26, was a bad influence on him. From this island, T. ruled Rome—this only gave rise to increased suspicions and misunderstandings. Rom. tradition (Suetonius, Tacitus) has stressed T.'s sensual propensities unnecessarily; he was a difficult character; his reign was marred by political trials for various offenses violating his dignity; his choice of Sejanus was a fatal mistake. Nevertheless, his government of the Empire, especially outside Rome, was just as favorable as

that of Augustus (see also VELLEIUS).

TIBULLUS, ALBIUS (c. 54-c. 19 B.C.). Rom. elegiac poet, a new member of the *equites,* and very rich. Like many others he sustained great property losses during the Civil War that followed the death of Caesar; nevertheless, he remained a prosperous man; therefore he did not need the support of Maecenas and was not a member of his literary circle. It is known, however, that he was a friend of Horace. T. obtained the favor of Messala Corvinus—a patron with more republican tendencies—whose circle he joined, and whom he accompanied on his Aquitanian campaign in 31. Several members of this circle, especially the poetess Sulpicia, contributed to the poems. The work is divided into four books, and has been handed down under T.'s name. Only the first two books can be definitely assigned to T. Like Propertius and Catullus, he expresses his love for a faithless mistress, Delia, the subject of his first book. The second book speaks of his mistress, Nemesis, who also embittered his love by her unfaithfulness. Most of T.'s other poems are about the peacefulness of country life.

TIBUR. City, now Tivoli, northeast of Rome on the Anio River. According to tradition, it was founded by the Siculi (see SICILY); it remained independent for a long time. After being granted Rom. civil rights in about 90 B.C., it became a luxurious country residence for Rom. aristocrats. Among others, Hadrian had his famous villa built there.

TIGELLINUS, OFONIUS. Commander of the Praetorians under Nero; of all Nero's favorites, the most hated by the Rom. people—a very deplorable successor indeed to Burrus. On the accession of Otho in A.D. 69, he was forced to commit suicide.

TIGRANES. King of Armenia from about 95-56, son-in-law and ally of Mithridates. He extended his power to a large part of Asia Minor, Syria, and the Parthian empire. Sulla, Lucullus, and Pompey were his opponents; they limited his empire to Armenia proper.

TIMAEUS. Name of:
—(1) T. of Tauromenium (c. 346-c. 250). Gr. historian, exiled from Sicily

by Agathocles, he lived in Athens for fifty years. T. wrote a history of Sicily, of which only a few fragments are extant. However, this work greatly influenced later historians (especially Diodorus Siculus).

—(2) T. of Locri in southern Italy (5th cent. B.C.). Philosopher of the school of Pythagoras. Plato named his dialogue, *Timaeus,* after him.

TIMGAD. City in Numidia, about 60 mi. south of what is now Constantine, founded in A.D. 100 by Trajan, nicknamed the "African Pompeii" because of the many beautiful antique structures found there.

TIMOLEON. Gr. statesman and general, born in Corinth. In 344 B.C. the Gr. cities of Sicily requested the aid of the Corinthians during civil dissensions within, and the threat of the Carthaginians without. T., in command of a small force, was sent there and succeeded in driving the tyrant Dionysius II from the fortress of Syracuse. He recalled the exiles, invited new colonists, and then stayed on to reorganize the constitution and to enact new laws—on a democratic basis. He also liberated other Gr. cities from the tyrants. The Carthaginians, fearing the renewed power of Syracuse, attacked the city with a large army, but T., although outnumbered, won a great victory in 341, after which a peace was made. In 337 he went blind and retired from public life. After his death he was honored everywhere as a liberator. For a short time peace and prosperity came to the island, which was so often torn by civil strife, but T.'s work was soon nullified by Agathocles.

TIMON. Name of:

—(1) T. of Athens (5th cent. B.C.). A famous Gr. misanthrope, semilegendary character, mentioned by Aristotle and Plutarch (*Antonius,* 70). Lucian named his dialogue after him; he is the subject of Shakespeare's play *Timon of Athens.*

—(2) T. of Phlius (c. 320-230). Gr. Skeptic philosopher, pupil of Pyrrho; he spread the Skeptic doctrine, not only in prose writings, but in tragedies, comedies, and parodic hexameters.

TIMOTHEUS. Name of:

—(1) T. of Miletus (447-357). Gr. dithyrambic poet and musician. Apart from fragments of a few other works, a large part of his *Persae,* a realistic portrayal of the battle of Salamis (480 B.C.), has survived; this text was the oldest Greek writing found on papyrus, and may well date from T.'s own time. T. introduced the eleven-string cithara.

—(2) T. of Athens (first half of the 4th cent. B.C.). General, son of Conon, organized the Second Attic League.

TIRO, MARCUS TULLIUS (104-4 B.C.). Freedman, secretary and friend of Cicero. Among other works, he wrote a (lost) biography of Cicero. T. is said to have invented a system of shorthand writing (*Notae Tironianae*).

TIRYNS. Ancient town in Argolis, south of Argos, one of the most important political centers of Mycenaean times. It was already important during the beginning of the Bronze Age (3rd millennium B.C.) and reached its peak in the 14th cent. B.C., when massive fortifications, the "Cyclops" walls, were built. A palace, constructed with a central hall of the *megaron* type (see HOUSES), dates, in its present state, from a more recent period. It was destroyed by a fire in about 1150, but T. remained in existence as an independent city for a long time afterward; it was destroyed by Argos in about 470 B.C.

TISSAPHERNES. Persian satrap of western Asia Minor in 413 B.C. He intervened in the Peloponnesian War by giving Sparta financial support. He warned King Artaxerxes II against Cyrus the Younger and after the battle of Cunaxa, lured Clearchus and his colleagues into his tent in order to arrest them. After his return to Sardes, T. decided to pursue a policy of aggression against the Ionian cities, but was defeated by Agesilaus. He was put to death by the order of Cyrus.

TITANS. The Gr. family of gods prior to that of Zeus; the best known T. are Cronus, Oceanus, and Rhea (see CYBELE). Their children were also called T. (Prometheus, for example). Zeus terminated their rule and threw them into the Tartarus, the darkest abyss of Hades. After that, the T. were seen as the personification of violence, especially in Orphism, where they represented the element of sin in human nature.

TITUS, FLAVIUS VESPASIANUS. (39-81). Rom. emperor, reigned from 79, son of Vespasian and his coregent from 71. He accompanied his father to Judaea in 67, where he suppressed the rebellion of the Jews in 70; his triumphal arch in Rome commemorates this victory. It shows the sacred objects being carried out of the temple of Jerusalem, the *menorah* (holy candelabrum) among them. He was unpopular during his father's reign, primarily for his liaison with Berenice, the daughter of Agrippa I, king of Judaea; however, when he became emperor himself, he became the favorite of the Rom. people. During his short reign, two great disasters befell Italy: the eruption of Mount Vesuvius in 79, and the great fire in Rome in 80. The Colosseum was completed during his reign.

TOGA. The formal dress of a Rom. citizen, and obligatory on public occasions. It was made of an oval, white woolen piece of cloth; it measured in length about three times, in width about twice, the wearer's height. It was draped around the body and arranged in a thick fold on the breast, to serve as a pocket. The *toga praetexta* had a purple border and was the official uniform of the curule magistrates and the priests of Rome. Young men also wore it; on becoming of age, the *toga virilis,* without the border, was worn (see also FABULA; MAGISTRATUS).

TOMB STELE. See STELE.

TOMI (or TOMIS). Colony of Miletus on the west coast of the Black Sea, founded in the 7th cent. B.C.; now called Constantia; brought under Rom. rule by Lucullus; famous as Ovid's place of exile.

TRACHIS. City west of Thermopylae; according to legend, the last home of Heracles. Locale of Sophocles' play *Trachiniae* (*The Women of Trachis.*)

TRAGEDY. Ancient Gr. T.—the most important cultural manifestation of the 5th cent. B.C.—originated in the lyric dithyramb, that is, in the song of a chorus during the Great Dionysia or other festivals in honor of Dionysus. This song expressed alternate joy and sorrow, following the ritual of the cult. That T.

originated in the Dionysiac cult is indicated by the word T. itself: A "tragedy" (literally "goat song" from *tragos,* hegoat and *ōidē,* song) was sung by the chorus, representing Satyrs or clad in goatskins, as a goat was sacrificed to the god. These "goat songs" were sung in the Peloponnesus (especially in Sicyon and Corinth) as early as the 6th cent. B.C., and received a certain dramatic form during the time of Arion, who flourished about 625 B.C., and who developed the dithyramb. Herodotus later likened them to the chorus in Attic tragedies. As the true drama, including tragedies and Satyric plays, developed, the once-dominant chorus gave way increasingly to dramatic elements.

According to tradition, Thespis of Icaria—a poet, actor, and leader of the chorus—produced the first true Gr. T. at the festival of Dionysus in Athens in 534 B.C. His tragedies consisted of a prologue, a series of choral songs connected with the action, and dramatic declamations between choruses. These plays were performed by Thespis himself, who played several roles, employing wooden masks. His pieces won the approval of the public, but were soon forgotten. Although the first tragedies were given in honor of Dionysus, soon other than religious subjects were introduced; for example, the sagas of Heracles, Troy, and Thebes. Historical subjects were used by Aeschylus in *The Persians* and by Phrynichus in *Phoenissae.* Euripides often wrote about topical subjects. Aeschylus was the first to add a second actor (*deuteragonistes*) to the first (*protagonistes*), thus making dialogue possible. Sophocles added to Aeschylus' two actors a third (*tritagonistes*), a practice that was adopted by Aeschylus in his later plays. With the death of Euripides and Sophocles, the creative period of Gr. T. declined—the plays of the three great tragedians were performed again and again.

In form, the fully developed Gr. T. consisted of alternating choral and dramatic episodes. The chorus included both song and dance. The T. typically contained a *prologos* (from the beginning to the first entry of the chorus), a *parodos* (first important choral part), *epeiso-*

dion (division between each choral song and the next), *stasion* (the song following the *epeisodion*), *kommoi* (lyric dialogue and lamentations between the chorus and the actor), and an *exodos* (concluding portion, which followed the last chorus). Four dramas (*tetralogia*) were enacted on a given day. They included three tragedies and a Satyric drama. Euripides often replaced the Satyric drama with a lighter T. Aeschylus sometimes gave the three tragic plays a single subject, to form a trilogy, and occasionally extended this technique to include the Satyric drama as well. Aristotle made interesting remarks about the form of Gr. T. in his *Poetica*. According to him, an ideal play is "economic," that is, the sequence of events must be logical, and no secondary plots should hamper the action; it contains a scene of "recognition" and a "reversal" from hopeful expectation to total disaster; finally, T. should provoke strong feelings of "pity" and "fear" in the spectators, which lead to the cleansing (*katharsis*) of these passions in the soul. A coercive precept of "unity of time, place, and action" has been incorrectly attributed to Aristotle. In some Gr. tragedies the locale of the scene does change; in others there are long time lapses in the action. In those cases the *stasimon* played the part of our curtain (see also AESCHYLUS; SOPHOCLES; EURIPIDES; AGATHON; THEATER; ORCHESTRA; METER; MUSIC; and DRAMA).

Rom. T. was founded entirely on that of the Greeks. At first there were crude satirical productions, but Livius Andronicus translated and staged Gr. dramas. He also created plays that were more or less versions of Gr. originals, as did his successors. Even the *Fabulae praetextae*, historical plays, drawn from Rom. history, were modeled on Gr. works. Naevius was the first of the Romans to write a *Fabula praetexta* (see also ENNIUS; PACUVIUS; ACCIUS). The philosopher Seneca wrote dramas, which were possibly intended for public recitation rather than for the stage; although they show great mastery of style, they are excessively rhetorical. From the scanty fragments of Rom. tragedies that have come down to us, it appears that Gr. T. was far superior to that of the Romans.

TRAJANUS, MARCUS ULPIUS (53-117). Commonly called Trajan. Rom. emperor, under whose rule the Rom. Empire reached its greatest size. Born in Spain, the son of one of Vespasian's generals, his career was military and political (consul 91); governor of Germania Superior in 97, he was adopted by Nerva, whom he succeeded to the throne in 98. He first consolidated the Rom. positions on the Rhine and the Danube, and then devoted himself to administrating the Empire, with great success. His financial and social policies were progressive; state aid for the education of poor children (*alimenta*) was increased. Large buildings arose, among them the Forum of T. Two difficult wars had to be waged in Dacia, during which King Decebalus was driven to commit suicide; T. made his capital, Sarmizegetusa, the center of this new Rom. province. Scenes from these campaigns are depicted on T.'s column in Rome. In the East, T. warred with the Parthians and conquered Armenia and Mesopotamia. Later, some of these excessive conquests proved to be impossible to maintain and, therefore, his successor Hadrian relinquished Mesopotamia. Although rebellions started early during T.'s campaigns, he managed to restore order, but, on his way home from an expedition against the Parthians, he died in Cilicia.

For a long time after his death, T. was honored as one of the best rulers. His special talents as a general were combined with great personal simplicity and a strict sense of justice. How carefully he attended to the government of the provinces, can be seen from the letters he exchanged with Pliny the Younger. The latter's panegyrics are perhaps too flattering, but in any case, a pessimist like Tacitus paid homage to his government. In final judgment it can be said that T.'s reign was one of the very best of the excellent governments provided by the adoptive emperors.

TRAJECTUM. Rom. settlement, remains of which have been found in Utrecht in the Netherlands.

TRAPEZUS. Colony of Sinope on the

south coast of the Black Sea, founded in in about 650 B.C. Later, S. was part of the kingdom of Pontus, but did, not flourish until it became part of the Rom. Empire and acquired good harbor installations.

TRASIMENUS. Lake in Etruria, where, in May, 217 B.C., the Rom. consul Flaminius and his army were ambushed by Hannibal. Hannibal had concealed his best troops in the mountains that overlooked the lake, and let the rest of his army be spotted at the end of the narrow pass between the mountains and the lake. When the Romans turned their flank to the hidden soldiers, Hannibal gave the signal for attack; the consul and the greater part of the Rom. army were killed (Liv. XXII, 4-7).

TREBIA. A tributary of the Padus, where Hannibal defeated the Rom. army under the command of Scipio (the father of Scipio Major) in December, 218 B.C.; this victory gave him access to the Po valley.

TREBONIANUS. See MILITARY EMPERORS.

TREVERI. Gallic tribe in the valley of the Moselle River, capital Augusta Treverorum; part of the tribe was Germanic. They furnished cavalry to Caesar, but later on they often rebelled against him.

TRIBE [Lat. *tribus*]. Originally there were three Rom. tribes, the three classes of Rom. patricians; later, the word was used only to denote a district or ward, four city (*tribus urbanae*) and twenty-six, eventually thirty-one, country tribes (*tribus rusticae*). By distributing new citizens (former *socii*, freedmen, etc.) into various tribes, an effort was made to limit their political influence because the voting in the *comitia tributa* was done according to tribes. In the imperial period the tribes lost all political importance.

TRIBUNI [Lat. plural of *tribunus*, chief of a tribe]. Civilian or military officials of the Romans. The T. *militum* had approximately the rank of senior officers. The best known T. are the T. *plebis* (tribunes of the plebs). This office was granted the plebeians in 494 B.C. after their secession to *Mons Sacer* (a hill in the Sabine country outside Rome) in protest of the oppression by the patri-

cians and consuls. The T. *plebis* had authority to intervene in favor of the plebeians before the magistrates, who originally all were patricians, and whose decisions and intended legislation they had the right to veto. They had authority to convene the *comitia tributa* and to preside over it. Later, they were also members of the senate and as such could convene it; from this moment on, there was no longer a great difference between the T. and the other magistrates. It was not until the time of the Gracchi that the revolutionary nature of the office was revived. Much later, the emperors saw to it that the T. *plebis* were always granted the *tribunicia potestas* (authority of the T.).

TRIGLYPH. See ARCHITECTURAL ORDERS.

TRIREME [Lat. *triremis*]. The typical warship (galley) of ancient times, having three banks of oars. The rowers in the uppermost row, receiving the highest pay, were called *thranitae*, those in the middle *zeugitae*, and the lowest *thalamitae*. The matter of the exact arrangement of their seats has not been established with certainty. The long, slim construction gave the T. easy maneuverability during naval battles, but made it very vulnerable during storms (see ARGINUSAE). The ship was equipped with an auxiliary sail which was used when the wind was favorable, but not during naval battles. In the Hellenistic period (and during the Punic Wars) the T. was temporarily replaced by the quinquereme.

TRITON. See NEREUS.

TRIUMPH [Lat. *triumphus*]. Procession by a victorious Rom. general through the streets of Rome, ending with a sacrifice to Jupiter on the Capitol. Only the holder of the highest command (*imperium*), a consul, praetor, or dictator, were accorded a T. by authority of the senate; the only body allowed to grant this honor. The triumphator rode in a chariot drawn by four white horses; his face was painted red with minium, probably in order to identify him with Jupiter himself. The senate and the principal captives marched in the procession. The soldiers sang jocular songs to offset the almost divine homage paid to the general. The T. was the only occasion on which an armed force was permitted to cross the pomerium. The army marched through a gate; later, in its place, a permanent triumphal arch was often erected. The presence of the armed legions gave the T. such dangerous aspects that only the emperor himself triumphed during imperial times when the generals commanded as his lieutenants (*legati Augusti*). Other generals might be awarded special triumphal insignia.

TRIUMVIRI [also written *tresviri* from Lat. *tres*, three, and *viri*, men]. Rom. college of three persons charged with an administrative assignment—for example, the T. monetales (mintmasters)—or a political task. The best known triumvirates are the first, of 60 B.C., which was a private arrangement between Pompey, Crassus, and Caesar, and the second, recognized by the state, between Octavian, Antony, and Lepidus. (For the consequences of these two triumvirates, see the articles on the persons named.)

TROEZEN [Gr. Troizèn]. City in the northeastern Peloponnesus, first inhabited by Ionians and later by Dorians. According to the saga, Theseus was born there; the scene of Euripides' *Hippolytus* is laid there. French archaeologists excavated it. (For an important historical inscription recently found there, see THEMISTOCLES.)

TROGUS, POMPEIUS (1st cent. A.D.). Rom. historian; wrote a history of the world (*Historiae Philippicae*), an excerpt of this work, written by Justinus, is extant. T. is said to have also written works on biology and zoology.

TROJAN WAR. According to the saga, the war between the Greeks under the leadership of Agamemnon, king of Mycenae, and the Trojans (see TROY) under King Priam (about 1200 B.C.). The story tells that the Greeks, angered by Paris' abduction of Helen, wife of the king of Sparta, Menelaus, Agamemnon's brother, set out to demand her return. When their request was refused they besieged Troy; it took more than nine years, as neither party was willing to make concessions. In the Gr. camp, it was young Achilles who was the most brilliant; among the Trojans, it was Hector, the son of Priam. In the *Iliad*, Homer described a few weeks

(to be more exact, only a few days) of the tenth year. After both the heroes had fallen, Troy was conquered in the tenth year through the ruse of the Wooden Horse (Virg. *Aen.* II). The events not described by Homer are the subject of the epic Cycle, the Gr. tragic poets also having portrayed several episodes. (For the historical background, see TROY).

Troy. Below: section of some of the cities excavated at Hissarlik

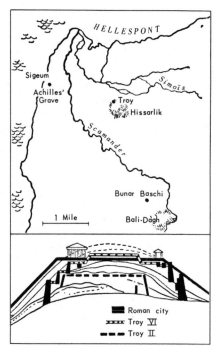

TROY. City in northwestern Asia Minor, capital of the region of Troas; according to tradition it was besieged by the Greeks during the Trojan War. In 1870, H. Schliemann excavated Hissarlik, a hill of ruins, which he had identified with T. The excavations were continued after his death by W. Dörpfeld and recommenced in 1932, with his cooperation, by an American expedition, which finished its work after the Second World War. Nine cities, one above the other, were found, of which the oldest dates back to before 3000 B.C.; Schliemann incorrectly believed the second city to have been that of Priam, and called the fortune in gold found there "Priam's treasure." The sixth city dates from Mycenaean times and was destroyed by an earthquake. The Americans identified the seventh settlement as Priam's T.; the Trojan War may then have coincided with the migration of peoples which led to the arrival of the Dorians in Greece. The ninth city is the Rom.-Hellenic T., usually called Ilium, a name that Homer already used for T.

TULLIANUM. The prison under the *comitium* (part of the Forum) in Rome, where many enemies and traitors were executed, among them Jugurtha, the followers of Catilina, and Vercingetorix.

TULLUS HOSTILIUS (673-642). According to tradition, the third king of Rome, probably a historical figure. He was said to have destroyed Alba Longa and built the *Curia Hostilia*. He was also said to have instituted the *fetiales*.

TUNIC [Lat. *tunica*]. A Rom. garment for men and women worn next to the person. Women covered it with a stola and sometimes a mantle; men wore a toga as their outer garment. A purple border indicated the wearer's rank: a narrow one for *equites*, a broad one for senators.

TU QUOQUE, BRUTE? "You too, Brutus?"; Lat. translation of the words Caesar spoke to Brutus when the latter, who was generally regarded as his son, stabbed him; also translated as *et tu, Brute?* (Suet. *Caes.* 82).

TUSCULUM. City in Latium near the present-day Frascati, the first city to be granted Rom. citizenship (381 B.C.). It was a favorite summer residence of noble Rom. families. Cicero, among others, had a beautiful country house there. Cato was a native of T.

TWELVE TABLES, LAW OF THE. See CORPUS JURIS; CLAUDIUS, APPIUS.

TYMPANUM. See ARCHITECTURAL ORDERS.

TYRANT [Gr. *tyrannos*, lord, king; the term probably originated in Lydia]. Absolute monarch of a Gr. polis, who was a member of the nobility, but had usually usurped power by violence with the support of the lower classes; sometimes he was a descendant of such a usurper. The history of Gr. tyrants can be divided into two main phases: the first was caused by the tensions in the 7th and 6th centuries B.C., when the transition to new means of existence (small industries, trade, etc.) was undermining aristocratic society. Many tyrants were excellent rulers, who promoted the prosperity and cultural development of their cities, but their suppression of freedom gave rise to discontent, which usually broke out in revolts in the second generation (see HARMODIUS; also CYPSELUS; PERIANDER; POLYCRATES; PHALARIS; THRASYBULUS; PISISTRATUS; HIPPIAS; and HIPPARCHUS). In the west of Greece, particularly in Sicily, tyranny was generally established later (see GELON, HIERO I, THERON). The second phase also started in the west, especially under the stress of foreign enemies, particularly the Carthaginians in Sicily (see DIONYSIUS; AGATHOCLES). In Greece itself, tyrants were concentrated mainly in Thessaly, during the 4th cent. B.C. (see PHERAE; JASON).

TYRTAEUS (7th cent. B.C.). Gr. elegiac poet. According to tradition, the Spartans, during the Second Messenian War (see MESSENIA), on the advice of the Delphic oracle, asked the Athenians for a general, and they sent them the crippled T., a schoolteacher. This derisive act proved to be a blessing—T., by the power of his martial poetry, united the divided factions of Sparta and roused them to such bravery that they won the war. It is possible that T. may have been a Spartan himself, or an Ionian from Miletus. His elegies, whose language and style were closely related to the epic, exhort men to fight and speak of the duty and honor of courage. Only fragments of his poems are extant.

UBI BENE, IBI PATRIA. "Where it is well with me, there is my country" (Cic. *Tusc.* V, 108).

ULIXES. Rom. equivalent for Odysseus; erroneously written Ulysses (see HOMER).

ULPIA NOVIOMAGUS. See NOVIOMAGUS.

ULPIANUS, DOMITIUS (c. A.D. 200). One of the greatest Rom. lawyers, born in the Phoenician city of Tyre. He held office under Caracalla; was exiled by Elagabal and recalled by Alexander Severus, under whom he served as *praefectus praetorio;* he was murdered in 228, as the result of a mutiny among the Praetorians, who considered his discipline too strict. He was a contemporary of the jurists Papinianus and Paulus. He was less original than the latter, but the clarity of his expositions was much greater. About one-third of the *Digesta* (see CORPUS JURIS) is from his writings.

UMBRIA. Region in central Italy, east of the Tiber. In the 3rd cent. B.C., Rome secured the strategic points of U., which served as a sally port to Gallia Cisalpina. The line of communication was along the Via Flaminia.

UMBRIANS. People in central Italy, who originally also ruled Etruria (they may have been the bearers of Villanovan culture); later, their power was confined to Umbria proper. Their language was one of the Oscan-Umbrian dialects (see OSCI).

URANIA. See MUSES.

UTICA. The oldest Phoenician colony in Africa, founded in about 1100 B.C. During the Third Punic War it supported Rome against Carthage and was promoted to be the capital of the Rom. province of Africa. Later, it took Pompey's side and opposed Caesar; Cato Minor committed suicide there after the Battle of Thapsus.

VAE VICTIS. "Woe to the vanquished," that is, the defeated have no rights; an utterance of Brennus, who threw his sword onto the scales when the Romans wanted to protest against fraud during the weighing of the tribute (Liv. V, 48, 9; compare Plaut. *Pseud.* 1317).

VALENS, FLAVIUS (328-378). Rom. emperor, coregent of Valentinian I; came into conflict with the Visigoths, whom he had initially admitted into the Empire. He fell at Adrianople.

VALENTINIANUS. Name of:
—(1) V. I (321-375). Commonly called Valentinian. Rom. emperor, brother of Valens, reigned from 364; was forced to defend the frontiers against the Germans constantly; supported Christianity, but was also tolerant toward paganism.
—(2) V. II (375-392). Rom. emperor, son of the preceding, coregent with his brother Gratianus; under the regency of his mother since 378. After having been driven out of Italy by the usurper Mag-

nus Maximus, he was restored to power by Theodosius in 388; murdered by Arbogastes, Frankish commander of his army.
—(3) V. III (419-455). Rom. emperor. He came to the throne in 425 under the regency of his mother Galla Placidia. During his reign the Empire almost met its downfall due to foreign wars and internal strife. Aetius' victory over Attilla on the Catalaunian Plains brought relief.

VALERIANUS. See MILITARY EMPERORS.

VALERIUS. Name of:
—(1) Gaius V. Flaccus Balbus Setinus (1st cent. A.D.). Rom. poet; wrote an unfinished epic, on the expedition of the Argonauts *Argonautica,* in eight books; it is broken off at the point where Jason and Medea flee from Colchis. The material is derived from Apollonius Rhodius, the style was influenced by Virgil and Ovid. It is less rhetorical than the works of Lucanus and other epic poets of his period. It was dedicated to Vespasian, whose expedition to Britain the poet wanted to commemorate. It was not rediscovered until 1416.
—(2) V. Maximus (1st cent. A.D.). Rom. writer on rhetoric and history. He dedicated a collection of historical anecdotes in nine books to Tiberius, the sources of which were Cicero, Livy, Sallust, and Pompeius Trogus.
—(3) Marcus V. Corvus. Hero of early Rom. history; military tribune under Camillus in 349 B.C.; consul six times. He is said to have fought a gigantic Gaul in single combat and to have won— helped by a raven which flew in his opponent's face. The (greatly exaggerated) stories about him originated with the annalist Valerius Antias (1st cent. B.C.), who claimed to be his descendant.

VANDALS. Germanic people, who migrated from the Baltic coast to the Danube countries in about A.D. 170. In 406 they crossed the Rhine and invaded the Rom. Empire; they went through Gaul to invade Spain. Some of them were annihilated by the Goths, but the survivors, the only Germanic people to build a fleet, established an empire in Africa, with Carthage as the capital. Their king Genseric led expeditions to Sicily, Sardinia, and Italy from there; in 455 they sacked

Rome. As Christians who followed the Arian doctrine, the V. ruled tyrannically over the Africans who were mainly Catholic. Belisarius (see JUSTINIAN) destroyed the V. empire in 533.

VAPHIO. Pre-Doric city in Laconia, bulwark of the Achaeans; site of a Mycenaean beehive tomb. Among other discoveries were two golden cups ornamented with bull fights. They are the most beautiful specimens of imported objects of art that were made in Crete during the Minoan period (about 1500 B.C.).

VARRO, MARCUS TERENTIUS (116-27). Rom. encyclopedic author and poet. He first studied in Rome and then at the Academy in Athens. Although he was a scientist at heart, he felt compelled to serve his country in the field of politics and became praetor. He joined Pompey's party during the Civil War and served as his *legatus* in Spain. He was forced to surrender to Caesar, who pardoned him and appointed him to take charge of the great public library in 47. In 43 he escaped proscription by Antony, but his library was plundered. He wrote 74 works in about 620 books, among them Menippean satires; also the first illustrated book in Latin, and an encyclopedia. His main work, *Antiquitates Rerum Humanarum et Divinarum,* has been lost, with the exception of a few fragments. Three books on agriculture, *Rerum Rusticarum Libri,* have been completely preserved; they are, with the work of Cato (2), our main source for knowledge of Rom. rural economy.

VARUS, PUBLIUS QUINTILIUS (c. 50-A.D. 9). Rom. general; consul in 13 B.C.; subsequently appointed governor of Syria, where, in 5 B.C., he suppressed a rebellion of the Jews. Augustus wanted to advance the frontier of the Empire from the Rhine to the Elbe, and in the fall of A.D. 9, V. led the Rom. army on an expedition to Germany. He was lured into a trap by Arminius in the Teutoburger Wald; his army was destroyed and V. committed suicide.

VASE FORMS. The Gr. potters usually used a limited number of standard shapes for their vases; in the course of time these might vary, but not so much that it prevented their classification according to type in archaeological museums. To designate them, these basic types were given Gr. names—some were used by the Greeks themselves—some were bestowed by archaeologists. The most important shapes are shown in the accompanying illustrations; the summary below lists the customary uses of each type:

Alabastron, small, elongated vase for perfume; often made of alabaster.

Amphora, jug with two handles for wine or oil, the size varies; diverse kinds are known (see also PANATHENAEA).

Aryballos, small vase for oils, ointments, or perfumes, worn on the arm by a strap through the handle.

Askos (literally: wine bag) small vase with a spout for wine.

Dinos, large bowl on a pedestal, used as a mixing bowl (see entries for Krater; Lebes below).

Hydria, water pitcher with three handles: two horizontal ones on either side for carrying it on one's head, and one vertical one behind for drawing or pouring.

Kalpis, a variant of the hydria.

Kantharos, cup with two handles set high, on a pedestal base; often made of metal with reliefs.

Kernos, small, open cups on a pottery ring for sacrifices.

Kotyle, general word for cup (see entries for Kantharos; Kylix; Skyphos).

Krater, bowl for mixing wine and water; various types are known. One of the most famous is the so-called François vase.

Kyathos, cup for ladling out wine.

Kylix, shallow drinking bowl.

Lebes, variant of the dinos; examples in bronze have been found in Etruria, which were given as prizes at games; another type is the wedding lebes, whose bowl and base are joined.

Lekane, bowl with a base and a cover, for toiletries.

Lekythos, small vase for oil or perfume, often buried with the owner; frequently polychrome with a white background. The custom originated in Greece of placing a monument in the form of a lekythos on the grave. Usually these were made of marble or terra cotta, often decorated with reliefs. A monument of this type is called a funeral lekythos.

Loutrophoros, tall vase, in which the water for the bridal bath was fetched. The L. that had not been her portion in life, was set on the grave of a girl who died unmarried.

Oechonoe, jug into which the wine was ladled from the krater, to be poured into cups.

Pelike, a more rounded type of amphora.

Phiale, bowl for making libations.

Psykter, large wine cooler.

Pyxis, box with a cover for toiletries.

Rhyton, cup shaped like a horn, used particularly by the Scythians who used them during funeral rites, and who drank from the wide opening (the Greeks drank from a small opening at the tip).

Skyphos, deep cup.

Stamnos, jug for wine or water, a cross between an amphora and a hydria.

VASE PAINTING. Because almost all Gr. monumental painting has been lost (for exceptions, see PINAX; PORTRAITURE) we can only form our opinions of styles, techniques, and creative ability from the painting on vases. It must be remembered that the Gr. vases, hundreds of which now enrich archaeological museums and a few private collections, were not ornamental objects in ancient times (again, with exceptions), but utensils (for their usage see VASE FORMS), products of industrial art. However, the Greeks decorated them with extreme care and originality. That they were useful as well as beautiful is a tribute to the innate artistry of the Greeks. The study of these vases does not only give us insight into the artistic capabilities of the artists, it also furnishes us with data concerning economic (see ARCHAEOLOGY) and political history.

During the geometric period (see GEOMETRIC ART), the most beautiful examples came from Athens; this indicates that the city must have been more important during the 9th-8th centuries B.C. than we would have assumed from other sources. Corinth began to dominate the

market in the late 8th and 7th centuries; first with proto-Corinthian and later with Corinthian pottery of Cypselus' and Periander's times; oriental motifs of the vases reflect the lively trade connections with the Near East. Besides Corinth, other centers developed: Chalcis, Rhodes, Ionia (see CAERE). The colonization of the West enabled Corinth and Chalcis, allies during the Lelantic War to ship their wares to Magna Graecia and Sicily in amicable rivalry. The export from Miletus to the coast of Pontus Euxinus is no less interesting; the splendid collections in Russia bear witness to that. Then, in the 6th cent., the market was gradually cornered by Athens.

At first the vases were decorated with black figures (for great masters of this art see FRANÇOIS VASE; AMASIS; ANDOCIDES; and especially EXECIAS). That we are now able to cite the names of the artists is also an important sign. We have reached the intermediate period of Gr. individualism, represented in literature especially by lyric poetry. The artist no longer hid behind his work, but announced with pride that he was the author; at times, the potter and the painter signed the vase. In about 530-525 a new style appeared: the figures took on the reddish brown of the clay; this is called the transition from the black-figure to the red-figure style. Some painters of the transitional period employed both techniques (Andocides), but soon only red-figured painting remained, with the exception of the Panathenaic amphorae (see PANATHENAEA; for great masters see EPICTETUS; BRYGOUS; and especially EUPHRONIUS). Several painters, undoubtedly masters, are not known by name; they have been named after their most famous works, for example the "Niobid painter," or after the museum where their most famous work is now exhibited, for example the "Berlin painter," etc. It is an interesting aspect of this period that we can recognize in the vases the charac-

---

Vase forms I: A. kylix (drinking bowl): 1. red-figured bowl; 2. miniature bowl; 3. bowl with eyes. B. wine and water jugs: 1. kalpis; 2. oenochoe; 3. stamnos; 4. psykter; 5. hydria. C. krater: 1. kalyx krater; 2. bell krater; 3. volute krater; 4. dinos (it was placed on a separate stand); 5. column krater.

A

1   2   3

B

1   2   3

4   5

C

1   2   3

4   5

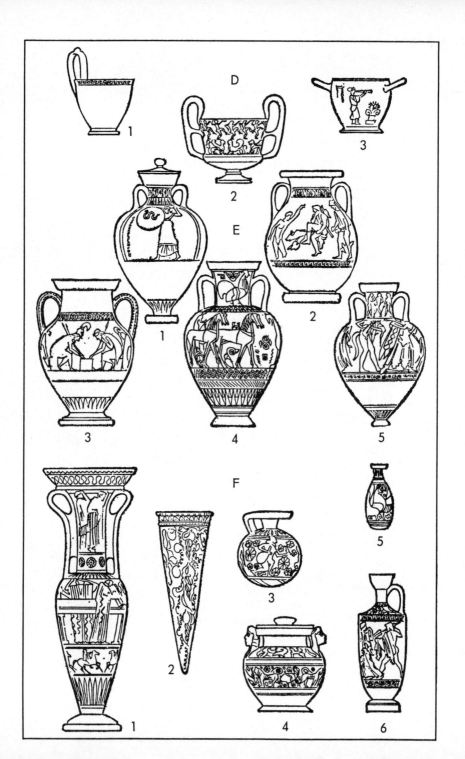

teristics of style of the monumental painters (see POLYGNOTUS; MICON; PARRHA-
SIUS) and make comparisons with the
descriptions in ancient literature. In the
middle of the 5th cent., in the south of
Italy, and under Athenian influence, the
production of red-figured vases began.
Soon they acquired their own characteristic features. In the 3rd cent. B.C., vases
were no longer decorated. In later centuries unpainted pottery was preferred
and sometimes black glazes were used in
the desire to imitate metal. Finally, it
was the red-glazed pottery, known as
Terra Sigillata, which became popular in
the Rom. Empire.

VEII. City in southern Etruria; for
nearly four centuries almost continually
at war with Rome (there are records of
fourteen distinct wars). Finally, after a
ten-year siege, it was conquered in 396
B.C. by Camillus. It was, and for a long
time remained, a large and prosperous
city, celebrated for its many sculptures,
among other things (see ETRUSCANS); in
Rom. imperial times it became a municipium without major importance.

VELIA.
—(1) Hill in Rome, between the Forum
and the Colosseum, on which the Arch
of Titus and important temples were
erected.
—(2) The Rom. name for the Gr. city
of Elea in Lucania (see also ELEATICS).

VELLEIUS PATERCULUS, GAIUS (c.
19 B.C.-after A.D. 31). Rom. historian,
originally from Capua. He served as
legatus under Tiberius on his expeditions
to Germany and Pannonia; he was praetor in A.D. 15. His abridged Rom. history
becomes more detailed when it treats of
his own period; he praises Tiberius highly.
What makes this book so important is
that it counterbalances the unfavorable
criticism of Tacitus and Suetonius; it is
also interesting to note that the author
digresses from his subject and writes
about the history of literature.

VENETI. Name of several ancient tribes;
the most important are: (a) the V. on

the coast of what is now Brittany, in
Morbihan; subjected by Decimus Brutus,
legatus under Caesar, after a violent
naval battle in 57 B.C. (Caes. B.G. III,
8-16); (b) the inhabitants of Venetia, a
region of northern Italy near modern
Venice; they were of Illyrian origin, and
settled in Italy in the 10th cent. B.C.;
from ancient times on they were allies
of Rome; after they were granted Rom.
citizenship in the 1st cent. B.C., they became Romanized.

VENI, VIDI, VICI. "I came, I saw, I
conquered"; Caesar's laconic message to
Rome after the victory over Pharnaces II
at Zela in 47 B.C. (Suet. Caes. 37).

VENUS. Originally a Lat. goddess of
vegetation, protector of gardens and vineyards. Her worship seems to have been
established at Rome in early times. Later,
she was identified with the Gr. Aphrodite, goddess of love and beauty. It is
not known how this came about, but the
earliest historical reference to V. as a
love-goddess is in 217 B.C., when a temple, dedicated to the V. of Mount Eryx
(V. Erycina) in Sicily, was built on the
Capitol in Rome. Sulla considered V. his
tutelary deity; Caesar erected a temple
in her honor as V. Genetrix, because, as
the mother of Aeneas and grandmother
of the latter's son Ascanius (Iulus), she
was considered to be the ancestress of
the Julian-Claudian house.

VERCELLAE. City of the Ligurians in
northern Italy, where Marius defeated
the Cimbri on the so-called Campi Raudii
in 101 B.C.

VERCINGETORIX. Nobleman of the
Arverni tribe, who, in 52 B.C., led a
general revolt of Gaul, which was already
almost completely subjected, against Caesar. Initially, he was very successful because he employed the scorched earth
policy and the strategy of exhausting his
opponent. The success of his defense of
Gergovia was the culminating point of
his strategy. But after a cavalry attack in
the field, during which V. was defeated,
he made the mistake of allowing himself

Vase forms II: D. kotyle (cup): 1. *kyathos;* 2. *kantharos;* 3. *skyphos. E. amphora*
(wine and oil jar): 1. *Panathenaic amphora;* 2. *pelike;* 3. *panel amphora;* 4. *neck*
amphora; 5. *amphora to stand in ring support. F. vessels with various uses:* 1.
loutrophoros; 2. *rhyton;* 3. *aryballos;* 4. *pyxis;* 5. *alabastron;* 6. *lekythos.*

to be trapped in Alesia. The taking of this city sealed his doom, and that of the Gauls. In 46 B.C. he was put to death, after Caesar's triumph (see TULLIANUM). Undoubtedly, V. was a national hero, and his statue deservedly stands in the market place of Clermont-Ferrand in France. On the other hand, according to Caesar (*B.G.* VII), his adventure shows the typical weakness in the Gallic national character: a highly enthusiastic and impetuous launching of a large movement, which collapses at the first real setback.

VERGIL. See VERGILIUS.

VERGILIUS MARO, PUBLIUS (70-19 B.C.). Commonly called Virgil or Vergil. The greatest Rom. poet; born in Andes, the son of a humble farmer, who had become prosperous by marrying his master's daughter. V. was not physically strong. He was educated in Cremona, Milan, and Rome, where he was taught by several teachers, including one from the school of Epicurus. Because of Octavian's land distribution in 41, his paternal home was confiscated, but it was returned to him through the intervention of influential friends, probably already including Asinius Pollio. In the meantime he worked on his ten *Eclogues,* which were later collected under the title *Bucolica,* and which attracted the attention of Maecenas. He was admitted to the latter's circle and dedicated *Georgica* to him; he also became the friend of Horace; through Maecenas he also met Augustus. The poet did not live in Rome, but in Neapolis, where he is also entombed. Augustus inspired him to write the national Rom. epic, the *Aeneid;* he constantly showed interest in the progress of the work and had the finished sections read to him. In 19, before completing the last part of his work, V. took a trip to Greece. On the return voyage he became ill, and died in Brundisium. His request that the unfinished epic be burned, was not complied with.

Apart from a few works of his early years, collected in the so-called *Appendix Vergiliana,* which comprises some poems incorrectly attributed to him (including the *Aetna;* there is a difference of opinion about the authorship of some of these poems), V.'s work consists of the three works already named: (a) *Bucolica* or *Eclogues,* ten pastoral poems modeled on Theocritus; the fourth eclogue, in which he predicts the coming of a child whose birth will bring about an ideal state on earth, is especially famous (see below). V.'s master hand is clearly discernible in all the poems adopted from Theocritus. The allusions to the politics of his day are also noteworthy. The work was written in 42-37; some parts may have been written earlier. (b) *Georgica,* a poem about agriculture in four books (written in 36-29); it, too, has a political background. This work was well adapted to the propaganda of the new government for the reestablishment of the Italian peasant class. Above all, this work reflects the personal interests of the author; he was well acquainted with farming from his youth and was particularly interested in beekeeping. Hesiod was his model; he gathered information from Cato Major and Varro; he was greatly influenced by Lucretius at that time—nevertheless, his work is unmistakably his own creation. (c) The *Aeneid,* a national epic in twelve books, written in 29-19. The saga of Aeneas, who survived the Trojan War and established a new empire in Italy, is very old. Homer (II. XX, 307) predicts a great future for the hero —in the work of Stesichorus and Hellanicus, the story that he came to Italy takes on an even more concrete form. His stay with Queen Dido in Carthage had also been mentioned before. Although a repetition of these narratives in unforgettably beautiful epic style could not fail to be attractive in itself (for Augustus traced his descent back to Aeneas through Caesar), it was not V.'s real aim. Above all, he wanted to prove that the greatness of Rome was the result of divine providence and of *fatum.* The character of his hero is modeled on the same principle. He is, above all, *pius,* that is, "loyal to his vocation." There is nothing Promethean about him; for this reason some later critics found him "weak." The pivot of the work is book VI, in which Aeneas, aided by the Sybil, descends to the underworld to see the future greatness of his race, and to learn what Rome's moral mission is (see PAX ROMANA); this book is also notable for the ideas adopted from Orphism and the school of Pythagoras. This epic too, V. modeled on others: Homer and Apollonius Rhodius, among the Greeks, and Ennius, in particular, among the Romans. But to repeat: V. transformed all these elements into a wholly personal creation.

V.'s fame was immediate, and increased in later imperial times, when he was known as the unique example of the classic poet. At that time also Servius' commentary was written. In the Middle Ages he was considered to have been a precursor of Christianity, mainly on account of his "messianic" *Eclogues,* but also because of the very religious nature of the *Aeneid* (by Dante, for example). Among other things, it is due to this interest in his works that we possess such excellent transmissions of the text.

VERONA. City in Gallia Cisalpina, birthplace of Catullus. A beautiful amphitheater has been preserved there. It was the residency of Theodoric.

VERRES, GAIUS. Notorious Rom. propraetor of the province of Sicily from 73-71, who made himself hated for his maladministration and extortions. He was successfully prosecuted by Cicero in his *Verrines;* some of the accusations were never voiced because V. went into voluntary exile in Massilia; in 43 he was proscribed by Antony. V. was a prototype of the corrupt Rom. magistrate during the years following Sulla's rule.

VERUS, LUCIUS AURELIUS (130-169). Coregent of Marcus Aurelius. At the request of Hadrian, he was adopted by Antoninus Pius in 148, and appointed coregent by Marcus Aurelius in 161. He died during an expedition against the Marcomanni.

VESPASIANUS, TITUS FLAVIUS SABINUS (A.D. 9-79). Commonly called Vespasian. Rom. emperor. In 66, Nero sent him to Judaea to conduct the war against the Jews. V.'s soldiers proclaimed him emperor against Vitellius in 69 (see YEAR OF THE THREE EMPERORS), and he was recognized by the senate on December, 22nd. He restored order and discipline in the Empire, which had been unsettled by Nero's maladministration and

the Civil War of 68-69. He reorganized finance, exhibiting extreme parsimony (see PECUNIA NON OLET). The frontiers of the Empire were consolidated through the annexation of vassal kingdoms. In Rome, the temple on the Capitol, destroyed by fire in 69, was rebuilt; the Colosseum was started. V. came into conflict with the senate, which was unable to appreciate the sometimes dictatorial tendencies of a man of humble birth. His son Titus was his coregent and successor.

VESTA. The ancient Rom. goddess of the hearth, honored in family worship, identified with the Gr. Hestia. In Rome, however, her cult became much more important because a state cult of V. was maintained, taking its origin from the hearth worship of the Rom. kings. The small round temple in the Forum, where V. was served by the Vestal Virgins, was the center of this cult.

VESTALS. Vestal Virgins, the priestesses of Vesta in Rome, a function that was originally held by the daughters of kings. They were chosen at the age of six to ten by the *pontifex maximus* (who represented the high priesthood of the former kings in this, see REX). He had parental authority over them. The V. originally served the goddess for five years, later for a period of thirty years. During this time they had to remain chaste, and see to it that the sacred fire never went out. They were considered very holy; a condemned man who met one of the V. was set free; on the other hand, any person who insulted or tried to seduce one of them, was sentenced to death; V. who violated their vow of chastity were buried alive.

VESUVIUS. Volcano in Campania. It was thought to be extinct, and it was a totally unexpected catastrophe when a violent eruption on August 24, A.D., 79, destroyed Pompeii, Herculaneum, and Stabiae (see also PLINY). The people should have been on guard: an earthquake in A.D. 63 showed that the volcano was still active. Spartacus found asylum on V. in 73 B.C.

VETERA. One of the chief Rom. army camps (*castra*) near modern Xanten on the Rhine. It was conquered by the Batavi under Civilis in A.D. 70. Later, the Rom.

colony of Ulpia Trajana was founded on the site of Xanten.

VETERANS [Lat. *veterani*]. Old soldiers of the Rom. army, who, after sixteen to twenty years of service, were exempt from heavy duty. In case of crises, they took up arms again and were considered to be a particularly trustworthy group. Since Marius's reign, the V. were regularly rewarded with a plot of land for their old age. The demobilization of enormous armies after the Civil Wars of the 1st cent. B.C. caused extensive expropriation of lands.

VETO. "I forbid"; an authorititative prohibition; interdiction (see TRIBUNI).

VIA [Lat. road or highway]. The con-

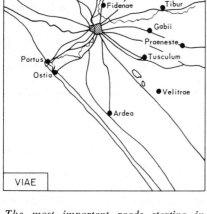

VIAE

The most important roads starting in Rome: Via Aurelia (S. of Caere), Via Cornelia (Caere), Via Triumphalis, S. of Veii, connecting with the Via Clodia, Via Cassia (E. of Veii, leading N.), Via Tiberina (W. of the Tiber), Via Salaria (E. of the Tiber), Via Nomentana (Nomentum), Via Tiburtina (Tibur), Via Praenestina (Praeneste), Via Labicana (E. of Tusculum, connecting with the Via Latina), Via Appia (S. of Velitrae), Via Ostiensis (Rome-Ostia), Via Severiana (Southeast from Ostia), Via Portuensis (Southern route Rome-Portus), Via Vitellia (Northern route Rome-Portus).

struction of large roads for rapid communications, particularly for troop movements, is one of the most striking aspects of Rom. organization. The more the Empire expanded, the more Rom. roads were built. They were marked with milestones, many of which have been found. The so-called *milliarium aureum* (golden milestone) in Rome was at the center of the network of roads (compare the expression "All roads lead to Rome"). The construction of roads was begun when Latium was conquered, and continued with the subjection of all of central Italy.

The most famous roads are:

The V. Appia from Rome to Capua, built in 312 B.C. by Appius Claudius Caecus, later extended to Brundisium, the main traffic artery to south Italy. The road can clearly be traced to Beneventum; from this point on, a different, shorter route superseded the V. Appia.

The V. Flaminia from Rome toward the northeast to Ariminum (modern Rimini), the main route to north Italy; constructed in 220 B.C. by Gaius Flaminius. Its extension to the Po Valley was called the V. Aemilia.

The V. Salaria (salt street) was the road along the left bank of the Tiber, on which the Sabines traveled to get their salt from the coast.

VIDEANT CONSULES. See CAVEANT CONSULES.

VILLA. Rom. country house or estate, originally for agricultural purposes, later, used more for luxurious summer residences of wealthy Romans, in Tusculum, Baiae, Tibur (Hadrian's V.), and other places. We have an elaborate description by Pliny the Younger (*Ep.* II, 17) of his V. in Laurentum.

VILLANOVA. Village in Italy near Bologna, where significant remains from the Early Iron Age have been found. Villanovan culture was named after the group of people who settled in this village. The discoveries date from between 1000 and 500 B.C. These people form the substratum of the population of Etruria especially (see ETRUSCANS; UMBRIANS). They also lived in Latium before the tribes who spoke Lat. dialects settled there.

VIMINAL HILL. One of the seven hills of Rome, north of the center; the remains of the so-called Servian Wall, built by Servius Tullius were found here.

VINDOBONA. The Rom. name for modern Vienna, camp of a Rom. legion. It played a part in the wars against the Marcomanni.

VIRGIL. See VERGILIUS.

VIRIATHUS. Shepherd from Lusitania. In 151 B.C. he had escaped the massacre of the people by the Rom. proconsul Sulpicius Galba. He led a resistance force against the Romans; the mountainous regions of Spain were especially favorable for guerilla warfare. Several successive wars were waged from 149-139 B.C., and after the Celtiberi had joined V.'s army, one of the Rom. proconsuls was forced to conclude a peace. V. was assassinated by negotiators he had sent to the Romans and who had been bribed by them (see NUMANTIA).

VITA BREVIS, LONGA ARS. "Life is short, art endures"; also used in reverse: *Ars longa, vita brevis* (compare Sen., *De Brev. Vitae* I, 1).

VITELLIUS, AULUS (A.D. 15-69). Rom. emperor during the Year of the Three Emperors (A.D. 69). On January 2nd of that year he was hailed as emperor by the troops in Germany, where Galba had sent him. His generals defeated Otho; after this victory V. marched into Rome. He ruled there for six months—incompetently and shortsightedly. In the meantime, Vespasian was proclaimed as anti-emperor in the East, and his generals defeated V.'s troops at Cremona. After Vespasian's troops had entered Rome, V. was murdered.

VITRUVIUS, POLLIO (2nd half of the 1st cent. B.C.). Rome. author of a work on architecture. From his own experience and extensive reading, he describes all kinds of structures, architectural styles, and ingenious implements. This book had great influence on Renaissance architecture. It contains many curious particulars and is the only book of its kind extant.

VOLATERRAE. The Rom. name for the Etruscan city of Velathri, modern Volterra, situated in Etruria in a high, predominating place. V. was particularly powerful during the 8th cent. B.C.; important remains from that period and the 9th cent. have been found.

VOLSCI. People of Italy, who, in the 6th cent. B.C., migrated from the Apennines to Latium, where they occupied Antium, Arpinum, and other cities. They were violently opposed to Rome (see CORIOLANUS). After 304 B.C. they were subjected by Rome and Romanized.

VOLUTES. The most striking characteristic of the Ionic style in architecture (see COLUMN).

VOX POPULI VOX DEI. "The voice of the people is the voice of God" (after Hom. *Od.* III, 214-5).

VULCANUS. See HEPHAESTUS.

VULCI. One of the most prosperous cities of Etruria. The large cemeteries discovered on the site in 1850 contained many Etruscan and Gr. artifacts; many were in a good state of preservation.

W-X

WEST ROMAN EMPIRE. The part of the Rom. Empire approximately west of the 20th meridian, definitely separated from the East Rom. Empire under Honorius in 395 B.C. It remained in existence until 476 (see ODOACER); its ideals lived on in the empire of Charlemagne and the German empire (962-1806). (See also VALENTINIANUS; ALARIC; STILICHO; GOTHS; and AETIUS).

WONDERS OF THE WORLD. Seven buildings or works of art, greatly admired in ancient times for their size or splendor. They were: the pyramids of Egypt; the Mausoleum of Halicarnassus; the hanging (terraced) gardens of Babylon; the lighthouse of Pharos; the Colossus (huge statue of Apollo) of Rhodes; the statue of Zeus by Phidias, at Olympia; and the Temple of Artemis, at Ephesus.

XANTHIPPE. The wife of Socrates, represented by tradition, but unjustly, as having been a quarrelsome and domineering wife (particularly by the Cynics). She was probably just an average Athenian housewife (see MARRIAGE) and, for that reason, no match for Socrates.

XANTHIPPUS. Athenian general and statesman, the father of Pericles. He prosecuted Miltiades in 490 B.C.; commanded the fleet that conquered the Persians at Mycale and took Sestos in 478.

XENOCRATES. Pupil of Plato and, after the death of Speusippus, president of the Academy from 339-314. He developed Plato's doctrine in a pythagorean sense (see PYTHAGORAS); he was also interested in practical morality; his theological studies foreshadow later Neoplatonism.

XENOPHANES of Colophon. (c. 565-470). Gr. philosopher and poet. After his native city was conquered by the Persians (545) he went to Greece, Sicily, and Magna Graecia as an itinerant poet and prophet of the Ionian spiritual movement. He wrote elegies and satiric poems (so-called *Silloi*), of which fragments remain extant, and possibly a longer poem about nature. X. is particularly significant as a religious thinker; he rejects the narratives of Homer and Hesiod, because they represent the gods as being anthropomorphous. There is, says X., only one god, who has not got a human shape, an unmoved master of the universe. This monotheistic conception of god, transferred to the field of natural philosophy, influenced the ideas of Parmenides (see also ELEATICS).

XENOPHON. Name of:

—(1) Gr. historian and moralist (c. 430-c. 354), a member of a prominent Athenian family. In his youth he was a none too loyal pupil of Socrates. In 401 he joined the expedition of Cyrus the Younger as an observer, and after most of the Gr. commanders had been treacherously murdered after the Battle of Cunaxa (see TISSAPHARNES), he led the retreat of the "Ten Thousand" (about 10,000 Gr. mercenaries hired by Cyrus) as commander of the rear guard. After 396 he served under the Spartan king Agesilaus, with whom he fought against his own native city at Coronea in 394; for this he was banished from this city (after Athens and Sparta had made peace in 369, this decree was revoked). Sparta gave him an estate at Scillus near Olympia, which he left in about 371, when Elis after the battle of Leuctra, again took possession of Scillus. He then settled in Corinth, where he died.

X.'s works do not possess great literary value, but they are written in pure Attic in a simple style, often fresh and lively; for this reason X. is usually required reading for students of Greek. In addition to the description of his campaign with Cyrus and the Ten Thousand, the Anabasis, his works are: (a) *Hellenica,* a history of Greece from 411-362, a continuation of the history of Thucydides; (b) *Memorabilia,* memoirs of Socrates, a rather unreliable portrait of the great philosopher; (c) *Cyropaedia,* an idealized biography of Cyrus the Elder. He also wrote lesser works on politics, horsemanship, finances, and other subjects. A highly interesting book about the Athenian state, written by a pertinacious oligarch, has been incorrectly attributed to X.

—(2) X. of Ephesus (3rd cent. A.D.). Gr. novelist, who wrote a love story called *Ephesiaca* about the adventures of a young couple; an excerpt of this work is extant.

XERXES (c. 519-465). King of Persia. He succeeded Darius I in 485 and advanced on Greece with the intention of conquering it in 480, after first having suppressed rebellions in his own empire. He failed (see TEMPE; THERMOPYLAE; ARTEMISIUM; SALAMIS; THEMISTOCLES); when he returned to Persia, he left Mardonius in Greece; he was defeated at Plataea in 479. Little is known about the rest of X.'s life; he was killed as the result of a court intrigue. He attempted to establish Ahura Mazda (see PERSIAN EMPIRE) as the sole cult. This religious zeal is in striking contrast to the concept the Greeks had of him. In Aeschylus'

The Persians he appears as the typical incarnation of *hybris,* the haughtiness which is incapable of respecting the boundaries between men and gods.

Y-Z

YEAR OF THE THREE EMPERORS. The year A.D. 69, so called because Galba, Otho, and Vitellius were Rom. emperors, one after the other, within a short period; if the final victor, Vespasian, who was officially recognized as emperor on December 22nd, is counted, we may even call it the Year of the Four Emperors. This episode is discussed extensively and extremely well by Tacitus in his *Historiae.* Galba had hardly entered Rome when the Praetorians proclaimed Otho emperor. He, in turn, had to deal with Vitellius, whose troops were advancing from Germany. The decisive battle was held at Bedriacum (in the Po Valley north of Cremona): after an unsuccessful fight by his troops, Otho committed suicide, although reinforcements were on the way. These troops soon joined the army of Vespasian, who had in the meantime been proclaimed emperor in the East. Again, the area between Bedriacum and Cremona was the scene of a civil war, now between the armies of Vitellius and Vespasian; Antonius Primus, the commander of Vespasian's troops, marched on Rome after his victory, where, in the interim, Flavius Sabinus, the brother of the future emperor, was trying to usurp power; he had to pay for that with his life. Domitian narrowly escaped; during these street fights the Capitol went up in flames. After a short, fierce battle, Primus' army entered the city and Vitellius was murdered. This aspect of the year A.D. 69 is particularly interesting in that Vitellius, in order to march on Rome, had to leave the Rhine frontier practically unprotected; this gave Julius Civilis an opportunity to incite the Batavi to revolt.

ZACYNTHUS. Island in the Ionian Sea, already mentioned in Homer as part of Odysseus' empire; conquered by Athens in 455 and a member of the Second Attic League; subsequently conquered by Macedonia and Rome.

ZAGREUS. A name for Dionysus in the mysteries, especially in Orphism.

ZALEUCUS. The lawgiver of the Locrians (see LOCRIS) in Magna Graecia. His legislation, the oldest Gr. code of law (c. 650 B.C.), was moderately aristocratic; his punitive laws were known to be extremely severe; many western Gr. cities adopted them.

ZAMA. Name of several places in Africa, of which the best known was Z. Regia. There, according to antique authors, Hannibal was finally beaten by Scipio Major in 202 B.C. Probably the battle took place to the west of Z. Later, Z. became successively a Rom. *municipium* and then a colony.

ZANCLE. See MESSANA.

ZENO. Name of:

—(1) Z. of Elea (c. 450 B.C.). Gr. philosopher, pupil of Parmenides (see also ELEATICS), whose doctrine he defended. Aristotle calls Z. the founder of dialectic. His example of the race between Achilles and the tortoise is famous: the tortoise has a head start and Achilles can never overtake him—during the time that he needs to reduce the distance between them, the tortoise will always have gotten a little farther still. This story probably was intended to prove absurd the doctrine of those who, in opposition to Parmenides, believed that matter was divisible to infinity.

—(2) Z. of Citium on Cyprus. (335-263). The founder of the Stoic school. The unmistakably Eastern elements in the Stoic doctrine are sometimes attributed to his Phoenician origin. He came to Athens in 313 and there became acquainted with the Cynic doctrine; he studied the writings of Antisthenes and other followers of Socrates, but, in contrast to them, he established a school of his own, in which the entire range of Gr. thought was introduced. It is difficult to ascertain just which elements of Stoicism can be attributed to Z. himself. However, his great ideal was known to have been "harmonious living," developed further by Cleanthes as "living in harmony with nature" (see SECUNDUM NATURAM).

ZENOBIA. Queen of Palmyra. Her native name was Septimia Bathzabbai. She reigned from 267/8-272 for her infant son. She was given a Gr. education by the philosopher Longinus, in a short time she established a large kingdom, comprising Syria and Asia Minor. Her kingdom was a threat to Rome, and Aurelianus and his general, the later Emperor Probus (see MILITARY EMPERORS) conquered it. Z. was shown at Aurelianus' triumph in 274 and spent the rest of her life in a villa in Tibur. To satisfy her personal ambition, she had sacrificed her small but prosperous kingdom.

ZENODOTUS of Ephesus (c. 325-c. 260). Gr. lexicographer, the first of the great Alexandrine philologists; became the first head of the library at Alexandria in about 284; undertook the textual criticism of various poets, particularly Homer. He was responsible for the classification of the *Iliad* and the *Odyssey* into twenty-four books each. His work was continued by Aristophanes of Byzantium and by Aristarchus.

ZEUS. The Gr. supreme god, the only Gr. god whose name can be definitely derived from the Indo-European: Zeus stands for *Dieus* from the Sanskrit *Dyaus* or *Diaus,* the bright heaven. Like the Rom. Jupiter, the name is derived from the root *diu* meaning radiant, clear, that is, the sky (god). The Greeks undoubtedly brought his cult with them from their northern homes in the 3rd-2nd millennium B.C., and when they immigrated they had him "marry" several pre-Hellenic goddesses, particularly Hera. They also identified him with a Minoan *kouros* (youthful god, actually a spirit of vegetation, which was born and died like nature: a "grave of Z." was displayed on Crete). In later times it was still said that Z. had been born on Crete. Of his many functions, three are particularly noteworthy: (a) The function of god of heavenly phenomena, principally that of cloud gatherer, lightning hurler, etc. (b) His place as the father in the family of gods on Mount Olympus, and thus his function as protector of the families of man, in a broader sense also of the state, society, and law. (c) His function as the protector of guests, strangers, and suppliants. Z. was worshiped primarily at Dodona and Olympia (the Olympic Games were also dedicated to him, as were the Nemean Games), and on Crete, as mentioned before. The Greeks drew the traditional image from the poems of Homer. In the course of the centuries, however, it underwent significant changes. Pindar and particularly Aeschylus gave an almost monotheistic portrayal of Z.; in later Gr. literature "Zeus" is practically identical with "God." This is particularly the case in Stoic philosophy, witness Cleanthes' famous hymn. The most celebrated image of Z. was Phidias' chryselephantine statue—Pausanias claimed that it shattered the viewer by its majesty. This statue has been lost; the best sculpture we have of Z. is a head, found at Otricoli (Rome).

ZEUXIS (2nd half of the 5th cent. B.C.). Gr. painter. He came from Heraclea in southern Italy; worked in the west of Greece and in Athens, where he competed with Parrhasius. His painting of Helen, created for the temple of Hera in Croton, was famous. It represents a female nude for which he used several models. His family of Centaurs, described by Lucian, was equally admired. Z. painted in a realistic style: according to an anecdote, the birds were deceived by the grapes he painted, and Lucian remarked on the subtle shading with which Z. rendered the transition from the human to the animal part of a female centaur. None of his work has been preserved.

Appendix

I. Constructional diagram of the Doric Temple of Aphaia in AEGINA.

II. Roman camp (see CASTRA). 1) Main gate; 2) Right gate; 3) Praetorian gate; 4) Decuman gate; 5) Main way; 6) Praetorium.

III. Some musical instruments of the classical world (see MUSIC). Above, from left to right: pipes, horn, and Pan's flute. Below: cithara (a type of lyre used by professional musicians), tuba, and lyre.

IV. Reconstruction of the BASILICA of Trajan at Rome (*ca.* A.D. 110).

V. Floor plan of the Basilica of Trajan.

VI. Exposed view of the ARA PACIS of Augustus, erected in 9 B.C. in honor of the Emperor.

VII. Example of an AMPHITHEATER: the COLOSSEUM at Rome.

VIII. CHITONS. At left: Dorian. Right: Ionian.

IX. Reconstruction of a fortified frontier (LIMES) with watch-tower.

X. Reconstruction of the Temple of Jupiter at Baalbek (see HELIOPOLIS).

XI. Different kinds of STELES. Above, left: representation of a stele on a funerary lekythos; above, right: a Spartan stele showing a heroic couple; center: stele of Hegeso; bottom, left: stele of Aristion; bottom, center: stele of Polycletus; bottom, right: an Ionian stele.

XII. Examples of MINOAN CULTURE. Above, left: a vase decorated with octopi (16th century B.C.); above, right: detail of a restored fresco dating from around 1500 B.C. It appears to represent women on a balcony, the "women in blue"; center: scene from a ritual bullfight—the figure shows the phases of jumping over the bull; below, left: the sacred bull of Crete, as represented on a vase; right: a stylized fresco showing, among other things, the horns of the bull (the Horns of Consecration).

XIII. Some examples of ETRUSCAN art. Above: schematic reconstruction of a temple; center, from left to right: Apollo of Veii; a vase in the form of a leg; a young man dancing, styled after a funerary fresco; below: sarcophagus of the necropolis of Caere.

XIV. Some examples of HAIR STYLES of the Greeks (top row) and the Romans. The Greeks maintained essentially the same styles over a long period of time. The Romans, on the other hand, knew many hair styles.

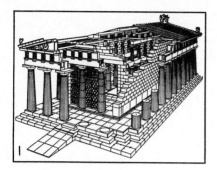

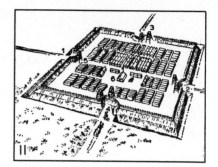

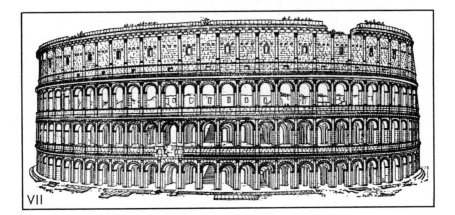

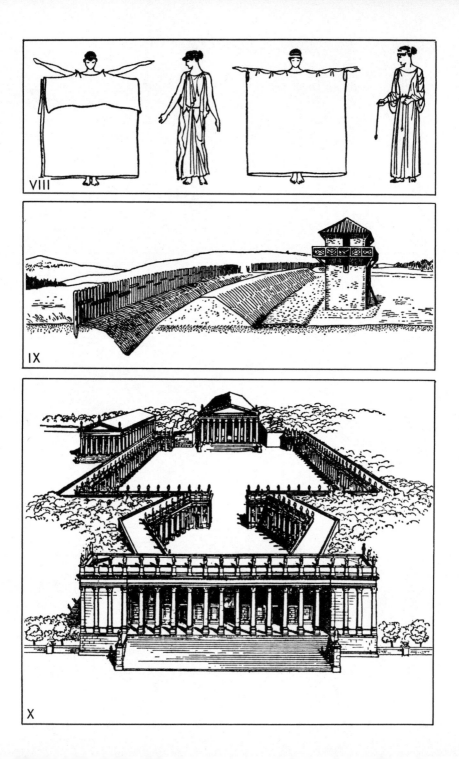

VIII

IX

X

XI

XII

XIII

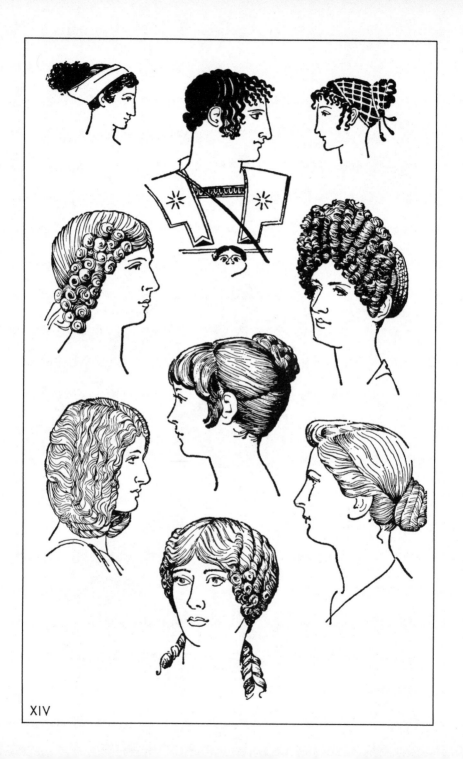

XIV

Other Spectrum  Encyclopedias

THE ENCYCLOPEDIA OF CLASSICAL MYTHOLOGY

A. R. A. Van Aken

This encyclopedia is a complete guide to classical myth and legend. Included, in addition to all the Greco-Roman deities and heroes, are principal religious festivals, significant locales, and such special items of mythological relevance as coins, temples, and oracles.

The encyclopedia also emphasizes the influence of mythology on art. It describes the surviving depictions of mythological figures by the ancients on friezes and bas reliefs, sculptures, coins, and ceramics. Also discussed is the influence of mythological themes on many of the masterpieces of Renaissance and Baroque art.

This work, the first English translation of the *Elseviers Mythologische Encyclopedie*, is designed to meet the needs of the art student as well as the casual museum-goer, of the literary scholar as well as the general reader. It provides the perfect complement to *The Encyclopedia of the Classical World*.

THE ENCYCLOPEDIA OF THE BIBLE

Edited by P. A. Marijnen

This complete reference work comprises thousands of persons and places, writings, institutions, and ideas associated with the Bible. Originally compiled by a team of leading Dutch experts on Biblical exegesis, including both Catholic and Protestant scholars, the Encyclopedia gives a complete listing of Biblical terms, together with the origins of many proper names (Jonah: "dove"; Methuselah: "spear bearer"); special articles on scriptural texts and sources (palimpsest . . . papyrus . . . Pastoral Epistles . . . Pentateuch); discussions of the meanings of theological concepts (Transformation . . . Tree of Life . . . Trinity); and articles that place in their scriptural context the most fundamental human ideas (life . . . light . . . love).

Noteworthy for scholarly completeness, yet lucid and readable, this new English edition of *Elseviers Encyclopedie van de Bijbel* will serve the scholar or theologian, as well as the layman.